Enigma Books

Also published by Enigma Books

Hitler's Table Talk: 1941–1944
In Stalin's Secret Service
Hitler and Mussolini: The Secret Meetings
The Jews in Fascist Italy: A History
The Man Behind the Rosenbergs
Roosevelt and Hopkins: An Intimate History
Diary 1937–1943 (Galeazzo Ciano)
Secret Affairs: FDR, Cordell Hull, and Sumner Welles
Hitler and His Generals: Military Conferences 1942–1945
Stalin and the Jews: The Red Book
The Secret Front: Nazi Political Espionage
Fighting the Nazis: French Intelligence and Counterintelligence
A Death in Washington: Walter G. Krivitsky and the Stalin Terror
The Battle of the Casbah: Terrorism and Counterterrorism in Algeria 1955–1957
Hitler's Second Book: The Unpublished Sequel to *Mein Kampf*
At Napoleon's Side in Russia: The Classic Eyewitness Account
The Atlantic Wall: Hitler's Defenses for D-Day
Double Lives: Stalin, Willi Münzenberg and the Seduction of the Intellectuals
France and the Nazi Threat: The Collapse of French Diplomacy 1932–1939
Mussolini: The Secrets of His Death
Top Nazi: Karl Wolff—The Man Between Hitler and Himmler
Empire on the Adriatic: Mussolini's Conquest of Yugoslavia
The Origins of the War of 1914 (3-volume set)
Hitler's Foreign Policy, 1933–1939: The Road to World War II
The Origins of Fascist Ideology 1918–1925
Max Corvo: OSS Italy 1942–1945
Hitler's Contract: The Secret History of the Italian Edition of *Mein Kampf*
Secret Intelligence and the Holocaust
Israel at High Noon
Balkan Inferno: Betrayal, War, and Intervention, 1990–2005
Calculated Risk: World War II Memoirs of General Mark Clark
The Murder of Maxim Gorky
The Kravchenko Case: One Man's War On Stalin
The Mafia and the Allies
Hitler's Gift to France
The Nazi Party, 1919–1945: A Complete History
Encyclopedia of Cold War Espionage, Spies, and Secret Operations
The Cicero Spy Affair
Hitler's Intelligence Chief: Walter Schellenberg
Becoming Winston Churchill
The First Iraq War: Britain's Mesopotamian Campaign, 1914-1918
Nazi Palestine: The Plans for the Extermination of the Jews in Palestine
Salazar: A Political Biography

Yuri Felshtinsky

Lenin and His Comrades

Enigma Books

Published by Enigma Books, New York

Printed in the United States of America

ISBN 978-1-929631-95-7
eISBN 978-1-936274-15-4

Publisher's Cataloging-In-Publication Data

Fel'shtinskiĭ, IUriĭ, 1956-
  Lenin and his comrades / Yuri Felshtinsky.

    p. : ill. ; cm.

  Includes bibliographical references and index.
  ISBN: 978-1-929631-95-7
  ISBN: 978-1-936274-15-4 (eBook)

  1. Lenin, Vladimir Ilich, 1870-1924. 2. Communist International--History. 3.
Soviet Union--History--Revolution, 1917-1921. 4. Russia--Politics and government--
1894-1917. 5. Communism--Soviet Union--History. I. Title.

DK265 .F45 2010
947.0841

Contents

Lenin and His Comrades

Introduction

The history of the revolutionary movement in Russia was never elegant. It was not a history of starched collars, white gloves, and polished shoes. It was a history of dirt mixed with blood. There are many different kinds of history—political, social, economic, diplomatic, military, and cultural. Many excellent books have been written about all of these subjects, both in Russia and elsewhere.

But Russia—which an American president once called "the evil empire," a label that the government of Gorbachev and Yeltsin came to agree with—also had a different kind of history, namely, a criminal history. That part of the past is the subject of this book. It focuses on the criminal side of the interactions and working methods of the Bolshevik leaders during the first quarter of the twentieth century. The Bolsheviks carried out expropriations prior to the Revolution to finance it; they murdered the millionaires Savva Morozov and Nikolai Shmidt to seize their inheritances; and they entered into mercenary collaborations with foreign intelligence services and governments that were hostile to Russia. At Lenin's urging the Soviet government signed a separate peace with Kaiser Wilhelm I in 1918 sabotage the revolution in Germany. The enemies of Lenin's Treaty of Brest-Litovsk—most importantly Felix Dzerzhinsky, the head of Russia's security services, the Cheka—organized the assassination of the German ambassador Count Mirbach in order to provoke Germany into breaking the treaty; and how Lenin, Trotsky, and Sverdlov used Mirbach's murder to destroy the Left Socialist Revolutionary Party and establish a single-party dictatorship in Russia. After the attempt to undermine the Treaty of Brest-Litovsk failed, it is our thesis that Dzerzhinsky and Yakov Sverdlov, the de facto general secretary of the party, organized an assassination attempt against Lenin on August 30, 1918 (the so-called "Kaplan assassination attempt"), during which

Lenin was wounded; and that Sverdlov's subsequent sudden death in March 1919 was not accidental, but may have been an act of revenge for his role in organizing the attempt. The murders of the heads of the German communist movement—Liebknecht and Luxemburg—in Germany: the theory supported here is that Karl Radek, a prominent Russian Bolshevik who was in Germany at this time, may have been involved in the murders of Liebknecht and Luxemburg. Beginning in 1922, Lenin was gradually ousted from power by Stalin and Dzerzhinsky, and as a result of this power struggle within the party he was murdered by them; and after which Trotsky was shunted aside, while Dzerzhinsky, Sklyansky, and Frunze—other prominent Bolsheviks—were eliminated. The leadership of the Bolshevik Party bore a striking resemblance to an organized crime group. Almost none of its members died of natural causes. And almost all the Soviet leaders of Stalin's generation, including Stalin himself, were done away with, in one way or another.

This book is based on wide-ranging sources, including both published and archival materials. Detailed references to these sources are given at the end of every chapter.

1.

The Money for the Revolution

When people talk about the Russian Revolution, the name that usually comes up first is that of Vladimir Ilyich Lenin. So let us honor this tradition and also begin with Lenin. So much has been said and written about him that truth and fiction, myth and anecdote, fantasy and reality, have long become confused in a torrent of information. Meanwhile, this political figure—who was to play a fateful role in Russian history—has remained concealed under countless "cultural layers" that have covered him in recent decades. The cult of Lenin's personality, which was originally created by his collaborators and followers for their own convenience and promotion, has never been formally debunked. He still stands on a political pedestal and knocking him down is no simple matter.

Of Lenin's character traits, the one that stands out is a passion for initiating schisms. It may seem that, given the revolutionaries' small numbers, their life-and-death conflict with the government, their exile, imprisonment, and emigration, their common goal of overthrowing autocratic rule in Russia should have tightly bound them together. It is all the more surprising, therefore, that the starting point of Lenin's political strategy was to foment a break within the Russian Social Democratic Labor Party (RSDLP).

On January 21, 1929, at a formal assembly commemorating the fifth anniversary of Lenin's death, A. V. Lunacharsky—a famous Bolshevik and the people's commissar of education—delivered a tedious speech with the mawkish title, "Radiant Precious Genius." In this vapid, soporific oration, Lunacharsky expatiated about the fact that Lenin viewed the internal enemy as far more dangerous than the external one:

> At an important meeting during the fight with Menshevism in 1905, Vladimir Ilyich expressed himself as follows on the subject of fighting [the internal enemy]. When he was told: "You're acting as if the Mensheviks were a more dangerous enemy for you than autocracy itself, and instead of fighting autocracy, you're trying to fight the Mensheviks," he replied: "Imagine that a commander is fighting a war against an enemy and that he has an enemy in his own camp. Before he goes to the front to fight the enemy, he must first clean out his own camp and make it free of enemies."[1]

In this way, by 1905 Lenin had already formulated the fundamental law of Bolshevism (which was then successfully applied both by Lenin himself and, many years later, by Stalin): one must always strike against the internal enemy first—even under the most unfavorable circumstances, even when the external enemy is approaching, even when the threat of common annihilation hangs over the party, the revolution, and the government—even if the internal enemy is the enemy of your enemy.

A classic example of this approach was the Lenin-engineered split within the RSDLP during the Second Party Congress, which took place in July-August 1903, first in Brussels and then in London. This split gave birth to two parties, which subsequently entered history as the Mensheviks (headed by the prominent Russian Social Democrat L. Martynov) and the Bolsheviks (headed by Lenin). From then on—while unsuccessfully attempting to take over the party's newspaper, *Iskra*, the party's Central Committee, and above all the party's treasury—Lenin waged a vicious verbal struggle, which descended to the level of invective and public insults, against the Social Democrats who refused to submit unquestioningly to his absolute leadership.

Whether Lenin wanted it or not, after the 1903 split the Bolshevik wing of the Social Democratic Party gradually became transformed into a mafia-like organization. Chronologically, the beginning of this transformation dates from the years 1905–1910. Organizationally, it was linked with the activity of the so-called Bolshevik Center, which was created by the Lenin-headed Bolshevik faction during the Fifth Congress of the RSDLP in 1907. Mafia-style morality, mafia-style principles, and mafia-style methods became the foundation of party work. The entire edifice of the party was built upon this foundation, which remained standing until the putsch of August 1991. "In essence, our party was one giant mafia," former KGB Major General Oleg Kalugin said in an interview in April 1996. "The Italian mafia is called the 'cosa nostra'—'our business'. Well, our business at the time was building communism. Our slogans sounded high-minded. But the mafia-style agencies that penetrated into all aspects of life, the complete control over everything, and the brutal punishment for everyone who 'deviated from the norm'—all this was typical mafia behavior."[2] The creator of this system was Lenin.

Fully aware that, in the work of the party, much if not everything depended on money, Lenin cynically exploited those who brought money to his organization, regardless of how this money was obtained. The money arrived from two basic sources: voluntary, semi-voluntary, or forced donations, which came from individuals; and "expropriations" of government funds, carried out by Bolshevik armed bands and groups connected to them in different parts of the country.

Among the Social Democrats, attitudes toward the expropriations varied. The issue first came up in April 1906 at the Stockholm congress of the Social Democratic Party. The Bolsheviks considered expropriations a form of "guerilla military action" directed against the government and viewed the expropriation of government resources for financing revolutionary activity as an acceptable course of action. The Mensheviks stressed the expropriations' demoralizing influence on the party and generally came out against them. In the end, the Stockholm congress passed the Mensheviks' resolution, which became the official party line concerning this issue. In May 1907, the decision to prohibit expropriations was approved by the Fifth Congress of the Social Democratic Party (in London). It was specifically stipulated that all of the armed bands and groups engaged in expropriations were to be dissolved. In spite of this, the Bolsheviks did not dissolve some armed bands and continued to conduct expropriations against the congress's resolutions. This work was overseen—through the Bolshevik Center, which was created specifically for clandestine activities—by Lenin, Leonid Krasin, and Alexander Bogdanov.

Among the armed bands, two were particularly active: one in the Urals and one in the Transcaucasus. At the head of the Ural group were the Kadomtsev brothers (Erazm, Ivan, and Mikhail), who called for the clandestine creation of a mass workers' militia and worked on plans for an uprising in the Urals. They carried out expropriations mainly in order to obtain funds for these objectives and gave the Bolshevik Center only part of their loot, which, however, was quite substantial. In 1906–1907, the Bolsheviks carried out dozens of expropriations in the Urals, mainly on a small scale, such as robbing state-run liquor stores. However, in August 1906, during a mail train robbery on the Dema River, near Ufa, over 200,000 rubles were stolen. Of this money, 60,000 rubles reached Lenin through I. A. Sammer (Lyubim), an agent of the Central Committee and the Bolsheviks' representative in the Urals.

The Transcaucasian groups had no significant projects of their own. They created a band of "merry men," headed by S. T. Petrosian-Kamo, whom Lenin amiably referred to as a "Caucasian outlaw," and sent their loot to the Bolshevik Center. Their assignments were discussed at the Center, developed by Krasin, approved by Lenin, and given to Kamo for implementation. All together, Kamo's group seized approximately 325,000–350,000 rubles. Their most significant expropriation, which took place on Erivan Square in Tiflis on June 25, 1907, brought them over 250,000 rubles, which were taken to the Bolshevik Center's headquarters in Kuokkala (Finland) by Kamo himself.

Of this money, 150,000 rubles, which were in small bills, were immediately transferred to the Bolshevik Center's "financial department," which consisted of the same three individuals: Lenin, Krasin, and Bogdanov. The remaining 100,000 rubles were all in large bills of 500 rubles each. The Russian government reported their serial numbers to all Russian banks and exchanging them within the Russian Empire presented considerable difficulties. Sewing up this money in his vest, the Bolshevik M. N. Lyadov took it out of the country in order to exchange it in banks abroad.

Since it was evident that after the first exchange the Russian government would send the serial numbers of the stolen bills to foreign banks as well, the decision was made to exchange the money in several European cities at once. In early January 1908, under Krasin's supervision, such an operation was indeed carried out in Paris, Geneva, Stockholm, Munich, and other cities. Unexpectedly for the Bolsheviks, however, the plan failed: all of the Bolsheviks who arrived in banks in order to exchange the money were arrested. Among them were people who were well known in Social Democratic circles, such as the future People's Commissar of Foreign Affairs in the Soviet government, M. M. Litvinov, who had been appointed shortly before by the Bolsheviks as the official secretary of the Russian Social Democratic delegation to the International Socialist Congress in Stuttgart in August 1907. When Litvinov was apprehended, twelve of the 500-ruble bills stolen in Tiflis were discovered on his person. The future People's Commissar of Public Health N. Alexandrov (N. A. Semashko, a distant relative of the founder of the Russia's Marxist movement, Georgi Plekhanov) was caught and arrested as well. Semashko was not directly involved in the attempt to exchange the bills, but he had received letters from one of the operation's participants. All together, the police obtained fifty 500-ruble bills, and the foreign press now quite openly reported that the Tiflis expropriation had been the work of the Bolsheviks.

The reason why the attempt to exchange the money had failed became clear only after the Revolution. Among those involved in developing the plans for the operation was Zhitomirsky (Otsov), a Bolshevik who was Lenin's deputy in dealing with Bolshevik emigrant groups starting in 1903–1904, as well as the main informer for the Paris branch of the Russian secret police, the so-called Okhrana. Through Zhitomirsky, the Okhrana kept abreast of all of Krasin's preparations and was able to alert European police departments in advance of the operation.

In 1906, Bolsheviks in St. Petersburg and Moscow developed a plan to issue counterfeit money. Krasin returned to this project in 1907 and ordered paper with watermarks in Germany for printing counterfeit three-ruble bills. However, this plan became known in Berlin and in Russia. In Berlin, arrests were made, the purchased paper was confiscated, and this project, as Bogdanov later recalled, "did not come to fruition due only to accidental and purely technical problems."[3]

After the plan to print counterfeit Russian money came to nothing and the attempts to exchange the 500-ruble bills failed, Lenin split off from Krasin and Bogdanov. Having previously held Krasin in great respect, Lenin now called him a "master at making promises and blowing smoke,"[4] and somewhat later even accused Krasin of embezzling 140,000 rubles of Bolshevik money obtained during the Tiflis expropriation (that is, almost all of the money, apart from the 500-ruble bills, that Kamo had delivered to the members of the "committee of three" in Kuokkala in July–August 1907).

Clearly Lenin's conflict with Krasin and Bogdanov was caused not by political differences, but by financial issues. What had occurred during the first half of 1908, then, aside from the unsuccessful attempt to exchange the ill-fated 500-ruble bills? As it happened, it was at this time that Lenin received news of the successful completion of another operation, which brought large sums of money to the Bolshevik Center's coffers. Such large sums, in fact, that it became advantageous for Lenin not to share them with his old collaborators, Krasin and Bogdanov, but to quarrel with them, by accusing them of appropriating the money from the Tiflis expropriation, and to keep the new money for himself. These funds came from the famous Russian furniture manufacturer Nikolai Shmidt (Shmit), a nephew of the even more famous Russian textile manufacturer Savva Morozov.

Morozov, a friend of the Revolution, has often been described as a "contradictory" figure who became disillusioned with everything at the end of his life and either went crazy and died or killed himself. Many attempts have been made to understand Morozov's behavior. Here is how the events were described by one knowledgeable eyewitness, Lidiya Osipovna Dan, the sister of one famous Menshevik, L. Martov, and the wife of another, Fedor Dan:

> The Bolsheviks received [money] from very wealthy people, too, for example, Savva Morozov—he was a Mason. Other Masons gave, also. No one will ever find out where the money came from. It necessarily had to be kept secret in the underground and no one will ever know about it. There are now almost no people left who knew about it and remember it.[5]

Nikolai Valentinov-Volsky, a Russian Social Democratic and journalist, devoted two chapters of his book, *The Little-Known Lenin,* to the sources of the Bolsheviks' money. He writes:

> With a false passport Lenin came from Geneva to St. Petersburg on November 20, 1905, and on the very next day he was already presiding in the editorial offices of the newspaper *Novaya Zhizn*.... The official publisher [of this Social Democratic newspaper was] M. F. Andreyeva was at the time the wife of Maxim Gorky. A footnote in the tenth volume of the fourth, "expurgated" edition of Lenin's collected works, on page 479, mentions that Gorky provided "substantial material assistance" to the newspaper. Gorky apparently invested nothing out of his own pocket in the newspaper. He was merely an influential middleman. He drew the merchants Savva Morozov and Shmidt into supporting the newspaper.... The Bolsheviks turned out to be great experts at extracting money from bourgeois pockets with the assistance of writers, artists, engineers, and lawyers who sympathized with them.... A big operator in this respect was the engineer L. B. Krasin, a member of the Bolshevik Central Committee. And an even more marvelous catcher of entrepreneurial and banking moths who were drawn to the Bolshevik flame was Maxim Gorky, who knew how to draw out money for *Novaya Zhizn*, for weapons, and all kinds of other enterprises.[6]

One could only marvel at Morozov's and Shmidt's generosity.

In 1990, during one of the first visits to Moscow after emigrating to the United States, I interviewed Savva Morozov's grandniece. With her permission, the interview was recorded. It was during this interview that she gave me her family's account of Morozov's death. I will quote the most vivid passages from this very important document:

Savva Timofeyevich had contacts with many revolutionaries.... In 1905, Savva Timofeyevich and [his wife] Zinaida Grigorievna traveled to Cannes. But prior to this he had most likely had an affair with Maria Fedorovna Andreyeva, Gorky's wife, since his life insurance policy—he had insured himself for 100,000 rubles—was made out payable to Gorky.... The life insurance was made out to Gorky so the lady wouldn't be compromised. And strange as it may seem, as soon as Savva Timofeyevich left for Cannes, Krasin immediately showed up there as well.... My mother said that he had to be eliminated since he had nothing more to give to the [revolutionaries]....

Zinaida Grigorievna was about to go out for a ride with [the banker and industrialist Pavel] Ryabushinsky. She was putting on her hat in front of the mirror. Suddenly, looking in the mirror, she saw the door open and the head of a red-haired man peek inside. Zinaida Grigorievna asked: "Who's there?" Savva Timofeyevich quickly replied: "No one, no one." Then she left. When she returned, Savva Timofeyevich was lying on his bed, his arm was hanging down, and a gun was next to him.... The police were called. They said that the bullet in his body did not match the revolver that was lying on the floor. That's the first thing. And the second thing is that, in the history of suicides, there has never been a single instance of a person shooting himself while lying in bed. This just doesn't happen. And third, they say that the red-haired man had some experience with these kinds of things.... The red-haired man was Krasin.... So, you understand, everything fits.... Very soon afterward, Gorky claimed the life insurance money, which amounted to 100,000 rubles.... And yet, what does it mean when hardly a week has passed and a person starts demanding money?... Three years later, in 1908, Plekhanov published an article in the magazine *Byloye*, in which he wrote: "It is time to ask Alexei Peshkov [i.e., Gorky] what he did with the 100,000 rubles, the price of Savva Morozov's life"....

Genya, the son of my mother's older sister, told me... directly: "Well, listen, everyone knows that Krasin shot him".... In our family, they knew. That generation knew.[7]

It should be noted that today we have further evidence that Morozov was killed by Krasin. In an article entitled "The Mysterious Death of Savva Morozov," T. P. Morozova, Morozov's great-granddaughter, writes that Zinaida Grigorievna, Morozov's wife, claimed that "Savva Timofeyevich was shot. She was near the room where Savva Timofeyevich was at the time, and she heard it. For a few moments, she remained frozen with fear. Then she ran into his room. The window was wide open and she saw a man running away through the park." Morozov was lying on his back with his eyes closed, his hands were folded on his stomach, the fingers of his left hand were singed. His right hand was open and a Browning gun was lying beside it. A piece of paper was lying on the floor by the bed—a suicide note. The French police, "experienced criminologists from Hungary and Yugoslavia, forensic doctors, ballistics experts" did not rule out the "possibility of a murder made to resemble a suicide."[8]

A photocopy of the suicide note was published in T. P. Morozova's article: "I ask that no one be blamed for my death."[9] The note, which was notarized in the Russian consulate in France shortly after Morozov's death, lacks a signature and constitutes clear evidence that Morozov was indeed murdered. In fact, a comparison between the handwriting in the note and a facsimile of Morozov's letter of December 21, 1904, leaves no doubt that the letters were written by two different people.

Who, then, was the author of Morozov's "suicide note"? There are reasons to suppose that the note was written by Morozov's murderer, Krasin. At least, the handwriting in the note and Krasin's handwriting (judging by his numerous letters, which are preserved in the archive of the International Institute of Social History in Amsterdam) bear a suspicious resemblance to one another. There was even a rumor that the note discovered by French police had actually read: "The debt has been paid. Krasin."[10]

The chronology of how the principal actors in these events met is important. Even before the Moscow Art Theater was formed, Maria Fedorovna Yurkovskaya, who took the stage name "Andreyeva," became interested in Marxism through her son Yuri's tutor, the student Dmitry Lukyanov. By the time she joined the Moscow Art Theater, "Andreyeva was already a committed Marxist, with close ties to the RSDLP and acting on this party's orders." It appears that one of her assignments was to become acquainted with Morozov. The actors of the Moscow Art Theater knew how much Morozov had donated to the theater. Without his help, the theater would not have been able to open or survive.

In 1898, Konstantin Stanislavski and Vladimir Nemirovich-Danchenko—the future directors of the theater—came up with a plan for the creation of the Moscow Art Theater and for this purpose formed a Society for Founding a Public Theater in Moscow. Among the donors was Savva Morozov. Of the initial donations of 28,000 rubles, Morozov's contribution was the largest: 10,000 rubles. These funds were used to rent the Hermitage Theater in Karetny Ryad Street, where in October 1898 the theater had its first production, *Czar Fedor Ioannovich* (based on the play by A. K. Tolstoy). From a commercial point of view, the theater was not very successful. By the end of the first season, it was 46,000 rubles in debt. According to Stanislavski, the situation was "almost catastrophic." Once again, Morozov came to the theater's aid. He not only furnished the missing 46,000 rubles, but also doubled his first contribution, bringing his expenditures for the first year of the theater's existence to approximately 60,000. Later, the other donors doubled their earlier contributions as well and the theater was saved.

In addition to financing the theater, Morozov took over its entire management, handling every detail and attending virtually every performance. Morozov was consulted on all questions connected with the selection of actors, the repertoire, and the distribution of roles. Not everyone was pleased by this arrangement. "Savva Morozov has become a fixture at the theater," Olga Knipper, an actress, wrote with irony to her husband, Anton Chekhov, in September 1899, emphasizing Morozov's tendency to interfere in discussions of directorial and performance problems.

The directors' views of Morozov's involvement in such discussions varied. Stanislavski realized that the theater would not survive a day without Morozov and was willing to tolerate all kinds of interference. Nemirovich-Danchenko protested desperately (although only in letters to third parties). "I didn't join forces with you to have a capitalist come and decide to turn me into... how shall I put it?—a secretary, perhaps?" he wrote to Stanislavski at the beginning of 1900. But in another letter, on August 14 of the same year, he already admitted: "I only now understand how much my job (and primarily my job) has been made easier by Savva Timofeyevich. After all, if it weren't for him, I would've had to go insane. I'm not even talking about the absence of material worries."

According to historians' estimates, Morozov contributed at least 200,000 rubles to the theater's operation during the years 1898–1902. In 1902, he spent an additional 300,000 rubles on a new building for the Moscow Art Theater. A house in Kamergersky Lane belonging to the oil magnate Georgi Lianozov, which had earlier been outfitted as a theater, was now completely remodeled by the architect Fedor Shekhtel. Krasin and Lenin could not allow such a philanthropist to slip away. It was Andreyeva who introduced Savva Timofeyevich to her friends from Lenin's circle.[11] This is how yet another key figure for the revolution became involved in this already convoluted narrative: the writer and revolutionary Maxim Gorky.

As revolutionaries, Lenin and Krasin were interested in Andreyeva having an affair with Morozov so that Morozov, who was famous for his wealth and philanthropy, would, first, start subsidizing Lenin's organization, and second, introduce Krasin to his friends and relatives. In fact, this was precisely how the Bolsheviks found another rich sponsor, Nikolai Shmidt. At the same time, Lenin and Krasin wanted closer ties to the proletarian writer Maxim Gorky. As a writer, Gorky was interested in having his plays produced at the Moscow Art Theater, whose repertoire was in many respects determined by Morozov. This could also be done with Andreyeva's help if she succeeded in becoming Morozov's lover. As an actress, Andreyeva wanted leading roles, and the easiest way to get them was to have Morozov put pressure on Stanislavski and Nemirovich-Danchenko.

Everything therefore depended on Andreyeva's "acting ability." It was not by accident that Lenin referred to her as "Comrade Phenomenon": Andreyeva carried out her most important Bolshevik party assignment successfully. It is very difficult to reconstruct the actual sequence of events. As an actress of the Moscow Art Theater, Andreyeva knew Morozov, who practically lived in the theater. The first meeting between Andreyeva and Maxim Gorky took place in the spring of 1900, in Sevastopol, according to some accounts, and in Yalta, according to others, while the Moscow Art Theater was on tour. Her affair with Morozov apparently began no later than 1901. Her husband, Councillor of State Andrei Zhelyabuzhsky, was eighteen years her senior and had married her when she was eighteen years old. In 1888, they had a son, Yuri, and in 1894 a daughter, Ekaterina. Shortly afterward, Zhelyabuzhsky became involved with another woman and broke up with Andreyeva. For the sake of appearances, however, everything remained just as it had been before: the couple continued to live together for the sake of the children. "My family knew about it, and most of my friends guessed it—some things are impossible to hide," Andreyeva wrote much later to her friend and party comrade Nikolai Burenin, a collaborator of Krasin and Yakov Sverdlov (and since 1901, an active participant in the revolutionary movement, known to party members as "Comrade German").

Gorky became involved in the revolutionary movement in 1901 at the latest. On April 17, together with the future Soviet writer Stepan Skitalets (Petrov), Gorky was arrested for disseminating revolutionary propaganda among Moscow workers. One month later, he was transferred to house arrest for health reasons, and in September he completed his play "The Philistines," which had been interrupted due to the arrest. Also in September, and probably not by chance, Gorky was visited in Nizhny Novgorod by Nemiro-vich-Danchenko, who took his play with him to be produced at the Moscow Art Theater.[12] This at the insistence of Morozov, and at Andreyeva's request.

In November 1901, Gorky was exiled from Nizhny Novgorod. A demonstration against his enforced exile was organized in the city, one of the participants was Yakov Sverdlov, the future chairman of the All-Russian Central Executive Committee (VTsiK). A detailed account of these events appeared in Lenin's newspaper, *Iskra*, on December 20, 1901. Lenin wrote an article on the same topic, entitled "The Beginning of Demonstrations."[13] In 1902, Gorky met the members of the Nizhny Novgorod committee of the

RSDLP, above all with Sverdlov, who was also arrested some time later and Gorky took part in organizing assistance for for him.

In 1902, the Moscow Art Theater began staging Gorky's plays. *The Philistines* opened on March 26 in St. Petersburg, where the Moscow Art Theater was on tour; *The Lower Depths* opened in Moscow on December 19. At the same time, Gorky strengthened his ties with Lenin (as yet only in writing) and with Krasin. 1903 may be considered a pivotal year for all concerned. As Gorky wrote, "It was among the Bolsheviks, in Lenin's articles, in the speeches and work of the members of the intelligentsia who followed them, that I first felt a genuine revolutionary spirit. By 1903, I had 'attached myself' to them." In the same year, for Andreyeva's sake, Gorky separated from his wife, Yekaterina Peshkova, although they remained on good terms. At the end of 1903, Andreyeva officially became Gorky's wife (they were both 35 at the time; Morozov was six years older). In December 1903, Andreyeva introduced Morozov to Krasin (she had already introduced him to Gorky, and from then on he and Morozov were considered friends). In 1904—perhaps as a reward for everything she had done—Andreyeva (along with Burenin) was admitted to the Bolshevik Party. Andreyeva's party name was "Strela" (or "Arrow"—but party friends called her simply Marusya).

Morozov met Krasin at Gorky's dacha in Sestroretsk, near St. Petersburg, where Krasin was able to obtain money for revolutionary work from Morozov. During the period 1901–1903, Morozov had been giving 2,000 rubles every month to support *Iskra*. The Bolsheviks managed to surround Morozov with several of their lawyers, who gave him advice that was profitable to the party. Gorky wrote about this openly only in 1918, during the brief period of his rift with the Bolsheviks:

> For your information, I will say that between 1901 and 1917 hundreds of thousands of rubles that went to the Russian Social Democratic party (the Bolsheviks) passed through my hands. Of this money, my personal earnings constituted tens of thousands, while the rest was drawn from the pockets of the "bourgeoisie." *Iskra* was published with money that came from Savva Morozov, who naturally did not lend these funds, but donated them. I could name a dozen respectable people—"members of the bourgeoisie"—who materially helped the growth of the Social Democratic Party [i.e., the Bolsheviks]. This is well known to V. I. Lenin and the other old party workers.[14]

In addition, Morozov donated money to the political Red Cross for helping political convicts escape from prison—the escape of Bolshevik convicts from the Taganskaya Prison was organized with help from Andreyeva—and for literature for the local Bolshevik organization. He purchased fur coats for those who were sent into exile and used his house to hide wanted Bolsheviks—Krasin and Nikolai Bauman. It may be said with absolute certainty that without Andreyeva, the Bolsheviks would have received no subsidies from Morozov.

Andreyeva's influence on Morozov expressed itself more and more in the selection of plays for the theater. Andreyeva insisted on producing works by revolutionary writers. And it was these works that had Morozov's backing. In March 1903, Nemirovich-Danchenko spoke out at a board of directors' meeting at the theater against staging plays by revolutionary writers, claiming that the theater was pandering to vulgar tastes. In February 1904, Andreyeva handed in her resignation from the theater (Stanislavski, still hoping for more money from Morozov, talked her into taking a year's leave of absence). Savva Timofeyevich then decided to create a new theater under the direction of Andreyeva and Gorky, with Vera Komissarzhevskaya's actors, in Yusupov's rebuilt mansion in St. Petersburg. But when the plans by architect A. A. Galetsky were ready, the 1905 revolution began and the project was abandoned.

At the beginning of January 1905, in Riga, Andreyeva was diagnosed with peritonitis and ended up in the hospital. Gorky and Morozov arrived in Riga on January 11, directly from St. Petersburg. On the same day, Gorky was arrested for having participated in a demonstration in St. Petersburg on January 9, 1905, and transported back there. On February 14, Andreyeva, who had by this time recovered, and Konstantin Pyatnitsky, the managing director of Znanie Press, its director since 1902 had been Gorky, put up bail for Gorky in the amount of 10,000 rubles. The money came from Morozov. On the same evening, Gorky was freed and exiled to Riga. Morozov left for Moscow.

At this time, Morozov asked his mother to be given full control over the affairs of their factory. In response, he was barred from any involvement in managing the factory and denied access to the family's money altogether. Unexpectedly for him and for those around him, he lost his fortune and was now forced to rely on his mother's generosity.

In the spring, rumors that Morozov had lost his mind began to circulate in Moscow and St. Petersburg. "Today, there are rumors and stories in the newspapers that Savva Timofeyevich has lost his mind," Stanislavski wrote to his wife on April 13, 1905. "I think they are untrue." The family had every reason to believe that Morozov was unwell. It turned out that Morozov's 100,000-ruble life insurance policy had been made out "to the bearer" and given to Andreyeva, and in fact Andreyeva had warned Morozov that she would transfer the money to the Bolshevik Party. On April 15, a board of doctors found that Morozov was suffering from "severe nervous collapse" and recommended that he seek a cure abroad (and far away from Andreyeva, Gorky, the revolution, and the revolutionaries). Accompanied by his wife and his personal doctor, N. N. Selivansky, Morozov left for France. He traveled first to Vichy and then to Cannes, where he stopped at the Hotel Royal. By this time, according to the accounts of many witnesses, he had definitively terminated his funding of the Bolsheviks. In the middle of April, immediately before leaving for France, Morozov had a final quarrel with Gorky. Prior to this, at the beginning of February, in the presence of Zinaida Grigorievna, he had refused to give Krasin money to organize the Third Congress of the RSDLP. After visiting Morozov a second time at the end of April, this time in Vichy, Krasin was refused once again. Zinaida Grigorievna overheard a part of their conversation from the next room: "No, no, and once again no! My kind sirs, I have no more money for you." On the next day, Morozov and his wife moved to Cannes.

On the evening of May 13—May 26 by the European calendar—at 4 p.m., Savva Timofeyevich was found in his bed with a bullet in his heart. "There's some mystery in this death," Gorky wrote to Yekaterina Peshkova after hearing about the incident and without yet knowing what had happened. "For some reason, I think he shot himself. In any case, there's something dark in this story."[15] What penetrating insight! The darkest episode in this story was Krasin's appearance in Cannes.

On September 6, 1906, Andreyeva, who at this time was staying in the resort town of Adirondack (in New York State), wrote a letter to her sister Ye. F. Krit, who was bringing up Andreyeva's abandoned children. In this letter, she explained exactly how the money was to be divided: not more than one thousand rubles would go to Morozov's lawyer, Malyantovich; 60,000 rubles would go to Krasin; 15,000 rubles would go to pay off a debt to Pyatnitsky; "the rest is for your expenses."[16]

Morozov's relatives tried to contest the life insurance money. A trial took place. Andeyeva won. After the case was closed, the "financial department" of the Bolshevik Center (Lenin, Krasin, and Bogdanov) received 60,000 rubles from Andreyeva. All of these operations were overseen by Krasin.[17]

Sixty thousand rubles was a lot of money. The revolution was in progress. Money was needed and needed urgently. What we know about the Bolsheviks gives us no grounds to suppose that it was impossible for them to kill a man for the sake of a large sum of money for the party's coffers. At the time, Krasin was the head of the technical combat group at the Central Committee, which was in charge of armed combat against the government of the Russian Empire, including acts of terrorism. Another member of this group was Burenin.

It was Krasin who oversaw the illegal transportation into Russia (through Stockholm and Helsinki) of weapons for the revolutionaries purchased in France, Bulgaria, and Macedonia. And as a chemical engineer, he personally supervised the work of the laboratory that manufactured "infernal machines," hand grenades, and bombs. Based on a late account by Trotsky, Krasin dreamed of creating a portable bomb "the size of a walnut." He had a workshop in Gorky's apartment in Moscow, in building 4/7 on the corner of Mokhovaya and Vozdvizhenka Streets. This apartment was guarded by Transcaucasian "expropriators" from Kamo's group. It was here that Krasin prepared the bombs that were used by the SR Maximalists in an assassination attempt against Russian Prime Minister Pyotr Stolypin, on August 12 (25), 1906, on Aptekarsky Island. The explosion at Stolypin's residence killed or wounded several dozen people (including Stolypin's children). Stolypin himself, however, was unharmed.

Krasin's bombs were also used on October 14 (27), 1906, during a robbery in Fonarny Lane in St. Petersburg, where the SR Maximalists stole approximately 400,000 rubles. In return for this, a substantial portion of the money stolen was given to the Bolsheviks, as were parts of the sums stolen by the SRs from the Moscow Society of Mutual Credit Bank in Moscow in April, 1906.

The person who oversaw the storage of the munitions in Gorky's apartment was Andreyeva. Her and Gorky's contributions to the revolutionary movement were given due recognition. In the fall of 1905, Gorky was admitted to the Bolshevik Party. On November 27, he and Andreyeva arrived in St. Petersburg and on the same day, in Pyatnitsky's apartment, Gorky met Lenin for the first time. Bogdanov and Krasin were also present. Evidently, they also expressed their gratitude to Gorky and Andreyeva for Morozov's money.

Gorky's second meeting with Lenin took place at the beginning of 1906 in Helsingfors. At the time, Gorky was preparing for a trip around the United States which had been organized by Krasin in order to collect money for the Bolshevik Center. On February 12, 1906, Gorky and Andreyeva left Finland, and at the beginning of April, together with Burenin, Krasin and Litvinov saw them off. They departed for New York, carrying a letter of recommendation from the RSDLP's Central Committee and a personal note from Lenin as the representative of the joint RSDLP within the International. And although the RSDLP had a Joint Bolshevik-Menshevik Central Committee at the time, all of the money collected in America was given by Burenin to the

Bolshevik Center. The RSDLP's Central Committee protested but did not receive a penny. With time, the issue was buried. The Bolshevik Center never returned the money. The exact amount of the money collected in the United States is unknown; in any event, it amounted to tens of thousands of rubles. As a result, during the first Russian revolution, the Bolsheviks ended up with so much money that, according to Krasin, they did not need to confine themselves to revolvers, but could buy cannons; however, there was no way to deliver cannons and no place to hide them.

If Morozov's were the only mysterious death that occurred during this period, it would be difficult to reach any significant conclusions. But this was merely the first step on the way to an even more profitable piece of business—the inheritance of Nikolai Pavlovich Shmidt, a 23-year-old manufacturer, the owner of Russia's finest furniture factory, located in Moscow, on Nizhnyaya Prudovaya Street, in the Presnya District.

Nikolai Shmidt was the son of the daughter of Vikula Yeliseyevich Morozov. He was therefore part of the Morozov dynasty. It was Morozov who introduced Shmidt to Gorky. Pleased to be acquainted with a famous writer, Shmidt began helping the Bolsheviks through Gorky, giving them money for the newspaper *Novaya Zhizn* and for weapons. The police called Shmidt's factory the "devil's nest," and after the armed uprising in Moscow in 1905, in which Shmidt himself and his factory both played active roles, he was arrested. His factory was destroyed by government troops. This is how Shmidt is characterized in the *Great Soviet Encyclopedia*:

> [Shmidt] was a student at Moscow University with links to the Bolshevik party. He was a prominent participant in the 1905 Revolution.... He played an active role in preparing the armed uprising of December 1905, buying a large quantity of weapons in order to arm his own and certain other militant groups. He provided the Moscow Bolshevik organization (through Gorky) with substantial funds to arm the workers. At the height of the December uprising, Shmidt was arrested.... On February 13 (26), 1907 (after a little over a year in prison), Shmidt was found dead in the prison hospital (according to one account, he had been stabbed by the prison authorities; according to another account, his death was a suicide).[18]

A less formal description of these events is offered by Alexei Rykov, the future head of the Soviet government, in his memoirs, published in 1918:

> During 1905–1906, I was in contact with the family of Nikolai Shmidt, who, after dying in prison, left his entire estate to the party. He was one of the most interesting figures of the time.... Beginning in 1905, he constantly assisted our

party in all kinds of ways.... He armed most of the workers in his factory and handed over the factory's management to a workers' committee. The well-known events in the Presnya District during the uprising of December 1905 [in Moscow] occurred mainly because of the participation of workers from his factory.... And it is still an unresolved question whether he committed suicide in Butyrskaya Prison or whether he was killed by a hired killer.... He was offered release on bail. But five days after the offer was made, he was found dead in one of the prison's towers.[19]

Krupskaya writes that Shmidt was "butchered" in prison, but that "before he died, he was able to make it known to people outside that he was bequeathing his property to the Bolsheviks." In other words, before being "butchered," Shmidt found time to make out a will and to leave everything to Lenin's organization. What foresight indeed!

It does not require exceptional acumen to realize that Shmidt was murdered not by the prison authorities, who were prepared to release him on bail, but by people who had been sent by the Bolsheviks, who already were in possession of Shmidt's genuine or forged will (which could be converted into actual money only in the event of his death). The Bolsheviks were also interested in Shmidt's death because he had started to divulge the names of his collaborators. Valentinov-Volsky writes:

> Shmidt was not subjected to any kind of physical torture. The Okhrana would have never dared to use on him, a member of the Morozov family, the methods of interrogation that would become standard practice in the [Soviet] GPU and NKVD. The gendarmerie officer from the Okhrana's Moscow bureau who was in charge of Shmidt's case "worked" on him in a different way.... He engaged him in "intimate" conversations, off the record, as if in secret.... The surroundings in which these "intimate" conversations to place looked more like a private room in a restaurant at a table set for a sumptuous meal than an interrogation cell. Naive and not knowing how to lie, Shmidt.... once revealed the names of the workers who had obtained weapons through him. He named other people as well. He talked about Savva Morozov and his subsidies for the revolution.[20]

Let us state more precisely what it was that Shmidt divulged to the police: "While under arrest, he indicated that he had given Gorky 15,000 rubles for the publication of the newspaper *Novaya Zhizn* and 20,000 for purchasing weapons."[21]

Clearly, once Shmidt started to provide information, he became dangerous for the Bolsheviks. Like Morozov, Shmidt was killed, but the will that he left behind brought the Bolsheviks far more money than Morozov's.

The Bolsheviks had to fight in order to obtain this money, however, and the very fact that they did so also confirms the assumption that Shmidt had been murdered by them.

Shmidt had two sisters (Yekaterina, who was a legal adult, and Yelizaveta, who was a minor) and a 15-year-old brother. In order for Lenin to acquire Shmidt's entire inheritance, it was necessary to get all three siblings to forfeit all claims to Shmidt's money. This was accomplished with the help of two Bolsheviks, Viktor Taratuta and Nikolai Andrikanis.

Viktor Taratuta had escaped from exile through the Caucasus and arrived in Moscow in November 1905 (before Shmidt's arrest in the second half of December). He became the secretary of the Bolsheviks' Moscow organization as well as its treasurer, and he took over the management of its press. The preliminary preparations for the Bolshevik Center's operation to obtain Shmidt's estate were apparently extensive. Taratuta began courting Shmidt's younger sister, Yelizaveta, even before Shmidt's death. In the spring of 1906, Taratuta left for a party congress in Stockholm. In the fall of the same year, possibly with Yelizaveta Shmidt, he traveled to Finland.

Beginning in 1906, various rumors began to circulate about Taratuta. On the one hand, a woman who came from the same town (R. S. Zalkind) and was well known among the Bolsheviks as a gossip—and such level-headed Bolsheviks as Ivan Sammer and Bogdanov—all claimed that Taratuta was an agent of the Okhrana. As we now know for certain, Taratuta was not a double agent. That role belonged another person within Lenin's circle, Dr. Zhitomirsky. However, at this time no one suspected Zhitomirsky and the leaks were blamed on Taratuta.

At a party congress in London in the spring of 1907, on Lenin's instructions, Taratuta was elected to the Bolshevik Center and became a candidate for the Central Committee of the RSDLP. Lenin's special patronage was due precisely to the fact that he was planning to obtain Shmidt's inheritance through Taratuta. For the first time in the history of the Social Democratic Party, a person who was accused of having ties with the police was being elected as a candidate for the Central Committee. Naturally, Taratuta's candidacy gave rise to serious objections, but Lenin was able to get his way and Taratuta was elected.

Soon after, apparently in the summer of 1907, Lenin became personally acquainted with Yelizaveta Shmidt, who had come to Finland together with Taratuta. The young woman was 18 or 19 years old. She had become involved with Taratuta, whose real biography she did not know, during the period of the 1905 revolution. His position within the party as the secretary of the Moscow committee of the RSDLP and a member of the Bolshevik

Center had undoubtedly made an impression on her. Lenin naturally understood this. Perhaps it was because of this that he was so intent on pushing through Taratuta's candidacy for membership in the Central Committee. After all, there were no formal guarantees that the money inherited by the young woman would be handed over.

Around this time, a conversation took place between Lenin and the social democrat Nikolai Rozhkov, which revealed a great deal about Lenin's position. When Rozhkov called Taratuta a "complete scoundrel," Lenin remained unfazed. Moreover, he objected, this was precisely why Taratuta was so valuable. "That's the good thing about him," Lenin said. "He will stop at nothing. You, for example—tell me the truth—could you stand to be maintained by a wealthy merchant lady for money? No? I couldn't do it either, I wouldn't be able to make myself do it. But Viktor did... This man is irreplaceable."[22]

Meanwhile, Taratuta, "by applying unacceptable threats,"[23] forced the legal custodians of Shmidt's 15-year-old brother to withdraw all claims to his inheritance. What was implied by these "unacceptable threats" was precisely the murder of anyone who might block the flow of Shmidt's money into the party's coffers. This was disclosed by Sergei Shesternin, an old Social Democrat from Ivanovo-Voznesensk, who was used by the Bolsheviks to acquire Shmidt's inheritance and to take the money out of the country.[24] During the very first meeting between the Bolshevik Center's representatives (Lenin, Krasin, and Taratuta) and Shmidt's brother and his lawyers in the spring of 1907 in Vyborg, Taratuta "in a harsh, metallic voice" announced that he would eliminate anyone who might hinder him from getting the money. Lenin "pulled on Taratuta's sleeve," while the younger Shmidt's St. Petersburg lawyers "displayed signs of discomfiture." Several days later, the lawyers gave notice that Shmidt's brother was ceding his rights to the inheritance to his two sisters.

Meanwhile, in 1907, a member of the Bolshevik Party's Moscow office named Nikolai Andrikanis—a young Moscow attorney and a government lawyer's assistant—married the older of Shmidt's two sisters, Yekaterina, but changed his mind about depositing what was now his own money into Lenin's treasury. The ever-resourceful Taratuta then threatened to kill both sisters as well as the older one's husband, Andrikanis, if they refused to hand over the money to the Bolshevik Center. Frightened, Andrikanis appealed to the party. The party held joint hearings, which were chaired by Mark Natanson, one of the leaders of the SRs, and it was resolved that Andrikanis must contribute either one-third or one-half of the inheritance to the Bolshevik Center.[25] And although Andrikanis clearly carried out the party's decision,

Taratuta remained unsatisfied by the outcome of the case and continued to threaten Andrikanis. The latter had no choice but to bring an appeal before the party once more. He therefore went to the Central Committee of the RSDLP to complain about Taratuta's actions, pointing out that the Bolshevik Center was demanding money that had been bequeathed to the Social Democratic Party as a whole, not just to the Bolsheviks alone.[26]

In his book *Two Parties,* Kamenev—a Bolshevik and the future head of the Soviet government—described the case of Andrikanis and Yekaterina Shmidt in greater detail:[27]

> The Bolsheviks put Andrikanis in charge of the money that they were supposed to get. When it came time to receive this money, it turned out that Andrikanis had become so "intimate" with it that we, as an underground organization, had almost no means of obtaining it from him. In light of a whole set of circumstances, which it would be unthinkable to discuss in print, Andrikanis could not completely deny the rights of the Bolshevik Center. But Andrikanis declared that only a part of this property (a negligible one) belonged to the Bolsheviks, that he was willing to pay this part, but that he was unable to say when he would pay it or how big the amount was. Meanwhile, aside from this part, everything else belonged to him, Andrikanis.... The only thing that the Bolshevik Center could do was to put Andrikanis before the court of public opinion, handing over their charges against him to an arbitration court.... In accordance with this court's ruling, we received the maximum amount that the court could obtain from Andrikanis. The court was forced to rely on the amounts of the legal guarantees that it had been possible to secure from Andrikanis before the trial. All the same, Andrikanis kept the lion's share of the estate.[28]

Kamenev further claimed that the legitimacy of the Bolsheviks' demands was confirmed by numerous documents, which could not be published for security reasons. But even after the Revolution, when security was no longer an issue, not one of the numerous documents mentioned by Kamenev was made public, although all of them were in the possession of the Bolshevik Center and were subsequently stored in the archives of the Central Committee of the CPSU—while Kamenev's book came out in a second edition in 1924.[29]

The ensuing discussion was noisy and complicated. Martov now claimed that the money bequeathed by Shmidt was the property of the Central Committee, and he described the situation as an "expropriation of party money by the Bolshevik Center."[30] Kamenev insisted that the argument with Andrikanis had not been about who should get the money that legally belonged to Lenin's Bolshevik Center, but about the portion of this money

Andrikanis had the right to retain for himself. Further, that Andrikanis's actions had been motivated not by a desire for justice (in this respect, Kamenev was undoubtedly correct), but by the desire to keep as much as he could for himself.

"At this time," N. K. Krupskaya, Lenin's wife, wrote in her memoirs, "the Bolsheviks obtained a solid financial foundation." So solid was this foundation, Valentinov-Volsky adds, that "at the end of 1908 [a part of it] showed up in Lenin's account at the Crédit Lyonnais on Avenue d'Orléans, No. 19, in Paris."[31] In late May 1908, Lenin received word that a part of Shmidt's inheritance had been sold, that all of the appropriate documents had been drawn, and that Shesternin was bringing them from Moscow to Paris. This was the money of Yelizaveta Shmidt, the mistress of Taratuta and the wife of A. M. Ignatyev, and it amounted to 510,000 francs or approximately 190,000 rubles in gold.[32] The financial crisis was over, and Andrikanis, in return for promising to drop the issue of Shmidt's estate being the rightful property of the Central Committee, was left in peace.

"The wealthy merchant lady," Yelizaveta Shmidt, who was in reality a young college student, turned out to be not as hopeless as Lenin had supposed. She began her adult life as a citizen by writing out a will whereby in the event of her death, all her money went to the Bolshevik Party. It is hard to imagine that this was done without pressure from Taratuta. "Yelizaveta Pavlovna Shmidt decided to transfer her share of the inheritance to the Bolsheviks," Krupskaya reports. But she does not specify how exactly this "transfer" took place.

What actually happened was the following. Since Yelizaveta Shmidt was not yet twenty-one, she could not, under Russian law, dispose of her inheritance until she was married. Therefore, a fictitious marriage was arranged for her and Ignatyev, an agent of Krasin's, who was in charge of organizing the armed bands of the Central Committee. At the end of 1907, with Ignatyev's formal consent, Yelizaveta Shmidt began signing all of the necessary documents in order to sell her share of her brother's estate (which had already been bequeathed to the party). For greater security, the party decided that Taratuta should remain the young woman's real husband. In this way, Lenin was guaranteed to get her money.[33]

Against the background of the squabble with Andrikanis and Martov's and Kamenev's argument over cash—far removed from the high ideals of socialism—Lenin dissolved his partnership with Bogdanov and Krasin. The break was seemingly based on the fundamental issue of the role of expropriations in the revolution and on how the remaining 500-ruble bills were to be exchanged. Unexpectedly for his partners, Lenin came out against further expropriations and risky ventures, particularly outside Russia. He insisted on abandoning all plans to exchange the remaining one hundred and fifty 500-ruble bills, preferring to lose 75,000. Krasin and Bogdanov had a different view. Bogdanov organized an attempt to exchange the money in North America, which also ended in failure. After a series of attempts, Krasin was able to alter the serial numbers on the 500-ruble bills and exchange some of them (this money was used by the group "Forward," which had split off from Lenin, to publish seven books between 1910 and 1913), although by this time all the banks in the world were closely monitoring Russian 500-ruble bills. With this development, Lenin's relations with Krasin and Bogdanov came to an end, and in 1909, at the insistence of the Mensheviks, the RSDLP resolved that all of the 500-ruble bills that had not yet been exchanged should be burned.

Lenin wanted to have complete control over finances. Krasin and Bogdanov insisted that financial issues be handled by the Bolshevik Center's "financial department" (Lenin, Krasin, Bogdanov). And when Krasin and Bogdanov refused to submit to Lenin's authority, the latter easily found political differences that could serve as pretexts for a much-needed quarrel. Lenin would have never resolved to split off from Bogdanov and especially from Krasin if this had not been financially expedient. Cunningly, Lenin decide to defame the two individuals who had been his close partners—to quarrel with them publicly, and after having quarreled, to expel Bogdanov and Krasin from the Bolshevik Center, thus keeping all of Shmidt's money for himself. In order to do this, Lenin needed to convene a conference. On July 1, 1908, several days after returning to Geneva, Lenin wrote a letter to Vatslav Vorovsky, Bolshevik, member of the Central Committee, and future Soviet ambassador to Italy:

> In August [new style], we are still definitely counting on your participation in the conference. Make sure to arrange things so that you can take a trip abroad. We will send travel money to all Bolsheviks.... We urgently request that you write for our newspaper. We can now pay for articles and we will pay without fail.[34]

From this letter it follows, first, that Lenin already disposed of large sums of money, and second, that he was convening a conference and using the money that was now in his possession to send for all of the people who were loyal to him. However, instead of a conference, a plenary assembly of the Central Committee took place on August 24–26, preceded by a meeting of the Bolshevik Center, which predetermined the outcome of the plenary assembly. A general assembly of the Bolshevik Center was not feasible. Over one third of the members of the Bolshevik Center were in prison and in exile. Nine members were outside Russia, but there are no definite records indicating whether or not they took part in the August 1908 meeting. It is known only that, in August 1908, four members sided with Lenin (Dubrovinsky, Zinoviev, Kamenev, and Taratuta) and two with Bogdanov and Krasin (Mikhail Pokrovsky and Virgilii Shantser). Lenin had the majority. Immediately following this, he dissolved the "committee of three" (Lenin, Krasin, Bogdanov) and the "financial group" (Lenin, Krasin, Bogdanov), and officially delegated the administering of the funds of the Bolshevik Center to a new "financial committee," loyal to Lenin that included Zinoviev, representative of the newspaper *Proletarian*; Lenin's wife, Krupskaya, the secretary of the Bolshevik Center; Kotlyarenko, responsible for deliveries; and Taratuta, who was responsible for the Bolshevik Center's treasury). A fifth member included in the committee—whose duties were not specified—was Zhitomirsky, an agent of the Okhrana. The Bolshevik Center's money was now fully and quite legally under Lenin's control.

The ideological break was reinforced by a philosophical work that Lenin wrote especially for the occasion, *Materialism and Empiriocriticism*. This book, which came out in 1909, was aimed against all philosophical theories, both in Russia and abroad, and consisted of a series of spiteful attacks. It is obvious that such a work had little to do with philosophy; and Lenin's attempt in this field should be considered highly unsuccessful. But because the anti-Bogdanov thrust of this dull volume was motivated not by philosophical disagreements, but by financial squabbles, the meaning of what Lenin wrote now appears to us in a completely different light.

The exact amount of money that went into Lenin's coffers was known only to a few individuals, first and foremost Lenin and Taratuta. Yemelyan Yaroslavsky, a Bolshevik and a future ideologue of Stalinism, indicated that Shmidt's estate amounted to 280,000 gold rubles.[35] After the Bolsheviks and the Mensheviks were reconciled in 1910 and all party treasuries were united into one, the Bolsheviks agreed to transfer 475,000 francs, or approximately 178,000 gold rubles, to Karl Kautsky, Franz Mehring, and Clara Zetkin, prominent German Social Democrats, who were appointed as the "custodians" of the Bolsheviks' funds. This was what remained of Shmidt's estate. Since Lenin's Bolshevik Center was expected to transfer its money to the Central Committee in installments, the Bolsheviks did not give up all of Shmidt's money. By the end of 1910, the Bolshevik-Menshevik coalition had fallen apart for good, and Lenin halted the transfer of the money to the "custodians." Moreover, he demanded that the money that had been given to the German Social Democrats earlier be returned to the Bolsheviks. A new "showdown" began—this time with prominent German Social Democrats.

All of this was not without repercussions for Lenin. He came to be viewed as a solitary fanatic, an extremist with an insignificant number of followers, who had emigrated from Russia as a political activist without a party or even an organization, only with money. The convening of the so-called Sixth Bolshevik Conference in Prague in 1912 was nothing but a desperate attempt on Lenin's part to break out of this isolation and to raise the status of his own group in the eyes of the socialists. Enlisting Joseph Stalin in absentia into the Central Committee and into the Russian bureau of the RSDLP was undoubtedly motivated by similar considerations: through Stalin, Lenin could obtain access to underground revolutionaries in Russia— this, at least, was what he was counting on.

During the First World War, mainly because of financial need, Lenin came in contact through intermediaries with representatives of the German government, including members of the Ministry of Foreign Affairs, military agencies, and the intelligence apparatus. The relations between the Bolshevik Party and the Kaiser's government during WWI remained a riddle for historians for a long time. When evidence first appeared that the German government, in order to weaken the Russian Empire and to encourage it to withdraw from the war, had found it expedient to finance socialist parties that stood for Russia's defeat and actively conducting defeatist propaganda campaigns, the discovery caused a sensation around the world. The German Social Democrat Eduard Bernstein, who was at one time the deputy finance minister in the German government, pointed out Lenin's ties to the Germans in an article entitled "A Dark History," which was published on January 14, 1921, in the morning edition of the German Social Democratic newspaper *Der Vorwärts*:

> Lenin and his comrades received enormous sums from the Kaiser's Germany. I learned about this at the end of December 1917.... However, at the time I knew neither the size of these sums nor the name of the intermediary who delivered them. Now I have obtained information from a reliable source that the amount in question was almost unthinkable, definitely surpassing 50 million German gold marks, so that neither Lenin nor his comrades could have had any doubts concerning the source of this money.

Apparently, Bernstein somewhat understated the amount. In a transcript of a conversation that took place at the beginning of January 1921, he indicated that the total sum amounted to 60 million marks:

I heard that the Bolsheviks had received money from the German government at a Reichstag committee meeting in 1921.... Apart from the members of
the Reichstag, those present at the meeting included high officials from the
Ministry of Foreign Affairs and the Military Department.... During the session,
one of the members of the committee said loudly to another: "After all, the
Bolsheviks received 60 million marks from the German government.".... The
next day, I visited Prof. Schüking, who was the committee chair, and told him
about the conversation regarding the 60 million marks. I asked him whether he
knew anything about this. He replied that he knew that the Bolsheviks had been
given that amount of money.[36]

However, Bernstein had touched on a problem that neither the
Communists, nor the German government, nor the German Social Democratic Party wished to discuss. It is not surprising that this question, which so
intrigued everyone, was left unanswered, and that Bernstein, like the German
Communists, chose not to insist on the formation of a commission to investigate the issue of the German gold marks. And when Vladimir Burtsev, a
Russian socialist revolutionary who was well known for uncovering agents
provocateurs and spies, offered a German Social Democratic publisher a
book that described how Lenin and the Bolsheviks had received money from
the German imperial government, the publisher declined:[37]

"I am far from certain that it is the right time to talk about this matter," the
historian and archivist Boris Nicolaevsky wrote to Burtsev in 1931, when the
latter complained to him about the Germans' rejection. "At any rate, the Germans themselves are decidedly convinced that it is too early to raise this set of
questions.... Forgive me, Vladimir Lvovich, but do you really believe that your
book can be accepted for publication by any German Social Democratic publisher? After all, this is a completely impossible work. You probably know that in
1920 [1921] E. Bernstein obtained certain materials describing the relations
between the German military and the Bolsheviks during the war, and that he was
about to publish them...but was compelled to call a halt to this business, and that
he still has not returned to it."[38]

In the end, Burtsev could only agree. "You are right, the Germans do not
want to talk about how they helped Lenin."[39]

Many years later, historians obtained access to documents that permitted
a deeper and more thorough examination of the now-legendary subject of the
German money and the sealed train car in which Lenin and a group of comrades came back to Russia from Switzerland, by way of Germany, in 1917.[40]
It is worth noting that these publications, which patently revealed the
connections between the German government and such famous revolu-

tionaries as the Swiss Social Democrat Karl Moor (Baier) and the Russian-Romanian-Bulgarian socialist Christian Rakovsky, caused a real furor among the revolutionaries who were still living at the time.

The picture that emerged was worthy of a thriller. It was clear that collaboration between the revolutionaries and Russia's principal enemies—Japan, Austria-Hungary, and Germany—had always existed. Thus, already in February 1904, the Japanese military attaché in Russia, Colonel M. Akasi, entered into contact with the head of the Finnish Active Resistance Party, Konni Zilliacus, and with one of the heads of the Party of Georgian Social Federalists, Georgi Dekanozov. At the same time, Akasi "developed a plan to provide financial assistance to revolutionaries in order to accelerate the start of an armed uprising in Russia."[41]

Japanese money paid for a Conference of Revolutionary and Oppositional Parties, which took place in Paris from September 30 to October 4, 1904, with the approval of Japanese intelligence and military headquarters (in 1905, Japanese money also paid for a similar conference in Geneva). In May 1904, Japanese money was used by Lenin and his future secretary Vladimir Bonch-Bruevich to establish the first large-scale socialist publishing enterprise, which began sending shipments of defeatist Social Democratic and SR literature to Japan for Russian prisoners of war. But by the summer of 1904, the leadership of the RSDLP had discovered the source of Lenin's and Bonch-Bruevich's money, and in July 1904 the Central Committee—which Lenin subsequently characterized as "appeasist"—categorically prohibited Bonch-Bruevich from "sending party literature to the Tokyo government since it compromises the party."[42]

Since Bonch-Bruevich did not comply with the Central Committee's orders and shipments of literature to Japan continued, the Central Committee was forced formally to bar Bonch-Bruevich from managing the project of forwarding books to Japan. When Plekhanov asked him directly whether he had made arrangements with the Japanese government to send literature to Japan, Bonch-Bruevich merely expressed his indignation at these allegations.[43] Only in 1915 did Plekhanov openly state that "already at the time of the Russo-Japanese War, Lenin's center was not above accepting assistance from the Japanese government, whose agents in Europe helped the distribution of Lenin's publications."[44]

At the beginning of March 1904 Akasi traveled to Cracow to meet with Roman Dmowski, a member of the privy council of the National League (Liga Narodowa). Armed with Akasi's letters of recommendation, Dmowski then left for Japan in order to meet with the deputy head of the Japanese military, General G. Komoda, and with the head of Japanese intelligence,

General Y. Hukushima. In the middle of May 1904, Dmowski "arrived in Tokyo, where at Komoda's request he wrote two extensive briefs on the domestic situation in Russia and the Polish question."[45] But since the National League was opposed to the creation of a Polish front at the rear of the Russian army, Dmowski assured the Japanese commanders that their hopes of using the Polish nationalist movement in order to weaken the Russian Empire were futile.

A different stance was taken by the Polish Socialist Party (PPS). Already in February 1904 the PPS had issued a call for a Japanese victory in the Russo-Japanese War. Hoping for Russia's defeat and the collapse of the Russian Empire, the PPS's Central Revolutionary Committee, together with other Polish revolutionary parties, started taking steps to organize an armed uprising in Poland. In the beginning of March 1904 Witold Jodko-Narkie-wicz, a member of the PPS Central Committee, presented plans for an up-rising to the Japanese ambassador in London, T. Hayashi. The plans included the dissemination of propaganda "among Polish soldiers in the Russian army" and "the destruction of bridges and railroads."

At the beginning of July a man whose name was to enter Polish and world history traveled to Japan in order to continue the negotiations. This was Josef Pilsudski, a member of the PPS Central Committee and the future head of independent Poland. He presented a memorandum to the Japanese Ministry of Foreign Affairs, in which he requested that the PPS be given money for an armed uprising and that a political alliance be formed between the PPS and Japan. Japanese military headquarters declined to enter into political agreements with the Polish socialists and decided to continue political contacts with Dmowski's revolutionary nationalists. At the same time, Pilsudski was given 20,000 pounds sterling (approximately 200,000 rubles) for intelligence and sabotage activities at the rear of the Russian army.

How much money, then, did Japan spend on the Russian revolution? And who in particular did this money go to and for what purpose? It is diffi-cult to give exhaustive answers to these questions. In the middle of March 1905 Japan's military made a decision to allocate one million yen to subsidize an armed uprising in Russia. At the end of March and the beginning of April, purchases of weapons began in Europe for delivery to Russia. Those who actively participated in the buying included Dekanozov, Zilliacus, Georgi Gapon, and the SRs Nikolai Tchaikovsky and D. Soskins, with the last two pretending that they were unaware of the source of the money.

Intermediaries from other parties participated in the purchases as well, for example, the anarchist Yevgeny Bo. Most of the money was received by the SRs, the PPS, the Party of Georgian Social Federalists, and the Finnish

Active Resistance Party. Several steamships were purchased to transport the weapons. However, their journey was beset by misfortunes. Two ships stayed behind in Denmark. The third one, the *Luna*, unloaded part of its weapons to the north of Vindau, but not finding anyone at the location where most of its cargo was supposed to be unloaded (on an island near Vyborg, Finland), it sailed back to Copenhagen. On September 4 and 6, the *Luna* successfully unloaded weapons in the Kemi district and near Pietarsaari twice. But on the early morning of September 7, the steamship ran aground in Finland, at a distance of 22 km from Jakobstad, and was blown up by the revolutionaries themselves (the crew sailed to Sweden on a yacht stolen from local residents).

Since the explosion of the *Luna* was organized as poorly as the sailing itself, two-thirds of the weapons ended up in the hands of the Russian government (Finland was part of the Russian Empire at the time); a great deal was appopriated by the local population; and only a small part went to the revolutionaries (the Wetterly rifles delivered by the *Luna* were used by revolutionaries during the December 1905 uprising in Moscow).

Only one attempt to transport weapons during this period was a complete success: at the end of 1905, the steamship *Sirius* delivered 8,500 rifles to the Caucasus. However, the scale of the Japanese-funded purchases should be judged not by the deliveries, but according to the purchases: Dekanozov and Bo bought 25,000 rifles and over four million bullets in Switzerland; in addition, 2,500–3,000 revolvers and three tons of explosives were also purchased. Zilliacus bought a load of Mauser cavalry carbines in Hamburg. And between the spring of 1904 and the end of 1905, the revolutionaries brought more than 15,000 rifles, approximately 24,000 revolvers, and large amounts of bullets, ammunition, and dynamite through Finland into Russia.[46]

Between the Russo-Japanese War (1904–1905) and the Russian-German War (1914–1918), beginning in approximately 1909 the revolutionaries collaborated principally with Austria-Hungary, which played on the national contradictions within the Russian Empire. First and foremost, they collaborated with the military intelligence wing of Austria's general headquarters; then with Austria-Hungary's Ministry of Foreign Affairs. Yakov Ganetsky, a prominent Bolshevik and a collaborator of Lenin's, was a key figure in this game. He was connected to the Austrians precisely between 1909 and 1914, and, with the consent of the Austro-Hungarian government, organized Lenin's move to Cracow, a part of Austria-Hungary at the time.

This move was connected to the Austrian government's policy of collaborating with Russian and Polish revolutionaries. The main representative of the Polish Social Democrats, in this instance, was Pilsudski, who after the end of the Russo-Japanese War was left without Japanese financial support. He needed to figure out how to continue financing his political activity.

The fact that the PPS had openly engaged in espionage and sabotage was not without repercussions for the party. In 1906, a split began within the PPS. In November 1906, at the Ninth Congress of the PPS, Pilsudski and his supporters broke away from the party for good, resigned from the PPS, and formed their own "Revolutionary Fraction of the PPS." A considerable number of the members of the PPS's militant wing, who were less interested in theoretical and literary activities than in armed combat, acts of terror, and expropriations, followed Pilsudski.

The last major expropriation executed by the PPS was the raid on a mail train at Bezdany, near Vilno (as Vilnius, the current capital of Lithuania, was called at the time), which took place in November 1908. Pilsudski himself took part in the robbery. Two hundred thousand rubles was stolen. And yet, this sum remained insignificant—not enough to blow up the Russian monarchy and liberate Poland. Gradually, Pilsudski reached the conclusion that the revolutionary base had to be organized abroad, with the support of Russia's current external enemy, whoever that happened to be. The natural choice at the moment seemed to be Austria-Hungary, which included Galicia—the eastern part of Poland, which enjoyed a certain autonomy.

Pilsudski's first negotiations with the Austrians began in 1906. On September 29, together with Jodko-Narkiewicz, he met with Colonel Franz Kanik, commander of the Tenth Army Corps in Przemysl. In his report to the general headquarters commander in Vienna, Kanik described this meeting as follows:

> They offered us various kinds of assistance with gathering intelligence against Russia, in exchange for certain favors from our side. These favors involve supporting the struggle against the Russian government in the following ways: assistance in acquiring weapons, a tolerant attitude toward secret weapon caches and party agents in Galicia, toward Austrian reservists who take part in fighting against Russia, and toward revolutionaries in the event of a possible intervention by our monarchy.

By the summer of 1908, firm contacts had been established with Major Gustav Ishkovsky of Austrian general headquarters, the commander of the Lwow Corps political intelligence unit. In 1908, Pilsudski, with the knowledge and permission of the Austrian authorities, began organizing Polish paramilitary units in Galicia. At the end of June, in Lwow (currently Ukraine), he created the Associations for Active Struggle, a militant organization that had 147 members by June 1909.

However, the clandestine nature of these activities contradicted the aim of creating a general Polish army. Therefore, in 1910 Pilsudski obtained permission from the Austrian government to create legal militant organizations in accordance with the Austrian law governing Riflemen's Associations: the Rifleman in Cracow and the Riflemen's Association in Lwow. Pilsudski's Association for Active Struggle remained these groups' secret command headquarters.

In the summer of 1912, Pilsudski established the Polish Military Fund, which oversaw the financing of his military-political activities. It is clear that the fund received most of its money from the Austrian authorities. At this time, Pilsudski disposed of sums that the impoverished emigrant Lenin could not even dream about. Lenin's move to the command center of Pilsudski's political and military activities in 1912 could not have been accidental: it could not have taken place without the permission of the Austrian government, without Pilsudski's permission, and without financial terms that were advantageous for himself. Cracow, a small city with a population of one hundred thousand, was the center of Pilsudski's movement. So by moving there, Lenin was moving directly under Pilsudski's wing, not submitting himself to Austrian control in some abstract Galicia.

Not everyone in the revolutionary camp supported such a policy. Lenin, undoubtedly, was aware of Pilsudski's "collaboration" with the Austro-Hungarian government and, finding it useful, supported it. However, in 1904, when the collaboration with the Japanese began, a part of the leadership of the Polish Socialist Party—first and foremost, the future head of the German Communist Party, Rosa Luxemburg, whose authority was already great not only within the Polish social democratic organization, but within the German one is well—came out first against collaborating with the Japanese military and then against Pilsudski's and Ganetsky's collaboration with the Austro-Hungarian government as well. It was precisely around the issue of Pilsudski's "Austrian orientation" that the final split within the Polish social democratic movement occurred. Ganetsky came out in favor of it. Prominent Polish revolutionaries—Luxemburg, Leo von Tyzka, Barsky, Dzerzhinsky, and others—were against it. At about the same time, officially for completely different reasons, Karl Radek—a future prominent member of the Bolsheviks' Central Committee and Soviet functionary—was expelled from the Polish Social Democratic Party, on the initiative of Luxemburg, due to suspicion that he was collaborating with Austro-Hungarian intelligence.

Austrian social democrats knew or suspected that Polish and Russian revolutionaries were collaborating with the Austro-Hungarian government. They did everything they could to avoid becoming mixed up in these relations, which sooner or later could only end in scandal. But Austria's social democrats also did not want to publicly expose the links between the socialists of other countries and their own government. They did, however, express their displeasure at these links in private conversations with social democratic "agents" of the Austrian government. Thus, Otto Bauer discussed this with Pilsudski when the latter visited the Austrian social democrats' office:

> "I understand," Bauer said, "that you, as a Polish socialist, may want to maintain friendly relations with Austrian socialists; I can accept that you, as a Polish nationalist, may consider it necessary to maintain relations with the Austrian government. But I do not understand how you cannot see that to maintain relations both with Austrian socialists and with the Austrian government simultaneously is impossible."

Pilsudski saw this very clearly. But, like Lenin, he simply found such a game useful. One might add that, also like Lenin, he derived a triple advantage from this double game.

With the beginning of the First World War, Pilsudski's collaboration with the Austrian government acquired the status of an open military-political alliance. With the support of Austria-Hungary's military headquarters, after the war began Pilsudski organized intelligence operations and created the Rifleman, an organization dedicated to terrorism and sabotage, in Galicia. At the same time, in August 1914, he formed the Polish Military Organization (Polska Organizacja Wojskowa). At the height of the war, Pilsudski was in command of the Polish Legions, which fought on the Austro-Hungarian side. When on November 5, 1916, the occupying powers of Germany and Austria-Hungary proclaimed a Polish state in Eastern Poland, Pilsudski became a member of the provisional governing council of the Regency Kingdom of Poland. In 1917, he went on to become the head of the military department in the government of the "independent" Polish state.

After the Russian revolution of February 1917, Pilsudski once again switched allegiances. With the recognition of Poland's right to independence by Russia's Provisional Government, it was unnecessary for him to maintain his allegiance to Austria, which did not want to hand over Galicia to Poland. After the United States entered the war, it became clear that the Central Empires would most likely not be victorious. And with the victory of the Triple Entente, the political career of the pro-Austrian Pilsudski would be coming to an end. Thus, he began searching for an excuse to break with Austria. In July 1917, he finally found one: on July 22, he was arrested for calling on Polish legionaires to refuse to take an oath of allegiance to Austria-Hungary and was imprisoned in the Magdeburg Fortress in Germany. Pilsudski therefore underwent a transformation from being a supporter of the Germans and Austrians to becoming a victim of the occupying powers. Each day of his imprisonment, he political stature grew.

In November 1918 the new German government released Pilsudski and he returned to Warsaw in triumph. In February 1919 the Polish parliament appointed him Chief of State and Commander-in-Chief, which he remained—with a three-year hiatus (1923–1926)—practically until his death in 1935. His past dealings in espionage and sabotage did not harm his career.

After the start of the First World War, Austria's military intelligence passed its connections with revolutionaries of the Russian Empire to German intelligence. In 1915 at the latest, Ganetsky began collaborating with the prominent German-Russian revolutionary and German government agent Alexander Parvus (Gelfand). They were joined by Georg Sklarz, on Parvus's side, and by Karl Radek, who was with Ganetsky. But things did not go according to plan. In Copenhagen, Ganetsky was arrested for trafficking in contraband. During the trial, documents emerged that proved that he was working with Parvus. It became equally clear that the German government's money—which Ganetsky received from Parvus—ultimately went to Lenin, that it was used to buy printing facilities, carry out propaganda campaigns, and feed the Bolsheviks in exile. Ganetsky himself was so compromised by his ties to Parvus and the Germans that at the beginning of 1918—after the October Revolution—he was expelled from the party, to be reinstated only following Lenin's personal intervention.

There is very little clear evidence proving the existence of collaboration between the Bolsheviks and the German government. Nonetheless, there is some. On July 24, 1917, two telegrams were sent to Parvus in Bern. One of them was signed by "Kuba," Ganetsky's assumed name. The other came from the Bolsheviks' foreign delegation. Both telegrams reached Parvus through the German Ministry of Foreign Affairs and were encrypted using the ministry's code. Since all the ministry's telegrams passed through Berlin, copies signed by the assistant to the German Secretary of State, Stumm, have survived in the archives. They were discovered in 1961, after the wave of "eye-opening revelations" had for the most part already passed. Meanwhile, these telegrams proved the existence of links between the Bolsheviks' foreign delegation and Ganetsky to Parvus, on the one hand, and the German government on the other.

Naturally, the answers to many questions could have been found in the archives of German and Austro-Hungarian intelligence. But the German archives were destroyed during the Second World War, while the Austrian archive was handed over to the Soviet government after the end of the war; indeed, the handing over of the archives was one of the secret conditions for the withdrawal of Soviet troops from Austria. Researchers have had no access to these materials since then.

One of the principal secret intermediaries between the revolutionaries and the German government was a prominent Swiss social democrat who came from a distinguished family with an Austrian background. He was born in 1853 and due to some scandal was forced to leave his place of birth, Austria, as a young man. Settling in Switzerland, he became a socialist and took the assumed name of "Karl Moor." In German intelligence documents and Ministry of Foreign Affairs dispatches, he is referred to by the covert name "Baier." Just like Parvus, Moor can undoubtedly be considered an agent of the German government. Since the 1880s–1890s, rumors about his ties to German intelligence were circulating within the Social Democratic Party, and he was treated with distrust. However, this did not prevent him, while maintaining an openly affluent lifestyle, from becoming one of the heads of the Swiss Social Democratic Party and organizing the passage of Russian Bolsheviks through Germany, Denmark, Sweden, and Finland into Russia in 1917. In July-August 1917, the Bolshevik Party received large sums of money through Moor, which were nominally referred to as loans out of his personal savings. The money was handed over to Ganetsky and Vorovsky. And after the revolution in Russia, he decided to get his "loan" back from the Soviet government.

On May 10, 1922, Ganetsky send a letter about this issue to the Central Committee. The letter was addressed to Vyacheslav Molotov, secretary of the Central Committee and future head of the Soviet government under Stalin:

> Up to now, I have not received any instructions from you regarding what I should do with the 85,513 Danish kroner that I brought from Riga.... This money is essentially the remainder of the sums received from Moor. The old man is still hanging around Moscow under the pretense of waiting for an answer concerning the money. Perhaps you might consider it expedient to give him this money, settle all accounts with him, and get rid of him?

On the same day, the letter was passed to Stalin, who sent a query to Lenin, who in turn sent the following response:

I vaguely recall that I've already dealt with this issue. But I've forgotten how and what. I know that Zinoviev was also involved. Please don't decide anything without a precise and detailed consultation, and make sure to ask Zinoviev.

Ganetsky reminded Lenin: "You were in favor of returning the money to Moor. In any event, it is necessary to settle things with the old man."

On May 20, Zinoviev sent the following response to Stalin: "In my opinion, the money (the sum is large) should be given to the Comintern. Moor will only drink the money away. Ganetsky and I have decided not to make any decisions before Radek arrives."

Moor waited patiently, wrote letters, knocked on doors, and continued to live in need of money, borrowing from acquaintances, including Radek, who knew Moor particularly well and who had borrowed a large sum from Moor with collateral from the Russian government in Germany in 1919. On August 23, 1923—that is, more than a year later—Zinoviev asked Stalin to give Moor "100 chervontsy [1,000 rubles], since he is milking Radek personally." On the same day, at a meeting of the Secretariat of the Central Committee, a decision was reached that went into the "special folder" of the Politburo, the Secretariat, and the departments of the Central Committee, which was used for safekeeping secret resolutions that were not included in the general transcripts of the meetings (this was one more indication of the fact that the money demanded by Moor was not Moor's money): "To agree with Comrade Zinoviev's proposal of a preliminary handout of 100 chervontsy to Comrade Moor, but on the condition that the issue be resolved jointly with Comrade Molotov."

Two more years passed. Moor remained in Moscow and continued to pester the government for money. On September 23, 1925, he sent a letter to the former executive secretary of the Council of People's Commissars (Sovnarkom), Nikolai Gorbunov:

> I urgently request that you do everything possible so that... $35,000 might be returned to me prior to your departure for a two-month vacation. If you leave before this issue is resolved, I will lose my last hope and I will die here.

A true bureaucrat, Gorbunov did not give Moor any money, but on September 26 he put together another brief on the subject of Moor's loans:

> I was visited by Karl Moor, who once again raised the matter of reimbursing him for the sum of money that he lent to the party in July-August 1917. His claims amount to $35,000. Moor tried to get an appointment with Comrade Lenin in 1921 and failed, but Vladimir Ilyich sent him a note in which he

flattered him and advised him to direct all questions about financial matters to me. Following Vladimir Ilyich's personal instructions, I spoke with you and with Comrade Radek at the time, conveying Vladimir Ilyich's view that Moor should be repaid at once, and sent Moor to you. Now Moor has again come to see me, announcing that he still cannot obtain the money which he is owed and that he considers himself to be in an extremely difficult and humiliating position, since he urgently needs this money and cannot do without it.

On October 30, 1925, Moor was invited to the Central Committee, where he was told that a final decision concerning his case had been reached: a sum of $25,000 would be given to him within a week, and the remaining $9,600 would be paid by November 1, 1926. However, even after this announcement, Moor was not given any money.

On November 15, in response to another request from Moor, another note was written, indicating that the money had been "borrowed" from Moor on faith, without the requisite paperwork: "In 1917 and at various later dates, the Central Committee's International Bureau borrowed sums of money from Karl Moor, specifically, Comrades Ganetsky, Vorovsky, and Radek received a total of $32,837. Moor's explanation of the accounts shows that Comrade Lenin was aware of this debt, but we have no documentary evidence of it."

During this whole time, Moor lived in Moscow in a small, damp room, without a telephone or any conveniences. He had come to Russia for the money in November 1921, for the third time since the October Revolution, as a healthy man. On December 11, 1925, he celebrated his seventy-third birthday in Moscow with a weak heart, shattered nerves, and a severe hernia. At the end of the year, he came down with pneumonia (and was graciously admitted to the Kremlin hospital, where members of the Soviet government were treated).

Almost two more years passed, and the 75-year-old Moor, who had become a permanent resident of hospitals and sanatoriums for veterans of the revolution, no longer capable of writing or asking for anything in person, appealed to the German revolutionary Clara Zetkin (who had acted as a judge when Shmidt's money was being divided), now living in Russia, and asked her for help. On August 19, 1927, Zetkin wrote a letter to Molotov:

> As a special concession to the well-deserving Swiss comrade Karl Moor, I cordially ask you to help him with his case.... Comrade Moor is anxiously waiting for a final resolution of his case, since in his weakened state of health he can no longer tolerate this climate.

On the impact of this letter, on September 9, 1927, the Secretariat of the Central Committee decided to pay Karl Moor $8,254 and to consider the debt to Moor settled. This was all that Moor could now count on. But he did not see this money either. In 1932, Moor died in Russia, in a sanatorium for party workers. He was buried with all the requisite party honors.

Leaving aside the question of how substantial the roles of Germany and Austria-Hungary were in the matter of organizing the Bolshevik coup and whether this coup could have taken place without German and Austrian assistance, it should be noted that Germany's support for sedition in Russia was only one part of a broader German policy aimed at weakening the enemy. Germany spent at least 382 million marks on so-called "peace propaganda" (in fact, prior to May 1917, more money was spent on Romania and Italy than on Russia, which did not prevent both of these countries from taking the side of the Triple Entente in the war). Tens of millions of marks were spent to bribe four French newspapers. In Russia, the Germans were apparently unable to bribe a single newspaper, and Germany's financing of Lenin's *Pravda* in 1917 constituted, it seems, the only exception to this rule.

These activities on the part of Germany were known to the counterintelligence services of Britain, France, and the democratic (Provisional) government of Russia, which was formed after February Revolution of 1917. After the Bolsheviks staged an unsuccessful attempt at a coup in July of that year, the Provisional Government, seeking to discredit the Bolsheviks, published information about the German-Bolshevik connection. This was done in a most ineffective manner, however. The Provisional Government had neither the intention nor the power to dispose of the Bolsheviks. And although a number of Bolshevik leaders were declared criminals, no leader was apprehended, while Lenin—who had avoided arrest—was able to emigrate to Finland in August 1917, where his work on organizing the next revolution in Russia continued at full speed.

2.

The Treaty of Brest-Litovsk

In October 1917 on the Russian calendar, and in November on the Western European calendar, which was twelve days ahead of the Russian calendar, the Bolshevik Revolution took place in Russia. We are used to thinking that Lenin was at the head of the Revolution. However, his unimpeachable authority among the Bolsheviks is one of many myths that do not correspond to reality. The Bolsheviks' own Central Committee, which ignored Lenin's directives; the Petrograd Soviet, at whose helm stood Leon Trotsky, an "interdistrictite" (not a Bolshevik) and an obvious rival for Lenin's place in the Russian Revolution; the Second All-Russian Congress of Soviets, which convened in October 1917 in Petrograd as a body of several socialist parties, of which the Bolsheviks were neither the largest nor the main party of the Russian Revolution—none of these organizations recognized Lenin as its head and leader, none of these constituent parts of the October armed uprising in Petrograd had any intention of submitting to his will.

But Lenin and his socialist rivals occupied unequal positions. The latter had to decide on the correct course of action in the interests of the Russian and the international revolution. He needed to determine what steps he had to take in order to end up at the head of the first Soviet government. It is not surprising that while his opponents argued and debated, Lenin—who made his first public appearance in Petrograd at the Congress of Soviets only on October 26, after Trotsky's Petrograd Soviet had carried out a coup on the night of October 25—went ahead and proclaimed the creation of a government, the Sovnarkom, that was to be run by a handful of Bolsheviks under his own leadership.

Lenin's declaration about the creation of the Sovnarkom, however, was of no inspiration to anyone. It introduced a split into the already weak and heterogeneous socialist movement, and proclaimed the overthrow of the Provisional Government and the creation of the Soviet government not by the will of the Congress of Soviets—which was an elected body, however small the number of voters that had elected it—but by the will of the Bolshevik party. And not by the entire party, since this question had not been discussed and its opinion on the matter was not known, nor the party's entire Central Committee, or the entire delegation at the Congress of Soviets, but only by the will of a small group of party comrades who had supported Lenin on this issue.

In the very first hours and days of the rule of the Bolshevik government, Lenin worked out a strategy that he successfully applied through all the years that followed. By using threats and blackmail, to the point of announcing his resignation, he would obtain support for his revolution—by a single-vote margin if need be—arranging for multiple rounds of voting until the exhausted opponents finally yielded to him and granted him a majority. Then he would pass a resolution to the effect that the entire Central Committee (or the entire delegation of the party) fully supported this majority, which in reality consisted of Lenin and a negligible minority, in all party policies. Then he would impose the minority's policies—in the name of the Bolshevik Party—on the VTsIK or the Congress of Soviets, splitting up or breaking up congresses at which the left wing lacked a majority. He rejected the idea of a "homogeneous socialist government" formed by a relatively wide circle of Soviet voters; and he rejected the idea of a nationwide Constituent Assembly—"the master of the Russian land"—elected by an even broader section of the population (although even here one could not speak of a secret ballot or a universal franchise, especially since the Kadet Party had been dismantled before the Assembly convened). Instead, Lenin proposed dictatorship, and not even the dictatorship of the party or the Central Committee, but his own, personal dictatorship, repeatedly giving his enemies and friends to understand that he would never cede this power to anyone as long as he was alive.

After announcing the creation of the Sovnarkom, Lenin overcame multiple crises, one after another. Making use of his opponents' departure from the Congress of Soviets, he started passing Bolshevik resolutions. Securing the Central Committee's support to establish a one-party government, he entered into negotiations with the Left SRs, whose political platform was close to the Bolsheviks', and obtained the ousting of VTsIK Chairman Lev Kamenev, who had come out against Lenin's diktat. Krupskaya recalled:

> On November 21 [Old Style], 1917, Yakov Mikhailovich Sverdlov was elected to replace L. B. Kamenev as VTsIK chairman. His candidacy had been put forward by Ilyich. The choice was remarkably successful. Yakov Mikhailovich was a very firm person.... He was irreplaceable.... What was needed was an organizer of the highest caliber. Yakov Mikhailovich was exactly such an organizer.[1]

Sverdlov was by no means a random choice "promoted" by Lenin. Since the Seventh All-Russian Conference of the RSDLP (Bolsheviks) in April, Sverdlov headed the Secretariat of the party's Central Committee—the Central Committee's executive arm. On August 6 (19), the Secretariat of the Bolshevik Party's Central Committee was formally established at a restricted meeting of the Central Committee, which included Felix Dzerzhinsky, Adolph Joffe, Matvei Muranov, Yelena Stasova, and Yakov Sverdlov. Sverdlov remained the chairman of the Secretariat. The *Encyclopedia of the October Revolution* indicates that the Secretariat "maintained contact with local party organizations," "directly oversaw the Bolshevik Party's military organizations and local party organizations," and assembled a "staff of traveling agents for delivering instructions from the Bolshevik Party's Central Committee to local party organizations."[2] In other words, as early as August 1917, the Secretariat was already in charge of the party's operations and the party's personnel. And Sverdlov was the head of that office.

By December 1917, the Cheka—the All-Russian Extraordinary Commission—was formed for the purpose of fighting opponents outside the party. The leadership of this crucial institution, which would form the foundation of the GPU and the NKVD, was assumed by Dzerzhinsky, one of the Secretariat's organizers. Meanwhile, the organizational, political, and ideological command over the army and the foreign policy of Soviet Russia went to Trotsky (formally, he became People's Commissar of War in March).

Leon Trotsky, one of the most prominent Russian and international revolutionaries, one of the ideologues of the first Russian revolution and chairman of the Petersburg Soviet, had emigrated after the defeat of the revolutions of 1905–1907. Returning to Petrograd in early May 1917, he was the organizer of the October coup in the capital. It appears he and Lenin formed an agreement literally on the day of the coup, October 24, 1917. Trotsky was the head of the Petrograd Soviet, the main lever of the Revolution. However, he did not have his own organization. The "interdistrictites" (*Mezhrayontsy*), headed by Trotsky, finally merged with the Bolshevik Party in July-August 1917. Also, unlike Lenin, Trotsky did not have his own private, mafia-style support structure. He was interested in leading the Revolution, while Lenin was interested in power: after seizing power, he planned to begin leading the Revolution. Lastly, Trotsky understood that, as a Jew, he could lead an uprising, but he could not become the head of the government of Russia.

The coalition between Trotsky and Lenin was a natural and mutually beneficial step. In return for giving up his "interdistrictites" to the Bolsheviks, turning the Petrograd Soviet into a tool for Lenin's policies, fully supporting Lenin in the extremely risky and in essence adventurist enterprise of seizing power and forming the Sovnarkom in circumvention of the will of the Second Congress of Soviets, influential socialist parties and labor unions, Trotsky obtained a Bolshevik Party membership card, became a member of its Central Committee, and received the minister of foreign affairs portfolio in the Sovnarkom. It was precisely because Trotsky was dealing with individuals who believed in power and valued it, such as Lenin, Sverdlov, and Dzerzhinsky, that his personal rise to power should be seen as a brilliant performance. Without endless petty fights against his real and imagined enemies, which perpetually preoccupied Lenin, without any shady "German money," without compromising himself by passing through German enemy territory, Trotsky became the number two man in the government with an ease that others might have envied. It was precisely this arrogant gesture—and his emphatic indifference to personal power, the ease with which everything came to him, and the popularity that he enjoyed among Communist activists—that was not forgiven by the members of the Bolshevik elite whom the October Revolution had passed by—Stalin, Zinoviev, Kamenev, and Bukharin.

In the end, Trotsky never became an equal member of Lenin's mafia. His position within the government was guaranteed only by his personal agreement with Lenin. It was clear that with Lenin's departure, Trotsky—the "non-Bolshevik"—would inevitably be ousted from power as well. Without knowledge of Lenin's agreement and the obvious weakness of his position, entirely dependent upon Lenin's personal power, one cannot correctly explain Trotsky's actions in the intraparty struggle of 1918–1924.

Trotsky's policies on the issue of a peace treaty with Germany became the first and most important test of his loyalty to Lenin. Because for many decades patent lies and slander were heaped upon him, first by Stalin, and then by the post-Stalinist Soviet leadership, it is extremely difficult to give an accurate description of Trotsky's actions during the negotiations at Brest-Litovsk in January-March 1918. Trotsky himself, remaining loyal to Lenin to the end of his days, did not reveal everything in his numerous articles, books, diaries, and memoirs. But since it was precisely his stance in Brest-Litovsk that was invoked as an example of his obvious non-Bolshevism and even treason when accusations against him were made, Trotsky's story cannot be told without an elucidation of the Brest-Litovsk agreement.

Up to 1917 Germany appeared to be the leader of the revolutionary movement—its Social Democratic Party was the most powerful in the world—a world revolution naturally assumed a revolution in Germany. The revolution did not necessarily have to begin there, but its victory in Germany seemed to all revolutionaries to be a requirement for success. The Social Democratic rhetoric of the time did not allow for any other conception of world revolution. And Russian revolutionary Lenin, prior to February 1917, saw no greater role for himself than as the leader of the extremist wing of Russia's Social Democratic movement, which was unquestionably secondary and subsidiary to the Communist movement in Germany.

In the days leading up to the war, it was to Germany's Social Democratic movement that the socialists in the world turned to. It seemed that by voting against giving the government war credits in the Reichstag, the German Social Democratic Party could stop the impending tragedy. However, the German socialists voted in favor of the war funding, in part because they hoped that the war would topple the monarchy in Russia, which they regarded as the main enemy of the international socialist movement.

The Bolshevik wing of the Russian Social Democratic Party believed—just as the Menshevik wing did—in the eventual triumph of socialism in the world. This seemed as obvious then as, say, the inevitable demise of colonial empires does today. The answer to the question, "Will the world revolution come?", was invariably positive, built entirely on their faith in ultimate victory. However, after October 1917, this once-theoretical question had to be examined from a more practical angle. Was it more important to preserve Soviet rule in Russia—where the revolution had already taken place—at any cost; or to try to organize a revolution in Germany, even at the price of seeing Soviet rule in Russia fail?

In 1918, the answer to this question was not as obvious as it might appear today. The consensus among Europe's socialist leaders was that in backward Russia it would be impossible not only to build socialism, but also to hold on to power for any extended period of time without the support of

European socialist revolutions, if only because (as the Communists believed) Russia's "capitalist encirclement" would consider it imperative to overthrow its socialist regime. The revolutionaries saw a revolution in Germany as the only guarantee for the Soviet government to remain in power in Russia.

Lenin thought otherwise. In October 1917, breaking out of oblivion in Switzerland and seizing power in Russia with lightning speed, he showed his many opponents how much they had underestimated this unique individual—the leader of a small extremist sect. Bolshevism not only seized the reigns of power in Russia, but created a real and unique base to launch a world revolution, to organize a Communist coup in Germany itself, where, as everyone assumed, the ultimate victory of socialism in the world would come from. For Lenin, the German revolution took second place to the already victorious revolution in Russia. Even more than that: it would be wrong to hurry toward a successful revolution in Germany, since when that happened, the center of gravity of the Communist world would shift to the industrialized West and Lenin would be left behind as nothing more than the head of the government of an "underdeveloped," "backward," and "uncultured" country.

It is in the light of Lenin's changed views about the revolution in Germany that one must examine the history of the negotiations in Brest-Litovsk between December 1917 and March 1918, which ended in a peace treaty between Russia, on the one hand, and Germany and the other Central Powers, on the other. His position at these negotiations—his insistence on forming a "Tilsit truce" for the sake of a respite from war with Germany— seems so reasonable that one can only marvel at the adventurism, naiveté, and carefree idealism of all of his opponents, from the Bukharin-led Left Communists headed to Trotsky with his formula "neither war nor peace." To be sure, Lenin's position seems correct mainly because it appeals to notions that most people find familiar: a weak army cannot fight against a strong one; if resistance is impossible, a peace treaty must be signed in the face of an ultimatum. But this is an ordinary person's way of thinking, not a revolutionary's. Such thinking would not have made it possible to seize power in October 1917 and to hold on to it against a coalition of socialist parties as Lenin had done, with Trotsky's help, during the days of November 1917. Indeed, such a way of thinking would have made it impossible to be a revolutionary. For some reason, the core of the party, with the exception of Lenin, was against signing the Treaty of Brest-Litovsk; in fact, a large number of party functionaries supported Trotsky's "demagogical" formula. And no one viewed the state of things as pessimistically as Lenin. Still, all of these people had to be governed by some kind of logic that we propose to discover.

The revolution and the revolutionaries were subject to their own special laws, which were perceived by the majority of the population as obscure, deranged, and irrational. But once it abandoned these laws, the revolution perished. In them lay the only source of power for the revolution and the only promise of victory. Lenin stepped back from these laws for the sake of preserving his power and leadership in the global Communist movement. From the point of view of absolute Communist interests, the Treaty of Brest-Litovsk was a catastrophe. It unequivocally destroyed any chance (however slight it had been) of a revolution in Germany, and consequently, of a swift revolution throughout Europe. The treaty, formed against the wishes of the majority of the revolutionary party, became the Soviet leadership's first pragmatic step, which set the stage for all of the USSR's subsequent unprincipled and inconsistent policies.

Ironically, it turned out that in order to secure victory for the revolution in Russia, a potential revolution in Germany had to be sacrificed. While in order to secure victory for the revolution in Germany, it might have been necessary to sacrifice Soviet rule in Russia. This was the choice that the treaty represented to the Soviet government. A peace treaty with Germany gave the German government a certain leeway from fighting and improved the general state of the country. By contrast, the Soviet government's refusal to sign a treaty would have impacted Germany's military and political situation negatively and increased the chances for a German revolution. This, at least, was the view shared by the German Communists, on the one hand, and the German government, on the other. As early as December 1917 German leftists had tried to prevent the formation of a separate peace between Russia and Germany. They distributed a declaration stating that peace negotiations would have a ruinous effect on a likely revolution in Germany and must be aborted.

The positions of Karl Liebknecht, the leader of the German Communists, and Lenin, the head of the Soviet government, were different. The German Communists demanded a revolution in Germany for the sake of a world revolution. Lenin's objective was to ensure that the Sovnarkom remained in power at any cost, so that he might keep power in his own hands and, in time, come to "reign over the international Communist movement."[3] By contrast, if Liebknecht did want to save the top position in the future Comintern for himself, this did not go against the interests of the European revolution.

It was initially believed that the Bolsheviks were engaging in peace talks with the German government exclusively for propaganda purposes and to gain some time, not in order to sign an actual treaty. Liebknecht emphasized that if the negotiations "did not lead to a socialist peace," it would be necessary "to curtail the negotiations, even if their [Lenin's and Trotsky's] government should fall because of this."[4] Lenin, however, was playing his own game and seeking to obtain a temporary peace with the German imperial government, seeing in this his only means of concentrating power in his own hands and splitting up the unified capitalist world; i.e., his aim was to form an alliance with the German Empire against England and France.

Liebknecht saw victory in a German revolution; Lenin wanted to influence the contradictions between the Central Powers and the Allied Powers. Liebknecht was interested in seeing Germany lose the war as quickly as possible; Lenin, by signing a separate peace, wanted Germany to avoid losing the war for as long as possible. He feared that Soviet rule in Russia would be overthrown by the joint efforts of Germany and the Allied Powers as soon as a peace treaty was signed on the Western Front. But by signing the Treaty of Brest-Litovsk and delaying Germany's defeat, Lenin did exactly what Liebknecht had effectively accused him of doing: sabotaging the German revolution.

In Russia itself, the Bolshevik Party was not unanimous regarding the negotiations with Germany even when they were understood to mean signing a peace treaty without annexations or reparations, conducting revolutionary propaganda, and playing for time while simultaneously preparing for revolutionary war. Those who supported an immediate revolutionary war (in time, they became known as the Left Communists) initially dominated the party organizations in Moscow and Petrograd. The Left Communists had a majority in the Second Moscow Regional Congress of Soviets, which took place from December 10 to December 16, 1917, in Moscow. Of the 400 members of the Bolshevik delegation in the Moscow Soviet, only 13 supported Lenin's proposal to sign a separate peace with Germany. The remaining 387 voted for revolutionary war.

On December 28, a resolution was passed at a plenary session of the Moscow regional party bureau calling for an end to the peace talks with Germany and in favor of breaking off diplomatic relations with all capitalist states. On the same day, the majority of the Petrograd party committee came out against Germany's peace conditions. Both organizations demanded that a party conference be convened to discuss the Central Committee's policies with regard to the peace talks. Since the delegations to such a conference would consist of the committees themselves and not the local organizations of the RSDLP, the Left Communists were assured a majority. Consequently, in order to avoid a defeat, Lenin began delaying the convocation of the conference.

The All-Army Demobilization Congress, which convened in Petrograd on December 15 (28) and remained in session until January 3 (16), 1918, also opposed Lenin's policies. On December 17 (30), Lenin prepared a special questionnaire for the congress. Delegates were supposed to answer ten questions about the state of the army and its ability to conduct a revolutionary war with Germany. He asked whether the German army could advance in winter conditions, whether German troops could occupy Petrograd, whether the Russian army could hold the front line, whether it was better to prolong the peace talks or to curtail them and start a revolutionary war. He hoped to obtain the congress's approval to continue the negotiations. But the delegates came out in favor of revolutionary war: their resolution called for conducting an intensive propaganda campaign against an annexationist peace, insisting that the peace talks be transferred to Stockholm, "prolonging the peace talks," conducting all necessary preparations to reorganize the army and provide for the defense of Petrograd, advocating and campaigning for the inevitability of a revolutionary war. The resolution was not published.

At the same time, the Moscow regional and Moscow city committees of the party—both headed by Left Communists—as well as a number of the largest party committees—from the Urals, Ukraine, and Siberia—all came out against Lenin. Lenin—who had just returned from abroad and had little enough influence as it was with "members of the underground" like Sverdlov, Dzerzhinsky, Stalin, and Kamenev, who believed (perhaps rightly) that the Revolution had been prepared by them, and not by the emigrants (Lenin and Trotsky) who returned once everything was ready—was losing his control over the party. The issue of peace was gradually becoming transformed into the issue of Lenin's power within the Bolshevik Party and his weight in the government of Soviet Russia. And so, he launched a desperate campaign against his opponents—a desperate campaign for the peace treaty, for his leadership in the party, and for power.

Lenin's original position was weak. Most party activists came out against Germany's demands and in favor of cutting off the peace talks and declaring a revolutionary war on German imperialism to establish a Communist regime in Europe. In addition, on January 7 (20), Trotsky reported to the Sovnarkom that Germany would not accept peace without annexations. But an annexationist peace—it would seem—should have been unacceptable to the leaders of the Russian Revolution. However, unexpectedly for the whole party, the head of the Soviet government, Lenin, once again came out for the peace treaty—and in favor of accepting Germany's annexationist conditions. He expressed his point of view in his 'Theses on the Question of an Immediate Conclusion of a Separate and Annexationist Peace," written on the same day.

The theses were discussed at a special party meeting on January 8 (21), 1918, with 63 people present, mainly delegates from the Third Congress of Soviets, which was to begin two days later.

Lenin tried to convince his listeners that without an immediate peace agreement, the Bolshevik government would fall under the onslaught of the peasant army. But if the threat to the Bolsheviks came from the peasant army, then it would have been expedient to disband it as quickly as possible and not leave it under arms, as Lenin in fact attempted to do both before and after the peace treaty was signed. If the army was ineffectual, then it should have been demobilized at once, as Trotsky suggested. If Lenin feared that that the Bolsheviks would be toppled by the Russian army in January 1918, when the army was so weak that it could do nothing—in Lenin's own words—to oppose Germany, then how could he have been so bold as to seize power in October 1917, when the army of the Provisional Government was far more powerful than the current one, while the Bolshevik government had not yet even been formed? Lenin's well-known pronouncement that if the Bolsheviks refused to sign a peace agreement, the Germans would sign it with another government, was probably not sincere. He must have understood that no other government would accept a separate, annexationist peace with Germany, just as no other government would agree to break off diplomatic, military, and economic ties with the Allied Powers. If only for these reasons alone, Germany could have had no better ally than Lenin.

During the first stage of the Brest-Litovsk negotiations, Lenin received support from Trotsky on the question of the peace agreement. However, Trotsky was for peace only as long as this was a peace "without annexations or reparations." And he turned against peace when it became clear that Russia would have to sign an annexationist agreement. It was obvious to him from the first day of the negotiations to the last that the Soviet government was in no condition to wage a revolutionary war. In this respect, he had no argument with Lenin. At the same time, he believed that the Germans would be unable to "quash a revolution that would proclaim an end to the war."[5] And on that point, he and Lenin differed. Lenin was betting on a peace treaty with Germany and was prepared to capitulate to the Germans on one condition: that they should not demand the resignation of Lenin's government.

At the beginning of 1918, it seemed that Trotsky's calculations were correct. The dragging peace talks and the deteriorating food situation in Germany and Austria-Hungary led to the rapid growth of the strike movement, and a general strike in Austria-Hungary. Workers' councils were organized in a number of districts on the Russian model. On January 9 (22), after the government promised to sign a peace treaty with Russia and to improve the food situation, the strikers returned to work.

A week later, on January 15 (28), strikes paralyzed Berlin's defense industry, quickly spread to other sectors and soon engulfed the entire country. The center of the movement was Berlin, where, according to official reports, about half-a-million workers were on strike. As in Austria-Hungary, workers' councils were organized, whose main demand was the formation of a peace agreement and the establishment of a republic. It was against the background of these events that Trotsky posed the question of whether "the German working class and the German army should be put to a test: on this side, a workers' revolution, which declares that the war is over, and on that side, the Hohenzollern government, issuing orders to crush the revolution."[6]

Lenin believed that Trotsky's plan was "tempting" but risky, since the Germans could launch an offensive. And taking a risky course, in Lenin's opinion, was out of the question, since "nothing [was] more important" than the Russian Revolution. Here, Lenin again disagreed with Trotsky, the Left Communists, and the Left SRs, the Bolsheviks' allies who believed that only the victory of the revolution in Germany would guarantee that the Soviets would hold on to power in backward, agricultural Russia. Lenin, on the other hand, believed only in the success of only those enterprises which he was personally in charge of, and therefore the revolution in Russia was far more important to him than the revolution in Germany. The risk of Trotsky's position did not consist in the possibility that the Germans might launch an offensive, but that, by formally signing a peace treaty with Germany, Lenin would remain in power, while without a formal agreement with the Germans, he might be driven from his position.

On January 21, at a party meeting devoted to the problem of peace with Germany, Lenin suffered another defeat. His theses, written on January 7, were not approved, despite the fact that on the day of the meeting Lenin added another paragraph, calling for a delay in finalizing the peace agreement. The transcript of this meeting, it turns out, "has not survived." The theses themselves were apparently not allowed to be published. In a final vote, only 15 people supported his proposal to sign a separate peace, while 32 voted for the Left Communists and 16 for Trotsky, who on that day for the first time proposed not signing a formal peace agreement, but making it known to the world that Russia would no longer participate in the war and would demobilize its army.

Trotsky's position, summed up in the formula "neither war nor peace," provoked arguments and objections. Nowadays, it is usually portrayed as an absurdity. However, his formula did have a perfectly concrete practical meaning. He based his reasoning on the premise that Germany was in no condition to engage in major offensive action on the Russian front (otherwise, the Germans would not have sat down at the negotiating table in the first place) and that that the Bolsheviks must preserve "moral purity before the working classes of all countries."[7] In addition, it was important to refute the general belief that the Bolsheviks had simply been bribed by the Germans and that everything taking place in Brest-Litovsk was nothing more than a well-played piece of theater, where each part had already been determined in advance. For these reasons, Trotsky now proposed resorting to a political demonstration: the plan was to discontinue military action due to the impossibility of engaging in it any further, but at the same time to not sign any peace accords with the Central Powers on principle. One of the undeniable advantages of Trotsky's position was that the formula "neither peace nor war" did not commit the Bolsheviks to any course of action with respect to a revolutionary war and even made it possible for them to initiate military operations at any moment. Here is what Trotsky himself wrote about this subject many years later, when he was no longer living in Russia:

> Many clever fellows use any available pretext to ridicule the slogan "neither peace nor war." It clearly appears to them, evidently, to go against the very nature of things. Meanwhile...several months after Brest, when the revolutionary situation in Germany became completely apparent, we dissolved the Treaty of Brest-Litovsk—without starting a war with Germany.[8]

However, after dissolving the treaty and not declaring war, the Red Army began a Western offensive (and quite a successful one, at that). If it was this—waging war without declaring it—that was called "Trotsky's middle line"—"neither war nor peace"—then it is clear that in time it won the support of the majority of the core of the party. The Left Communists with Bukharin at their head proposed waging a war in a gentlemanly fashion, by declaring it beforehand. Trotsky proposed making a declaration of peace, waiting until Russian forces gathered sufficient strength, and then initiating military operations without declaring anything to anyone.

Traditionally, war had been seen by mankind in terms of the loss or gain of territory. Defeat in war meant a loss of land, while victory meant gain. This ancient approach was, of course, rejected by the revolutionaries. Neither Lenin, nor Trotsky, nor Bukharin saw victory or defeat as consisting in the gain or loss of territory, especially since the Bolsheviks had always favored the breakup of the Russian empire and popular self-determination. The Left Communists put more value on preserving the purity of the Communist principle of not compromising with the imperialists, even if this meant the defeat of the revolution in Russia. Trotsky found a less worrisome solution: he did not trample on any principles, but he also did not take the risk of declaring a revolutionary war that would have left Germany with no other choice than to topple the Soviet government.

Trotsky's formula, therefore, exhibited neither the demagogy that has been attributed to it by Soviet historiographers (it was in Lenin's theory of "peace" that the real demagogy was to be found), nor the reckless adventurism of those who, under Bukharin's leadership, supported an immediate revolutionary war. By the standards of the revolutionary times, Trotsky's position was moderate. Like the Left Communists, he believed that signing a peace treaty would not guarantee the cessation of military operations, that the revolutionaries had no reason to trust the "imperialists," that Germany would continue to take offensive action when it could. And under such circumstances, it was better to sign no documents at all, but to appeal to the proletariat of all countries and even to make use of the Allied Powers' assistance. In addition, during those months there was a widespread view in revolutionary circles that Germany was in no condition to take offensive action, and that even if it did manage to launch an offensive, it would not be able to hold on to occupied territories without risking an uprising in Berlin.

Lenin alone stubbornly insisted on a separate agreement with the Germans on terms dictated by Germany. At a Central Committee meeting on January 11 (24), he presented his theses on forming a peace agreement—and suffered a defeat. Bukharin, sharply criticizing Lenin's speech, declared that the "most correct" position was that of Trotsky, whose formulation—"end the war, conclude no peace, demobilize the army"—was passed by nine votes to seven. At the same time, twelve members to one voted in favor of a proposal introduced by Lenin, for face-saving purposes, "to prolong the signing of the peace treaty for as long as possible": Lenin was inviting people to vote for an obvious truth, namely, that in purely formal terms it was his resolution that had received the majority of the votes. He did not dare to submit the issue of signing a peace treaty to a vote that day. On the other hand, eleven votes against two, with one member abstaining, rejected the Left Communists' resolution, which called for revolutionary war. A joint assembly of the RSDLP's and the Left SRs' central committees, which convened on the following day, likewise voted for Trotsky's formula.

The majority stood behind Trotsky. For the second time since October 1917, Lenin's fate was in the hands of this lucky individual, to whom everything came with great ease, and who therefore never did manage to learn the value of power. Trotsky was too involved as a revolutionary and totally worthless as a tactician. Not seeing any of this, not suspecting that by effortlessly getting the party to embrace his political line—"neither war nor peace"—he was also exerting control over Lenin's personal power. At the end of January (New Style) he departed for Brest-Litovsk in order to break up the peace talks.

Thanks to the efforts of Soviet historiography, which for decades republished the same lies in book after book, there is a common belief that after returning to Brest-Litovsk to renew negotiations with Germany, Trotsky had orders from the Central Committee and the Sovnarkom to sign a peace treaty. This myth is based on a statement made by Lenin to the Seventh Party Congress, which took place on March 6–8, 1918: "It was agreed that we would hold back until the Germans handed over an ultimatum and consent after the ultimatum was given."[9]

It appears, however, that Lenin maligned Trotsky in the eyes of the congress, trying to lay the blame on him for the breakdown of the peace talks and for the German offensive. That this is the case can be inferred from the absence of documents that confirm Lenin's words, and from the existence of materials that refute them. In his recollections of Lenin, published in 1924 initially in *Pravda* and then as a separate book, Trotsky elucidated the meaning and contents of the agreement:

> Lenin: "Suppose your plan is accepted. We refuse to sign a peace treaty, and then the Germans attack. What do you do then?"
>
> Trotsky: "We sign a peace treaty at gunpoint. Then the situation will be clear to the working class around the world."
>
> "Will you not then support the call for a revolutionary war?"
>
> "By no means."
>
> "Putting it that way, the experiment might not seem so dangerous. We risk losing Estonia and Latvia.... It would be a great pity to sacrifice a socialist Estonia," Lenin joked, "but for the sake of a good peace treaty, I suppose we'd have to agree to that compromise."
>
> "And what if we sign a peace treaty immediately—would that rule out the possibility of a German military intervention in Estonia and Latvia?"
>
> "Let's say you're right. But in this case, it's only a possibility, whereas in the other case, it's almost a certainty."[10]

Thus, they had in fact agreed that a peace treaty would be signed, not after a German ultimatum, but after the start of a German offensive.

Trotsky touched on this matter more candidly in November 1924 in an article entitled "Our Disagreements," which was not published at the time. Concerning the Brest-Litovsk talks, he wrote:

I cannot, however, avoid mentioning here the absolutely shameless distortions of the Brest-Litovsk story.... Supposedly, after leaving for Brest-Litovsk with party instructions to sign a peace treaty in the event of an ultimatum, I independently went against these instructions and refused to give my signature. This lie goes beyond all limits. I left for Brest-Litovsk with a single instruction: to prolong the negotiations for as long as possible, and in the event of an ultimatum, to negotiate an extension and come back to Moscow to participate in the Central Committee's decision. Only Comrade Zinoviev proposed giving me instructions to sign a peace treaty immediately. But this was rejected by everyone else, including Lenin. Everyone agreed, of course, that prolonging the negotiations would worsen the terms of the agreement, but they believed that this negative would be outweighed by the positive agitational purpose that such a strategy would serve. What course of action did I follow in Brest-Litovsk? When things came to an ultimatum, I arranged for an extension, returned to Moscow, and the question was decided by the Central Committee. Not I alone, but the majority of the Central Committee at my suggestion decided not to sign the peace treaty. This was also the decision of the majority of the all-Russian party convention. I left for Brest-Litovsk for the last time with a perfectly clear decision from the party: to not sign the peace treaty. All of this can be easily verified by the Central Committee's transcripts.[11]

The same picture emerges from the directives that were sent to Brest-Litovsk by Lenin on orders from the Central Committee. The directives called for a cessation of the peace talks in the event that the Germans should introduce another condition to the negotiating table: recognition of Ukraine's independence under the leadership of the "bourgeois" Rada.

However, in the case of Brest-Litovsk, Trotsky still came out looking like the villain. Out of loyalty, he could not begin clearing his name while Lenin was alive. But after Lenin's death, it was already too late. Those who were struggling against Trotsky for power had no interest in the historical truth.

On February 5 (NS), Trotsky met with Czernin, the Austro-Hungarian foreign minister. The head of the Soviet delegation to Brest-Litovsk was prepared to break off the peace talks and generally tried to provoke the Germans and Austrians into presenting unacceptable demands, declaring that he would "never agree" to the formation of a separate peace treaty between the Central Powers and Ukraine. The Germans accepted the challenge. On the same day, at a meeting in Berlin chaired by Chancellor Georg von Hertling and attended by Ludendorff, a decision was made to "conclude a peace agreement with Ukraine, and discontinue negotiations with Trotsky regardless of whether their outcome was positive or negative." The form of the interruption (with or without an ultimatum) was left to the discretion of the German delegation in Brest-Litovsk.

On January 27 (February 9), opening the morning session, German foreign minister Kühlmann, and then Czernin, made an offer of peace to the Soviet delegation. At the same time, at a meeting of the political committee, the representatives of the Central Powers announced that they had signed a separate agreement with the Ukrainian Republic. According to the terms, the Rada was recognized as the only legitimate government of Ukraine, and moreover Germany pledged to provide Ukraine with military and political assistance in order to stabilize its regime. The Rada, in its turn, pledged to sell to Germany and Austria-Hungary one million tons of bread, up to 500,000 tons of meat, 400 million eggs, and other food supplies and raw materials, before July 31, 1918. There was also a secret agreement to deliver one million tons of grain. It was stipulated that the peace treaty would be cancelled by the German government if Ukraine failed to make these deliveries.

On the evening of January 27 (February 9), Trotsky wired the Smolny Palace that Kühlmann and Czernin had "offered to resolve the main issue tomorrow once and for all." The historian A. O. Chubaryan interprets the telegram as referring to the signing of a peace treaty between Germany and Austria-Hungary, on one side, and Ukraine, on the other. "Thus, I repeat," Trotsky went on, "the final decision will be made tomorrow evening." Meanwhile, in Kiev, the Bolsheviks were attempting to form a government and announce a takeover of power. "If we receive definite and reliable information from you before 5 p.m. that Kiev is in the hands of the Soviet people," Trotsky wired Petrograd, "this might have major significance for the negotiations."[12] Within several hours Trotsky's request was honored, and he received a telegram from Petrograd about the victory of the Soviet government in Kiev. He reported this news to the Central Powers' delegation. But it is obvious that even if he had been telling the truth, the Germans and the Austrians had no intention of following his advice and tearing up their treaty with Ukraine, which was also useful to them as a means of exerting pressure on the Bolsheviks.

An exchange of opinions regarding the Ukrainian question was scheduled for 6 p.m. on January 28 (February 10). "Today, around 6 p.m., we will give our final answer," Trotsky wired Petrograd on the same day. "It is necessary to make its essence known to the whole world. Take the necessary measures."[13]

What instructions was he given? In a telegram sent to Trotsky at 6:30 a.m. in response to his query, Lenin wrote: "You know our point of view; it has only become firmer in recent days[14] and especially after Joffe's letter. We repeat once more that nothing is left of the Kiev Rada and that the Germans will have to accept this fact if they have not already accepted it. Report to us more often."[15]

Lenin didn't mention a peace agreement. Meanwhile, if the "point of view" that was known to Trotsky was to agree to a German ultimatum and to sign a peace treaty, Lenin would have had no need to speak in such veiled terms. He could have given explicit orders to sign. The answer to this puzzle, of course, is found in Joffe's letter. Its subject was not the peace treaty, but the Soviet government's attempt to get Germany to recognize the Soviet Ukrainian delegation in Brest-Litovsk as a legitimate participant in the peace talks. It was the Central Committee's point of view concerning this question that Trotsky knew so well: no concessions, refusal to recognize the "bourgeois" Rada in Kiev, and in the event of German persistence—an end to the peace talks. At this moment—so decisive for the fate of the Ukrainian Communist revolution—the Soviet government could not recognize the Ukrainian Rada even for the sake of a separate peace with Germany, even if Lenin insisted on it.

Differences of opinion regarding the peace issue had divided not only the Bolsheviks, in those days, but the Germans as well. On February 9 (NS), Kaiser Wilhelm II sent a telegram to Kühlmann at Brest-Litovsk with a directive to conclude the negotiations within 24 hours on conditions dictated by the Germans (and unacceptable to the Bolsheviks). Kühlmann disagreed. In a telegram, he advised the Chancellor that the situation would become completely clear on February 10 (NS) at a Sunday meeting at which the Soviet delegation would have to either accept or reject the German conditions. If the latter happened, the negotiations would end within 24 hours; and then the truce would be broken as well. But if Trotsky accepted the German conditions, then it would be highly unreasonable to break off the peace talks, since this would lead to a conflict with Austria-Hungary and to unrest in Germany. Kühlmann characterized Wilhelm's demands as "unacceptable both from the political point of view and from the perspective of peoples' rights," pointing out in addition that it would be absolutely impossible to secure support for these demands from Germany's allies.

On February 10, Kühlmann discussed the newly emerging complications with Czernin, who gave his full support to Germany's foreign minister and indicated that if the Germans changed their course from seeking to achieve a peace agreement with the Bolsheviks, then Austria-Hungary would not be able to support Germany and would go its own way. Kühlmann's response to this was that it would be "completely impossible" for the foreign ministry to pursue a new, hard-line agenda, and that if Berlin should insist on an ultimatum, then he, Kühlmann, would resign. He gave the Kaiser and the

Chancellor four hours to reply: if no reply came, Kühlmann would remain at his post and not present Trotsky with an ultimatum. Four hours passed. There was no reply from the Kaiser. Kühlmann remained at his post. The peace talks continued.

On the evening of January 28 (February 10), in response to Germany's repeated request to "discuss only those conditions which can lead to concrete results," in accordance with directives from the RSDLP's Central Committee and Lenin's telegram, Trotsky—speaking for the Soviet delegation—announced the termination of the peace talks: "We are withdrawing from the war, but we must decline to sign a peace treaty."

General Hoffmann recalled that after Trotsky's announcement, the assembly hall fell silent: "The dismay was unanimous." On the same evening, the Austro-Hungarian and German diplomats held a consultation, to which Hoffmann was invited. Kühlmann believed that General Hoffmann's proposal to discontinue the peace talks and to declare war was "completely unacceptable," and that it was far more reasonable, just as Trotsky had suggested, "to maintain a state of war, without interrupting the truce."

"Under the right circumstances," Kühlmann observed, "we could... reach the environs of St. Petersburg within a few months. However, I don't think that that would give us anything. No one will be able to prevent the [new] revolutionary government, which will perhaps replace the Bolsheviks by that time, from moving to another city or even beyond the Urals.... With Russia being as large as it is, we can conduct a campaign against it for a very long time...and still not attain our goal; that is, we won't sit people down at the negotiating table and we won't force them to sign an agreement. The degree of military pressure that will influence people, that is, the highest degree...has already been reached. Further war would have no higher aim than the simple destruction of the enemy's forces. We know from the example of small countries—in particular, Serbia—that even after the whole territory of the state has been occupied, the government in exile...remains the government of the country. And no degree of military pressure (raising this degree is no longer possible, since everything that could be occupied has already been occupied) is capable of forcing people to sign a peace agreement.... War cannot be considered a suitable means to achieve the peace agreement that we seek."

After Kühlmann's speech, the German, Austro-Hungarian, Turkish, and Bulgarian diplomats unanimously declared that they accepted Trotsky's proposal: "Although the declaration does not constitute a peace treaty, it nonetheless reestablishes a state of peace between the two sides." Hoffmann was left completely alone: "I was unable to convince the diplomats of the correctness of my view," he wrote. Trotsky's formula "neither peace nor war" has been accepted by the conference, Czernin stated.[16] And the Austrian delegation was the first to telegraph Vienna that a "peace agreement with Russia has already been concluded."[17]

Hoffmann did not remain passive, but immediately informed German army headquarters of the outcome of the meeting. Germany's supreme command, which had long been searching for a pretext for new conflicts with the foreign ministry, decided to support Hoffmann against Kühlmann. Feeling powerful forces behind him, Hoffmann began to insist that it was necessary to respond to Trotsky's declaration by ending the truce, marching to St. Petersburg, and openly taking the side of Ukraine against Russia. But on February 10–11 (NS), Hoffmann's demands were ignored. And at a ceremonial, final meeting on February 11 (NS), Kühlmann "fully embraced the point of view expressed by the majority of the delegations to the peace talks and supported it in a very persuasive speech."[18] Trotsky had won. His calculations had proven accurate. A state of "neither war nor peace" became a fact. The only thing left to be done was to disband the old, Russian, anti-Bolshevik army, which was not controlled by the capital. And Trotsky issued orders for its demobilization.

During this time, events were taking place in Berlin that would decide Germany's destiny. Hertling, who on the whole supported the supreme command, turned to Wilhelm, insisting that Trotsky's declaration was a "factual violation of the truce." By contrast with Hoffmann, however, Hertling did not intend to declare a resumption of the war: his plan was to declare the truce over on February 10 (according to the terms of the truce agreement, this would give Germany freedom of action by February 18). And although Hertling was not yet announcing the beginning of military action against Russia, that was the clear implication of his proposal.

Once again, the foreign ministry came out against this plan, citing domestic political considerations. Nonetheless, in the early morning of February 13, the Kaiser presided over a Crown Council meeting in Hamburg at which a final decision was made to continue military action against Russia and to regard Trotsky's declaration as being tantamount to a termination of the truce as of February 17 (since Trotsky had made the declaration on February 10). It was planned that the German government would officially announce the termination of the truce as soon as the German diplomatic mission in Petrograd, headed by Count Wilhelm von Mirbach, left Soviet Russian territory (the German military offensive did indeed begin on February 18—immediately following the departure of the German diplomatic mission).

Upon returning, Trotsky gave a speech before the Petrograd Soviet. He indicated that Germany would most likely be unable "to deploy troops against a socialist republic. The odds are nine to one that they will be unable to mount an offensive, and there is only a ten percent chance of an offensive. But I am certain that there will be no offensive."[19] "This was the only correct decision..." Zinoviev commented. "Despite all the cries of desperation from the right...we are profoundly convinced that there can be no offensive by the German imperialists at this point."[20]

A majority of the Petrograd Soviet supported the decision of the Bolshevik delegation to Brest-Litovsk. A day earlier, the executive committee of the party's Petrograd bureau had also come out in favor of breaking off the peace talks with the Germans and against the policy of an "obscene peace."[21] On January 30 (OS), the Moscow Soviet voiced its support for terminating the negotiations. Trotsky's position was endorsed by the Left SRs and approved by the German Communists. Like Trotsky, the latter believe that "with the collapse of the peace talks, the Central Powers will unlikely be able to inflict new major military damage on Russia, despite the current state of Russia's armies. War on the Russian border must increasingly dwindle down."[22]

Austria-Hungary's political leaders, apprised of the Germans' intention to declare the truce over on February 17, were thrown into confusion. "Our view that the truce expires on February 17 is in most cases not shared here even in government circles," wrote Count von Wedel, the German ambassador in Vienna, to Germany's foreign ministry on February 15. Austria-Hungary's ambassador to Rome, Baron von Merey, was literally "stunned" and stated that without a formal reply to Trotsky's declaration, which had not yet been made, it was impossible to take February 10 as the starting date for the time that had to elapse before hostilities could resume. Thus, on February 16, the German government sent an official press release to the Wolfe Bureau News Service, stating that Germany viewed Trotsky's declaration as a termination of the peace talks and the truce. "February 10," the press release indicated, "must be seen as the date marking the termination of the truce... Upon the expiration of the seven-day period stipulated by the agreement, the German government shall consider itself at liberty to act as it chooses."

A copy of the press release was forwarded to the headquarters of Germany's Eastern Front. From there, on February 16 at 7:30 p.m., a notification was sent to Russian military command: "at 12 p.m. on February 18, Germany and Russia shall resume a state of war." At least this was the message wired to Petrograd from Brest-Litovsk by General Samoilo on February 17. At 1:42 p.m., Trotsky sent an urgent query to Berlin, indicating that the Soviet government considered the telegram to be a provocation, since even if Germany had decided to terminate the truce, "notification of this, according to the terms of the truce, must be given seven days in advance, not two, as has been done." The Soviet government demanded an immediate explanation.

On February 18, Germany's high command sent an explanation, bearing Hoffmann's signature, which pointed out that "the seven-day period provided for by the agreement began...on February 10 and expired yesterday. Because the Russian government has refused to conclude a peace agreement with Germany, Germany considers itself free from all obligations and reserves the right to pursue whatever course of action it deems necessary."

Germany's ultimatum was not supported by its ally Austria-Hungary, whose government came out against resuming military action and lodged an official protest with Germany because of this. The Germans, however, had asked the Austrians to "wait before making their position known," until the Soviets could be formally notified of Germany's conditions. Czernin naturally agreed, promising "not to undertake anything" without contacting Berlin beforehand. By this time, Czernin already had on his desk a radiogram from Trotsky, who had inquired "whether the Austro-Hungarian government also [considered] itself to be in a state of war with Russia," and if not, whether it considered it "possible to enter into a practical agreement." In addition, it was well known that the Germans had redeployed all battle-ready troops from the Eastern Front to the West. Lastly, Germany's envoys—who had arrived with diplomatic instructions on December 16 (29)—were still in Petrograd: Count Mirbach, the head of the German economic mission, and Vice Admiral Count Kaiserling, the head of the naval mission. Thus, there was still some hope that the Germans themselves had not yet made a final decision to begin an offensive.

Based on these considerations, at a meeting on the evening of February 17 the Central Committee rejected—by six votes to five—Lenin's proposal to agree to the German conditions and to sign a peace treaty immediately, and instead came out in favor of Trotsky's formula, resolving to wait before renewing any peace talks until a German offensive should actually materialize and its influence on the proletarian movement in the West might be gauged. Those who voted against immediately resuming negotiations, even under the threat of a German attack, included Trotsky, Bukharin, Lomov, Uritsky, Joffe, and Krestinsky. Voting in favor of Lenin's proposal were Sverdlov, Stalin, Sokolnikov, Smilga, and Lenin himself.

During a Central Committee session on the morning of February 18, Lenin's resolution was once again defeated by one vote: six to seven. A new session was scheduled for the evening. Only in the evening, after protracted debate and under the pressure of a German attack, was Lenin's proposal accepted by seven votes to five. Voting in favor were Lenin, Trotsky, Sverdlov, Zinoviev, Sokolnikov, and Smilga. Uritsky, Joffe, Lomov, Bukharin, Krestinsky voted against. The task of preparing an official statement for the German government was given to Lenin and Trotsky. In the interim, the Central Committee resolved immediately to send a radio message to the Germans about their decision to sign a peace agreement. Meanwhile, Sverdlov had to go to the Left SRs, notify them about the Bolshevik Central Committee's decision, and about the fact that a joint resolution by the Central Committees of the Bolshevik Party and the Left SRs would stand as the official decision of the Soviet government.

On February 18, at a joint meeting of the Central Committees of the Bolsheviks and the Left SRs, the latter voted to accept the German conditions. Lenin therefore hurried to schedule for February 19 a joint meeting of the Bolshevik and Left SR delegations to the VTsIK, agreeing to regard the new resolution as final. On the night of February 19, certain of his victory, Lenin, together with Trotsky, in accordance with the Central Committee's resolution, composed a radio message to the Germans. The Sovnarkom expressed a grievance about the German decision to launch an offensive against a republic "that had declared the state of war over and had begun to demobilize its army on all fronts"; but it also declared its "intention to sign a peace treaty on the conditions that have been put forward by the delegations of the Quadruple Alliance [Central Powers] in Brest-Litovsk."[23]

On the morning of February 19, the radio telegram—signed by Lenin and Trotsky—was sent. By 9:12 a.m. it was received by the Germans, and General Hoffmann was notified immediately. Lenin had done all of this before any formal joint decision had been made by the Bolshevik and Left SRs delegations to the VTsIK. But while he had been able to skip over formalities in dealing with the Left SRs, he was unable to do so in dealing with the Germans. The latter, not wishing to call a halt to a successful offensive, demanded an official written document; and Lenin replied that a courier was on its way. Germany took this declaration under advisement, but did not stop the offensive.

The Germans occupied several cities during those days: on February 18, Dvinsk; on the 19th, Minsk; on the 20th, Polotsk; on the 21st, Rezhitsa and Orsha; on the 22nd, Wolmar, Wenden, Walk, and Hapsal; on the night of the 24th, Pskov and Yuryev; on the 25th, Borisov and Reval. Remarkably, the Germans carried out this offensive without an army. They made use of small, dispersed units of 100–200 men, made up of volunteers. Due to the panic that reigned under the Bolsheviks and to false rumors about approaching

German troops, cities and stations were given up without any fighting even before the enemy's arrival. Dvinsk, for example, was taken by a German detachment of 60–100 men. Pskov was occupied by a small troop of Germans on motorcycles. In Rezhitsa, the German soldiers were so few in number that they were unable to take over the telegraph office, which continued to operate for another 24 hours. The Germans did not capture cities as declare that they had occupied various locations that had been abandoned in a panic by the hastily retreating Russian army. On February 22, 1918, the military commissar Vadim Podbelsky wired from the front: "I have no reliable new information, apart from the fact that the Germans, generally speaking, are advancing inexorably, for lack of any resistance."[24]

In Ukraine, the offensive proceeded mainly along the railways, reaching a "speed that impressed even the soldiers themselves,"[25] as Hoffmann put it. Here and there, some resistance was offered by the Soviet Red Guards, who were advancing in order to occupy Ukraine, and by Czechoslovakian troops, who supported the Allied Powers and put up the strongest opposition. Nonetheless, on February 21, the Germans entered Kiev.

On February 19, Lenin made a two-hour speech in defense of his theses on signing the peace treaty at a joint meeting of the Bolshevik and Left SR delegations to the VTsIK. Evidently, he expected a victory. But to his surprise, and to the surprise of many members of the Central Committee of Left SR Party, a majority in the VTsIK voted to reject Germany's peace conditions. The transcript of the meeting from February 19 "has not survived," but on the following day, the newspaper *Sotsial Demokrat*—the media outlet of the Bolsheviks' Moscow organization—published a brief account of the meeting: "The majority was of the opinion that the Russian Revolution would survive this trial; it was decided to resist as long as possible."[26]

Then, on February 19, Lenin called a meeting of the Sovnarkom to discuss "questions of foreign policy in connection with Germany's offensive and the telegram" sent by him to Berlin. By a majority of the votes—with only two members opposed—the Sovnarkom approved the contents of his nighttime telegram, mailed prematurely and against the will of the VTsIK. And since he had already passed a resolution that provided for transferring all questions connected with the peace treaty to the Sovnarkom, all of the requisite formalities had been taken care of.

Due to the newly passed decision to sign a peace treaty with Germany, a schism effectively took place within the Bolshevik Party at a Central Committee session on February 22. Bukharin resigned from the committee and relinquished his duties as editor of *Pravda*. A group consisting of Lomov, Uritsky, Bubnov, V. Smirnov, I. Stukov, M. Bronsky, V. Yakovleva, Spunde,

M. Pokrovsky, and G. Pyatakov submitted a statement to the committee expressing their disagreement with its decision to discuss the very idea of signing a peace treaty, and reserving the right to agitate against its policies in party circles. Joffe, Dzerzhinsky, and Krestinsky also declared their disagreement with its decision to sign a peace treaty, but refrained from joining Bukharin's group, since this meant splitting up the party, which they did not dare do.

At 10:30 a.m. on February 23, the Germans presented an ultimatum that would expire in 48 hours. The ultimatum was read by Sverdlov at a Central Committee meeting. The Soviet government had to agree to the independence of Kurland, Lifland, Estland, Finland, and Ukraine, with which it had to make peace, facilitate the transfer of the Anatolian provinces to Turkey, recognize the Russian-German trade agreement of 1904, which was unfavorable to Russia, grant Germany most favored nation status in trade until 1925, grant Germany the right to export ore and other raw materials freely and without tariffs, and refrain from any agitation or propaganda against the Central Powers and on territories occupied by them. The agreement had to be ratified within two weeks. Hoffmann believed that the ultimatum contained every demand that could possibly be made.

Lenin called for the immediate acceptance of Germany's terms and announced that he would resign if no agreement was forthcoming. Then, apparently by prior agreement with him, Trotsky took the floor:

> We cannot wage a revolutionary war with a split inside the party.... Under the conditions that have developed, our party is powerless to conduct a war.... V. I. [Lenin's] arguments are hardly convincing; if we had unanimity, we could undertake the task of organizing a defense, we could manage it...even if we had to surrender Petersburg and Moscow. We would keep the whole world in suspense. If we sign the German ultimatum today, then we might get a new ultimatum tomorrow. Everything is formulated so as to leave open the possibility of further ultimatums.... From the international point of view, we would stand to gain a great deal. But that would require the greatest possible unanimity; and since there is none, I cannot take upon myself the responsibility for voting for war.[27]

Following Trotsky, two other Left Communists refused to vote against Lenin: Dzerzhinsky and Joffe. Uritsky, Bukharin, and Lomov took a firm stand against signing the agreement. Stalin initially did not commit himself to the peace treaty: "We can start the peace talks again, without signing it."[28] In the end, Trotsky, Dzerzhinsky, Krestinsky, and Joffe—opponents of the Treaty of Brest-Litovsk—abstained from voting. Uritsky, Bukharin, Lomov, and Bubnov voting against it. But Sverdlov, Stalin, Zinoviev, Sokolnikov, Smilga, and Stasova supported Lenin. By seven votes to four, with four abstaining, the German ultimatum was accepted. At the same time, the Central Committee made a unanimous decision "to immediately prepare for revolutionary war."[29] This was another one of Lenin's nominal concessions.

However, the victory of Lenin's minority in such an important vote threw the Central Committee into even greater disarray. Uritsky, speaking for himself and for Bukharin, Lomov, Bubnov, candidate member Yakovleva, as well as Pyatakov and Smirnov, declared that he did not wish to bear the responsibility for a decision that had been passed by a minority, since the abstaining members were against signing the peace agreement; he threatened that all of the aforementioned Bolsheviks would quit the committee. A panic set in. Stalin said that for the opposition to leave their posts was to "murder the party." Trotsky said that he "would have voted differently if he had known that his abstention would lead to the comrades' departure." Lenin now agreed to "silent or open agitation against signing," as long as people did not leave their posts and signed the agreement for the time being. But the Left Communists departed, reserving the right to agitate in favor of the war in party newspapers.

A joint meeting of the Central Committee of the Bolshevik Party and the central committee of the Left SR Party was scheduled for the evening of February 23. The transcript of the meeting has not been found, and nothing is known about what took place. Various pieces of evidence indicate that the majority of the Left SRs supported Trotsky. The question was then given over for discussion to the two parties' VTsIK delegations, which remained in session all night on February 23, both separately and jointly. The small hall given over to the Bolshevik delegation was packed. Apart from the delegation, the members of the Petrograd Soviet and the city's party workers were also in attendance. The meeting was chaired by Sverdlov. Lenin came later and made a speech in which he argued that every possible way of delaying and sabotaging the peace talks had already been tried.

A majority of the Bolsheviks' VTsIK delegation voted in favor of a resolution to accept the German peace terms. The Left Communists tried to get the Bolshevik delegation to allow each member to vote as he or she saw fit, but they were defeated: the Bolshevik delegation then passed a resolution that obligated each member of the delegation either to vote for the peace treaty or to abstain from voting. At the joint session between the Bolshevik and the Left SR contingents of the VTsIK, the Left Communists again spoke out against signing the peace treaty, but failed to gather a majority of the votes.

Finally, at 3 a.m. on February 24, a VTsIK meeting began in the great hall of the Tauride Palace. There were five main delegations in all: the Bolsheviks, the Left SRs, the SRs, the Mensheviks, and the Anarchists. In the early morning, a roll call vote began. Every attendee was called to the podium and, facing the audience, spoke out in favor of peace or war. All kinds of scenes were played out. Bukharin, despite the Bolshevik delegation's directive not to vote against signing the peace agreement, came out against it, "and his words were drowned out by the applause of half the people present."[30] He was supported by Ryazanov. Lunacharsky did not know what to say until the very last second: as a Left Communist, he had to be against the peace, yet as a disciplined Bolshevik, he had to be for it. Coming up on the podium, he uttered "yes" and "covering his spasmodically twitching face with his hands, [ran] down from the podium."[31] Apparently, he was crying. Most of the Left Communists, not wishing to vote for peace, but not daring to violate party discipline, left the hall even before the voting began thus deciding the outcome in Lenin's favor.

An analogous split took place among the Left SRs, the only difference being that their delegation as a whole decided to vote against the peace treaty and obligated Lenin's supporters to abstain from voting. Just as with the Bolsheviks, not everyone agreed to uphold party discipline if that meant going against their own principles. Spiridonova, Malkin, and a number of other notable members of the Central Committee voted in favor of the peace treaty. The SRs and the Mensheviks voted against it. But Lenin still won the majority that he needed: 116 VTsIK members voted for Lenin's resolution, 85 voted against it (SRs, Mensheviks, Anarchists, Left SRs, Left Communists), and 26—Left SRs who were in favor of the peace treaty—abstained from voting.

At 5:25 a.m. the meeting was adjourned. An hour and a half later, messages were sent from the Sovnarkom to Berlin, Vienna, Sofia, and Constantinople, notifying the Central Powers that the German terms had been accepted and that a duly authorized delegation was leaving for Brest-Litovsk. A courier was sent from Petrograd to Brest-Litovsk so that the Soviet agreement might be submitted in written form. By 10 p.m., Germany's Eastern Front headquarters—responding to a radiogram about the Soviet government's acceptance of Germany's terms—demanded that a peace treaty be signed within three days of the Soviet delegation's arrival in Brest-Litovsk.

February 24 was spent discussing who would be part of the delegation that would sign the peace treaty. No one wanted to go. Joffe refused. Zinoviev pointed to Sokolnikov, Sokolnikov pointed to Zinoviev. Everyone pointed to Joffe. Joffe made his participation contingent on hundreds of "ifs," Sokolnikov threatened to resign (if he was sent). Lenin asked the comrades "not to get upset," pointing out that "Comrade Petrovsky can go as a People's Commissar." Lomov, Smirnov, Uritsky, Pyatakov, Bogolepov, and Spunde all resigned from their posts in the Sovnarkom. Trotsky remembered that five days earlier he had already tendered his resignation from the post of People's Commissar of Foreign Affairs and now insisted upon it. Zinoviev urged Trotsky "to remain [at his post] until the peace treaty is signed, because the crisis is not over yet." Stalin talked about the "pain that he feels about the comrades" who are leaving their posts, especially because "there is no one to replace them." Trotsky declared that he "no longer wished to bear responsibility" for the peace policy at the People's Commissariat of Foreign Affairs, but, not wanting to split up the party, he was prepared to announce his resignation in the "least conspicuous fashion"; "the routine work can be supervised by Chicherin, while the political leadership must be taken over by Lenin." Zinoviev begged Trotsky to "delay his departure by two or three days." Stalin also asked him to "wait a couple of days." Lenin stated that Trotsky's resignation was unacceptable. The arguments began again. Trotsky described a split within the party:

> In the party now there are two very sharply separated factions. If we look at it from a parliamentary perspective, then we now have two parties, and from a parliamentary perspective, the minority should yield to the majority; but this isn't happening in our case, because what we have is a struggle between groups. We cannot surrender our positions to the Left SRs.[32]

After long debate, Sokolnikov agreed to put his signature on the peace treaty. The delegation left on the night of February 24. Sokolnikov was accompanied by Grigory Petrovsky, Georgy Chicherin, Lev Karakhan, and Joffe, who had finally been persuaded to go along as a consultant, without any responsibility to sign the agreement.

On February 28, the Soviet delegation arrived in Brest-Litovsk only to learn that the German government was going even further in its demands. They were now demanding that Kars, Ardagan, and Batum be handed over to Turkey (although these territories had never been occupied by Turkish troops during the war). Sokolnikov made an attempt to object, but Hoffmann let it be understood that discussion of the ultimatum was out of the question. The three-day period during which the peace treaty had to be signed had been defined by the Germans as starting at 11 a.m. on March 1, when the first official meeting in Brest-Litovsk was to take place.

On March 1, the conference resumed its work. On both sides, the negotiations were now conducted by secondary figures. Foreign ministers Kühlmann, Czernin, Talaat (Turkey), and Radoslavov (Bulgaria) were all at peace talks in Bucharest at this time, and they had sent their deputies to Brest-Litovsk. At the very first meeting, Rosenberg—the German envoy who was to sign the agreement—proposed to the Soviet delegation to discuss the draft of the peace treaty that he had brought with him. Sokolnikov asked him to read the entire draft, and after the reading declared that he refused "to discuss any of it because that is absolutely useless under the present circumstances"[33]—especially since the world-wide proletarian revolution was already drawing nigh.

The Treaty of Brest-Litovsk was literally the only point of contention between Trotsky and Lenin during the first and most crucial years of the Soviet government. The history of their disagreements is quite telling: on February 23, 1918—when the issue was not really the peace treaty as much as Lenin's power in the party—Trotsky refused to speak out against the peace treaty, thereby securing for Lenin a majority of the Central Committee's votes. If would be absurd to think that Trotsky was motivated by gentlemanly considerations. By leaving Lenin in power, he was first and foremost protecting his own position, knowing that without Lenin he would not be able to survive in the government and would be squeezed out by rivals. So he had no alternative. Lenin, the great party strategist, of course understood this. Nor was Trotsky supporting Lenin for disinterested motives: on the very next day after the Treaty of Brest-Litovsk was signed, March 4, 1918, Trotsky was appointed head of the Supreme Military Council, and on March 13, People's Commissar of Army and Navy Affairs. It is difficult to believe that these appointments, which took place as soon as the peace treaty was signed, were not Lenin's reward to Trotsky for the outcome of the February 23 vote. It is possible that, even before the vote, Lenin had obtained from Trotsky a promise not to speak out against him in return for important ministerial posts, which significantly strengthened Trotsky's position in the government.

In insisting on the Treaty of Brest-Litovsk, Lenin clearly understood what he was doing. While his opponents on the issue of the peace agreement were trying to ascertain what course of action would most benefit the cause of world revolution, he had to calculate which path guaranteed him personally the greatest chances of remaining in power. By not signing a peace treaty with the Germans, he would have lost his position of leadership, since a continuation of the German-Russian war might have led to the toppling of the Sovnarkom government. Furthermore, victory over the Germans could only be achieved through national unity, and for this he would have had to relinquish his personal leadership position and enter into an alliance with other socialist parties. On the other hand, in order to get the peace treaty signed, Lenin needed to overcome only one kind of opposition: the one within his own party. To achieve this, according to a strategy already familiar to him, he had to overwhelm the resistance of the majority of his own Central Committee. And to reach this goal, according to a strategy that was entirely familiar to him, it was enough to threaten to resign. This was precisely his way of proceeding. By yielding to the Germans on all counts, by signing off on conditions that contemporaries described as "humiliating," Lenin remained the head of the Sovnarkom. However, the opposition to the separate peace within the party and the Soviet apparatus forced him to change tactics. He gradually shifted his stress from "peace" to "respite." Rather than talking about a peace treaty with the Central Powers, he was now arguing for signing a noncommittal nominal agreement for the sake of a brief pause—even if it was one that lasted only a couple of days—which was required in order to prepare for revolutionary war. By formulating the matter this way, he almost erased the distinction between himself and the Left Communists. Their disagreement now was about timing. Bukharin was in favor of immediate war. Lenin was in favor of war after a short respite. The separate peace vanished from his lexicon.

Just like Trotsky's formula "neither war nor peace," Lenin's "respite" was a middle course. Without renouncing the call for a revolutionary war, it made it possible to delay its beginning indefinitely. By giving the Left Communists hope for a quick declaration of war, the "respite" enabled him to conclude the Treaty of Brest-Litovsk, which was so important to his survival. The "respite" formula also seemed more convenient than a separate peace in terms of solving the Soviet government's foreign relations problems. By signing a peace treaty, the Bolsheviks compromised themselves both with the German socialists and with the Allied Powers, provoking the latter's intervention. A "respite" gave both of them a hope that war between Russia and Germany would soon resume. One drawback to this policy, from Lenin's point of view, consisted in Germany's growing fears that the Bolsheviks had no serious intentions to honor the peace. But since Germany would not have been able to obtain more advantageous peace terms from any other Russian government, Lenin understood that Germany would remain interested in the Sovnarkom.

As for the Allied Powers, the Bolsheviks' initial intention to conclude a separate peace and thus break up Russia's alliance with England and France seemed in 1918 to be an act of unprecedented duplicity. Not wishing to deal with a government of "Maximalists" in Russia, and doubting its ability to remain in power, the Allied Powers nonetheless tried to maintain contact with the Soviets, at least on an unofficial level, in order to convince the Soviet government not to sign—and after the signing, not to ratify—the Treaty of Brest-Litovsk.

In the eyes of the Allied Powers, Lenin, who had traveled through Germany in a sealed train, and who had received money from the Germans (which England and France, at least, there was not doubt), was, of course, a puppet of the German government, if not a true German agent. This was how the British and the French explained Lenin's pro-German policies. Clearly, Trotsky's formula "neither war nor peace" did not cut Russia off from the Allied Powers as categorically as Lenin's peace proposal. By signing a peace treaty, Lenin was pushing the Allied Powers toward war with Russia. Trotsky tried to maintain a balance between the two opposing camps. After March 3, however, this course became quite difficult to maintain. Lenin's "respite," without ridding Russia of the German occupation, provoked the intervention of the world powers—England, France, Japan, and the United States—and unleashed a civil war in Russia.

One can understand the reasons that, in this instance as well, drove Lenin to pick what would seem to be the most risky course for the Revolution (and the least dangerous course for himself). The Germans demanded territories. But they did not demand that Lenin relinquish power; just the opposite, they were interested in him, since they understood that, in order to conclude a separate peace, they would find no better ally. By contrast, the Allied Powers were not interested in territories. What they needed was to keep the Eastern Front active. By forming an alliance with Germany, Lenin secured his personal power. In an alliance with the Allied Powers, he would have unquestionably lost it, since he was a supporter of a pro-German orientation.

The Treaty of Brest-Litovsk could go into effect only after it was ratified by three bodies: the party congresses, the Congress of Soviets, and the German Reichstag. Therefore, those who supported the peace and those who opposed it had two weeks at their disposal as stipulated by the Germans as the deadline for the ratification. The Moscow regional party bureau had passed a resolution of no confidence in the Central Committee, and Lenin, before doing anything else, tried to get it revoked. The opportunity came at a Moscow municipal conference of the RSDLP, convened shortly after the peace was signed, on the night of March 4. All three points of view were represented in the reports of the conference's participants: Lenin, Trotsky, and Bukharin. Lenin's position was defended by Zinoviev and Sverdlov. Obolensky (Osinsky) spoke for the Left Communists, proposing that the conference pass a resolution of no confidence in the Central Committee. The Left Communists were defeated: only five people voted for Osinsky's resolution; 65 conference delegates voted for a resolution of confidence in the Central Committee, and came out in favor of preserving party unity by any means necessary. However, on the question that was of greatest importance to Lenin, Trotsky came out the winner: a majority of the participants in the conference, 46 people, voted against signing the peace treaty (Pokrovsky's resolution).

In a fight, Lenin always had a clear grasp of the interconnections between minor details. This distinguished him from Trotsky, who was perpetually striving for the unreachable horizon and did not set immediate goals for himself. For Lenin in March 1918 the objective was the ratification of the Treaty of Brest-Litovsk at the upcoming Seventh Party Congress. By this time, the Bolshevik Party had effectively split in half. The most striking manifestation of this split was the beginning of the publication of the newspaper *Kommunist* by the Left Communists. The newspaper, which was first published on March 5 and edited by Bukharin, Radek, and Uritsky, became the press organ for the St. Petersburg committee and the St. Petersburg regional committee of the RSDLP. In Moscow, the Left Communists began to publish a magazine under the same name. Lenin tried to oppose the Left Communists, mainly through *Pravda*. Thus, before the opening of the congress, on March 6, he published an article entitled "A Serious Lesson and a Serious Responsibility." But the article was very persuasive. The main idea was that "from 1 p.m. on March 3, when the Germans called a halt to military action, until 7 p.m. on March 5," when Lenin wrote the article, the Soviet government had had a respite which it had already successfully made use of.[34] Such an argument could only elicit a smile. It was premature to talk about the Germans calling a halt to military action. In addition, it was obvious that no measures for the defense of the state could be enacted over two days.

On March 6, at 8:45 p.m., shortly after a joint meeting between the presidium of the VTsIK and the Sovnarkom at which Sokolnikov delivered a report about the work of the peace delegation, the Extraordinary Seventh Congress of the party, convened specifically for the ratification of the peace treaty with Germany, opened in the Tauride Palace. The congress did not represent the full membership. "Only party members with more than three months' standing could take part"[35] in the voting, i.e., only those who had joined the RSDLP before the October coup. In addition, the number of delegates was small. As late as March 5 it had still not been clear whether the congress would take place, and whether it would be allowed to make any rulings. At a preliminary meeting, Sverdlov admitted that "this is a conference, a meeting, but not a congress."[36] And since such a "congress" could in no way be called "ordinary," it was labeled "extraordinary."

The congress met in a great hurry. There are no precise records about the number of delegates participating; it is assumed that there were 47 delegates with the right to vote and 59 consultative delegates, formally representing 169,200 members of the Russian Communist Party (Bolsheviks). As for the actual size of the party as a whole, according to inaccurate and unverified records it had as many as 300,000 members—not that many, considering that at the time of the Sixth Congress in July 1917, when the party did not yet control the government, its ranks had already swelled to about 240,000; indeed, between April and July 1917, the size of the party had tripled. Now, however, Lenin was compelled to point out that "many organizations have effectively not grown over the recent period."[37] And Sverdlov, who delivered a Central Committee report before the Seventh Congress, drew the delegates' attention to two other deplorable factors: "members' dues were coming in extremely haphazardly," while *Pravda*'s circulation had fallen from 220,000 in October 1917 to 85,000—and moreover the newspaper was being distributed effectively only in Petrograd and the surrounding areas.[38]

On March 7, at 12 p.m., the first report at the congress—about the Treaty of Brest-Litovsk—was delivered by Lenin, who attempted to convince the delegates of the need to ratify the agreement. It may be considered genuinely remarkable that the text of the agreement was kept secret and not shown to the delegates at the congress. Meanwhile, the terms of the treaty were harsher than those of the Treaty of Versailles. With respect to territorial changes, the Brest-Litovsk agreement stipulated that Russia would withdraw from the provinces of Eastern Anatolia—the Ardagan, Kars, and Batum regions—and ensure "their orderly return to Turkey"; sign an immediate peace treaty with the Ukrainian Republic; and recognize the peace treaty between Ukraine and the Central Powers. Effectively, this meant handing over Ukraine—which had to be cleared of all Russian and Red Guard units— to German control. Estland and Lifland were also to be cleared of Russian troops and Red Guards. Estland's eastern border would now more or less follow the Narva River. Lifland's eastern border would run through Lakes Chudskoye and Pskovskoye. Finland and the Åland Islands were also to be cleared of Russian troops and Red Guards, while the Finnish ports were to be freed from the Russian fleet and naval presence.

The surrendered territories, with a total area of 780,000 square kilometers with a population of 56,000,000 (one-third of the population of the Russian Empire), before the Revolution contained 27% of the country's agricultural land, 26% of its entire railway system, 33% of its textile industry, 73% of its iron and steel production, 89% of its coal mines, 90% of its sugar industry, 918 textile factories, 574 breweries, 133 tobacco factories, 1685 distilleries, 244 chemical enterprises, 615 cellulose factories, 1073 machine shops, and most importantly, 40% of its industrial workers, who would now be placed under "the capitalist yoke." Obviously, without all this it would be impossible to "build a socialist economy"[39] (which was the point of the Brest-Litovsk respite). Lenin compared the peace agreement with the Treaty of Tilsit, in which Prussia had lost about one-half of its territory and 50% of its population. Russia was losing only a third. But in absolute numbers, the territorial and demographic losses were immeasurable. Russia's territory would now be smaller than it was before Peter the Great.

This was the agreement that Lenin was defending. He read his speech as an inveterate supporter of world revolution, speaking above all of the hope for a revolution in Germany and of the fundamental impossibility of co-existence between socialist and capitalist states. In substance, Lenin expressed solidarity with the Left Communists on all of the main issues: he welcomed the revolutionary war, the guerilla struggle, world revolution; he admitted that war with Germany was inevitable, that coexistence with capitalist countries was impossible, that Petrograd and Moscow would most likely have to be surrendered to the Germans, who were preparing for another advance, that the "respite" could not last for more than a day. But still from all this the Left Communists concluded that the proper course of action was to declare a revolutionary war. Lenin, on the other hand, felt that a respite, even one that lasted only one day, was worth a third of Russia and, more significantly, a retreat from revolutionary dogma. In this, the Left Communists could never agree with Lenin.

Bukharin responded to Lenin with his own speech. He indicated that the Russian Revolution would either be "saved by the international revolution or perish under the blows of international capital." Therefore, there was no point in talking about peaceful coexistence. The advantages of a peace agreement with Germany were illusory. Before signing the agreement, it was necessary to understand the purpose of the reprieve proposed by Lenin. He claimed that it was "needed in order to regulate the railways," to organize the economy, and to "establish the same Soviet apparatus" that "we have been unable to establish over the last four months."

Bukharin believed that "if there was any chance for such a respite," the Left Communists would agree to sign the peace treaty. But if the lull would last only a few days, then the game wasn't worth the candle, because the problems that Lenin had enumerated could not be solved in a few days: they would require at least a few months, and neither Hoffmann nor Lieb-knecht would grant the Bolsheviks that much time. "The point is not that we are protesting against shameful and ignominious peace terms as such," Bukharin continued. "We are protesting against these terms because they in fact do not provide us with this lull," since they leave Russia without Ukraine and bread, without the Donets Basin and coal, splitting up and weaking the workers and the workers' movement. Even such pro-Soviet territories as Latvia are surrendered to German occupation. The Soviet government's measures to nationalize foreign industry are in fact cancelled, because "the peace terms contain clauses that pertain to safeguarding the interests of foreign subjects." In addition, the agreement would forbid Communist agitation by the Soviet government in the countries of the Central Powers and in the territories occupied by them, which, in Bukharin's opinion, would negate the international significance of the Russian Revolution that in the end will depend on "whether or not the international revolution will triumph," because the international revolution is its only "salvation."

Lastly, Bukharin categorically objected to a new item in the Brest-Litovsk agreement, "added only afterward," according to which "Russia must preserve the independence of Persia and Afghanistan." Bukharin believed that this alone was reason enough not to sign a peace treaty that provided a two-week delay. The only solution, according to him, was to begin a revolutionary war against "German imperialism," which, in spite of inevitable defeats during the initial stage of such a war, would bring victory in the end, because "the more deeply the enemy penetrates into Russia, the more unfavorable will be the conditions in which he will find himself."[40]

After Bukharin's speech, the meeting was adjourned. In the evening, during the debates about Lenin's and Bukharin's speeches, Uritsky argued that Lenin had failed to prove "the correctness of his position." One could try to obtain a prolonged respite. But to "settle for a pause of two-three days," which "will give us nothing, but threatens to destroy the remaining railroads and the small army," which the Bolsheviks have only begun to create, means to agree to "a pause that no one needs, that is useless and harmful," only to have to resume fighting "on the very next day, under much worse conditions," retreating "to infinity," all the way to the Urals, evacuating "not just Petrograd, but Moscow as well," since, as is obvious to everyone, "the general situation can deteriorate significantly."

Uritsky disagreed with Lenin's comparison between the Brest-Litovsk treaty and the Treaty of Tilsit. "It was not the German working class that signed the Treaty of Tilsit," he said. "It was signed by the other side. The Germans had to accept it as a fait accompli." Uritsky therefore proposed "not to ratify the agreement," although he understood that a break with Germany "would initially bring a whole series of defeats on the battlefield," which, however, "might contribute a great deal more to the outcome of the revolution in Western Europe" than the "obscene peace" advocated by Lenin.[41]

Bubnov commented that at a moment when a "revolutionary crisis [was] already gathering steam in Western Europe" and the "international revolution [was] preparing to turn into the most acute, the most large-scale form of civil war, to sign a peace agreement" would mean to deal a fatal "blow to the cause of the international proletariat," which was now "facing the problem of starting a civil war on an international scale," a problem that was "not fanciful, but quite real." This was the meaning of the call for "revolutionary war." Lenin, however, from his leftist position of October 1917 had shifted to a rightist position and was now contending that the "masses do not want to fight, the peasants want peace." "Since when do we pose the question in the way that it is now being posed by Comrade Lenin?" asked Bubnov, hinting at hypocrisy.[42]

The point of view of those who favored a pause was also critiqued by Radek. He described Lenin's policies as impossible and unacceptable, pointing out that the Bolsheviks had never hoped that "German imperialism would leave us in peace." On the contrary, everyone assumed the inevitability of war with Germany and therefore "stood for a demonstrative policy of peace, a policy aimed at stirring up the masses in Europe." It was such a policy on the part of the Soviet government that had "brought forth a general strike in Germany" and "strikes in Austria."

Even now, after the new German offensive, Radek believed that the opponents of the peace treaty were right when they argued that "the Germans have no major forces" and that they are prepared to accept an agreement "without a formal peace treaty" (as was reported in the German press). He said that the plan to declare a guerilla war against German occupying forces was more than empty words and that if the Bolsheviks surrendered Petrograd and retreated deep into the country, they would be able to "create new military cadres" within three months, during which time the Germans would be unable to advance further into Russia "in view of the international situation, in view of the state of affairs in the West."[43]

Ryazanov, who also spoke out against signing the peace treaty and in favor of revolutionary war, effectively charged Lenin with treason. If Petrograd was to be evacuated, only government agencies should leave the city. "Any attempt to surrender Petersburg without resistance by singing and ratifying this peace treaty" would constitute "an inevitable betrayal of the Russian proletariat," since "it would encourage the Germans to continue their offensive." Lenin, Ryazanov went on, was prepared to give up "Petersburg, Moscow, the Urals, he is not afraid of going to Vladivostok if the Japanese let him," he was prepared to retreat and retreat; "this retreat has a limit."[44]

Kollontai, another opponent of the peace treaty, indicated that there would be no peace and that even if the treaty was ratified, the Brest-Litovsk agreement would exist only on paper. The proof of this was the fact that even after the signing of the treaty, the war was set to continue. She believed that there was no possibility of a pause, that peace with Germany was impossible, that the current situation should be used in order to form an "international revolutionary army," and that if the Soviet government in Russia collapses, the Communist banner will be "picked up by others."[45]

The Seventh Party Congress was remarkable as a majority of the delegates present voted in favor of the peace treaty, while a majority of the speakers came out against it, and even the minority that supported Lenin—and indeed even Lenin himself—qualified their arguments for the peace treaty in different ways (Zinoviev, Smilga, Sokolnikov, and others). Sverdlov, another supporter of the peace agreement, spoke in defense of Trotsky, who had been misrepresented by Lenin, stating that Trotsky's policies at the Brest-Litovsk peace talks had been the policies of the Central Committee:

> We were all equally in favor of drawing out the peace talks for as long as possible... All of us supported the position that was initially taken by our Brest delegation, under the leadership of Comrade Trotsky... Therefore, the claim that the Central Committee was pursuing an incorrect policy does not correspond to reality. We still continue to say that, under certain circumstances, we will inevitably have to wage a revolutionary war.[46]

After this, Trotsky elaborated a "third position" for the delegates—the position of neither peace nor war—and said that he had abstained from the Central Committee vote on signing the peace treaty because he did not see "this or that attitude to this issue as being decisive for the destiny of the revolution." He acknowledged that the chances of victory were greater "not on the side that has been taken" by Lenin, and pointed out that the peace talks with Germany were above all a form of propaganda and that, if it had really been necessary to form a genuine peace agreement, then the peace treaty should not have been delayed, but ought to have been signed in November, when the Germans were willing to accept terms that were most favorable to the Soviet government.

Trotsky rejected the argument that if the Soviet government failed to ratify the peace treaty, the Germans would take over Petrograd, and referred to a conversation that he had had with Lenin. Even Lenin believed, he noted, that "the capture of Petrograd would have a revolutionizing an effect on German workers." "Everything depends on the speed with which the European revolution will come,"[47] Trotsky concluded, but he did not speak out against ratifying the peace treaty: "I will not argue that you should not ratify it," he said, adding that "there is a certain limit" beyond which the Bolsheviks could not go, since "that would really constitute a betrayal in the full sense of the word." This limit was the German demand that the Bolsheviks sign a peace treaty with the Ukrainian Rada.[48] And since the contents of the Treaty of Brest-Litovsk were unknown to the delegates, no one corrected Trotsky by pointing out that the treaty—which had already been signed by the Soviet government and which was now supposed to be ratified by his listeners—did in fact require the Bolsheviks to sign a peace treaty with the Ukrainian Republic.

At 9:45 p.m. on March 7, the session ended. On the following day, at 11:40 a.m., the fourth and penultimate session of the congress began. Bukharin again spoke, calling for revolutionary war: "Is war today even possible? We must decide whether it is objectively possible or not." If war was possible and if it would begin anyway "in two or three days," what was the point of paying "such a price for this peace treaty," which brought incalculable harm and besmirched the Soviet government "in the eyes of the entire global proletariat"?[49] In reply, Lenin acknowledged that he was "ninety percent" in agreement with Bukharin,[50] that the Bolsheviks were maneuvering "in the interests of revolutionary war," and that there was agreement on this score between "both halves of the party"; the argument concerned only the question of "whether the war should be continued without any pause or not." Lenin likewise argued that Bukharin's apprehensions about signing the peace treaty were mistaken, since the treaty could be torn up at any time: "In war, one must never let oneself be bound by formal considerations; the peace treaty is a means to gather our strength." "The revolutionary war will come, we have no disagreement here." But for the time being, Lenin threatened to resign in the event the congress failed to ratify the treaty.[51]

In a recorded vote, 30 people supported Lenin's resolution, 12 voted against it, and 4 abstained. The Left Communists' resolution received 9 votes, with 28 people voting against it. However, Lenin's resolution, which won the majority of the votes, did not mention an actual armistice, but only talked about a respite in order to prepare for a revolutionary war. Publishing such a resolution was absolutely out of the question, since the Germans would have taken it as a repeal of the truce. Therefore, Lenin insisted that the congress add an amendment: "The present resolution will not appear in print, and only the fact that the peace treaty has been ratified will be made public."

For Lenin, it was important to sign the peace treaty and get it ratified. In every other respect, he was willing to yield to the Left Communists. In particular, he proposed an amendment to the effect that the Central Committee would have the right to repeal the agreement at any time: "The congress grants authority to the Central Committee of the party both to repeal all peace treaties and to declare war on any imperialist power and on the whole world whenever the Central Committee deems appropriate." Naturally, such an amendment infringed not only on the VTsIK's prerogatives, but on the Sovnarkom's as well. But it gave freedom of action to the core of the Bolshevik party, which now had the right not to convene a special congress in order to annul the peace treaty. Obviously, Lenin himself had no interest in this amendment, but after winning the vote on the ratification issue, he was attempting to lull the opposition by yielding on all possible (and, to him, insignificant) points. As it happened, however, Sverdlov refused to put Lenin's amendment to a vote, on the grounds that the Central Committee "naturally" had the right to make fundamentally important decisions between party congresses, including decisions about war and peace.[52]

Since the resolution passed by the congress concerned a delay rather than an armistice—that is, since the congress was in fact announcing that it would shortly resume war with Germany—Lenin tried to do everything in his power to prevent this information from going beyond the halls of the Tauride Palace. In the end, fearing the possibility that the Left Communists might sabotage his plans directly (for example, by publishing the congress's resolution in *Kommunist*), he demanded that "personal signatures be obtained on this matter from all those present" in view of the "importance of the matter to the state."[53] The congress approved the amendment as well. And it was only his demand that the delegates return the text of the peace resolution in order to "safeguard a military secret" that met with resistance, especially from Sverdlov: "Every delegate, returning home, will have to report to his organization, at least to the main office, and you will need to have these resolutions with you." Lenin persisted, arguing that "messages that contain military secrets are delivered orally."[54] But he lost the vote and this amendment was rejected by the congress on Sverdlov's initiative.

By forcing the party to sign the Treaty of Brest-Litovsk, Lenin achieved a brilliant tactical victory. However, his position was made more difficult by the fact that Russia's main socialist parties, which had representation in the VTsIK, remained in the opposition on this issue: the Left SRs, the Mensheviks, the SRs, and the Anarchist Communists. The battle with these parties still lay ahead, at the ratification of the Brest-Litovsk treaty by the Congress of Soviets. Lenin also had to take into account the likelihood that the Left SRs and the Left Communists would try to form their own party. In the end, in the heat of the struggle over the peace treaty, he overlooked another possible danger: Sverdlov, who was becoming an increasingly prominent figure during those months—overshadowing himself, who was losing his power, authority, and control—blocked the formation of an alliance between the Left Communists and the Left SRs by attempting in March-April 1918 to unite the Bolsheviks and the Left SRs for an inevitable and imminent revolutionary war with Germany.

The German government was informed about the struggle taking place within the Bolshevik Party regarding the peace treaty. On March 11 State Secretary Kühlmann of Germany's foreign ministry indicated in a telegram to the ministry that the general situation was highly "uncertain" and proposed to "refrain from any commentary about" the upcoming ratification of the treaties at the Congress of Soviets. The transfer of Russia's capital from Petrograd to Moscow (where the Congress of Soviets was to meet), farther away from the front lines, likewise pointed to the fact that the Soviet government's intentions were far from peaceful.

The congress opened in Moscow on March 14. Like the Seventh Party Congress, the Congress of Soviets was not representational and labeled "extraordinary." It was attended by 1172 delegates, including 814 Bolsheviks and 238 Left SRs. For the first time, 1000 copies of the text of the Treaty of Brest-Litovsk were printed for the delegates. In the final vote, the peace treaty was ratified by a majority of 784 against 261, with 115 abstaining. The consequence of this vote, however, was the departure of the Left SRs from the government, although this decision by the Left SR delegation was by no means unanimous. At least 78 Left SR delegates voted against resigning from the Sovnarkom and in favor of signing the peace treaty. Nonetheless, on March 15, all of the people's commissars who were members of the Left SR Party resigned from their posts, after which they, like the Left Communists, reserved the right to criticize the Sovnarkom's Brest-Litovsk policy.

In connection with the departure from the Soviet government of all of the Left SRs and some of the Left Communists, on March 18, one day after the Fourth Congress of Soviets concluded its work, the Sovnarkom took up the issue of the "general ministerial crisis." A speech on the subject was delivered by Sverdlov, who was not formally a Sovnarkom member, but was gradually beginning to take over Lenin's duties in the Sovnarkom. At congresses and conferences, Sverdlov had long ago become the presenter or co-presenter for the head of the Sovnarkom. He would also deliver the reports of the Central Committee, as at the Seventh Party Congress, which in the future would be done by the general secretary. On Sverdlov's initiative, the Sovnarkom began negotiating with the Bolshevik Party's Moscow regional committee, whose members had resigned from the government earlier in opposition to the Brest-Litovsk policy, for them to return. Sverdlov himself began negotiating with a number of Bolsheviks who were seen as potential candidates for the posts of People's Commissars of Agriculture, Property, Justice, and for the chairmanship of the Supreme Soviet of the National Economy, to replace the Left SRs and Left Communists who had tendered their resignations and who were, in turn, discussing the issue of removing Lenin from power and forming a new government out of a coalition between the Left SRs and Left Communists. At the same meeting of the Sovnarkom, Sverdlov delivered a report about the Supreme Military Council, which had expelled the Left SR Prosh Proshyan following the departure of the Left SRs from the Sovnarkom.

The longer the "delay or pause" lasted, the more evident Lenin's miscalculations became. The Treaty of Brest-Litovsk remained nothing but a declaration on paper. Neither of the sides viewed it as practical, feasible, or final. If Germany won the war, the treaty was to be reviewed and given a concrete form within the framework of the overall European agreement. If Germany lost, the treaty would obviously become void both because it would be dissolved by Russia, since it would not be recognized by the Allied Powers. The population of the former Russian empire that did not find itself under Soviet rule did not recognize the Treaty of Brest-Litovsk at all unless it was under German, Austro-Hungarian, or Turkish occupation. Within the Soviet camp, both those who had voted for the treaty under pressure from Lenin, and those who had supported an agreement with the Germans under the influence of circumstances, regarded the Brest-Litovsk peace agreement as nothing other than a delay. Not surprisingly, shortly after the ratification of the treaty, Stasova, Sverdlov's assistant and secretary of the Bolshevik Party's Central Committee, indicated in a letter to local organizations: "There is no doubt that Germany, although it has agreed to a peace treaty, will make every effort to eliminate the Soviet government."[55]

From the military point of view, the Brest-Litovsk agreement did not make things easier either for Germany or for the RSFSR. The fall of Petrograd and its occupation by the Germans was expected at any moment. On March 4, one day after the peace treaty was signed, the Petrograd committee of the RSDLP queried the Central Committee about the possibility of operating as an underground organization should the Germans occupy the

city—so little did everyone believe in the newly signed agreement. In the
event that it might have to operate as an underground organization, the
Petrograd committee requested several hundred thousand rubles. It also proposed not to convene the Seventh Party Congress in Petrograd, but to transfer it to Moscow and evacuate all the delegates who had come for the
congress to Moscow as well, so as not to "lose our best comrades" should
the city be captured.[56] As the head of the Petrograd Soviet, however,
Zinoviev tried to remain calm:

> The actual balance of forces on the two sides reveals that at the present
> moment German imperialism has the power to demand a pound of meat from
> us without paying customs duties, but it still lacks the capacity to demand the
> extradition of the head of the Soviet.... Germany will not continue its offensive,
> no matter how tempting the possibility of occupying Petrograd and destroying
> the Smolny Palace might be.... And if Wilhelm does remain capable of con-
> tinuing his offensive against us, what then? Then we have no other choice but to
> continue the war, and in this case the war will for the first time acquire a truly
> revolutionary meaning.[57]

No one paid any attention either to the peace treaty or to the fact that it
had been ratified by the congress. Thus, concurrently with the Seventh Party
Congress, a city conference of the Bolshevik Party also took place in Petrograd. Like the earlier Moscow conference, the conference in Petrograd was
devoted to two issues: the Brest-Litovsk agreement and preventing a split
within the ranks of the Bolshevik Party. Also as in Moscow, the majority of
the people at the conference voted against the split, demanded that the Left
Communists "end their independent organizational existence," and resolved
that the publication of the Left Communists' newspaper, *Kommunist*, must be
terminated as well;[58] *Petrograd Pravda* was declared to be the official newspaper
of the Petrograd party organization.[59] However, on the question of Lenin's
middle course—the delay—he once again met with disappointment. Even
Zinoviev, who represented his position at the conference, concluded his
speech with a declaration of compromise:

> Not for a second can we create the impression that a period of peace has
> arrived. A delay is a delay. We must sound the alarm. We must prepare and
> mobilize our forces. Under the crossfire of our enemies, we must create an army
> for the revolution.[60]

The majority of the conference voted in favor of Trotsky's formula
"neither war nor peace."

The main fault in Lenin's plans was that the Brest-Litovsk agreement turned out to be a total and unconditional capitulation. The closer one came to the line of demarcation (or to the regions of the intervention), the more obvious it was that the peace treaty which Lenin had signed was only the beginning of the problems connected with the issues of war and peace. This was true first and foremost of those regions that had been surrendered to Turkish and German occupation: the Transcaucasus and Ukraine (in the Transcaucasus, Lenin had surrendered not just three districts—Kars, Batum, Ardagan—but the Transcaucasus as a whole). If the revolutionaries, whose gaze was fixed on the West, were willing to forgive Lenin for the loss of the southern territories, which could have been of use only to launch attacks on India, Turkey, Iran, or Afghanistan, they viewed Lenin's consent to surrender Ukraine—now almost Soviet—to the German occupation as an outright betrayal of the revolutionary cause. This was the very threshold that Trotsky, at the Seventh Party Congress, had promised not to cross. This was "betrayal in the full sense of the word."[61]

From the economic, political, military, or emotional point of view, the transfer of Ukraine to German control was a singularly dramatic step for the revolutionaries. Soviet rule, which was already succeeding in Ukraine (or perhaps this was merely the impression of the credulous Communists?), was being sacrificed for the sake of the same old whim of Lenin's: in order to obtain a delay for Soviet Russia. For those who were genuine internationalists, it was difficult not to feel that the Russian Bolsheviks were betraying their Ukrainian comrades, who had been attempting to seize power since December 1917.

As in Petrograd, the Bolsheviks in Kiev had initially tried to stage a coup by relying on the Congress of Soviets of Workers' and Soldiers' Deputies. However, the Ukrainian Peasant Union—having sent its representation to the congress beforehand—neutralized this first attempt. The Bolsheviks there abandoned Kiev, made their way over to Kharkiv, and there declared themselves to be the organ of the Soviet government in Ukraine. From Russia, the Sovnarkom sent troops to aid the Ukrainian Bolsheviks. The Soviet detachments were carrying out a successful offensive, were about to take Kiev, and the government of the Ukrainian People's Republic had no other choice but urgently to declare independence—on January 9 (22), 1918—and sign a separate peace treaty with the Central Powers in order to avoid occupation by the Soviets in exchange for German occupation.

As in the case of the Transcaucasus, Russia was losing a great deal more than had been stipulated by the Brest-Litovsk agreement. Initially, the designnation "Ukraine" was taken to refer to the provinces of Kiev, Chernihiv, Poltava, Kharkiv, Kherson, Volyn, Podolsk, Yekaterinoslavsk, and the Tauride Province—nine in all. Soon, however, the RSFSR also lost the provinces of Kursk and Voronezh to the Ukraine, as well as the Don Voisko Oblast and the Crimea.

Germany assumed the role of Ukraine's defender against anarchy and the Bolsheviks. However, the peace treaty that it had signed with the Rada was based on food, not politics. And the fact that the Germans and Austrians were taking food supplies out of the country made Germany and Austria-Hungary responsible for economic disruptions, not necessarily Germany's fault, in the eyes of the populace. The recent threat of a Soviet occupation was soon forgotten. The devotees of Ukrainian independence were now predisposed against the Germans, since they saw them as occupiers. The supporters of reunification with Russia were also against the Germans, since they believed, rightly, that it was under pressure from Germany that Ukraine had declared independence and separated from Russia. Within a short time, all sections of the Ukrainian population were turning against the Germans.

If in Ukraine the population believed that Germany was robbing their food supplies, then the opinion in Russia was that the famine and shortages were the results of Germany's occupation of Ukraine. Whether or not this had any relation to reality was beside the point. What was important was that the cause of the food shortages in Russia was attributed to the German occupation of Ukraine and to the Sovnarkom's Brest-Litovsk policy.

To these objective factors were added some subjective ones. German troops in Ukraine behaved as an occupying force, in part because of provocations from the opponents of the Brest-Litovsk treaty. This was most conspicuously confirmed by the establishment of German courts-martial in Ukraine, which according to German law could operate only during a time of war on occupied enemy territory. There were cases of German troops disarming Ukrainian units, although such units had a right to exist according to the terms of the Ukrainian-German agreement. The Ukrainian government had to obtain permission for a May Day celebration from the head of the German forces in Ukraine. More eloquent proof of the absence of any real peace agreement would have been difficult to imagine: Ukraine was not under allied, but under enemy, occupation.

Clearly, the hardening of the occupying regime in Ukraine was connected, first to Germany's own deteriorating food supply situation. It was precisely to secure the regular export of Ukrainian food products that the German army engaged in various military actions in Ukraine. The "peace for bread" strategy had been advertised thoughtlessly to the German and Austro-Hungarian public. Ukrainian bread became a legend. Everyone in Germany and Austria-Hungary—from government officials to simple workers—believed that it would save them. Therefore, Germany's military policies in Ukraine were governed by objectives connected to the food supply. In order to organize the export of food products from Ukraine, it was necessary to establish a stable regime there, to station troops in the region, and to secure a reliable means of transport. Many fields lay fallow. Not all arable land was being used. This greatly preoccupied the German leadership, that chose the path of coercion: on orders from General Eichhorn, the head of Germany's occupation forces in Ukraine, peasants were forced to plant crops on all available land.

The order called for coerced cultivation of the fields by the peasants and military requisitioning of agricultural products with "due compensation" to the owners; it required landowners to make sure that peasants were planting crops and to report to the military authorities if they refused to do so. Local land committees were obligated under penalty of punishment to provide the necessary working animals, farm equipment, and seeds. But since the order did not indicate who exactly had to do the planting, it led mainly to arbitrary takeovers of other people's fields. German officers on location interpreted the order in various ways, "sometimes chasing the land-grabbers away, sometimes encouraging them."[62] And this naturally led to the growth of rural banditry in Ukraine, i.e., to results that were diametrically opposed to the objectives set by the German government—to stabilize Ukraine's regime in order to provide for the peaceful export of food supplies to Germany.

Such policies could be called neither wise, nor reasonable, nor consistent. In time, even the Rada government—which was dependent on Germany—began to speak out against them. For reasons of political expediency, it directed its criticism at Eichhorn, the head of Germany's forces in Ukraine, and attempted to appeal to the German government and the Reichstag for help. Key meetings devoted to German policies in Ukraine took place in Kiev on April 27 and 28, shortly after Eichhorn's orders to establish German courts-martial and capital punishment were made public. The criticism was universal. At a meeting on April 27, Lyubinsky, who had himself signed the German-Ukrainian peace treaty in Brest-Litovsk, proposed to stand firm this time and to demand the recall of Eichhorn and Mumm, the German envoy. In opposition to Eichhorn's order, he proposed that the Ukrainian government issue its own decree, cancelling the German commander's instructions. On the following day, Vsevolod Golubovich, the head of Ukraine's Council of People's Ministers, told the members of the Lesser Rada that, according to the existing treaty between the German and the Ukrainian governments, "all orders must be issued by mutual agreement and after joint discussion";[63] meanwhile, Eichhorn's orders were being given unilaterally.

Given that, on April 17, the Ukrainian government had already refused to sign the Ukrainian-German military convention, which the Germans were insisting on, it was obvious that it was no longer loyal to Germany. The German government drew its own conclusions: on April 28, during a meeting of the Lesser Rada, at 3:45 p.m., the Ukrainian government was arrested by German troops. Since Germany, was not interested in maintaining a government that was (in its opinion) sabotaging its food supply policies, it organized the coup d'état. The old government was replaced by the new government of the Hetman Pavlo Skoropadsky, which pursued a more pro-German course.

The Treaty of Brest-Litovsk became the Achilles heel of Bolshevik rule. In the final analysis, they would either have to yield to their political opponents, to acknowledge the fundamental soundness of their criticism, and both formally and factually to terminate the delay, or else deepen their ties to the German government even further and to increase their dependency on Germany. In the former case, Lenin might be removed from power as the initiator of a flawed policy. Obviously, therefore, he preferred the second option. Under pressure from him, the Central Committee agreed to exchange ambassadors with "imperialist Germany." Today, this move does not seem extraordinary. But in April 1918, when the German revolution was about to erupt at any moment, the official recognition of the "Hohenzollerns" by the Soviet government—which could in no way be justified by the need to maintain Lenin's "delay"—was no longer simply a mistake from the point of view of the interests of the German and world revolution: it was a crime. And if Joffe, a Left Communist who supported the world revolution and opposed the Treaty of Brest-Litovsk, had been told in March 1918 that he would become Soviet Russia's first authorized representative in imperialist Germany, he would likely have considered this a bad joke, and the very idea that the Soviet republic and the Kaiser's Germany might exchange embassies would have seemed to him like sheer mockery.

As it turned out, however, the Central Committee, which disagreed with Lenin on the issue of Germany and the German revolution, nonetheless yielded to him step by step in all practical matters. Obviously, it was first and foremost he who insisted on establishing diplomatic relations between the RSFSR and Germany. Giving the ambassadorship to Germany to a Left Communist and an ardent opponent of the Brest-Litovsk treaty constituted a compromise, allowing the majority of the Central Committee to agree to establish diplomatic relations with the imperialist state: Joffe was going to

Germany in order to coordinate the activities of German and Russian Communists toward organizing a German revolution.

The Germans appointed Count Mirbach as ambassador to the RSFSR; he had already spent several weeks in Petrograd and was thus familiar with the general outlines of the situation. Mirbach arrived in Moscow on April 23. The embassy occupied a two-story townhouse that belonged to the widow of the sugar manufacturer and collegiate counselor von Berg (today at Vesnin Street, no. 5). The ambassador's arrival coincided with the coup d'état in Ukraine, the occupation of Finland by German troops, and the Germans' gradual and systematic advance eastward of the line demarcated by the Brest-Litovsk agreement. Naturally, the Soviet government expressed its displeasure to Mirbach as soon as the opportunity presented itself—when his credentials were being presented on April 26. Three days later Mirbach informed Hertling that the German offensive in Ukraine "became the first cause of complications." Finland was the second problem. Chicherin voiced his displeasure with a diplomatic formula; Sverdlov was more severe, expressing the hope that Mirbach would succeed in "eliminating the obstacles that still stand in the way of a genuine peace." The ambassador's letters credentials were given in a cold and perfunctory manner. After the official ceremony ended, Sverdlov did not invite anyone to sit down and engage in private conversation.[64]

As a diplomat, Mirbach was unprejudiced and subtle. His reports to Hertling and to State Secretary Kühlmann of Germany's foreign ministry on the whole speak of an accurate understanding of the situation in Soviet Russia. On April 30, in a report on the political situation in the RSFSR, Mirbach did not hesitate to describe the central issue: the state of anarchy in the country and the weakness of the Bolshevik government, which lacked the support of the population. "Moscow, the holy city, the symbol of czarist rule, the sacred site of the Orthodox Church," Mirbach wrote,

has become in the hands of the Bolsheviks the symbol of the most flagrant violations of good taste and style, unleashed by the Russian Revolution. Anyone who knew the capital during the days of its glory has difficulty recognizing it now. In all parts of the city, particularly in the central commercial district, the walls of buildings are riddled with bullet holes—evidence of the battles that took place here. Artillery fire has turned the magnificent Hotel Metropole into a heap of ruins, and even the Kremlin has suffered great damage. Various gates have been severely hit.

The streets are full of life, but one gathers the impression that they are filled exclusively with the proletariat. Well-dressed people are virtually not to be seen—as if all the representatives of the former ruling class and the bourgeoisie have suddenly fallen off the face of the earth. Maybe this is partly explained by the fact that most of them are trying outwardly to adapt to the new appearance of the streets, so as not to excite the passion for plunder and unpredictable excesses on the part of the new ruling class. Orthodox priests, who had previously constituted a significant proportion of the pedestrians, have likewise vanished from view. In the stores, one can buy almost nothing—only the dusty remnants of former luxury and at unheard-of prices. The central leitmotif of the whole picture is unwillingness to work and idleness. Since the factories are still not operating, and the land is still not being cultivated—or so it appeared to me, at least, during my journey—Russia seems to be moving toward an even more frightening catastrophe than the one that has already been brought about by the revolution. Security is quite poor, but during the day one can walk anywhere freely without escorts. However, to go out in the evening is unwise, and even during the day one keeps hearing gunfire, and more or less serious clashes take place constantly.

The former owning class has fallen into a state of profound unrest: one order by the government would be enough to deprive them of all their possessions. Sinister warrants of requisition hang on almost all of the palaces and large mansions, resulting in the owner ending up on the street, often in a matter of hours. The desperation of the representatives of the former ruling class knows no limits, but they are in no condition to gather sufficient strength to put an end to the organized robbery to which they are being subjected. The desire to establish some kind of order extends to the lowest strata of the population, while their sense of their own powerlessness compels them to hope that salvation will come from Germany. The same circles that had formerly been the loudest in railing against us now view us, if not as angels, then at least as a police force....

The Bolsheviks' power in Moscow is provided mainly by Latvian battalions, as well as by the large number of automobiles, requisitioned by the government, which constantly circulate throughout the city and can, if necessary, deliver troops to locations where disorders arise.

To predict what all of this will lead to is impossible. At the present time, one can only suppose that the basic situation will remain the same.

Mirbach believed that it was still in Germany's interest to deal with Lenin's government, since those who would replace the Bolsheviks would try, with the Allied Powers' help, to reunite with the territories that had been cut off by the Treaty of Brest-Litovsk, first and foremost with Ukraine, and that therefore it was most advantageous for Germany to provide the Bolsheviks with a minimum of supplies and maintain them in power, since no other government would have agreed to a treaty that was so advantageous to Germany.

Mirbach heard these arguments once more from Lenin himself, during a meeting that took place on May 16 in the Kremlin. Lenin acknowledged that the number of his opponents was growing and that the situation in the country was more serious than it had been a month before. He likewise noted that his opponents were not the same people as in the past. Previously, these had been the representatives of the right-wing parties; now, however, he had to face an opposition within his own camp, where a left wing had emerged. The main contention of this opposition, he went on, was that the Treaty of Brest-Litovsk, which he was still prepared staunchly to defend, was a mistake. More and more Russian territory was under German occupation; the peace treaty with Finland had still not been ratified; there was no peace treaty with Ukraine; famine was spreading. The situation was still very far from a genuine armistice, Lenin indicated, while a number of recent events had confirmed the soundness of the left opposition's arguments. He therefore was working toward securing peace agreements with Finland and Ukraine as a top priority. Mirbach noted the fact that Lenin did not threaten him with a possible re-orientation of Soviet policy toward a partnership with the Allied Powers. Lenin had simply emphasized that his own position within the government was extremely unstable.

Mirbach's report about his conversation with Lenin is literally the only document that contains an admission by Lenin that the Brest-Litovsk policy was a failure. Theoretical and ideological mistakes, however, were far less noticeable than practical ones. The Treaty of Brest-Litovsk, despite the fact that the Bolsheviks had acceded to all the German demands, had resulted neither in the coveted armistice, nor in the "delay" promised by Lenin. From the point of view of the German leadership, the Brest-Litovsk agreement was a military measure to help the Western Front while simultaneously using the Eastern districts for economic purposes in order to continue the war. This being the case, the deterioration of Germany's position in the West had to increase its appetite in the East. After the peace treaty was signed, military activity did not stop for a single day on most of the territory of the former Russian empire. Germany continued to present new ultimatums and occupy entire districts and cities located to the east of the demarcation line established by the Brest-Litovsk treaty.

The Treaty of Brest-Litovsk turned out to be merely an agreement on paper precisely because the two main participants in the peace talks—the Soviet and the German governments—did not take it seriously, did not consider it final, and most importantly, signed it not to secure peace, but only in order to continue the war, under conditions that were more favorable to them. The Bolsheviks were thinking of a revolutionary war, the Germans of a war for a stable peace. As it turned out, even if the Treaty of Brest-Litovsk did provide a delay, then it was only for the benefit of Germany, and only until November 1918.

There is no point in arguing that Lenin could have foreseen the consequences of the treaty. But it is evident that the majority of the party's activists saw the worst of their fears realized. They had supported Trotsky's formula "neither war nor peace" before signing the peace treaty, and after it was signed they entered a period of crisis that resulted in—as Trotsky put it—a "strategy of desperation." The Bolsheviks themselves during this period believed that their days in power were numbered. With the exception of the two capitals, they had no support in the country. On May 22, a circular letter from the Central Committee—published in *Pravda* and written, evidently, on Sverdlov's initiative—acknowledged that the Bolshevik Party was going through "an extremely critical period," whose urgency was compounded on top of everything else by the grave "internal state of the party," since "due to the departure of a large number of senior officials from the party" many party organizations had grown weak. One of the main causes of the crisis, the authors of the letter noted, was the secession of the left wing of the Bolshevik Party. They went on to conclude: "We have never before gone through such a difficult period."[65] Two days later, in his article "On the Famine (A Letter to the Workers of Petrograd)," Lenin wrote that due to problems with the food supply and the famine that had spread to vast regions of the country, the Soviet government was near collapse.[66] He refused, however, to acknowledge that both of these developments were the results of his Brest-Litovsk policy.

On May 29, the Central Committee addressed party members in yet another letter, apparently also written on Sverdlov's initiative, which stressed that the "crisis" which the party was going through was "very, very grave"— membership was falling, internal conflicts were becoming more and more frequent, clashes between party organizations and the party's representatives in the Soviets and in executive committees were not uncommon. "The harmony and integrity of the party apparatus have been compromised. There is no longer the former unity of action. Discipline, which had always been so solid," has grown weak. "There is an unquestionable general decline in party work and disintegration within the organizations."[67]

The moribund state of the Soviet government became the reason for increasing panic in Bolshevik ranks. "However strange it may seem," Vacietis later recalled, the expectation at the time was that "the center of Soviet Russia would become a stage for internecine war and that the Bolsheviks would unlikely be able to hold on to power and would fall victim to the famine and to the general discontent within the country." People were not ruling out "the possibility of a Moscow offensive by the Germans, the Don Cossacks, and the White Czechs. This last notion was particularly widespread at the time."[68] Georgy Solomon, Krasin's agent and good acquaintance with close ties to the Bolsheviks, wrote in his memoirs about the confusion prevailing in Bolshevik ranks during the summer of 1918. Solomon noted that it was approximately during these months that a prominent Soviet diplomat in Berlin (probably Joffe) confessed that he was certain that the Bolshevik revolution in Russia would fail and suggested to Solomon that he should disappear as soon as possible.[69]

The catastrophic state of the Soviet republic was discussed at a VTsIK meeting on June 4. Many prominent Bolsheviks delivered speeches, including Lenin and Trotsky. Lenin acknowledged that "we are now, in the summer of 1918, facing what may be one of the most difficult, one of the most severe, and one of the most critical transitions in our revolution," and not merely "from the international point of view," but domestically as well: "we are constrained to undergo enormous difficulties within the country...an agonizing food crisis, an extremely agonizing famine."[70] *Intra muros,* the VTsIK was even more pessimistic: "We are already effectively dead men; now it is up to the coffin-maker."[71]

On June 15, at a meeting of the Petrograd Soviet of Workers' and Soldiers' Deputies, Zinoviev delivered a report about the situation in Western Siberia, in the Urals, and in the eastern parts of European Russia in connection with the Czechoslovak offensive. "We are defeated," he concluded, "but we are not crawling at anyone's feet. If war must come, then we would have our class enemies choke on blood as well." After speeches from the opposition—Mensheviks and SRs—Mikhail Lashevich, who was also present, spoke in response, taking out a gun and concluding with the following words: "Remember just one thing: whatever happens—maybe it is our lot to die—fourteen bullets are for you, the fifteenth for us."[72] These fourteen bullets were enough—one month later, on Lenin's and Sverdlov's orders—to exterminate the Russian imperial dynasty.

The May-June crisis in the Soviet government was undoubtedly the result of Lenin's Brest-Litovsk policy, which had led to general discontent. Everyone was tired. Even those who had originally had illusions no longer believed in Soviet rule. In the opposition socialist press, particularly critical pronouncements were made by the Mensheviks, who had once been a part of a united Social Democratic organization along with the Bolsheviks, and who in many respects understood Lenin better than his other political opponents did. The "right" did not lag behind either. At a conference during that time, a speaker—apparently a member of the Kadets—stated in a report on foreign policy that he was obliged to speak "about the international position of a country about which it is not known whether it is in a state of war or peace," and which was ruled by a government that was recognized "only by its enemies." "As the story of the Brest-Litovsk treaty has shown," the speaker observed, "the key point is not the signing of the agreement, but the guarantee that it will be executed." And obviously, "no new paper agreements with Germany, no improvements on the Treaty of Brest-Litovsk," will restrain Germany "from its future encroachments." After all, Ukraine, Belorussia, the Caucasus, the Crimea, and the Black Sea fleet had been occupied and taken by the Germans outside the signed agreement.[73]

The Left SRs, who as a Soviet and ruling party could oppose the Brest-Litovsk policy in an official capacity, also directed severe and perceptive criticism against the Bolsheviks. In 1918, a whole series of pamphlets attacking the Brest-Litovsk treaty was penned by prominent opponents of the delay. The Left SRs argued that Lenin's respite was a betrayal of the revolutionary cause that had given nothing to the Soviet government: "not bread, not peace, not the possibility to continue socialist construction";[74] that the Brest-Litovsk treaty had brought with it a "snuffing out," an "exhaustion, a revulsion of the spirit," since it was "not in a final decisive engagement and not from the blow of a knife raised overhead that the Russian revolution surrendered," but "without making an attempt to fight,"[75] that the signing of the peace treaty had caused a "sharp break" in the entire foreign policy of the RSFSR, since the path of accepting German ultimatums, the path of compromises, "represents a turning away from that straight path that the Revolution had followed so triumphantly," leading not only to territorial and economic losses, but to ruination, since "even after losing its innocence, worker-peasant Russia [had acquired] no capital" from the delay, while the German army was penetrating "more and more deeply" into Russian territory, and the "power of the bourgeoisie" was now restored "in more than one third of the federation."[76]

The Left SRs believed that the Bolsheviks' Brest-Litovsk policy would doom not only the Russian Revolution, but the world revolution as well. The RSFSR, Steinberg wrote, "wants to extend and expand its united states gradually, first over Europe, then over America, and then over the entire world." The Treaty of Brest-Litovsk had "cut [us] off from this task of self-expansion," depriving Russia "of the assistance and revolutionary collaboration" of other countries, while leaving the Western world without any "help and collaboration" from Soviet Russia.[77] "All of the natural wealth of Ukraine, the Don, the Caucasus" had ended up at the disposal of the German government; and in this way the Sovnarkom had done militant Germany a great disservice: "the inflow of fresh natural products from the East" had weakened "the revolutionary will" of the German populace; "one of the most frightening threats"—"the threat of hunger, emaciation, impoverishment"— has been significantly weakened by Germany's and Austria-Hungary's food supply agreements.[78] "These are the consequences of the Treaty of Brest-Litovsk," which "cannot be described otherwise than as a counter-revolutionary treaty," Steinberg summed up; "it is becoming clear that it should have never been signed." After a lapse of "a mere three months since the day of its signing, all of the arguments that were made in its favor seem strange and lifeless." People had talked about a "respite," a "rest." But the "rest" had turned out to be an "empty hope": "Soviet Russia's imperialist enemies are pressing down upon it from all sides" and giving "[us] neither a rest nor any extra time."[79]

The Left SRs saw a popular uprising against the occupiers as the only way out of the existing situation. What they had in mind, naturally, was an uprising in the territories occupied by the Germans and Austrians, above all Ukraine. Speaking out against the "demoralizing preaching of weakness, fatigue, helplessness, the preaching of the inevitability of a pact with the foreign bourgeoisie,"[80] the Left SRs proposed to "uphold the revolutionary idea of uprising and armed resistance in the face of the foreign bourgeoisie's intimidations" until revolutions should break out in Germany, Austria, and other countries.[81] As for the chances of success that such an uprising would have, in the opinion of the Left SRs "no regular army, which always fights under the lash," would compare "with the insurgent people itself, when from behind every bush, from every ravine...the vengeful hand of the insurgents" would threaten the "punitive expedition coming from abroad." Only after this would "the German nation, worn out by long war and a half-starved existence, terrorized by the guerilla struggle of the entire insurgent Russian nation," finally understand that it was "attacking a nation that had opened its borders, withdrawn from the war"; and then "the muzzles of rifles and cannons would finally turn against the instigators and leaders of the punitive expedition" and point to the governments of Germany and Austria-Hungary.[82]

Although the proposal to lie in wait for the enemy "behind every bush" might have appeared naive from a military point of view, the Bolsheviks— during this summer of 1918, when guerilla actions and sabotage had become a reality in Ukraine—declined publicly to reject the idea of an uprising.

All of this criticism probably would not have been enough to be considered critical were it not for the fact that the Bolsheviks themselves were unhappy with Lenin's Treaty of Brest-Litovsk. And given the pervasive resistance to the Brest-Litovsk agreement, the realization of Lenin's policies became a practical impossibility, Germany—the country for whose sake Lenin had made so many concessions—was now also unhappy with the Treaty of Brest-Litovsk as well.

Ludendorff, who had never relished the idea of collaborating with the Bolsheviks, was sincerely irritated by what was happening. "The Soviet government," Ludendorff wrote to Kühlmann, "as anyone can see, has taken the same position toward us as at the beginning of the peace talks in Brest-Litovsk. It is delaying all decisions that are important to us in all kinds of ways and, as far as possible, acting against us. We have nothing to expect from this government, even though it exists only because we allow it. For us, it is a constant danger, which will abate only when it unconditionally recognizes us as the dominant power and submits to us out of fear of Germany and out of fear for its own existence."

In signing the treaty, Germany had hoped to have at its rear "a peacefully-minded Russia, from which the famished Central Powers might obtain food and resources." The reality has turned out to be the exact opposite. "Rumors that come from Russia every day are more and more dismal." The Germans were getting neither peace nor food. "There has been no real peace on the Eastern Front." Germany, "although relying on weak forces," was keeping the front active.[83] The German government was no less preoccupied than Lenin's government, unable to see how to get the Sovnarkom—which was pretty much helpless—to fulfill various ultimatum-backed demands.

On May 13, Kühlmann, Ludendorff, and Kühlmann's deputy Bussche, taking into account the fact that "the Bolsheviks are under a serious threat from the left, that is, from a party that holds even more radical views than the Bolsheviks" (the Left SRs and the Left Communists), found that it was in Germany's interest to "declare once and for all that our operations in Russia are over," "the line of demarcation has been drawn," and "thus the offensive has been concluded." It is not clear, however, that this assurance was really made to the Soviet government. It is even less clear how anyone could have believed it, since the German offensive continued after May 13. Even at the beginning of June, Radek voiced the belief that the balance of forces created by the Brest-Litovsk agreement "threatens us with further profound upheavals and great economic losses," that the "territorial losses that are the consequence of the Treaty of Brest-Litovsk are not yet over," that a "period of intensive fighting" over Soviet territories still lay ahead.[84] (And indeed, the evacuation of Kursk began a few days later.)

Given this predicament, it is clear that Lenin could find comfort only in the thought of retreating further into the depths of Russia. When Trotsky asked him what he proposed to do "if the Germans nonetheless continue their offensive" and "aim for Moscow," Lenin replied:

> We will retreat further, to the east, to the Urals.... The Kuznetsk Basin is rich in coal. We will create a Ural-Kuznets republic, supported by the industry of the Urals and the coal of Kuznets, the Ural proletariat and the Moscow and Petersburg workers that we manage to take with us.... If necessary, we will go even further to the east, past the Urals. We will go all the way to Kamchatka, but we will not surrender. The international situation will change dozens of times, and from the borders of the Ural-Kuznets republic, we will expand once again and come back to Moscow and Petersburg.

Trotsky explained that the "conception of a Ural-Kuznets republic" was "organically necessary" for Lenin, so that "he might steel himself and others in the conviction that nothing has been lost yet and that a strategy of desperation was absolutely out of the question."[85] Indeed, for Lenin it was more important to be at the head of the Kamchatkan republic than to yield his power, even for the sake of a revolution in Europe. But did anyone else besides Lenin believe in a Soviet Kamchatkan republic? Apparently not. In any case, the idea of retreating to Kamchatka while the Far East was under the threat of a Japanese occupation inspired no one. And on May 10, at a Central Committee meeting, Sokolnikov put forward a resolution to abolish the Treaty of Brest-Litovsk:

> The Central Committee believes that the coup d'état in Ukraine represents the emergence of a new political situation, characterized by an alliance between the Russian bourgeoisie and German imperialism. Under these conditions, war with Germany is inevitable and the respite provided by the Treaty of Brest-Litovsk is over. The party's task is to begin immediate open and large-scale preparations for military action and to organize resistance through broad mobilization. At the same time, it is necessary to conclude a military pact with the British-French coalition with a view to military cooperation on well-defined terms.[86]

Until April 1989, this resolution was considered "lost."[87] But the "Theses on the Present Political Situation," which Lenin outlined at a meeting on May 10, were never lost were:

> The foreign policy of the Soviet government must not be changed in any way. We are still facing the very real threat—which at the present time is

stronger and closer than it was yesterday—of Japanese troop movements meant to divert German troops deeper into European Russia, and on the other hand, of German troop movements aimed against Petrograd and Moscow in the event of a victory by Germany's war party. We must respond to these dangers as before with a strategy of retreating, biding time, and maneuvering, while keeping up the most intensive military preparations.[88]

Sokolnikov's resolution was defeated. He alone voted for it. Stalin abstained, while Lenin, Sverdlov, Shmidt, and Vladimirsky voted against it. Yet Lenin's theses were not put to a vote on that day either. Sokolnikov lost. But neither did Lenin come out a winner. A second discussion of Lenin's theses took place at the next Central Committee meeting, on May 13. Sokolnikov's resolution was also discussed a second time, and its text has not survived among the materials from this meeting either.[89] The Central Committee, with the same members present, came to the conclusion that Lenin had greatly overestimated the military threat posed by Germany. Nonetheless, his theses were passed, with certain amendments. Sokolnikov's resolution—his proposal to abolish the Treaty of Brest-Litovsk and to seek the support of the Allied Powers in the fight with Germany—failed to win a single vote, apart from its author's. Stalin voted against Lenin (but did not back Sokolnikov). Trotsky and Zinoviev, in Petrograd at the time and not present at the meeting, had voiced their support for Lenin's theses.

In May and June 1918, an increasingly important role was assumed by Sverdlov. In March-April, he had been mainly coordinating collaboration between different political coalitions. In May-June, he took up all party work and the functions of the "general secretary" and was appointed as Lenin's co-presenter by the Central Committee, i.e., he began to play the role of party commissar to Lenin. It was Sverdlov—in place of Lenin—who read the "Theses of the Central Committee on the Present Political Situation" at a Moscow municipal party conference on May 13. In the transcript of a Central Committee meeting on May 18, his name is at the top of a list of those present. The Central Committee meeting of May 19 was a complete triumph for Sverdlov: he was assigned absolutely every party task. The transcript of this meeting was first published in April 1989:

"The committee heard a report from Dzerzhinsky, who stressed the need to provide the Extraordinary Commission [Cheka] with responsible comrades capable of replacing him." It was resolved that Latsis would be transferred from the NKVD to the Cheka. "Comrades Yakovleva and Stukov will also be transferred to the Cheka and become the heads of the counter-revolutionary department. Responsibility for notifying them has been assigned to

Sverdlov." Trotsky made a statement "about a conflict that he was having with the representatives of the Zamoskvoretsky District Soviet." Sverdlov "reports that he has already instructed the Moscow committee to tighten discipline in the districts." He "reports that the presidium of the TsIK [Central Executive Committee] was discussing the future fate of Nicholas, that the same question is being discussed by the Ural Regional Soviet and by the [Left] SRs. It is necessary to decide what to do with Nicholas. A decision has been made not to do anything with Nicholas for the time being, only taking the necessary precautionary measures. Responsibility for notifying the Ural Regional Soviet has been assigned to Sverdlov."

The question of military experts was also discussed, with some speakers noting that there was "widespread discontent among the lowest circles, in the rank and file of the party, about the fact that excessively broad rights have been granted to former counterrevolutionary officers and generals," while the original intention had been to put them "in the position of consultants." A decision was made to schedule a special meeting of the Central Committee for May 26 in order to discuss this question, and to invite certain prominent Bolsheviks who had served both in the pre-Revolutionary and the Soviet army. "Responsibility for organizing the meeting and selecting comrades from the military has been assigned to Comrades Trotsky and Sverdlov." It was decided to propose to the Moscow party committee to call a municipal conference "in order to discuss the position of the party organizations and the aims of the party. Comrades Trotsky and Sverdlov have been delegated to the conference from the Central Committee." The participants also voted to establish a Supreme Revolutionary Tribunal. Sverdlov was instructed "to order Stuchka and Krylenko to draft an urgent resolution for the Sovnarkom in accordance with this decision." It was agreed "to institute death sentences for certain crimes." Sverdlov was instructed to order Stuchka "to draft a resolution in accordance with this decision first for the Central Committee, and then for the Sovnarkom and the TsIK."[90]

Lenin was given only one assignment at this meeting, and it could hardly be characterized as crucial: "to get the Sovnarkom to grant permission to Steklov to be present there."[91]

It is impossible to trace the further growth of Sverdlov's influence (and the decline of Lenin's authority) in Central Committee transcripts because the transcripts from May 19 to September 16, 1918, have not been located. Evidently, numerous Central Committee transcripts from that time "did not survive" precisely because in them Lenin's position appeared in a highly unfavorable light. Only fragmentary evidence of this exists. Thus, on June 26 the Central Committee discussed the issue of preparing a draft of the constitution of the RSFSR to be ratified at the Fifth Congress of Soviets. The Central Committee found the work on the preparation of the draft unsatisfactory, and Lenin, supported by several other members of the Central Committee, proposed to "remove this issue from the agenda of the Congress of Soviets." But Sverdlov "insisted that the question remain in place,"[92] going against Lenin and other Central Committee members and winning; later he played an active role in writing the constitution.

Beginning in May—in keeping with the policy of the Secreteriat of the Central Committee (i.e., Sverdlov), and against Lenin's will—Ukraine became the theater of intense, subversive, anti-German activity. On May 3—in order to weaken Germany's military might and to set the stage for a Communist takeover—the Central Committee of the Bolshevik Party passed two resolutions concerning the creation of a Ukrainian Communist party.[93] The texts of these resolutions do not appear in the transcript of the Central Committee's meeting, but on May 9 *Pravda* published the following report:

> The Central Committee of the Russian Communist Party, having discussed the question of separating a special Ukrainian Communist party from the Russian Communist Party, found no objections to the creation of a Ukrainian Communist party, because Ukraine is an independent state.

This was one of the resolutions passed by the Central Committee on May 3, and it was published. The second resolution was not subject to publication and is considered "lost," since "it concerned the fact that the Ukrainian Communist party [was] a component part of the Russian Communist Party (Bolsheviks),"[94] in other words, its meaning was precisely the opposite of the resolution that was published in *Pravda*. The point of this maneuver is clear: by loudly proclaiming the independence of the Ukrainian Communist party, the Central Committee absolved itself of any formal responsibility for the subversive activity which the Bolsheviks were preparing in German-occupied Ukraine. Anti-German actions could now be carried out effectively in the open, without the risk of complicating poor Soviet-German or Soviet-Ukrainian relations. Germany's objections were dismissed by Chicherin on the grounds that the Bolsheviks in Russia had no connection to the Bolsheviks in Ukraine. At the same time, the second resolution reminded the Ukrainian Bolsheviks that they did not constitute an independent party, but were subordinate to the unified Central Committee of the Russian Communist Party.

In the summer of 1918, the inevitability of Germany's defeat in the world war—following the failure of the last major German offensive on the

Western Front and the arrival of American forces in France—became apparent. German leaders therefore recognized that an offensive deeper into Russia was now ill-advised not only from a political, but also from a military point of view. On June 9, in a memorandum to the State Secretary of Foreign Affairs, the usually self-assured Ludendorff indicated that, due to troop shortages on the Western Front, the army's command was forced further to weaken the divisions on the Eastern Front. "They are sufficiently strong to solve problems of an occupational nature," Ludendorff continued, "but if the situation in the East deteriorates, they will be unable to manage it." If the Bolsheviks were to fall, Germany's prospects would be even worse. Ukraine would reunite with a non-Bolshevik Russia, and, as Riezler believed, Germany could end up "in an extremely difficult situation" and would either have to "oppose a powerful movement with only a few divisions" or to "accept this movement," and yield to the demands of the new government and revise the Brest-Litovsk agreement.

After the failure of the Germans' March offensive on the Somme and around Amiens, in Hoffmann's words, "there were no more good troop replacements, and supreme command gathered men from everywhere for troop replacements, paying attention only to their numbers and not taking into account any other considerations." This is how "all young soldiers were pulled from the Eastern divisions and redirected to the Western Front." The artillery was particularly affected by this policy: "all men with any amount of ability have been taken out of the squadrons on the Eastern Front." The divisions that remained on the Eastern Front were in Hoffmann's opinion unfit for any serious fighting.[95]

If even Ludendorff and Hoffmann admitted the German army's inability to conduct an effective offensive in the East, if it was clear that Germany would have to negotiate with a new government—whatever it might be— from a position of weakness, it was expedient to seek a political decision. Kühlmann therefore instructed Mirbach to continue providing the Bolsheviks with financial assistance in order to keep them in power. "From here, it is very difficult to say who should be given support if the Bolsheviks should fall," Kühlmann wrote. "If there is truly powerful pressure, the Left SRs will fall along with the Bolsheviks," and these "are the only parties that base their positions on the Treaty of Brest-Litovsk." The Kadets and the monarchists are against the treaty. The latter stand for a unified Russia, and "it is not in our interest to support the monarchic idea, which will reunify" the country. On the contrary, it is necessary, as far as possible, to preclude "Russia's consolidation and with this aim to support the extreme left-wing parties" (the Bolsheviks and the Left SRs).

It appears that Mirbach did not consider the task set by the foreign ministry feasible. As he observed the collapse from the windows of the embassy, Mirbach was convinced that the Bolsheviks were living out their final days. In the event that the Sovnarkom should fall, he proposed to take precautionary measures in advance and to form a government with pro-German leanings. The foreign ministry agreed to his proposal. "Practically speaking," Riezler wrote on June 4, "this means that we must stretch a thread to Orenburg and Siberia over the head of General Krasnov, keep the cavalry [ready for battle] and oriented toward Moscow, and prepare a future government" with which Germany could sign a treaty; revise those terms of the Brest-Litovsk agreement which are directed against Germany's economic hegemony over Russia; attach Ukraine to Russia, and perhaps Estonia and Latvia as well. "To facilitate the rebirth of a Russia that would once again become imperialistic," Riezler concluded, "is not a pleasant prospect, but such a development might turn out to be inevitable."[96] Riezler believed that the change in Germany's eastern policy must take place within six to eight weeks.

During this period, Ambassador Mirbach sent a similar report to Hertling. In view of the "ever-increasing instability the Bolshevik position," he recommended preparing for a "military regrouping, which may become a necessity," and suggested relying on the Kadets, a group with a "predominantly right-wing orientation," often called "monarchists." These people, in his opinion, could form the "kernel of a future new order," and therefore it would be useful to establish contact with them and to provide them with necessary financial resources.

On June 5, Trautmann—a foreign ministry advisor—spoke out in favor of a change in Germany's Eastern policies, but envisioning a more passive role for Germany itself. He believed that the Bolsheviks should be supported "by every available means," in spite of the obstacles that the German demands had created. Nonetheless, Trautmann recommended taking into account the possibility that the Bolsheviks might fall, not breaking off relations with other political parties, and "providing for a maximally secure transition for ourselves."[97]

More or less the same course of action was recommended by Ludendorff: despite the existence of diplomatic relations with the Soviet government, it was advisable to maintain simultaneous "relations with other movements in Russia, in order not to find ourselves suddenly in complete isolation"; "to establish contact with right-wing, monarchist groups and to influence them in such a way as to render the monarchist movement, as soon as it acquires any influence," beholden to Germany's interests.

The interests of Germany's political leadership, foreign ministry, and military command finally converged. A reorientation took place in its eastern policy. On June 13, Mirbach notified Berlin that he had been approached, directly and through intermediaries, by various political leaders seeking to learn if the German government would be willing to offer assistance to anti-Soviet forces aiming to overthrow the Bolsheviks, on the condition, however, that the terms of the Brest-Litovsk agreement would also be revised. The most serious of these groups Mirbach considered to be the coalition of right-wing organizations headed by former minister of agriculture Krivoshein. Through the members of the Octobrist Party, Krivoshein had queried Mirbach whether the German ambassador was prepared to establish ties with members of Krivoshein's organization, and receiving an affirmative response, instructed two members of the central committee of the Kadet Party to take further action; these were Baron Nolde, former assistant to the foreign affairs minister in Lvov's cabinet, and Leontiev, former assistant to the minister of internal affairs in the same cabinet.

On June 25, Mirbach wrote to Kühlmann that "after two months of careful observation" he could no longer "give Bolshevism a favorable diagnosis. We are, without question, standing by the bedside of a dangerously ill person, whose condition might now and again improve, but who is doomed." Based on this fact, he proposed filling the "newly formed vacuum" with new "government organs, which we will keep ready and which will be wholly and entirely at our service." Since it was obvious that no new government would agree to honor the Treaty of Brest-Litovsk, he proposed substantially easing its terms, above all by uniting Ukraine and Estonia with Russia. On June 28, in his last dispatch from Moscow, the ambassador wrote that he was observing the coup that was being prepared by Krivoshein's group and that was supposed to take place literally in a few weeks.

The change in Germany's position did not go unnoticed in Russia. By the middle of May, "right-wing" circles noted that the "Germans, whom the Bolsheviks had brought to Moscow—the treaty between the two being the only basis for the Bolsheviks' existence—are themselves ready to overthrow the Bolsheviks."[98] The diplomatic representatives of the Allied Powers were informed about the anti-Soviet activities of the German embassy. Given such extensive leaks, it is hardly surprising that the shift in the embassy's mood was also no secret to the Soviet government. At the beginning of June— around the time when Mirbach and Riezler were sending their letters to Berlin arguing that Germany's eastern policy had to change—a new department was created in the Cheka, either on orders from above or by the Cheka itself, for the purpose of monitoring "possible criminal activity by the embassy." The Cheka, it will be recalled, was run by the Left Communist Dzerzhinsky. The top post in this new department was given to the future murderer of the German ambassador, the Left SR Yakov Blumkin, a young man of nineteen or twenty.

It must be said that, for quite some time, the German embassy's employees had been living with a premonition of unpleasant and unforeseeable events. On June 4, in an astonishingly clear-sighted dispatch to Berlin, Riezler described the future in the bleakest tones imaginable:

> Over the past two weeks, the situation has become critical. Famine is encroaching upon us; they are trying to stifle it with terror. The Bolshevik fist comes down on everyone indiscriminately. People are tranquilly executed by the hundreds. All of this in itself is still not so bad, but now there can no longer be any doubt that the Bolsheviks' material resources are running out. Fuel reserves are waning, and even Latvian soldiers, sitting in their trucks, can no longer be counted on—let alone workers and peasants. The Bolsheviks are terribly nervous, probably feeling their end approaching, and therefore the rats are beginning to flee from the sinking ship.... Karakhan has stored the original copy of the Treaty of Brest-Litovsk in his desk. He intends to take it with him to America and to sell it there, getting vast sums for the emperor's signature....
>
> No one is able to predict how they [the Bolsheviks] will meet their end, and their death throes may last for another few weeks. It may be that they will attempt to flee to Nizhny Novgorod or Yekaterinburg. It may be that they are intending, out of desperation, to get drunk on their own blood, or perhaps they will invite us to get lost in order to tear up the Brest-Litovsk agreement (which they call a "respite")—their compromise with imperialism—thus saving their revolutionary consciousness at the hour of their death. These people's actions are absolutely unpredictable, particularly in a state of desperation. In addition, they have once again started to believe that the increasingly open "military dictatorship" in Germany is giving rise to enormous resistance, especially as a result of further advances to the east, and that this must lead to a revolution. This was recently written by Sokolnikov, obviously based on Joffe's reports.... I apologize for this lyrical digression about the state of chaos, which even by Russian standards is now completely unbearable.[99]

Trautmann offered a similar impression, writing a day later that "in the coming months a political struggle might flare up. It might even lead to the Bolsheviks' downfall." Trautmann added that, according to his intelligence, "one or even two" Bolshevik leaders had "already reached a certain level of desperation with regard to their own fate."

During these weeks, the usually-dynamic Lenin was idle, as if he were paralyzed. Yet he did talk more and more often about Germany's weakness.

On July 1, in an interview with a Swedish newspaper, he effectively acknowledged that the failure of the Brest-Litovsk policy in Ukraine was due to an underestimation of the power of the guerilla movement: "The Germans need peace. It is telling that in Ukraine, the Germans want peace more than the Ukrainians themselves." Meanwhile, "the Germans' position in Ukraine is very difficult. They get no bread at all from the peasants. The peasants are arming and large groups of them are attacking German soldiers," and "this movement is growing."

Any Left Communist would have concluded that, precisely for this reason, the Treaty of Brest-Litovsk should be repealed. But Lenin thought otherwise. "We in Russia must now wait for the development of the revolutionary movement in Europe," he said. "Sooner or later, things everywhere must come to a political and social collapse." He emphasized that the Bolsheviks had time on their side also because "due to the German occupation, Bolshevism in Ukraine has become a kind of national movement," and that "if the Germans occupied all of Russia, the result would be the same."[100] Again and again, Lenin proposed retreating in the face of German demands and remaining inactive even if the Germans should occupy "all of Russia." He took up this subject again at the Fifth Congress of Soviets in early July:

> The frenzied forces of imperialism are continuing to fight, while in the three months that have elapsed since the last congress they have moved several steps closer to the abyss.... This abyss over three and a half months...has unquestionably moved closer.... The Western powers have taken an enormous step toward this abyss into which imperialism is falling faster and faster with every week of the war.... Over three-and-a-half months...of war, the imperialist states have moved closer to this abyss.... This wounded beast [Germany] has torn many lumps of flesh from our living organism. Our enemies are nearing this abyss so fast that even if they had more than three-and-a-half months at their disposal, and even if the imperialist carnage were to bring us new losses as heavy as before, it is they who would perish, not we, for the speed with which their resistance is waning is rapidly bringing them nearer to the abyss.

But in this schizophrenic speech with multiple repetitions of almost identical phrases, Lenin found a way to urge the Soviet leadership to do the same thing that he had urged them to do in March—to wait things out, to remain inactive, and not to tear up the Brest-Litovsk agreement: "Our position cannot be anything else but to wait...until these frenzied groups of imperialists, which are now still strong, shall tumble into this abyss which they are approaching—this everyone can see."[101]

Only it was hard not to ask: if Germany was on the brink of demise three and a half months after signing the Treaty of Brest-Litovsk, while conducting large-scale military action on only one front, receiving food supplies from Russia and Ukraine, and using the Red Army to fight the Czechoslovak forces, which, if the Bolsheviks had not prevented them, would have long ago been fighting in Europe against the Germans, how deep in this abyss would the Kaiser's Germany have already been if it had been forced to fight on two fronts? What would have been the condition of the Central Powers now? And where would the borders of the Communist state have been?

Driven into a dead end by Lenin, brought to a state of crisis, split up and losing power, the Bolshevik Party could now do nothing but grasp at the straw that in March 1918 had been offered to it by Trotsky: "No matter how much we equivocate, no matter what kind of strategy we invent, we can be saved in the full sense of this word only by a European revolution."[102] And in order to encourage it, it was necessary, first of all, to repeal the Treaty of Brest-Litovsk, and second of all, to form a Red Army. On April 22, the question of creating a regular army had been raised by Trotsky at a session of the VTsIK, and he had emphasized that such a new trained and disciplined army was necessary above all to fight the foreign enemy[103]—"specifically to renew the world war together with France and England against Germany." At the same time, Trotsky and Mikhail Bonch-Bruevich began discussing plans for joint military operations with the representatives of the Allied Powers. This new army began to be called the "People's Army." By the summer of 1918 it formed the kernel of the Moscow garrison, was built up on a contractual basis, was considered apolitical, came under the jurisdiction of the Supreme Military Council headed by Trotsky, and was under the military leadership of Mikhail Bonch-Bruevich, a former officer in the headquarters of the tsar's army. The forces were under the direct command of Muralov, who was in charge of the troops in the district. In June, the People's Army admitted the Latvian Rifle Division to its ranks on Trotsky's orders.[104]

It seemed that only a breakdown of the Brest-Litovsk agreement could cut through the knot of Soviet-German relations and reunite the divided Bolshevik Party. Perhaps to start the war in the summer of 1918 was no less risky than to have continued it in March. But in June, the Bolsheviks had no options left. Lenin's "respite" policy had been tried and yielded no positive results for the revolutionaries. By June, it was irrelevant whether he had been correct in March. During the three months of the delay, the Revolution had lost its uncompromising dynamic force. The agony and despair of the Bolshevik regime had reached its peak. The critical moment came on July 6, 1918, when Chekists bearing a mandate from Dzerzhinsky and Ksenofontov arrived at the residence of the German embassy and demanded a meeting with German ambassador Mirbach on extremely urgent business. Right then and there, the Bolshevik government was saved, and along with it—even more ironically—Lenin's Brest-Litovsk "delay."

3.

The Assassination of Count Mirbach and the Destruction of the Left SR Party

The conspiracy of July 1918 was possibly one of the most multifaceted plots of the time. Without a doubt, on July 6–7, 1918, the objectives of several conspiracies were accomplished at the same time.

First, the conspiracy of Dzerzhinsky against Lenin: the murder of German ambassador Count Mirbach by two agents of Dzerzhinsky's Cheka, Blumkin and Andreyev, seeking to provoke the Germans to repeal Lenin's Brest-Litovsk treaty.

The second conspiracy consisted in preparations by the Bolshevik leadership—above all, Sverdlov, Lenin, and possibly Trotsky—to organize the arrest of the Left SR Party representatives, including almost all the members of the party's central committee, at the Congress of Soviets taking place on that day in the Bolshoi Theater. What was at stake was quite literally a new government coup that was to lead to the establishment of a single-party, Bolshevik dictatorship in Soviet Russia (which indeed happened on July 6).

The third conspiracy that unfolded on July 6 was Blumkin's plot with certain members of the Left SR Party's central committee—who were unaware that Dzerzhinsky was behind Blumkin and who were acting in secret from the rest of the Left SR Party's central committee and from the Central Committee of the Bolshevik Party—to assassinate the German ambassador, Count Mirbach, in Moscow and the German consul in Petrograd. In order to carry out the assassination in Petrograd, long before July 6, Blumkin had sent two Cheka agents there—the Left SRs "Mikhail" (M. A. Bogdanov) and "Baron" (Ye. N. Malm). As Bogdanov and Malm later testified, on July 6 they arrived at the Petrograd and asked Bokiy, the head of the Petrograd Cheka, to use the Cheka telephone in order to receive instructions from Blumkin in Moscow. However, "instead of giving us permission, Bokiy, looking pale, informed us that news of the assassination of Count Mirbach had just been received from Moscow by telephone, and that the wire was no longer working. Hearing this long-awaited news, we immediately rushed to the German consulate [in order to kill the consul], but we found out that the consul had left for a conference with other consuls, and that from there he would proceed to Moscow. After discussing the situation, we decided to go to Moscow on the following day."

Clearly, Blumkin had begun preparations for the murder of the ambassador in Moscow and the consul in Petrograd not in early July, but much earlier.

It is possible that there was yet a fourth conspiracy: the conspiracy of Left SR Party's central committee to oppose possible attempts by the Bolsheviks to arrest the Left SR representatives at the Bolshoi Theater. Apparently, it was for this reason that Left SR troops from the provinces had started moving toward Moscow (although not in time to arrive in the city itself).

The principal conspiracies of the day were, of course, the murder of Count Mirbach by Dzerzhinsky's men, and the arrest of the Left SR delegation at the Congress of Soviets in the Bolshoi Theater by Sverdlov, Lenin, and Trotsky. So then...

On the morning of July 6, 1918, Cheka agent Yakov Blumkin, according to his later testimony, went to the Cheka, obtained a blank piece of official stationery from the secretary, and typed that he and Revolutionary Tribunal representative Nikolai Andreyev were authorized "to enter into direct negotiations" with German ambassador Count Mirbach "on matters directly related" to the ambassador. Dzerzhinsky's signature on the paper, according to Blumkin, was forged—by a "member of the central committee" of the Left SR Party. Ksenofontov's signature was also a forgery—Blumkin had signed in his place. After waiting for the arrival of Dzerzhinsky's deputy and member of the Left SR Party's central committee Vyacheslav Alexandrovich, "who knew nothing," Blumkin "asked him to put the Cheka's seal on the warrant." Blumkin also obtained Alexandrovich's permission to use an automobile and then proceeded to the First House of Soviets, where in the "apartment of a central committee member" Andreyev was waiting for him. After obtaining two trotyl bombs, revolvers, and final instructions, the conspirators left the Hotel National around 2 p.m., ordering the driver to stop near the building of the German embassy, to wait for them with the motor running, and not to be surprised by noise and gunfire. The car had a second driver, a sailor from a Cheka unit under the command of Popov. The sailor "had been brought by a member of the central committee" of the Left SR Party, and he apparently knew that Mirbach's assassination was being planned. Like the terrorists, the sailor was armed with a bomb.

At around 2:15 p.m. Blumkin and Andreyev rang the doorbell at the German embassy. They were shown in. After they presented the mandate from Dzerzhinsky and waited for a short while, two embassy employees came out to talk to them—Riezler and Lieutenant Müller (acting as interpreter). All four of them proceeded to the reception hall and sat down around a large marble table. Blumkin informed Riezler that he had to speak with Mirbach on a matter of personal interest to the ambassador, and, citing Dzerzhinsky's strict orders, he continued to insist on a private conversation with the Count, despite Riezler's objections that the ambassador was not receiving any visitors.

Finally, Riezler returned with the Count, who had agreed to speak with the Chekists in person. Blumkin informed Mirbach that he had come to discuss the case of "Robert Mirbach, a member of the distant Hungarian branch of his family, not known to the Count personally," who was involved in a "case of espionage." For confirmation, Blumkin presented documents of some kind. Mirbach replied that he "had nothing in common with this officer" and that "this matter was completely foreign to him." Blumkin responded that in ten days the matter would be taken up by the Revolutionary Tribunal. Andreyev, who had not taken part in the conversation up to this time, asked whether the German diplomats would like to know what kinds of measures would be taken by the tribunal in the Robert Mirbach case. The same question was repeated by Blumkin. Evidently, this was a cue. Mirbach, suspecting nothing, replied in the affirmative. With the words "I will now show you," Blumkin, who was standing behind the large marble table, pulled out a revolver and fired it across the table first at Mirbach, and then at Müller and Riezler (but missed). They were so stunned that they remained seated in their deep armchairs (they were unarmed). Then Mirbach jumped up and ran out to the room that adjoined the reception hall, but at this moment he was struck down by a bullet fired by Andreyev. Blumkin meanwhile continued shooting at Riezler and Müller, but kept missing. Then there was an explosion, after which the terrorists jumped out the window and rode off in the car that was waiting for them. When Riezler and Müller came to and rushed to help Mirbach, the latter was already lying dead in a pool of blood. Next to him they saw an unexploded bomb, and at a distance of two or three paces from the ambassador a large hole in the floor—left by another bomb that had gone off.

The sailor from Popov's unit was driving the car that drove the terrorists away. Maybe it was because of this that they were taken (unbeknownst to them) to Trekhsvyatitelsky Lane, the headquarters of the Cheka's troops. From that moment on, Blumkin, who had hurt his leg while jumping out the window and had also been wounded in the leg by a sentry who started firing at the fleeing terrorists, did not directly participate in the ensuing events. Andreyev—the killer of the German ambassador—had vanished earlier. And for reasons unclear, his success was attributed to Blumkin.

But the assassination had not been well executed. In the confusion, the terrorists had left behind the briefcase containing "the case of Robert Mirbach" and the mandate made out to Blumkin and Andreyev and signed by Dzerzhinsky and Ksenofontov. Moreover, two highly dangerous witnesses of the crime—Riezler and Müller, whom Blumkin had repeatedly tried to shoot—were still alive. One can only guess how the events of July 6 would have developed if the terrorists had not made these accidental blunders.

When did preparations for the assassination of Mirbach actually begin and who was in charge of them? Who was behind the murder of the German ambassador? These questions remain difficult to answer. The fact is that that no documents exist which could prove the involvement of the Left SR Party's central committee in organizing the killing. The most complete collection of materials pertaining to the events of July 6–7 was published in 1920 under the title *The Red Book of the Cheka*.[1] But it, too, contains no documents confirming the charges made against the Left SRs—above all, against the central committee of the Left SR Party—of organizing the assassination of Mirbach and for "insurrection." Historians have therefore resorted to freely paraphrasing the documents in *The Red Book*, rather than quoting them directly. The well-known Soviet historian of the SR party K. V. Gusev writes: "On June 24, 1918, the central committee of the Left SR Party made a decision to assassinate the German ambassador to Moscow, Count Mirbach, and to begin a counter-revolutionary revolt."[2]

Meanwhile, nothing tangible is mentioned in the transcript of the Left SR Party's central committee meeting of June 24.[3] There are no direct indications of its intention to kill Mirbach in the June 24 transcript. Who was behind the plot of the German ambassador's murder? Blumkin claimed that it was the central committee of the Left SR Party. On July 4, before the evening session of the Congress of Soviets, he had been invited "from the Bolshoi Theater 'by one of the members of the central committee' for a political conversation." The "member of the central committee" informed Blumkin that the central committee of the Left SR Party had decided to kill Mirbach "in order to appeal to the solidarity of the German proletariat" and, "by presenting the collapse of the Brest-Litovsk agreement to the government as an accomplished fact, forcing it at long last to become more decisive and uncompromising in the struggle for the international revolution." After this, the "member of the central committee" asked Blumkin—as a Left SR acting in line with party discipline—to tell him what he knew about Mirbach. Blumkin therefore believed that the "decision to assassinate Count Mirbach was made suddenly, on July 4." However, Blumkin himself was not present at the meeting of the central committee where, according to him, the decision to kill the ambassador was made. On the evening of July 4, he was invited by the same "member of the central committee," who again asked him to "relate all the information about Mirbach" that Blumkin had in his possession as the head of the department to fight against German espionage"; indeed, he was told that "this information is necessary to carry out the assassination." It was at this point that Blumkin offered to kill the ambassador. On that very night, the conspirators decided to carry out the assassination on July 5. However, the murder itself was postponed by a day, since "it was impossible to make the necessary preparations in such a short time."[4]

We know that Blumkin was lying at that point in his account, since he himself was simultaneously preparing the murder of the German consul in Petrograd, and that the organizer of that operation was also Blumkin and it was carried out by the Cheka. Otherwise, Bogdanov and Malm would not have been able to ask Bokiy, the head of the Petrograd Cheka, to let them call Blumkin from his office. But who was it that oversaw the actions of Blumkin and Andreyev (another Left SR and agent of Dzerzhinsky's Cheka)? Who was the mysterious "member of the central committee"?

There are reasons to believe that this individual was Proshyan, who in March had "jokingly" proposed in conversation with Radek to arrest Lenin and declare war on Germany. One of the leaders of Left SR Party, Maria Spiridonova, wrote explicitly about Proshyan's responsibility in the German ambassador's assassination: "The initiative with Mirbach, the first moves in this direction, were his."[5]

Proshyan had always been to the left of the revolutionary spectrum. Probably it was because of this that he made a strong impression on people as different as Lenin and Spiridonova. Lenin wrote about him that he was "distinguished at once by his profound commitment to the revolution and to socialism," that one could see in him a "convinced socialist" who decisively took "the side of the Bolshevik Communists against his colleagues, the Left Socialist Revolutionaries." And it was only the issue of the Brest-Litovsk treaty that had led to "a complete divergence" between Proshyan and Lenin.[6]

Indirect evidence of Proshyan's hand in Blumkin's actions may be seen in the fact that his name (and none other) appears in Blumkin's testimony in connection with his, Blumkin's, letters to Proshyan—"demanding that [Proshyan] explain the party's behavior following the Mirbach murder"—and "Proshyan's return letters." What did these letters contain, then, and on what grounds did a rank-and-file member of the Left SR Party demand something of a central committee member? Blumkin's demands are easy to guess. It turns out that the mysterious "member of the central committee" with whom Blumkin had made arrangements about Mirbach's murder had assured the Chekist Blumkin that the Left SR Party's central committee was interested "only in the assassination of the German ambassador." As Blumkin testified:

The general question of the consequences of Count Mirbach's assassination was not raised during my conversation with the aforementioned member of the central committee. For my part, I bluntly posed two questions which I considered highly important and for which I demanded exhaustive answers, namely: (1) would the assassination of Count Mirbach pose a danger, in the central committee's opinion, to Soviet Russia's representative in Germany, Comrade Joffe; and (2) does the central committee guarantee that its objective is limited to the assassination of the German ambassador with the aim of presenting the Soviet government with the breakdown of the Brest-Litovsk agreement as an accomplished fact?

If Proshyan was in fact the central committee member who met with Blumkin, then Blumkin's demand to him to explain the behavior of the Left SR Party following Mirbach's assassination becomes clear. After all, Blumkin had spent July 6 and 7 in a hospital and had information about the events of these days only from Soviet newspapers, where the Bolsheviks were all referring to an uprising, something that in Blumkin's view could not have possibly happened. As Blumkin testified:

In September, when the events of July became clearly understood, when the government was carrying out repressions against the Left SR Party and all of this marked a watershed in the Russian Soviet Revolution—even then I wrote to a member of the central committee that I was frightened by the myth of an uprising and that I had to give myself up to the government in order to destroy this myth.

But the "member of the central committee" forbade him to do so, and Blumkin, submitting to party discipline, obeyed. Only at the beginning of April 1919, after Proshyan's sudden death in December 1918, did he go against wishes of the deceased and went to the Cheka in order to disclose the "secret" of the Left SR conspiracy.[7]

The list of suspects in the conspiracy of Mirbach's murder is not limited to the names of Proshyan and Blumkin. One must look for them not only among the members of the Left SR Party, but also among the Left Communists. The individual whose behavior calls attention to itself is Dzerzhinsky, a Left Communist and the head of the Cheka. It was within the walls of his agency, and with his knowledge and consent, that Cheka agent Blumkin had started keeping a file on "the nephew of the German ambassador," Robert Mirbach, in early June. This was Blumkin's first "assignment." He had come to the Cheka at the beginning of June, when he was appointed to work on "German espionage" as head of the counterintelligence department responsible for "monitoring the embassy's guards and possible criminal activity by the embassy." As Latsis later testified, "Blumkin exhibited a strong urge to expand the department" for fighting with espionage and "more than once submitted projects to the Cheka." However, the only assignment that he really worked on was "the case of the Austrian Mirbach"; indeed, he had "devoted himself entirely to this case" and spent "whole nights interrogating witnesses."[8]

Here was an opportunity for the young Chekist to show what he could do. The case was rather out of the ordinary because, first of all, Robert Mirbach apparently was not a nephew of the German ambassador, but mpt even Austrian. According to some sources,[9] the Russified baron Roman Mirbach, "a member of the economic council at the Smolny Institute," was living peacefully in revolutionary Petrograd. Unfortunately, we know almost nothing about him.[10] The only person who could have known about the Russified baron was Vladimir Bonch-Bruevich, who at that time was in constant contact with the Smolny Institute, including its economic section. Information about the Russian Mirbach may have passed from Bonch-Bruevich through Dzerzhinsky to Blumkin. The Russified baron, who was a member of the economic council at the Smolny Institute vanished, and was replaced by the nephew of the German ambassador—an Austrian officer, prisoner of war, and the ambassador's distant relative, whom the ambassador had never met. According to the Chekists' information, Robert Mirbach had served in the 37th infantry regiment of the Austrian army, was taken prisoner, wound up in a camp, but was released after the ratification of the Treaty of Brest-Litovsk. While waiting to go back to Austria, he had rented a room in a hotel in Moscow where he lived until the beginning of June, when the Swedish actress Landström suddenly committed suicide in the same hotel. Whether or not the suicide was set up by the Chekists is difficult to judge. In any case, the Cheka claimed that Landström had committed suicide in connection with her counter-revolutionary activities and arrested all of the hotel's residents. Among them, supposedly, was the "nephew of the German ambassador," Robert Mirbach.

The Chekists' subsequent actions—Blumkin's above all—were undeniably inventive. The Cheka immediately notified the Danish consulate, which represented Austria-Hungary's interests in Russia, of Robert Mirbach's arrest. On June 15, the Danish consulate entered into negotiations with the Cheka concerning "the case of the arrested officer of the Austrian army, Count Mirbach." During these negotiations, the Chekists suggested to the consulate's representative that Robert Mirbach might be related to the German ambassador. On June 17, a day after the negotiations began, the consulate gave the Chekists a document which they were not expecting:

> The Royal Danish Consulate General hereby informs the All-Russian Extraordinary Commission [Cheka] that the arrested officer of the Austro-Hungarian army, Count Robert Mirbach, according to the written report of the German diplomatic representation in Moscow addressed to the Danish Consulate General, is indeed a member of a family that is related to the German ambassador Count Mirbach, residing in Austria.[11]

Since the first document by the Danish consulate is dated June 15 and the second June 17, one must assume that the written response of the German embassy to the Danish consulate's query was given on June 16, immediately after the consulate's query was received, and that it was humane in intent: it was decided in the German embassy that the unknown Count Robert Mirbach could be considered a relative of the German ambassador in the hope that this would make things easier for the unfortunate Austrian officer and that he would be immediately released, especially since the charges against him seemed frivolous to Riezler. The German ambassador's own involvement in the case of the "nephew" was apparently limited to his permission to refer to Robert Mirbach as a relative.

The German embassy had already forgotten about the matter. The Danish consulate was waiting for Robert Mirbach's release from the Cheka. But two weeks had passed and he was still not released. Consequently, on June 26 Haxthausen, the consul general of Denmark, sent the Cheka an official request to "release from arrest the Austrian prisoner of war Count

Mirbach on the condition of the consulate's guarantee that the said Count
Mirbach will appear before the Extraordinary Commission [Cheka] as soon as
he is requested to do so until the investigation [of the Landström case] is concluded."[12]

Haxthausen's request, however, was denied. And not by accident: "the
case of the ambassador's nephew" became the basis for the case against the
German embassy and the ambassador personally. The main piece of evidence
in Blumkin's possession was a document signed (freely or under duress) by
Robert Mirbach: "I, the undersigned, a German subject, prisoner of war and
officer of the Austrian army Robert Mirbach, pledge voluntarily and of my
own free will" to convey to the Cheka "secret information about Germany
and the German embassy in Russia."[13]

However, neither the Austrian officer nor the Smolny Institute employee
could be considered a "German subject" or provide the Chekists with any
secret information about Germany and the German embassy in Russia.
Therefore, when *The Red Book of the Cheka* was reissued by Politizdat in 1989,
Prof. A. S. Velidov, the editor of the volume, changed "German" to
"Hungarian," naively assuming that the Chekists had made an accidental mistake.[14] The whole matter was clearly a fabrication. The "pledge" itself had
been written in Russian by one person. The signatures in Russian and
German had been added by another, and in the German signature the
"Count" had made a mistake, which can be explained only by the fact that
the "nephew" did not know German. It is quite possible, however, that
Robert Mirbach did not see this document at all, did not read it, or sign it,
and that the signature had been forged by the Chekists themselves. No signed
text of the "pledge" in German existed.

All of this caused the Germans to worry. The ambassador now denied
any relation to Robert Mirbach, and suspected that the fabricated case was a
provocation. The Chekists' interest in the German embassy was now known
even in Berlin. And shortly after the Mirbach assassination, Soviet representatives in Berlin learned "that the German government has no doubt that
Count Mirbach was killed by the Bolsheviks."[15] "The assassination was prepared in advance," the German embassy in Moscow reported to Berlin at the
time. "The case of the Austrian officer Robert Mirbach was only a pretext
used by Cheka agents to gain access to the Kaiser's ambassador."[16]

Blumkin claimed that his work fighting German espionage in the Cheka
"in light of its significance had obviously been carried out under the direct
supervision" of Dzerzhinsky and his deputy Latsis. According to Blumkin, he
had been in "constant consultation" with the presidium of the Cheka and
with Karakhan, the deputy of the people's commissar of foreign affairs,

concerning all of his activities, such as his "inside intelligence work" in the embassy.[17]

After Mirbach's murder, Dzerzhinsky tried to absolve the Cheka of any responsibility in the death of the German ambassador. He claimed that at the very beginning of July Blumkin had been removed from the Robert Mirbach case. As grounds for his dismissal, he cited complaints brought to him about Blumkin's abuse of authority, several days prior to the ambassador's murder, by the well-known Russian poet Osip Mandelstam and Larisa Reisner (the wife of Bolshevik people's commissar Raskolnikov). This meeting had been arranged by Raskolnikov.[18] According to Dzerzhinsky, immediately following his conversation with Mandelstam and Reisner at a meeting of the Cheka , he proposed to "dissolve the department of counterintelligence, and to leave Blumkin without a position for the time being,"[19]. Latsis also testified that Blumkin had been dismissed, emphasizing (albeit after Mirbach's murder) that he "especially disliked" Blumkin and had "decided to dismiss him after colleagues complained about him." A week before July 6, as Latsis testified, he was no longer a member of the department, "since the department had been dissolved by a decision of the Commission, and Blumkin was left without a specific assignment."

Nonetheless, in Latsis' testimony Blumkin is referred to as "head of the secret department," not "former head."

It would appear that, in claiming that Blumkin had been removed from his post several days before the assassination, Dzerzhinsky and Latsis were not telling the truth. Documents regarding Blumkin's dismissal were never published. During the first week of July he was doing the same work as before. At 11 a.m. on July 6, Latsis gave him the Robert Mirbach file from a safe, which of course could have never happened if Blumkin had been dismissed from the job.[20] More likely, Nadezhda Mandelstam, the poet's wife, offers the correct assessment: "Mandelstam's complaint about Blumkin' terrorist impulses" was ignored. "If people had become interested in Blumkin then," she went on, "the famous assassination of the German ambassador might have fallen through, but this did not happen: Blumkin brought his plans to fruition without the slightest obstacle."[21]

There was no interest in Blumkin because it didn't suit Dzerzhinsky. The latter apparently knew about the preparations for the assassination—at the very least because he had already been twice notified about it by the German embassy. Thus, around the middle of June, representatives of the embassy had informed Karakhan, and through him, Dzerzhinsky, "about preparations for the assassination of members of the German embassy." The case was assigned to Peters and Latsis. "I was convinced," Dzerzhinsky later testified, "that someone was deliberately giving false information to the members of the embassy in order to blackmail them or for other, more complicated purposes." On June 28, Karakhan gave Dzerzhinsky "new materials received by him from the German embassy about the developing conspiracies."

Dzerzhinsky, however, was interested not in the conspirators, but in the names of the German embassy's informers; and the head of the Cheka told the German diplomats that without knowing the informers' names, he would not be able to help the embassy uncover the conspiracies. Not surprisingly, after this Riezler became convinced that Dzerzhinsky was "turning a blind eye to conspiracies that are directly concerned with the safety of the members of the German embassy." But because Dzerzhinsky needed to learn the source of the information "about the developing conspiracies" (i.e., about the source of the leak), he had Karakhan arrange a private meeting for him, Riezler, and Müller. During this meeting, Riezler told Dzerzhinsky that "the individuals who are giving him information receive no money from him" and that he therefore trusted his informers. Dzerzhinsky objected that "there might be political motives" and that "there's some kind of intrigue here," aimed at preventing him from finding the "real conspirators, whose existence, on the basis of all of the existing" evidence, he didn't doubt. "I feared assassination attempts against Count Mirbach," Dzerzhinsky testified, but "my hands were tied by the distrust evidenced toward me by those who were giving me materials."

Yielding to Dzerzhinsky's entreaties, Riezler named one of his sources and arranged for a meeting between Dzerzhinsky and the other source. The first informer was "a certain Benderskaya." The second was V. I. Ginch, whom Dzerzhinsky met at the Hotel Metropole in Riezler's and Müller's presence approximately two days before the murder. At the beginning of June (i.e., when the Robert Mirbach affair began), Ginch had said somewhere that there were plans to assassinate Mirbach. Several times after that he came to the Cheka in order to say the same thing, and even went to Popov's Cheka unit, "but they wouldn't listen." Riezler, for his part, after receiving information from Ginch about plans for a terrorist attack, reported it to the People's Commissariat of Foreign Affairs. The information passed to the Cheka, where the warning was once again ignored. Then Ginch again warned the embassy; in fact, about ten days before the assassination he gave a precise date for the terrorist attack—between July 5 and 6—and during his meeting with Dzerzhinsky at the Metropole, he openly told him that certain Cheka agents were mixed up in the case.

Dzerzhinsky declared that all this was nothing but a provocation and, after leaving the Metropole, had Karakhan request the German embassy for permission to arrest Benderskaya and Ginch.[22] The Germans did not reply, but on the morning of July 6, shortly before Mirbach's murder, Riezler went to the People's Commissariat of Foreign Affairs and asked Karakhan to take some kind of action, since rumors about an imminent attempt to assassinate Mirbach were reaching the embassy from all sides. Karakhan said that he would notify the Cheka about everything.

Various pieces of indirect evidence indicate that Dzerzhinsky knew about the planned assassination of Mirbach by Blumkin. Thus, according to Latsis's testimony, when he learned about the assassination at 3:30 p.m. on July 6, he went to the Cheka and found that people there already knew that Dzerzhinsky "suspected Blumkin of murdering Mirbach." Dzerzhinsky was not at the Cheka: he "had gone to the scene of the crime," from where Latsis soon received a query about "the case of Mirbach, the ambassador's nephew," whether it had been closed and "who was now in charge of the file, since it had been discovered at the scene of the crime." Only now did Latsis realize that "Mirbach really had been assassinated by Blumkin."[23] But Dzerzhinsky had somehow guessed this even before going to the embassy.

The person who gained the most from Mirbach's murder, as it turned out, was Lenin. Most likely, he had not known about the preparations for the assassination. There are no indications of his complicity in the act, not even indirect ones. On the contrary, it must have been obvious to him that the murder was a provocation organized by the opponents of the Brest-Litovsk treaty, the Left Communists and the Left SRs. It was equally obvious that the conspiracy against Mirbach had been envisioned as a strike against himself[24] and that one of the main organizers of this strike was the head of the Cheka, the Left Communist Dzerzhinsky.[25]

Yet, remarkably, the Bolsheviks turned out to be better prepared for this unexpected event than the Left SRs, who, as the Bolsheviks claimed, had prepared this act of terror. From the moment the first news of Mirbach's assassination came through, Lenin's interest in the destruction of the Left SR Party was unrelenting: he decided to use the murder in order to put an end to them. Georgy Solomon, a representative of the Soviet government in Berlin, described how Leonid Krasin, returning to Germany from Moscow shortly after the July events, had told him "with profound disgust" that he had not thought Lenin capable of "such profound and cruel cynicism." On July 6, telling Krasin about how he intended to get out of the crisis created by Mirbach's murder, Lenin added "with a little smile, I repeat, with a little smile": "In short, we will take out an internal loan from our comrades, the [Left] SRs...and in this way both preserve our innocence and acquire capital." Solomon goes on to write that "during his trip [to Berlin], Krasin repeatedly

came back to this topic in conversation, as though unable to rid himself of a
terrible, nightmarish thought, and several times repeated" Lenin's words. He
also came back to this matter in conversations with Solomon later on.[26]

By "taking out an internal loan," Lenin meant nothing other than
charging the ingenuous Left SRs with plotting Mirbach's murder.[27] But Solomon's testimony is by no means unique. Here is what Aino Kuusinen (the
wife of Otto Kuusinen, head of the Finnish Communist Party) writes in her
memoirs:

> In reality, the [Left] SRs were not guilty. I came home once and found Otto
> in his study with a tall, bearded young man, who was introduced to me as Com-
> rade Safir. After he left, Otto told me that I had just seen the assassin of Count
> Mirbach, whose real name was Blumkin. He was a Cheka agent and was about to
> go abroad on an important mission for the Comintern. When I pointed out that
> Mirbach had been killed by the [Left] SRs, Otto burst out laughing. Un-
> doubtedly, the assassination was only a pretext for getting the [Left] SRs out of
> the way, since they were Lenin's most serious opponents.[28]

So serious, in fact, that in the summer of 1918 the proportion of Bolsheviks in local Soviets had fallen—compared to what it had been in March—
from 66% to 44.8%;[29] and at the Fifth Congress of Soviets the Left SR Party
ended up with an effective majority. The Bolsheviks' position was unstable
and had to be made more secure. The simplest course of action appeared to
be to arrest the Left SR Party delegation at the Congress of Soviets and to
declare the party illegal (as had been done in June 1918 with the SRs and the
Mensheviks). This was exactly what Lenin did on July 6–7. One can only
marvel at his adroitness and decisiveness: hearing about the assassination of
the German ambassador, he charged the Left SRs with insurrection against
the Soviet government—an insurrection that never existed.

During the first fifteen minutes following the murder, confusion reigned
in the embassy. Colonel Schubert, the head of the commission on the re-
patriation of prisoners of war, began organizing the defense of the building,
which was soon transformed into a small fort (the Germans did not rule out
the possibility that the assassination of Mirbach was the beginning of a
planned destruction of the embassy by the Bolsheviks). Attempts to notify
representatives of the Soviet government about what had happened remained
ineffective: for some reason, the embassy's telephone was not working (and
to the Germans, this probably did not look like an accident). Then, a little
after 3 p.m., Karl von Botmer, an embassy official, and Müller, the interpreter, took the embassy's car and drove to the People's Commissariat of
Foreign Affairs, at the Hotel Metropole, to see Karakhan.

Seeing the German diplomats, Karakhan leapt out of his chair and ran to his secretary's office.[30] From the visitors' excited appearance, he understood that something had happened and decided that the Germans had come to kill him. Soon he calmed down, returned to his office, heard out his visitors, and assured them that representatives of the Soviet government would come to the German embassy at once. He telephoned Chicherin, who telephoned the Sovnarkom's executive secretary, Vladimir Bonch-Bruevich, who asked whether any details were known. Chicherin said no.[31] Bonch-Bruevich telephoned Lenin, told him what had happened, and was ordered to go to the German embassy with a unit of Latvian riflemen—the military guard of the Soviet government—and to report back by telephone. Meanwhile, Lenin telephoned Dzerzhinsky and informed him of the beginning of the "rebellion."[32]

Then Lenin summoned Sverdlov, telephoned Trotsky at the army commissariat, and told him that "the Left SRs have thrown a bomb at Mirbach."[33] How did Lenin find out, then, that they had been involved in the terrorist attack? The names and party affiliation of the terrorists could have been known only to Dzerzhinsky (and only if he had been a co-participant in the assassination and had personally signed Blumkin's and Andreyev's mandate). It may be assumed that even in this case Dzerzhinsky would have been unlikely to reveal Blumkin's name and thus betray to Lenin his own participation in the conspiracy. Of the details of the assassination, Lenin could have known only that Mirbach had been fatally wounded.

Within several minutes, Trotsky and Sverdlov came to Lenin's office.[34] Soon, they found out that Mirbach was dead. It was important to "influence the character of the German report to Berlin";[35] therefore, Lenin, Sverdlov, and Chicherin headed for the German embassy in order to express their condolences on account of the ambassador's murder. Lenin made a joke: "I've already discussed this with Radek. Wanted to say 'Mitleid', but the proper word it 'Beileid.'"[36] And "he started laughing a little, under his breath," at his own joke; then he "got dressed and said to Sverdlov firmly: 'Let's go.'" His face "changed, became stone-gray," Trotsky recalled. "It was not easy to go to the Hohenzollern embassy to express condolences for Count Mirbach's death. In terms of his own inner trials, this was probably one of the most difficult moments" in Lenin's life[37]—another payment for the delay. Trotsky, as an opponent of Lenin's policy, refused to go to the embassy—and the formula "neither peace nor war" did not require him to do so.

However, in July 1918, when the Soviet regime was going through an extremely serious crisis, Mirbach's assassination—strange as it may seem—actually helped the position of Lenin's government. With his death, the tangled knot of Soviet-German relations was severed and an opportunity pre-

sented itself to eliminate the Left SR Party, and thus to cut the second and no
less tangled knot of Bolshevik-Left SR relations. After preparing for a
possible confrontation with the Left SRs during the very first days of the
Fifth Congress, Lenin, Sverdlov, and Trotsky—as soon as they heard the
news about the German ambassador's assassination—began to take "urgent
measures to suppress and terminate the rebellion,"[38] although they could not
yet have known who was behind Mirbach's murder, especially because there
was no evidence of any kind of anti-government insurrection. Thus, Malkov,
the commandant of the Kremlin, who was at the Bolshoi Theater at the time,
wrote that around 4 p.m. Strizhak, the manager of the Bolshoi Theater,
"came running" to him, "out of breath," and conveyed to him Sverdlov's
order to "come to the Kremlin at once." Five minutes later, he was in the
Kremlin and "from the few phrases" that he had been able to exchange with
VTsIK and Sovnarkom officials on the way, he understood that "the Left
SRs had started a rebellion." "Everything happened remarkably quickly, precisely, smoothly," Malkov recalled. "Vladimir Ilyich and Yakov Mikhailovich
were right there writing telephone messages, instructions, orders on sheets of
notebook paper." In five minutes, the entire Kremlin garrison was made
ready for battle.[39] Meanwhile, the Left SRs who were inside the Kremlin—in
the garrison or among the personnel—were immediately arrested.

The first official government announcement about the assassination of
Mirbach came at 4:20 p.m. It was a telephone message from Lenin to Bolshe-
vik-controlled organizations: to the district committees of the Russian
Communist Party, to the district Soviets of Deputies in Moscow (where there
were practically no Left SRs), and to the headquarters of the Red Guards. In
this first telephone message Lenin announced that "at around 3 p.m. two
bombs were detonated inside the German embassy, seriously wounding Mirbach." Lenin indicated that the assassination attempt had been perpetrated by
"monarchists and provocateurs" who were trying to draw "Russia into war in
the interests of English-French capitalists," and demanded that "all forces be
mobilized, brought into action immediately in order to catch the criminals,"
"all cars stopped and searched three times."[40]

Thus, Lenin's official telephone message did not mention the Left SRs,
while in the orders given to specific party leaders, "the rebellion of the Left
SRs" was mentioned as an accomplished fact. This divergence appears suspicious and not accidental. If one believes that Lenin had no inkling of the
Left SR "rebellion" (and that indications to the contrary in the memoirs of
contemporaries were a misunderstanding), then it seems surprising that he
did not inform the Congress of Soviets, which was meeting in the Bolshoi
Theater, about what had happened. If Lenin did suspect the Left SRs, it is

difficult to understand his reference to "monarchists" and nameless "provocateurs."

The meaning of Lenin's instructions is explained by Bonch-Bruevich: "This was a strategic move in order to avoid scaring the [Left] SRs." The Left SRs could not be alerted[41] until a plan for the military destruction of the Left SR Party had been fully worked out, until Popov's military unit had been surrounded, and the Left SR delegation at the Congress of Soviets had been arrested. Until then, the Left SRs could not be told that they were being seen as an insurgent party. A precise plan to destroy Popov's unit was approved by the Bolsheviks at 5 p.m. on July 6.

Until then, not only did Lenin not consider it possible to announce the death of the German ambassador (although the 47-year-old Count died at 3:15 p.m., an hour before Lenin's first telephone message),[42] but he tried to keep silent even about the wounding of Mirbach. In the draft of his telephone message, the following, subsequently deleted, sentence was added as a postscript: "We have now received news that the bombs did not explode and that no one was hurt."[43] In this attempt to show that the terrorist attack had failed, the same strategy appears to conceal the truth for some time both from the Germans and from the opponents of the Treaty of Brest-Litovsk, because the likelihood was too great that the news of Mirbach's death would elicit applause from all the delegates at the Congress of Soviets, from the Left SRs to the Bolsheviks, and that in an outburst of revolutionary enthusiasm the congress would approve of the assassination and repeal the Treaty of Brest-Litovsk. In order to insure itself against a possible annulment of the treaty by the congress, the Soviet leadership decided to arrest the Left SR delegation at the congress before it could find out about the murder of the German ambassador. This was the second reason why the news of Mirbach's death had to be kept secret and why the Left SRs could not be allowed to see that events were taking a serious turn, since the ambassador had been killed and the Treaty of Brest-Litovsk was possibly already defunct.

The first person to arrive at the German embassy was the omnipresent Radek. After him came Karakhan, People's Commissar of Justice Stuchka, and Bonch-Bruevich, who brought with him a unit of Latvian riflemen from the Ninth Regiment. Dzerzhinsky arrived at embassy to investigate the terrorist attack. Müller met him with a rebuke—"What do you say now?"—and showed him Blumkin's and Andreyev's mandate with the signature of the head of the Cheka. The authorization read:

> The All-Russian Extraordinary Commission authorizes its member Yakov Blumkin and Revolutionary Tribunal representative Nikolay Andreyev to enter

into negotiations with the German ambassador to the Russian Republic concerning a matter that has a direct relation to the ambassador. Chairman of the
All-Russian Extraordinary Commission: F. Dzerzhinsky. Secretary: Ksenofontov.[44]

On the face of it, judging by a photocopy of the document, Dzerzhinsky's signature did not look forged. Whether the investigative commission
submitted the signature for expert analysis is hard to say. The results of such
an analysis, at least, have not been found by historians. "I signed no such
authorization," Dzerzhinsky later testified. "Examining my signature and that
of Comrade Ksenofontov, I saw that our signatures had been copied, forged.
The figure of Blumkin...immediately emerged as a provocateur. I gave orders
to find and arrest him immediately (I did not know who Andreyev was)."[45] It
took Ksenofontov over three weeks to repudiate his signature. Only on July
31 did he declare that "the signature of the secretary on this document is
forged: I did not sign such a document."[46]

     After 4 p.m., Gil—Lenin's personal chauffeur—drove up to the main
entrance of the Sovnarkom; Lenin, Sverdlov, and Chicherin got inside the car
and drove to the embassy. The Germans were informed of their arrival by
Bonch-Bruevich, who said that "the heads of the government...wish to have
an official talk with the representatives of the German embassy." The visitors
were shown into the embassy's main hall. Everyone sat down. Lenin "made
some brief remarks in German, expressing the government's apologies for
what had happened inside the embassy building," that is, on territory not
controlled by the Soviet government. He added that "the case will be investigated immediately and the guilty parties will be duly punished."[47]

     Of course, his "remarks" could not satisfy the officials of the German
embassy. In essence, Lenin was absolving the Soviet government of any
responsibility for the German ambassador's murder, indicating that it was not
accountable for what had happened inside the embassy. He offered his
remarks sitting down. The Germans noted Lenin's "cold politeness,"[48] but
could do nothing about it. The members of the Soviet government then went
out to the inner courtyard of the embassy. Only Stuchka remained inside the
building; he began to conduct an "investigation" of the crime scene. The
results of this very first investigation were never made public by the Soviet
government. But one thing is certain: the file with the case of Robert Mirbach, hastily left behind by the terrorists in the embassy's reception hall, and
the Cheka's mandate with Dzerzhinsky's and Ksenofontov's signatures,
which would have been dangerous pieces of evidence in the hands of the
German government, ended up in the possession of the Bolsheviks.

     Meanwhile, in the central committee of the Left SR Party—or more precisely, in the building of Popov's Cheka unit, where the leadership of the Left SR Party met—everything was perfectly calm, although the "rebellious party" should have been behaving differently, especially since by midday on July 6 rumors about an imminent assassination attempt against Mirbach had reached not only the forewarned Dzerzhinsky (if he was not himself an organizer of the conspiracy) and Karakhan, but some of the Left SRs as well. Around noon, Alexandrovich had been told about the impending assassination attempt by Blumkin. Between 1 and 2 p.m., the plans for the terrorist attack became known to Proshyan (if, of course, he was not doing the planning himself), Karelin, Cherepanov, and Kamkov.[49]

Meanwhile, after killing Mirbach, the terrorists drove to the Morozov mansion in Trekhsvyatitelsky Lane, to Popov's unit. Popov himself apparently took no special notice of what was happening. His Cheka unit, at any rate, continued operating as usual. When Blumkin and Andreyev arrived, Popov was in his office, talking to Abram Belenky, a Bolshevik and an agent of the Cheka's crime department; Andreyev and the wounded Blumkin— fresh from committing their terrorist attack—were introduced to him. Belenky soon left Popov's unit and proceeded to look for Dzerzhinsky. When he finally found him with the other Soviet leaders at the German embassy in Denezhny Lane, it was past 4 p.m.[50]

After talking to Belenky, Lenin, Sverdlov, and Bonch-Bruevich left for the Kremlin. They began discussing how to destroy Left SRs. "The case is so clear," Lenin said, "yet we've been discussing it for over an hour. But the [Left] SRs like to talk even more than we do. They're probably having a heated discussion right now. This will help us until [troop commander] Podvoisky gets going," he added, laughing.[51]

Indeed, at that moment the central committee of the Left SR Party was debating how to react to Blumkin's announcement that he had killed the German ambassador and (as he mistakenly believed) Riezler and Müller, and whether to react at all. It was obvious that there would be a search for Blumkin, since the orders with Dzerzhinsky's and Ksenofontov's signatures, made out to Blumkin and Andreyev, had been "left in Count Mirbach's office." It was decided to wait.[52]

After 5 p.m., accompanied by three Bolshevik Chekists—Belenky, Trepalov, and Khrustalev—Dzerzhinsky proceeded to Popov's headquarters in order to arrest "Blumkin and those who are hiding him."[53] By this time, the names of the terrorists were already known, and it was natural that the Bolsheviks would publicize them in order to facilitate the search. However, the names of Blumkin and Andreyev were kept secret until the Left SR Party was destroyed. Blumkin was first referred to by name only on July 8, in an official note written by Trotsky. This note indicated that "a certain Blumkin, on orders from" the central committee of the Left SR Party, "had carried out the assassination of the German ambassador, Count Mirbach."[54] Andreyev's name was first mentioned on July 14.[55] But Andreyev, who in the eyes of the German embassy's employees was Mirbach's true assassin, had vanished.

Lenin, Sverdlov, and Trotsky apparently viewed what was happening as a joint conspiracy between the Left SRs and the Cheka against Lenin's government. It was for this reason that, on Trotsky's orders, the "artillery and other military units" were brought into position against the Left SR Party, the Cheka was declared officially dissolved, Dzerzhinsky was removed from its chairmanship, and Latsis was appointed in his place (he was to hire new personnel for the agency at his own discretion). Since at the end of the operation to eliminate the Left SR Party the Bolshoi Theater was to be surrounded, Trotsky appointed the Bolshevik Fomin as head of the guard of the outer ring of the theater. Peters and Polukarpov had the job of arresting the Left SR delegates to the congress.[56] Meanwhile, Latsis was attempting to replace the ordinary guard at the Cheka building, made up of Chekists, with a military guard. In accordance with the decision of the Sovnarkom, Trotsky also gave Latsis orders to arrest all Cheka agents who were Left SRs and to declare them hostages. Dzerzhinsky's deputy, Zaks—a Left SR—was at the Cheka at the time, but he was so genuinely perplexed by what was going on that Latsis did not arrest him. When board member M. F. Emelyanov—another Left SR—was stopped by the Cheka, he "immediately gave orders to have him arrested"[57] as a hostage.

The central committee of the Left SR Party was informed of the successful execution of the terrorist attack by Blumkin himself, who came to Popov's headquarters at approximately 3 p.m. Nonetheless, the Left SRs did nothing before Dzerzhinsky and the Chekists Belenky, Trepalov, and Khrustalev arrived there as well, after 5 p.m. If the central committee of the Left SR Party had really been preparing a terrorist attack, it would have immediately reported to the delegates at the Congress of Soviets that it had been successfully carried out, since it was the congress that could decide to abolish the Treaty of Brest-Litovsk, which was what the Left SRs wanted. Instead, it spent over two hours—from the moment of Blumkin's arrival until Dzerzhinsky's arrival at Popov's headquarters—deciding how to react to the murder: whether to claim responsibility for the terrorist attack or to dissociate themselves from it and give Blumkin up to the Bolsheviks.

The next session of the Congress of Soviets was to begin at 4 p.m. The Left SR delegation, as yet unaware of Mirbach's murder, took its seats on the right-hand side of the orchestra and boxes, but the presidium remained empty. Contrary to everyone's expectations, Lenin had not appeared. "The session did not begin," an eyewitness recalled. "The lights in the hall were still dimmed. The tables on the stage were empty. The stenographers loitered about on the side. The diplomatic box was also empty."[58] Only a few Left SR leaders were in the hall.

It was expected that Sverdlov would open the session, but he did not do so. Instead, "he summoned the most trusted comrades who were then inside the Bolshoi Theater" and told them the plan of action. Peters was to be responsible for arresting the Left SR Party delegation. On Sverdlov's instructions, he came out on the stage and announced that the Bolshevik delegation was meeting in a room behind the stage; that the exit was through the orchestra, all other doors being closed; that there were guards posted at the exit; and that Glafira Okulova, the deputy secretary of the VTsIK, was checking comrades' credentials and letting out only members of the Bolshevik delegation, with instructions to proceed to 6 Malaya Dmitrovka Street, where the Bolsheviks were gathering.

The Bolshevik delegates went behind the stage and left the theater through the rear entrance. The Left SRs were told to conduct the meeting of their own delegation inside the main hall of the theater—in other words, they were simply not allowed to leave. The Left SRs still knew nothing about Mirbach's assassination. Some of them began to worry and ask what was going on. It was clear that the Bolsheviks were leaving the building, with everyone else under guard inside, but the Left SRs "did not react to this in any way."[59]

By about 6 p.m., the congress's Left SR guard was removed and the theater was now completely in the Bolsheviks' hands. In addition, it was surrounded by an outer ring of Latvian riflemen and armored vehicles. Only now were the Left SRs told that they were uner arrest in connection with events that had taken place in the city. Rumors immediately began circulating that Mirbach had been killed, that "the Bolshoi Theater must become the nucleus and center of an uprising of the Left SRs, about 300 of whom are on the left side of the orchestra, armed with bombs and waiting for a signal." People headed for the exit. A large crowd formed in the main lobby and began demanding that the doors be opened. "But the doors were closed," the eyewitness recalls. "Red Army soldiers were standing with their backs to them, with rifles at the ready, and not allowing those who wished to leave to come near them. No one was allowed even to stand on the lobby staircases." Everyone was making noise, "arguing with the soldiers, demanding to be released, shouting, threatening."[60] It was between 6 and 7 p.m.[61] Altogether, 450 people had been detained (353 were Left SRs, the rest were Mensheviks and independents).

Dzerzhinsky played one of the most important roles in the events of July 6. The most significant part began, possibly, with his departure from Denezhny Lane. When he arrived at Popov's headquarters, he was met by Popov himself. In response to the Cheka chairman's question, "Where is Blumkin?", Popov informed him that he was no longer in the building and "that he had gone to some hospital." Dzerzhinsky demanded to "see the guards who were standing at the gates and who could confirm that Blumkin had indeed left"; but, noticing "Blumkin's hat on the desk," "he demanded to be allowed to search the premises."[62]

The hat, however, did not belong to Blumkin: the terrorists had left their hats behind in the embassy, and Dzerzhinsky, who was coming from the embassy, knew this. But he needed a pretext to conduct a search. With his three companions, he went through the entire building, breaking down several locked doors in the process. He did not find Blumkin, of course, but in one room he came upon a meeting of some of the members of the central committee of the Left SR Party. At this point, he called an end to his search and "declared Proshyan and Karelin under arrest," telling Popov that if he did "not submit and hand them over," he would "put a bullet in his head and shoot him as a traitor immediately."[63] With regard to Proshyan and Karelin Dzerzhinsky said that one of them must become the "sacrificial lamb for Mirbach,"[64] that is, be executed.

What was Dzerzhinsky attempting when he arrived at Popov's head-quarters? He had a small guard to "conduct an investigation into the Mirbach affair," but instead of doing so he declared two members of the Left SRs' central committee under arrest, announced his intention to have one of them executed, and threatened Dmitry Popov—a VTsIK member, a Cheka collegium member, and head of the Cheka's military unit—to "immediately put a bullet in his head as a traitor." Obviously, faced with such prospects, the central committee of the Left SR Party preferred to detain Dzerzhinsky, and indeed it could not have done otherwise. Neither the central committee members nor Blumkin were handed over to him, since the Soviet government had never punished anyone for the murder of an "imperialist." Blumkin himself, according to his own testimony, took the high ground in this matter. He asked the central committee to bring Dzerzhinsky to him at the infirmary. But he was convinced that the Soviet government could not execute him "for killing a German imperialist." The central committee, however, decided to not sacrifice Blumkin and denied his request.[65]

Instead, shortly after 6 p.m., in order to "defend her party," Left SR leader Maria Spiridonova—accompanied by a group of sailors from Popov's unit—went to see the Bolsheviks at the besieged Bolshoi Theater. In November 1918, in an "Open Letter to the Central Committee of the Bolshevik Party," Spiridonova explained her obviously rash action as follows:

> I came to you on July 6 so that you could have someone from the central committee of our party on whom to vent your anger and whom you could use in order to give compensation to Germany.[66]

The Bolsheviks fulfilled Spiridonova's request and arrested her at the entrance of the Bolshoi Theater, telling her that the Left SR Party delegation to the Congress of Soviets had been detained. Nonetheless, she told them that the central committee of the Left SR Party was claiming responsibility for the assassination of the German ambassador and that Dzerzhinsky had been detained. From this moment, the Bolsheviks had every right to charge the Left SRs with conspiracy. Hearing about Dzerzhinsky's arrest, Sverdlov proceeded to the Kremlin, where he informed Bonch-Bruevich about what had happened, and Bonch-Bruevich told Lenin. When the sailors who had accompanied Spiridonova returned to Popov's headquarters and told about the arrests, the central committee of the Left SR Party was thrown into confusion and "with every new piece of news, the mood in the detachment grew progressively downcast."[67] "For us it was evident," Sablin—a member of the central committee—later testified, "that aggressive action against us had begun. This was confirmed by the appearance of patrols in the vicinity of Popov's headquarters, and by the fact that automobile traffic had been stopped—except for those who had a special pass signed by Lenin, Trotsky, and Sverdlov."[68]

But it was precisely the arrest of the Left SR delegates at the congress, with Spiridonova at their head, that was the last straw for Popov and the members of the central committee of the Left SR Party who were still at liberty; they decided to do something. First, they published "Bulletin No. 1," in which they stated that at 3 p.m. a "flying squadron" from the Left SR Party had "killed the envoy of German imperialism, Count Mirbach, and his two close assistants." Relying on Blumkin's words, they continued to believe that Riezler and Müller had also been killed. The bulletin then went on about the arrest of Dzerzhinsky, the detention of the Left SR Party's delegation to the Congress of Soviets by the Bolsheviks, and the fact that Spiridonova had been taken hostage.[69] At the same time, a group of sailors from Popov's detachment under Zharov's command arrived at the Cheka and took away Latsis and several other Bolsheviks. On the way, Emelyanov—who had been freed by the Left SRs—questioned Latsis about who had given the order to arrest him and why; Latsis remained silent. At the headquarters of Popov's

Cheka unit, Popov asked Latsis the same question: "Who gave the order to arrest Emelyanov?" Latsis replied that he had arrested him on orders from the Sovnarkom. Then Popov declared him under arrest by order of the central committee of the Left SR Party and began berating him for the fact the Bolsheviks were standing up for "scoundrels like Mirbach" and arresting those who had helped get rid "of this scoundrel."[70]

At 3 a.m. the Left SRs detained Pyotr Smidovich, the head of the Moscow Soviet, near the Post Office; Smidovich testified a day later that he was met "with surprise and politeness" and not searched, but nonetheless taken "as a hostage to the same building where about 20 communists, along with Dzerzhinsky and Latsis, were already being held." At Popov's headquarters, Proshyan explained to Smidovich that he was "being detained as a hostage in view of the fact that the Sovnarkom had given orders to detain Spiridonova and a number of other members" of the Left SR Party.[71]

By the morning of July 7, the number of Bolsheviks arrested by the Left SRs had grown to 27. But an outside observer could not have failed to notice that the "rebels" were acting without a plan. On July 10, Smidovich testified before an investigative commission that, in his opinion, "these people were not controlling the course of events, the logic of events was controlling them, and they did not realize what they had done. They had no system, no plan."[72] Popov's unit effectively remained idle. This did not go unnoticed by Vacietis, the commander of the Latvian riflemen, who wrote that "information about the insurgents was extremely scanty and inconsistent," "the Left SR leaders missed the moment for decisive action," and the Bolsheviks' position was "quite solid." The Left SRs, in his opinion, "had few forces, and these were not distinguished by exceptional fighting power, lacking a talented and energetic commander; had they had such a commander, then they and the Left SRs would not have spent July 6 and the whole night until July 7 doing nothing. The Kremlin, for the Left SRs, was an unassailable citadel."[73]

The Left SRs indeed were not contemplating any offensive action. Sablin testified that, in response to proposals to "take action against the Sovnarkom, which was taking obviously hostile" measures against the central committee of the Left SR Party and Popov's unit, "the central committee would emphasize the need to adhere to a strictly defensive course of action, on no account going beyond defending the district occupied by the Cheka unit." Popov's headquarters was only a kilometer from the Kremlin and the Bolshoi Theater, where the Fifth Congress of Soviets had been taking place and where the Left SR Party delegation to the congress—353 people—had been arrested. But neither immediately following Mirbach's assassination nor at any later time did the "insurgents" attempt to attack the Kremlin or the Bolshoi Theater.

All of this leads to the conclusion that the Left SRs' actions following the assassination of Mirbach can only be understood as a form of self-defense against the Bolsheviks,[74] who, however, using Mirbach's assassination and Popov's careless steps as formal pretexts for repression, were busy demolishing the Left SR Party.

The night passed peacefully in Moscow. The "rebels" took no action. Sporadic shootouts in the city were a commonplace occurrence. At 5 a.m. the Latvians began their offensive. It is difficult to say whether they and Popov's unit engaged in any fighting as the former approached Trekhsvyatitelsky Lane. There had been thunderstorms and rain all night. On the morning of July 7 a thick fog "covered the city with a gray, impenetrable mist. One could see 15–20 steps ahead, and it was absolutely impossible to distinguish friend from foe, since both were dressed in gray."[75] It is possible that Popov's detachment offered some resistance. But proof of firm resistance by the Left SRs would have consisted, of course, of casualties, either among the "rebels" or the among the Latvians. However, when Podvoisky and Muralov delivered a report about the quelling of the "rebellion" on the evening of July 7, they indicated that Bolshevik casualties constituted "isolated incidents."[76] Popov's casualties were few in number as well: by 10 a.m., two or three men in his unit had been killed, and 20 wounded.

The fact that the "rebels" put up little resistance is also evidenced by their attempt to enter into negotiations with the Bolsheviks: shortly after the beginning of the Bolshevik offensive, Popov tried to resolve the conflict peacefully. Four envoys from his unit went over to the Latvian division, stated that the unit stood "for the Soviet government with Lenin at its head," and that "the reasons for the insurrection are completely unclear and incomprehensible" to it.

The Latvians referred the matter to Vacietis, but he ordered that the envoys be sent away. Trotsky was informed about what had happened, and Sklyansky entered into negotiations with the Left SRs. They were conducted by Sablin, who had emerged from the Morozov mansion. The Bolsheviks presented the them with an ultimatum that expired at 11:30 a.m. The Left SR activists inside the mansion discussed the terms of the ultimatum, decided not to surrender, and attempted to sneak out of the besieged building. At precisely this moment, apparently as soon as the ultimatum expired, Sklyansky ordered Eduard Berzin, the commander of the Latvian rifle squad, to begin firing from a range of 200 meters. In a few minutes, both of the buildings in which the Left SRs were holed up were hit by "16 delayed-action artillery shells that went through the walls splendidly and exploded inside." Altogether fifty-five to sixty shells were fired. Afterwards there was no more

128 *Lenin and His Comrades*

resistance from Popov's unit.[77] None of the Bolshevik hostages were hurt. Fifteen or twenty minutes after the beginning of the attack, Dzerzhinsky had joined the artillerymen of the Latvian division. There were few casualties. The Latvians suffered one killed and three wounded; in Popov's unit, 14 men were dead and 40 had been wounded.[78]

On July 7, regardless of whether or not they had taken part in the "insurrection," Left SRs were arrested across the entire city on orders from the Extraordinary Five-Man Council, which had been created specifically to eliminate the Left SR Party, and that consisted of Lenin, Trotsky, Sverdlov, Podvoisky, and Muralov. Bolshevik political commissars were sent to review the troops; revolutionary committees were established. By noon on July 7, it was all over: Popov's unit had been defeated and had fled to the Kursk Station. Vacietis was given a monetary reward. "You've destroyed one of the biggest political plots and you don't know whom you have destroyed," said Trotsky, ambiguously, as he handed Vacietis the packet with the money.[79]

At 4 p.m. the Sovnarkom announced to the public that "the insurrection of the Left SRs in Moscow has been demolished," and that "the Left SR detachments" have fled. The total number of people arrested in Moscow reached 444.[80] When on the evening of July 7, Malkov reported to Lenin on the results of the pursuit of the Left SRs, Lenin heard him out attentively but calmly, without particular interest. "It was obvious that for him the Left SR rebellion was already a thing of the past."[81]

On July 7, by order of Moscow Soviet collegium member Feldman, all Left SRs who had occupied government posts were dismissed and replaced by Bolsheviks.[82] On the same day, the Sovnarkom formed a special investigative commission, consisting of Stuchka, the People's Commissar of Justice; Viktor Kingisepp; members of the Revolutionary Tribunal's investigative department in the VTsIK; and Yakov Sheynkman, head of the Kazan Soviet and delegate to the Fifth Congress.[83] Rozmirovich was appointed commission head. It was given all documents and materials connected to the events of July 6–7, as well as information about the ensuing arrests. The arrested individuals were released only with the commission's consent.[84]

When on the morning of July 7 Kamenev arrived at the Bolshoi Theater, the Left SRs demanded to be released immediately and called for a ceasefire on both sides. Spiridonova accused the Bolsheviks of using violence. She was backed up Kolegayev, who declared that the Bolshevik Party had violated their constitutional rights. Kamenev replied that it was inappropriate to talk about constitutional rights, since what was taking place was an "armed struggle for power," during which only one law was in effect, "the law of war"; and that those who were arrested "are now not delegates to the Fifth

Congress of Soviets or VTsIK members, but members of a party that has mounted a rebellion against the Soviet government."[85]

The conversation went nowhere. The day had to be spent somehow and the arrested delegates staged a talent show. On the night of July 7 the Bolsheviks compiled a list of all those who had been arrested and confiscated all weapons. Spiridonova was subjected to a search and her revolver was taken from her by force. On July 8, Sverdlov, Trotsky, and Lenin, who signed their names in that order,[86] passed a Central Committee resolution "to determine, on the night of July 8, the attitudes of the Left SR delegates at the Fifth Congress to this reckless undertaking." All of the resulting materials were to be handed over to the investigative commission. The Left SRs spent the third night of their incarceration filling out the questionnaire "Questions of the Special Investigative Commission". Altogether, 173 were filled out. Approximately 40% condemned the assassination of Mirbach; half the delegates gave vague, evasive responses; and the rest refused to answer. The vast majority of the arrested delegates spoke out against war with Germany, arguing that Soviet Russia was not yet ready for war.[87] In the end, it became clear that the Congress of Soviets would not have abolished the Brest-Litovsk delay, as Lenin had feared.

Since the congress was scheduled to renew its work in the Bolshoi Theater on July 9, the Left SRs were transferred to the Maly Theater. Having been denied the right to take part in meetings, excluded from the government, partially arrested, and politically destroyed, the Left SRs were no longer a danger to the Bolsheviks. On July 9, Trotsky announced that the Left SR Party "had committed political suicide for good" and "can no longer come back to life."[88] On the same day, the Congress of Soviets—which now, in effect, consisted entirely of Bolsheviks—demanded "severe punishment for the criminals" and declared that the Left SRs "can have no place in the Soviets."[89] All of this allowed Sverdlov—by July 10—to assure the Bolshevik delegates to the Fifth Congress that the majority of those arrested "would be released tomorrow, or the day after tomorrow at the latest, because they were clearly not implicated in the actions." The Bolsheviks were no longer accusing the Left SRs of rising up against the Soviet government.

The easing of the Soviet government's attitude toward them on July 10 was possibly aimed at dividing them. Thus, in a speech before the VTsIK, Sverdlov indicated that only those members of the Left SR Party would not be expelled from the VTsIK who "submit declarations of their lack of solidarity with the actions" of the Left SRs' central committee.[90] On the whole, Sverdlov's maneuver was successful: on July 15, "a whole series of organizations submitted such declarations."[91] On July 19, the Moscow regional Soviet

expelled all Left SRs from its ranks (there were ten of them), executive
committee members who had refused to condemn Mirbach's murder. For
analogous reasons, Left SRs were excluded from Moscow's city and district
Soviets. At the same time, the Moscow provincial Soviet resolved to "consider the Left SR delegation expelled as a whole," and "to consider [those
Left SRs] who had condemned the enterprise and expressed their solidarity
with the party of the proletariat as fully legitimate members of the
presidium."[92] Here, too, the divisive strategy met with success. By the end of
July, the Left SR Party had given up practically all posts in the government of
the country.

Of the Bolsheviks, only Dzerzhinsky remained under suspicion. The fact
that he had been arrested by the Left SRs on July 6–7 did not wipe out the
question of his possible involvement in the German ambassador's murder.
His testimony about his connections with the German embassy were quite
murky, and his self-justifying arguments were also dubious. He claimed, for
example, that the German embassy's informers, Ginch and Benderskaya,
were provocateurs, but he left out the fact that their information was accurate
and did not specify whom these "provocateurs" were working for. Meanwhile, it is obvious that Ginch and Benderskaya were not working for either
the Bolsheviks or the Cheka. They were not arraigned in connection with the
Mirbach assassination and it is unlikely that they were working for the Left
SRs. They were, evidently, the German embassy's informers. But because by
agreement the Cheka could not arrest Mirbach's intelligencers, Benderskaya
and Ginch were arrested only on July 6, shortly after the murder of the
German ambassador, when, in fact, the Chekists were no longer afraid of
going against the interests of the German embassy. The materials from the
interrogation of these informers were not made public, and Ginch and
Benderskaya themselves, on that same day, disappeared forever from the
Germans' and the Bolsheviks' field of vision.

The suspicion that fell on Dzerzhinsky caused Sverdlov, Trotsky, and
Lenin to remove him from his post as head of the Cheka in order to avoid
any possible inconvenient revelations. This matter was discussed at a special
meeting of the Central Committee of the Bolshevik Party. On July 7,
Dzerzhinsky submitted an official resignation to the Sovnarkom, in view of
the fact that he was "one of the main witnesses in the case of the murder of
the German envoy Count Mirbach."[93] Apparently, in order to somewhat calm
the Germans, the resolution to dismiss Dzerzhinsky was made into a public
gesture: it was not only printed in newspapers, but also pasted up everywhere
in the city.[94] Peters was appointed temporary head of the Cheka, and its
collegium was dissolved; it was to be reorganized within a week. Anyone with

any direct or indirect involvement in the murder was subject to "elimination."[95] However, Dzerzhinsky's dismissal was fictitious. As Peters recalled six years later, he remained the real "head of the Cheka, and the collegium was formed with his direct participation."[96]

On July 14, the newspapers reported that Vyacheslav Alexandrovich had been executed. He had been arrested on July 7 "while trying to get into a car and escape."[97] Before the execution, Peters had had a long one-on-one conversation with him. The latter testified that, as a member of the central committee of the Left SR Party, he had followed party discipline, and this was his only justification. "He cried, he cried for a long time," Peters remembered, "and it became hard for me, perhaps because, of all the Left SRs, he had made the best impression."[98] During his interrogation, Alexandrovich said that the orders which he had given—including the orders to arrest Latsis and Peters—were based on instructions from the central committee of the Left SR Party. He refused to answer other questions.[99] On the night of July 8, he was shot, apparently by Dzerzhinsky personally,[100] and indeed it is possible that Alexandrovich was executed "to satisfy German demands,"[101]

Perhaps it was for this reason that the Bolsheviks began to sing Alexandrovich's praises after he was executed. "He was a revolutionary, and I was told that he died with dignity," Trotsky said at the congress on July 9. "I trusted Alexandrovich completely," noted Dzerzhinsky. "He almost always agreed with me," "this fooled me and was the source of all the trouble. Without this trust, I...would not have instructed him to investigate the complaints that were sometimes being lodged against Popov's unit, would not have trusted him when he vouched for Popov in those cases when I had doubts in connection with rumors about his drinking bouts. Even today I cannot reconcile myself to the thought that he was a conscious traitor, although all the evidence is there and there can be no two opinions about him."[102]

The wily Alexandrovich had fooled the gullible Dzerzhinsky. In return for this, the gullible Dzerzhinsky executed the wily Alexandrovich. Only, who would ever believe in Dzerzhinsky's naiveté?

Until the destruction of the Left SR Party on July 6 and 7 was over, one of the principal initiators of the attack on them—Lenin—remained firm and cool. But evidently he could not help feeling some emotional discomfort, for it was in accordance with his orders that the Bolsheviks had opened fire at close range on their friends and recent allies, who had been talking about merging with the Russian Communist Party (Bolsheviks) and were committed supporters of the Revolution. Only this can explain the strange fact that, on the evening of July 7, Lenin himself came to the Morozov mansion, where the Left SRs had been holed up.[103] Together with Krupskaya, the only witness of such a strange action on Lenin's part, he walked around the rooms of the ruined house in Trekhsvyatitelsky Lane, crushing with the soles of his shoes the pieces of fallen plaster and broken glass that were lying on the floor. He remained thoughtful and silent, and soon asked to be driven back to the Kremlin.[104]

On July 10, the special investigative commission began its investigation of the terrorist attack and the "insurrection" of the Left SRs. The commission did not try to find Mirbach's murderers. Andreyev was strangely forgotten by everyone. In the resolution of the Fifth Congress of Soviets, passed on July 9 on the basis of Trotsky's report, "On the Assassination of Mirbach and the Armed Insurrection of the Left SRs," only Blumkin was mentioned. He also was not arrested. The German government protested many times that "the assassination of Count Mirbach has not been compensated for with a corresponding punishment for the guilty parties and the perpetrators of the crime," and that the terrorists "have not been arrested."[105]

For want of Mirbach's assassins, the special investigative commission tried to convince some of the leaders of the Left SR Party to confess to the central committee's plot;[106] however, the committee refused to take responsibility for the clashes of July 6–7 and claimed that it had not been "in charge of these military actions."[107] Unable to obtain a confession from any of the members of committee, the commission began to question ordinary participants in the "rebellion"—rank-and-file Left SRs and men from Popov's unit, who likewise denied that there had been any "insurrection" or any intention to overthrow the government.[108] Altogether, the special investigative commission questioned about 650 individuals, but its conclusions were entirely at odds with the claims of Sverdlov, Lenin, and Trotsky about an "insurrection against the Soviet government." The testimony of the members of Popov's unit made it perfectly obvious that the charges about the "insurrection" were absurd. After hearing the confessions of hundreds of the "insurrection's" participants, the members of the commission confirmed their innocence. Kingisepp wrote in connection with this that a significant portion of the Left SRs who had taken part in the events of July 6–7 had lacked any knowledge or understanding of what was happening even on July 7, when shells were exploding around them. Thus, two Finnish units that were part of Popov's unit had been convinced that they were defending themselves against Austro-Germans, who had "dressed up in Red Army uniforms and were intending to overthrow the Soviet government."[109]

If such conclusions were being reached by the members of the commission—i.e., by Bolsheviks themselves—then what were the Left SRs supposed to think? Svetlov, speaking on their behalf at a VTsIK meeting on

July 15, was at a complete loss. He pointed out the groundlessness of the charges that the Left SR Party had attempted to overthrow the Soviet government and raised doubts about the involvement of the party as a whole in the assassination of Mirbach, indicating that the results of the investigation conducted by the special investigative commission had not yet been made public, and that "a calmer assessment of what has happened" would lead one "to reject the characterization of the actions" of the central committee of the Left SR Party "as an attempt to take over or overthrow the Soviet government." "This was absolutely and positively a terrorist attack," Svetlov stated. "There was no attempt to take over or to topple the Soviet government."[110]

The investigative commission effectively reached an analogous conclusion. But this was the conclusion most feared by the leaders of the Bolshevik Party—Lenin, Trotsky, and Sverdlov. Therefore, the commission, which had only begun its work, was quickly dissolved. Stuchka was sent to Berlin at the beginning of September. Sheynkman was sent back to Kazan (where on August 8 he was shot by White troops that had entered the city). On September 13, the board of the People's Commissariat of Justice passed a resolution to hand the case over to the VTsIK's Revolutionary Tribunal. But the investigation was essentially terminated, even though the main culprit—Blumkin—had not yet been heard from. He gave his testimony about the July events only in April-May 1919. In response to questions about the Left SR insurrection, he said:

> I know only one thing, that neither I nor Andreyev would have under any circumstances agreed to assassinate the German ambassador in order to start an uprising. Did the central committee trick us and try to attempt an insurrection behind our backs? I...know that it could not have done such a thing. The party...was always preoccupied with the idea that it was necessary, at any cost, to unite with the Communists. All conscientious workers and such party members as M. A. Spiridonova were looking for this unification at the time and if they failed to find it, then it was through no fault of their own. What happened on the 6th and 7th in Trekhsvyatitelsky Lane, in my opinion, was only an act of self-defense by the revolutionaries. And that would not have been necessary if the central committee [of the Left SR Party] had agreed to hand me over to the authorities.... There was no insurrection.... The assassination of Mirbach had completely unexpected political consequences. From an act of protest against the cupidity of German imperialism, from an act of revolutionary self-defense by Soviet Russia, the assassination of Mirbach was transformed into an act of party strife between the Left SRs and the Communists, and into an act hostile to the Soviet government. Moreover, this act was interpreted by the Soviet government as a signal for the start of an insurrection by the Left SRs against it. Instead of

being directed against German imperialism, it was turned into an armed conflict between two Soviet parties.[111]

In 1922, a letter written by Spiridonova on July 17, 1918, in which she denied any conspiracy against the Soviet government, was published for the first time:

> I read the newspapers with disgust. Today I was seized by mad laughter. I saw how cleverly they have arranged it. They themselves have invented the "conspiracy." They themselves are conducting the investigation and the interrogations. They themselves are the witnesses and they themselves are appointing the main participants—and executing them.... If only they killed a single "conspirator"—because they are executing only people who are innocent, innocent.... How can one convince them that there was no conspiracy, that there was no coup....? I'm beginning to think that they have convinced themselves, and if earlier they knew that they were fanning and manipulating [rumors], then now they themselves believe that there was a "conspiracy."[112]

However, the admissions of both Blumkin and Spiridonova came too late. On July 6, the Left SR Party went into a headlong decline from which it never recovered. If at the Fifth Congress of Soviets it had over 30% of the delegates, then at the Sixth Congress, which took place only four months later, the Left SRs had only 1% of the votes; 98% of the delegates were now Bolsheviks.

The assassination of the German ambassador in a remarkable fashion briefly reunited the Bolshevik leaders—Lenin, Trotsky, and Sverdlov—who had hitherto been divided over the question of Brest-Litovsk. By shrewd and decisive action, they demolished their principal political opponent, the Left SR Party, and effectively annihilated the Left Communists, who had quietly bowed their heads before the threat of new "anti-Soviet" actions (which was the charge leveled against the Left SR Party). This did not mean, however, that the core of the Bolshevik Party had reconciled itself to the "Tilsit" peace treaty. In July-August 1918, the threat to Lenin's personal power became more acute than ever before. On the political horizon, the figure of a new party leader was emerging: he was not an orator and an ideologue, like Trotsky, and not an authoritative leader, like Lenin, but an inconspicuous party *apparatchik*, a functionary known only within narrow party circles. This was the profile of Yakov Sverdlov.

VTsIK chairman, Central Committee member, Central Committee secretary, Sverdlov had gradually concentrated all party work in his own hands. His signature appeared on documents more often than any other. In July 1918, he began using his official titles in place of a signature: secretary of the

Central Committee of the Russian Communist Party (Bolsheviks) or even simply "secretary"; or else documents would be signed "for the secretary" by Klavdia Novgorodtseva, his wife; and more or more often letters would be sent from the "Secretariat of the Central Committee" (not the "Central Committee," as had been the rule). On August 26, 1918, Sverdlov sent a letter to the Vologda committee of the Russian Communist Party, signing it with his new official title: "Secretary of the Central Committee of the Russian Communist Party Ya. Sverdlov."[113] In other words, he assumed the functions that several years later would pass to his comrade-in-exile, another dark horse of the Revolution, Joseph Stalin—the functions of the general secretary of the party.

4.

Vladimir Lenin and Yakov Sverdlov

"Yakov was mischievous and restless as a boy; he organized games for all the children on his street."

Klavdia Sverdlov (wife of Yakov Sverdlov),
Yakov Mikhailovich Sverdlov
Moscow, 1976, p. 60

For the sake of caution, we will call this chapter an assumption, one that has as much right to exist as, for example, the hypothesis that Yakov Sverdlov and Vladimir Lenin were friends; or that Lenin was friends with Stalin. Or, finally, that Lenin was shot by Fanny Kaplan and that Sverdlov died of the Spanish flu. All of Soviet history is riddled with theories and hypotheses. What remains to be determined are those that are correct and those that are not.

The subject herer is another conspiracy: the one by Dzerzhinsky against Lenin. In August 1918, Dzerzhinsky, having failed to undermine the Treaty of Brest-Litovsk through the assassination of Mirbach, attempted to destroy the Brest-Litovsk agreement by getting rid of the promoter of this policy, the chairman of the Sovnarkom, Lenin. This conspiracy is usually known to historians as the Kaplan assassination attempt of August 30, 1918. Like the murder of the ambassador in July, the attempt to assassinate Lenin was carried out through other people, not by the main conspirators themselves. And as will be shown in this chapter, it was the result of a broad anti-Lenin conspiracy within the upper echelons of the party—so broad, in fact, that the plan to eliminate Lenin was evidently known to Sverdlov, who was subsequently eliminated either by Lenin or by the other conspirators—who in March 1919, during the intraparty war between Lenin and Sverdlov, after the abrogation of the Treaty of Brest-Litovsk and the end of the First World War, chose to side with Lenin rather than Sverdlov.

Those who do not understand how Sverdlov could have planned to eliminate Lenin at the height of the mortal struggle with "international imperialism," and how Lenin could have allowed himself to settle scores with Sverdlov at a time when the whole party depended upon him, are referred to Lenin's pronouncement, cited above and quoted by Lunachasky in his speech "Radiant Precious Genius": "Imagine that a commander is fighting a war against an enemy and that he has an enemy in his own camp. Before he goes to the front to fight the enemy, he must first clean out his own camp and make it free of enemies."[1]

This notion captures the essence of the relations among the Bolshevik leaders. In 1918–1919, the Soviet commander Lenin did nothing but go to the front, but also cleaned out enemies in his own camp. And Sverdlov did his own cleaning, too, just not as successfully. His mistrust of those around him was so serious that after his death, the keys to his personal safe could not be found. The safe was sent to the inventory warehouse of Pavel Malkov, the commandant of the Kremlin, where it remained until July 26, 1935, when it was finally opened. On July 27, People's Commissar of Internal Affairs Genrikh Yagoda submitted a list of the safe's contents to Stalin. It contained czarist-era gold coins in the amount of 108,525 rubles; gold articles, many with precious stones—705 items altogether; seven blank czarist-era passports; czarist bank notes in the amount of 750,000 rubles.[2]

Also discovered were nine traveling passports, including a passport made out in Sverdlov's name, prepared in the event that he would have to flee Soviet Russia. From the dispatches of the German diplomatic mission (one of the few that was working in those days in Soviet Russia), it is known that in August 1918, even before the assassination attempt against Lenin, "something resembling a state of panic" settled over Moscow. On August 1, 1918, the German embassy notified Berlin that the leadership of Soviet Russia was transferring "substantial monetary resources" to Swiss banks; on August 15, the embassy wrote that people were procuring traveling passports and that "the air of Moscow... is pregnant with assassination as never before."[3]

The memoirs of Yelena Stasova, secretary and member of the Central Committee and assistant to Sverdlov, were published in 1957. According to her, the Bolsheviks were in a state of panic in 1919 as well:

> 1919 was a very difficult year. The fact that fourteen countries had launched an offensive against the Soviet republic created such a dangerous situation that it was possible that the party would once again have to go into hiding, if the forces of the domestic counter-revolution and the foreign interventionists should temporarily gain the upper hand. And so passports had to be made for all the members of the Central Committee and above all for V. I. Lenin. Material resources had to be secured for the party as well. To this end, a large sum of czarist-era money was printed (so-called "yekaterinki," i.e., 100-ruble bills with a portrait of Catherine). In order to keep this money safe, the bills were packed in identical boxes and given to Nikolai Yevgenyevich Burenin for safekeeping in Petrograd. He buried them, as far as I know, outside of the city, somewhere in Lesny, and later even photographed how they were dug up, when the position of the Soviet government finally became secure. At the same time, a document was made out in Burenin's name (he was a merchant by birth), stating that he was the owner of the Hotel Metropole. This was done in order to provide for the party financially.[4]

In 1957, Stasova's revelations were greeted with surprise, since the Bolsheviks did not like to talk about their period of panic. As soon as he received her memoirs, the prominent Menshevik Rafail Abramovich reported about what he had read to another Menshevik and the author of several books, Nikolai Valentinov-Volsky. "The episode with the passports and the money at the beginning of 1919, at the most dangerous moment for Bolshevism in the civil war," Valentinov-Volsky replied, "is known not only to me, as one of the main members of what was then the Mensheviks' central committee, but also, independently from me, to four other people [Mensheviks] in New York: L. O. [Dan], B. I. Nicolaevsky, [Yu. P.] Denike, and B. Dvinov. At the time, we ourselves were offered passports by Enukidze and Kamenev, which were prepared for us and for the Bund, and the Bund, which was then operating in Belorussia, even received a rather substantial sum in those very 100-ruble bills that you write about.... I know, as you probably know also, as does [B. K.] Suvarin, that at the same time or some time earlier, they sent a large amount of gold abroad through Mark Natanson; this gold was supposed to be deposited in Swiss banks, in accounts named by the Bolshevik Party. Some part of this gold they gave to Left SRs of Natanson's stripe, who then used this money to establish Skify Press in Berlin."[5]

Lenin was no stranger to panic either. Bukharin recalled how, at moments of crisis, Lenin would "just in case give orders to take such-and-such measures in order to recommence underground operations. He [does not] doubt for a second that he would die if defeated."[6]

Thus, Sverdlov was not the only government leader who was making arrangements to flee abroad. But it was the Secretariat of the Central Committee, and Sverdlov first and foremost, that was responsible for preparing the party's transition to an extralegal footing should the Bolsheviks be defeated due to Lenin's defeatist Brest-Litovsk policy, which had brought the Bolsheviks to a dead end and to the brink of their downfall.

It is remarkable that in his speech about Lenin, which we have already cited, Lunacharsky constantly brought up another genius: Sverdlov. Initially, he explained, it was Sverdlov who was in charge of selecting party workers, i.e., it was he who carried out the duties of the general secretary of the party:

> Thus, Comrades, our Bolshevik underground lived under this terrible weight, under this pressure of several thousand atmospheres, and one could watch a person and see whether he was active, whether he was energetic, whether he was an organizer, how well groups crystallized around him. Ya. M. Sverdlov knew all of these types very well. For example, Ivanov or Petrov—who is he? Sverdlov knew when he had joined the party, when he had fled, when he had been released, and so on. This trait was so phenomenally developed in Ya. M. Sverdlov—all of us in party knew about it; therefore, when we were electing people for our Central Committee and the editorial board of our main newspaper, we elected them not because we liked their noses, but following an enormous vetting process. And the people in these positions of leadership had to be tested by life in the most severe, the most merciless fashion. This is how the best men among the intelligentsia and the proletariat gradually filtered through to the best organization in the country: great leaders were being created for the Revolution, which would come later. It is perfectly clear that such an organization and such leaders were unique in the world.

Sverdlov was pointedly placed by Lunacharsky on the same level as the "shining precious genius," Lenin:

> [Lenin] valued Sverdlov very highly. As you know, Sverdlov played a big role in the history of the party—he was the secretary of the Central Committee, worked on selecting and sorting out new personnel, and thus stood at the head of the Soviet government, doing an enormous amount of the most vital work together with Vladimir Ilyich. When Sverdlov died, Vladimir Ilyich said...: A man has died whom no one can replace. We have no other such man in the party.... He must be replaced by a collective.[7]

In other words, already in 1919 Lenin was making the same accusation against Sverdlov that he would go on to make against Stalin in his "Last

Testament": that he was concentrating unlimited power in his own hands. The unfolding of Lenin's struggle against Dzerzhinsky and Stalin in 1922–1924—and its final outcome—is described below. How, then, did the struggle between Lenin and Sverdlov—the party's first general secretary—play out and what was its final outcome?

Historians have usually viewed August 30, 1918, as the date that marked the beginning of the campaign of Red Terror, which came in response to the assassination attempt against Lenin. The accepted view has been that he had been shot by Kaplan, an SR who was arrested, confessed to everything, and either shot or, according to another account, secretly pardoned, and that the terrorist attack had been organized by the leaders of the SRs' combat group. However, August 30 became a watershed in the history of the Bolshevik Party for quite a different reason. For the first time since seizing power, the Bolsheviks were disposing of one of their own leaders: Lenin was shot by his own party.[8]

The Russian Federation's General Prosecutor's Office has twice started new investigations into the circumstances surrounding the assassination attempt against Lenin on August 30, 1918. On June 19, 1992, Russia's General Prosecutor's Office, which began looking into the justifiability of the arraignment, sentencing, and execution of Fanny Kaplan on September 3, 1918, by an extrajudicial resolution of the presidium of the Cheka, passed a resolution to reopen this old criminal case:

> Yu. I. Sedov, senior judicial advisor at the General Prosecutor's Office of the Russian Federation and prosecutor at the department for the rehabilitation of the victims of political repressions, after examining the materials of criminal case No. N-200 against F. Ye. Kaplan, has resolved that:
>
> F. Ye. Kaplan (Roydman) was criminally prosecuted and subsequently executed for attempting to carrying out a terrorist attack against Sovnarkom Chairman V. I. Ulyanov (Lenin).
>
> The materials of the case reveal that the investigation was conducted in a superficial fashion. No forensic or ballistics tests were conducted; witnesses and victims were not questioned; other investigative procedures necessary for a full, comprehensive, and objective investigation of the circumstances of the crime were not conducted.
>
> Therefore, the prosecutor has resolved, under articles 384 and 386 of the penal code of the RSFSR, to commence proceedings in the light of newly discovered evidence.[9]

The aim of the investigation was to establish "whether Kaplan shot Lenin, and what were her motives and subsequent fate."[10] The investigators were expected to examine her files and those of the Right SRs, who had been convicted in 1922 on charges which included the assassination attempt against Lenin. And since the relevant files were stored in the archives of the former KGB and remained classified until 1992, the investigation of the matter was assigned to the investigations directorate of the Russian Federation's Ministry of Security (the former KGB and the current FSB). After the Ministry of Security was abolished in late February and early March of 1994, the Kaplan case passed to Vladimir Solovyev, a criminal prosecutor at the General Prosecutor's Office.[11]

By the summer of 1996, the Kaplan case had been examined by six investigators, who had replaced one another (which could only have had a detrimental effect on the work). The idea of reexamining the terrorist attack did not please the FSB. Although the General Prosecutor's Office of the Russian Federation instructed the FSB to get to the bottom of all the circumstances surrounding Fanny Kaplan's assassination attempt against Lenin on August 30, 1918, outside the Mikhelson Factory, during which the head of the Sovnarkom received two gunshot wounds, the FSB's staff did not display any zeal in carrying out their instructions.[12]

So what did happen on August 30, 1918? Lenin's secretary, Vladimir Bonch-Bruevich, recalled: "Comrade Kozlovsky arrived late at night. As a member of the collegium of the Commissariat of Justice, he had been ordered to question Kaplan first.... Kozlovsky told me that Kaplan made an extremely undistinguished, stunted, high-strung, almost hysterical impression. She acted confused, rambled when she talked, and was in a state of depression. Kozlovsky said that the SR organization was undoubtedly behind this, although Kaplan denied it, and that it had a clear connection to the events in St. Petersburg (the murders of Volodarsky, Uritsky), and that, of course, other acts of violence are to be expected. Kozlovsky did not yet know any details about the assassination itself."[13]

Immediately following the shooting, even before Kaplan's first interrogation, which began at 11:30 p.m., the Soviet government accused the SR Party of organizing the terrorist attack. Sverdlov, as head of the VTsIK, signed the resolution: "To everyone, to everyone, to everyone.... Several hours ago a villainous assassination attempt was carried out against Comrade Lenin.... We have no doubt that here, too, we will find traces of the Right SRs, traces of the hirelings of the British and the French."[14]

It should be noted that Sverdlov knew about the involvement of the SRs and the "British-French hirelings" in the assassination attempt before he received the first reports about the shooting. For him it was important to make use of the attempt against Lenin in order to dispose of the SRs and to initiate a large-scale terror campaign against all "enemies of the revolution,"[15] just as Mirbach's murder had been used to destroy the Left SR Party.

After Sverdlov's announcement, the VTsIK issued a decree declaring the transformation of the Soviet republic into an armed camp and the Sovnarkom issued a decree announcing the beginning of the Red Terror. On September 1, Yakov Peters, the deputy head of the Cheka and the head of the Revolutionary Tribunal, reported in *Izvestiya* that "the arrested woman who fired at Comrade Lenin is a member of the Right SR Party," but that the terrorist (who had not yet been named) "stubbornly refuses to provide information about her collaborators or to reveal the source of the money that was found on her.... Eyewitness testimony has revealed that a whole group of people participated in the assassination attempt, since as Comrade Lenin was approaching his car, several people stopped him under the pretence of wanting to talk to him. A congestion of people was deliberately created at the exit."

Thus, a whole group participated in the assassination attempt, but Kaplan, who was first named only on September 3 in the morning edition of *Izvestiya*, had for some reason been transferred on September 1 from her solitary cell in the Cheka jail to the Kremlin jail; and on September 3 at 4 p.m. she was shot by Pavel Malkov, the commandant of the Kremlin. On September 4, *Izvestiya* reported that "Fanny Roydman (Kaplan), who shot at Comrade Lenin, has been executed in accordance with a Cheka resolution."[16]

Descriptions of the assassination attempt and of Kaplan's arrest are numerous and contradictory. She was arrested by S. N. Batulin, an assistant to the military commissar of the Fifth Moscow Soviet Infantry Division, who testified that she had been picked up far from the scene of the shooting and following a chase:

> Approaching the car in which Comrade Lenin was to depart, I heard three sharp, dry sounds, which I interpreted not as gunshots but as ordinary motor noises. Following these sounds, I saw the crowd of people who had previously been standing peacefully by the car now starting to run in different directions, and I saw Comrade Lenin behind the car, lying immobile with his face to the ground. I understood that an assassination attempt against Comrade Lenin had taken place. I did not see the person who had shot Comrade Lenin. I did not lose my head and I shouted: "Hold the murderer of Comrade Lenin!"—and shouting this, I ran out to Serpukhovskaya Street, where people who had been scared by the shots and by the general disorder were running in different directions, alone and in groups.... On Serpukhovskaya Street...behind me, beside a tree, I saw a woman holding a briefcase and an umbrella, whose strange appearance caught my attention. She had the appearance of a person who was

being chased; she looked harassed and frightened. I asked this woman why she was here. She replied: "Why do you need to know?" Then, searching her pockets and taking her briefcase and umbrella, I told her to follow me.... On Serpukhovskaya Street, someone from the crowd recognized this woman as the person who had shot Comrade Lenin. After this I asked her again: "Did you shoot Comrade Lenin?" She replied in the affirmative, refusing to name the party on whose orders she did the shooting.... In the military commissariat of the Zamoskvoretsky district, this woman, whom I had arrested, named herself as Kaplan and confessed to attempting to assassinate Comrade Lenin.[17]

Lenin's driver, Gil, did not see the assassin.[18] Moreover, as it later turned out, none of the questioned witnesses who had been present at the scene of the shooting had seen the person who shot Lenin face-to-face and none of them were able to identify Fanny Kaplan as the guilty party.[19] There was only indirect evidence against her, and the witnesses' testimony was full of contradictions. Some had seen a strange woman in some kind of hat; others had seen a woman with no hat, but a kerchief on her shoulders; some had seen a woman in a short jacket, others in an autumn coat; the majority could remember nothing more than a hand with a gun. There were even greater discrepancies in witnesses' accounts of the perpetrator's arrival at the factory. Some claimed that she had entered the building several minutes after Lenin's arrival. Others asserted that a strange woman had turned up at the factory workshop even before the meeting, and that workers had seen her smoking constantly. The circumstances of her arrest were altogether vague: she had either been arrested immediately in the factory yard, or else she had had time to run away and was arrested at a considerable distance from the scene of the shooting. According to some witnesses, she had been chased down the street; according to others, she had walked down the street calmly, then stopped, tossed papers of some kind out of her briefcase, and then for some reason collected them again. Someone had even noticed that she tore something up in front of her pursuers.[20]

The first interrogation took place at the Zamoskvoretsky military commissariat. According to the transcript, which Kaplan refused to sign, she admitted that she was guilty of attempting to assassinate Lenin: "Today I shot Lenin. I shot of my own volition."[21] However, this response must be considered extremely peculiar. It could have been given only by a person who did not know when exactly the assassination attempt had taken place. The interrogation was conducted by A. M. Dyakonov, head of the Moscow Revolutionary Tribunal and member of the collegium of the Cheka, and Abram Belenky, the future head of Lenin's guard. Kaplan was requested to provide some kind of proof that she had really done the shooting. But she could not give any details about the assassination: "How many shots I fired—I don't remember." "I won't tell you what gun I used; I don't want to talk about details."[22] Kaplan further informed her questioners that she had been arrested "at the entrance to the meeting." Not "at the exit," as might have been said by someone who had just fired at Lenin as he was leaving the meeting, but "at the entrance." Naturally, her testimony that she had been arrested there also contradicted the recollections of witnesses who claimed that she had been apprehended at some distance from the scene of the crime.

From the Zamoskvoretsky commissariat, on Peters' request, Kaplan and M. G. Popova—a woman who was wounded along with Lenin—were taken in separate cars to the Cheka. Chekist Grigory Alexandrov rode in Kaplan's car; Zinaida Legonkaya, the "Chekist-scout," accompanied Popova on a Red Cross truck. At the Lubyanka, those arrested were met by People's Commissar of Justice Dmitry Kursky; Mechislav Kozlovsky, a member of the collegium of the People's Commissariat of Justice; Varlam Avanesov, VTsIK secretary; Peters; and Nikolai Skrypnik, the head of the Cheka's counter-revolution department. Sverdlov arrived later. Over a period of four days—from August 30 until September 2—more than 40 witnesses were questioned. The last interrogation of Kaplan that is known to us is dated August 31.

The Kaplan interrogations at the Cheka were dry and formal. All six were conducted during the twenty-four hours following her arrest and were very short. She was interrogated by different people who asked the same questions. Apparently, there was no doubt that she had carried out the shooting. But she had to provide all of the evidence against herself. The investigators had nothing incriminating: no one could identify her, no weapon had been found on her. Kaplan agreed to sign the transcripts of only two of the interrogations. She possessed no information that was of interest to the Cheka. One of the interrogations was described as follows: "The interrogation went smoothly, without complications; everything that was said was carefully recorded. Although reluctantly, Kaplan told about her childhood and her family.... And she said nothing illuminating about her participation in the assassination attempt against Lenin. How did she get into the meeting at the Mikhelson Factory? Who gave her orders and helped her by watching the scene? Who provided her with money and a weapon? Not a word about any of this."[23] And, naturally, this was not because the Chekists were incapable of beating the information out of her.

Popova, a common citizen who had asked Lenin questions while standing beside his car and was hit by one of the bullets, was treated in a completely different fashion. Her wound was dressed in a hospital; then she was taken to the Zamoskvoretsky military commissariat (where Kaplan was also brought); and from there to the Cheka jail in Lubyanka Square. She was arrested because of the testimony of police officer A. A. Sukhotin:

> About four paces from Lenin, a woman was lying on the ground. She looked about 40 years old. She was crying, "I'm wounded, I'm wounded," while people in the crowd were shouting, "She's the killer." I rushed to this woman.[24]

On the morning of August 31, Popova's husband and two daughters were also arrested and put in the Cheka jail. *Izvestiya* reported: "On the day of the fateful assassination attempt against Comrade Lenin, Popova was wounded by a bullet that went through her left breast, shattering a bone on her left side. Her two daughters and husband were arrested, but soon released."[25] Nikolai Skrypnik, Cheka collegium member and head of its counter-revolution department, felt that parents could be arrested on account of their children, but "to keep the children under arrest because their mother was a victim is somewhat indecent."[26] And indeed, the husband and daughters who had been taken hostage were released by the beginning of September, and at the beginning of October Popova herself was let go, her case having been dismissed for lack of evidence. She was given a lump-sum compensatory payment,[27] and after Lenin's death in 1924 she began receiving a personal pension due to the work disability caused by her wound.[28]

Thus, the suspect Popova was held in jail and questioned for over a month, while Kaplan—who was involved in the assassination attempt and who confessed to carrying out the terrorist attack—was interrogated for one day! So what did Kaplan's role consist of? Many authors who have studied this issue have come to the conclusion that her job was to establish the time and place of Lenin's appearances at meetings for the actual terrorists who had designs on his life. After all, according to her testimony, she had come "to the meeting at about 8 p.m."[29] (and it was at this time that she was noticed by numerous witnesses). After learning that Lenin would be speaking at the factory, Kaplan "herself left before the meeting began and conveyed the information about Lenin's arrival at the factory to the local operative, who was waiting at a prearranged location on Serpukhovskaya Street. She remained behind to wait for the outcome of the assassination attempt on the spot where Commissar Batulin later found her."[30] So why did the conclusions which were easily reached by historians and journalists many years later fail to tempt the Cheka's investigators in 1918? For some reason unknown to us they preferred to consider her the lone gunwoman—Kaplan, who was arrested with an umbrella in one hand and a briefcase in the other, and, as was revealed later, with nails in her shoes that made it painful for her to walk and to run.[31] Furthermore, the Chekists discovered another unexpected complication in dealing with Kaplan: she turned out to be half-blind and half-deaf, half-insane and not an SR.[32]

Could a half-blind and, apparently, not entirely normal woman have fired several well-aimed gunshots, late at night? Indeed, where did Kaplan learn how to shoot a gun? The experts' opinion is that "only the firm, well-trained hand of a professional marksman" could have "hit a target from a pistol (or a revolver) under such crowded conditions."[33] On September 2, 1918, Cheka investigator Kingisepp conducted a reenactment of the crime, staging the assassination. Gil played himself. N. Ya. Ivanov was "Lenin," Kingisepp was "Fanny Kaplan," and Sidorov, a trade union committee employee, was "Popova."[34] As a result, it was determined that "the shooter was positioned near the front left fender of the car, while Lenin was within a yard of the rear fender. The shots were fired from a distance of 4–4.5 meters, at an angle of 45–50 degrees, and most likely from the car's fender."[35] It seems unlikely that such shooting could have been done by someone who had no experience firing a gun.

File no. 2162, which contains materials pertaining to the assassination attempt against Lenin on August 30, 1918, has several pages missing: 11, 84, 87, 90, and 94. They were removed from the file and hidden from the eyes of future investigators because they contained the testimony of witnesses who claimed that Lenin had been shot by a man.[36] Lenin himself, who was never questioned about the incident, had also seen that the person who fired the gun was a man.[37]

The question of Lenin's personal security deserves to be examined separately. "The day of August 30, 1918, got off to a lousy start," Malkov recalled. "Grim news was received from Petrograd"—M. S. Uritsky (the head of the Petrograd Cheka) had been killed. Dzerzhinsky "immediately took off for Petrograd, in order to oversee the investigation in person." Lenin "was supposed to speak on that day at the Mikhelson Factory. People close to him, learning about Uritsky's death, tried to stop Lenin, and talk him out of going to the meeting. In order to calm them, Vladimir Ilyich said at lunch that maybe he would not go, but then he called for a car and drove off."[38] We should add: drove off without bodyguards. Moreover, at the factory where he was to speak, there were no bodyguards either.

This behavior—so atypical for the ordinarily cautious Lenin—was apparently dictated by the fact that on August 29, Sverdlov had sent Lenin the following directive, which was not cancelled despite Uritsky's murder:

> Vladimir Ilyich! Please schedule a meeting of the Sovnarkom for tomorrow, not earlier than 9 p.m. Major meetings will be held in all districts tomorrow

according to the plan that you and I have agreed on; advise all Sovnarkom members that, if anyone receives [an invitation] or an appointment to a meeting, no one has [the right] to refuse. The meetings will begin at 6 p.m.[39]

On orders from Sverdlov, Sovnarkom member Lenin went off—without bodyguards—to deliver a speech that had been announced in the district in advance.[40] "Somehow it happened that no one met us: neither the members of the factory committee nor anyone else," testified Lenin's driver, Gil.[41]

Like Gil, we are also surprised: how was it that, on the day when Uritsky was killed, Lenin arrived at the meeting without bodyguards?

All this stands in stark contrast to the security that he had been provided with when he delivered a speech at the same factory on June 28. The event took place in the same hall, in front of the same several thousand people. Responsibility for supervising the security was assigned to A. D. Blokhin, military commissar and head of the Zamoskvoretsky garrison. He was armed with a mauser gun and a revolver. Lenin was met in military fashion, with an official report. Blokhin was accompanied by Red Army soldiers. Together with Lenin, they came out onto the stage. Lenin was embarrassed by such obvious security presence at the factory. He requested that the soldiers be taken away. Blokhin did not rush to carry out the Sovnarkom chairman's orders, but called his supervisor on security issues, Dzerzhinsky, since it was precisely Dzerzhinsky who had instructed district military committees and garrison commanders to provide security at meetings. Dzerzhinsky gave orders to inform Lenin that he, Dzerzhinsky, would allow the security personnel to be removed from the stage. And this was his only concession.

To identify the organizers of the attack on Lenin, it was extremely important to determine the time at which the shooting took place. This seemingly banal topic turned out to be incredibly convoluted. His driver, S. K. Gil, testified on the night of August 30, i.e., immediately following the shooting, that he had "arrived with Lenin around 10 p.m. at the Mikhelson Factory.... After the end of V. I. Lenin's speech, which lasted about an hour, a crowd of about 50 people rushed from the building in which the meeting was held toward the car and surrounded him."[42] It is hard to believe that Gil was mistaken and did not remember the time at which he had let Lenin off at the factory gates. If what he says is accurate, then Lenin's speech ended around 11 p.m. The testimony of police officer A. Sukhotin—which was given at 1 a.m. on August 31, i.e., immediately after the shooting—agrees with this account: "Comrade Lenin arrived around 9 p.m. In about one or two hours, Comrade Lenin finished his speech and headed for the exit."[43]

On that day, decree time was shifted back one hour. Due to this, witnesses' testimony could differ by an hour because of the time change. It is also known that Lenin was the last to speak at the meeting. Therefore, the assassination attempt could have taken place not earlier than 10 p.m., and more likely around 11 p.m., when it was completely dark. It would seem that Gil's testimony is the most reliable, since the transcript of Fanny Kaplan's first interrogation clearly indicates the time when it took place: 11:30 p.m. Assuming that her arrest and delivery to the nearest military commissariat, where the interrogation began, took 30–40 minutes, then the time indicated by Gil should be considered the most accurate. And there is another piece of evidence to suggest that the shooting did indeed take place at such a late hour: the meeting at the Mikhelson Factory was not the first at which Lenin had spoken. Before that, he had attended a meeting at the opposite end of Moscow, in the Basmanny district, inside the Grain Exchange building. Several people had given speeches, and his own lasted from thirty minutes to an hour. Travel time from one end of Moscow to the other must have been at least an hour.[44]

Therefore, Lenin arrived at the factory at approximately 10 p.m. according to the old decree time or at 9 p.m. according to the new decree time, and spoke for about an hour, concluding his speech between 10 and 11 p.m. according to the new decree time. To the great regret of historians, it is impossible to establish the time of the attack on him any more precisely. But it is the exact time of the attack that contains the answer to another puzzle about the organizers of the shooting. It is obvious that some time must have passed between the shots fired at Lenin and the report about these shots that was delivered to Sverdlov.[45] But Sverdlov's announcement about the assassination attempt was signed by the chairman of the VTsIK at 10:40 p.m. This could have happened only if the announcement had been written beforehand, if Sverdlov had been informed about the assassination attempt that was being planned, if he had deliberately allowed the terrorist attack to happen or perhaps was—through the Cheka and Dzerzhinsky—its direct organizer.

Another peculiar item in Sverdlov's announcement—in addition to the time of its writing—is its first sentence. After clearly defining the enemy of the Revolution—the Right SRs and the British-French hirelings; and after specifying to the minute the time at which the announcement was written—10:40 p.m.; Sverdlov was all too imprecise about the point that called for the greatest precision: the time of the attack itself. "Several hours ago a villainous assassination attempt was carried out against Comrade Lenin..." Meanwhile, no more than half-an-hour could have elapsed since the shooting.

Let us compare this text with the telephone message sent out by Lenin after the murder of German ambassador Count Mirbach on July 6, 1918, which was written at 4:20 p.m.: "At around 3 p.m. two bombs were detonated inside the Germany embassy..."[46] Lenin had reacted to the assassination of Mirbach after about an hour and a half. When exactly did Sverdlov write his announcement? When did he find out about the attack that was being planned or had taken place?

Yet Sverdlov's instructions to Lenin to attend the August 30 meeting without fail and the time at which Sverdlov wrote his "announcement" are not the only and not even the most significant pieces of evidence against him. The interrogations of Kaplan at the Cheka ended on August 31. On September 1, on Sverdlov's orders, she was transferred from the Cheka jail to a cell in the Kremlin, located under Sverdlov's office. We know about the details of her transfer there from the memoirs of Malkov, commandant of the Kremlin:

> One or two days [after the assassination attempt] I was summoned by [the secretary of the TsIK, who was accountable to Sverdlov, the head of the VTsIK], Varlam Alexandrovich Avanesov.
> "Go to the Cheka at once and get Kaplan. You will put her here, in the Kremlin, under reliable guard."
> I called for a car and drove to the Lubyanka. Taking Kaplan, I brought her to the Kremlin, to a semi-basement room underneath the children's half of the Bolshoi Palace. The room was spacious, with high ceilings.... Another day or two passed and Avanesov again summoned me and showed me a Cheka resolution: Kaplan was to be executed, the sentence was to be carried out by the commandant of the Kremlin, Malkov.... "When?" I asked Avanesov quickly.... "Today. At once."[47]

A page later Malkov indicates that he shot Kaplan on September 3 at 4 p.m.[48] And although Malkov really did not want to admit it, it is easy to figure out that, on the night of August 31 at the latest, Sverdlov interrupted the interrogations and took Kaplan away to the Kremlin in order to have her shot "at once." The perplexity of researchers concerning this matter has been expressed by one author as follows:

> Probably the reader has become convinced that many details about the assassination attempt against Lenin remain unclear, casting serious doubts on the generally accepted account of the event. What is remarkable is the feverish haste with which Fanny Kaplan was convicted and eliminated in circumstances that are so dark and unnatural that it is difficult to find a reasonable explanation for them. Why was she transferred from the completely secure cellars of the Cheka at the Lubyanka to the Kremlin? Even if we make allowances for the harsh conditions that existed at the time, it is impossible to understand why it was necessary to eliminate Kaplan specifically inside the Kremlin, where the Soviet government was located. Why was the Cheka's death sentence not carried out by

the Chekists themselves? For what reason did the chairman of the VTsIK assume personal responsibility for organizing the execution, appointing the commandant of the Kremlin as its executor? One forms the impression that the organizers of this execution were afraid of something. Kaplan's last recorded interrogation took place on August 31, and she was shot on September 3. Could she have, perhaps, begun giving testimony that did not suit the investigators and was for this reason so hastily transferred from the Cheka to the Kremlin? Could it have become increasingly likely that she would have to be returned to the Lubyanka? Could this increasing likelihood have been linked to Dzerzhinsky's return from Petrograd? Could this not have been the reason why the execution was carried out in such haste, inside the Kremlin, where no one could inter- fere?[49]

We shall try to unravel the reasons for such strange behavior on Sverd- lov's part. The basic facts of the case are as follows. A certain woman, who was referred to as "Kaplan," was arrested, subjected to several brief and quite general interrogations by various people, and, not earlier than August 31 and not later September 3, was taken to the Kremlin on orders from Avanesov, who was acting on orders from Sverdlov. In the Kremlin, she either was or was not subjected to further questioning, and on September 3 she either was or was not shot by Malkov. And since Sverdlov, for reasons that are quite mysterious, gave orders to "destroy the remains without a trace,"[50] we have no material proof of Kaplan's execution apart from one author's assertion that Kaplan's corpse was doused with gasoline and burned in an iron barrel in Aleksandrovsky Garden.[51] Malkov did state, however, that the execution had been witnessed by the Bolshevik poet Demyan Bedny, who was living in the Kremlin and who had come out to the courtyard of the Kremlin after hearing a strange noise. During executions, to keep the public from hearing the shots, the Bolsheviks would usually run the motors of trucks that were standing nearby (usually, the same trucks on which the victims had been brought). Commandant Malkov recalled:

> To my displeasure, I ran into Demyan Bedny here, who had come running at the sound of the motors. Demyan Bedny's apartment was located right above the car squadron, and he had taken the back stairs, which I had forgotten about, and come out right into the courtyard. Seeing me with Kaplan, Demyan imme- diately understood what was going on, nervously bit his lip, and silently took a step back. However, he had no intention of leaving. So what, then? Let him be a witness.[52]

But all that Bedny could have witnessed was the execution of some woman, who—he was told—was the Kaplan who had attempted to assassinate Lenin.

Recalling that the assassination of German ambassador Mirbach on July 6 was also directed against Lenin and carried out by the agents of the Cheka, the Soviet government could have again had reasons to suspect the Chekists, above all the Left Communist and opponent of the Treaty of Brest-Litovsk Felix Dzerzhinsky, of organizing a conspiracy against Lenin. It is possible that it was precisely for this reason that Lenin, Sverdlov, and Trotsky had considered it necessary, in July 1918, to keep the arrested leadership of the Left SR Party not in the Cheka jail, under the control of Dzerzhinsky, but behind the walls of the Kremlin, the key to which was in the possession of Commandant Malkov, who answered to only two people: Lenin and Sverdlov. He took no orders from anyone else.[53]

Let us note once more who was subordinate to whom. Lenin's assistant and secretary was Bonch-Bruevich. Sverdlov's assistant and secretary was Avanesov. Malkov answered to Lenin and Sverdlov, but he did not answer to Bonch-Bruevich and Avanesov. With Bonch-Bruevich and Avanesov, he was on an equal footing.

Had Malkov carried out similar orders in the past? The answer is yes. On the evening of July 7, 1918, he had taken Spiridonova and Sablin—members of the central committee of the Left SR Party and of the VTsIK—to the Kremlin and placed them under arrest. Ordering Malkov to remove Kaplan from the Cheka before Dzerzhinsky's return from Petrograd would have been a natural move if Sverdlov was not a participant in the conspiracy against Lenin and suspected Dzerzhinsky of organizing the terrorist attack. By removing Kaplan from the Cheka, Sverdlov would have been, first, preventing the murder of Kaplan by Chekists—above all, by Dzerzhinsky—who wished to keep her from testifying; second, preventing Dzerzhinsky from seeing and questioning Kaplan; and third, have an opportunity to question Kaplan inside the Kremlin and to find out what really happened. As it turned out, however, she was taken to the Kremlin only so that she could be shot. And here, of course, there is some missing link that makes it difficult to understand what really happened. After all, if she was executed in the Kremlin with Demyan Bedny as a witness, then someone must have really been in a big hurry.

We have only Malkov's word to prove that he carried out the execution in accordance with a Cheka resolution. No one ever saw such a resolution. Kaplan's execution was most likely never officially formalized. It was not even mentioned in the records of the Cheka's judicial committee. Nor is it very clear how the Cheka could have resolved not only to execute her, but also to order the commandant of the Kremlin to carry out the sentence. The assignment is too routine for such a distinguished revolutionary. But let us suppose that a Cheka resolution did indeed exist. Why would Sverdlov have had to execute Kaplan immediately—and destroy her remains? There is only one conceivable reason: it was important not only to stop her from talking, but also to forestall the identification of her body by the witnesses of the terrorist attack—Lenin, Gil, Batulin, and others.

If the description of the arrest of the woman with a briefcase and an umbrella makes it clear that she was not the one who did the shooting, then Malkov's account of the events suggests that someone (evidently, Sverdlov) considered it very important to cover up the traces of the crime: a destroyed corpse cannot be identified. After September 3, it was impossible to determine anything: whether the woman with the umbrella and the briefcase who was arrested by Batulin was indeed Kaplan; whether the woman arrested by Batulin was the same one who had spoken to Gil before the start of the meeting, prior to the attack; whether Kaplan was the one who had carried out the attack, i.e., whether she was the woman who had shot Lenin; whether the woman who was shot in the Kremlin was indeed Kaplan; whether the woman who was shot in the Kremlin was the same one who was arrested by Batulin; whether the woman who was shot in the Kremlin was the same one who was seen by Gil and other witnesses near the Mikhelson Factory; whether Kaplan was half-blind and half-deaf; and who exactly was shot in the Kremlin on September 3, 1918? The list of these questions is endless. With Kaplan no longer a living witness, and with her dead body eliminated, it was impossible to answer them. It was Sverdlov who closed the Kaplan case by destroying the most important piece of evidence—the arrested party herself. He could have done so only if he personally wished to avoid an investigation and if he directly was involved in the conspiracy. No other explanations for Sverdlov's behavior exist.

Nor was it possible, without Kaplan, to answer any questions about her accomplices. Yet Lenin had been shot four times with two guns of different caliber,[54] apparently a revolver and a Browning. Kingisepp had discovered four shells while inspecting the scene of the attack and reenacting the crime. On Monday, September 2, he was given the gun by which Lenin had been shot on August 30. According to some accounts, this was a revolver from which three bullets had been fired; according to others, it was a "Browning No. 150489," with four unused cartridges. It was this Browning that ended up in Moscow's Historical Museum as the weapon used in the attempt. On April 23, 1922, a bullet "from a medium-size Browning"[55] was removed from Lenin's body. All of this meant that two or three shots could have been fired at Lenin with the Browning, because the seventh bullet—a 6.35 mm type from Browning's 1906 model—could have remained in the barrel of the gun.

After the case was reopened in 1992, the Russian Ministry of Security (today's FSB) conducted a comprehensive criminal examination of the Browning No. 150489, the empty shells, and the bullets that had hit Lenin. But the results of this examination were inconclusive. Experts determined that, of the two bullets, one had probably been fired from this gun, but it was impossible to establish whether the second bullet had been fired from it as well. While conducting a reenactment of the crime in 1996, the FSB asked the Historical Museum for the woolen coat and the black jacket that Lenin had worn at the time of the shooting, the four empty shells that were found on the scene of the crime, the two bullets, and the Browning. (Lenin's coat and jacket had last been examined in 1959; the materials from that examination are stored at the Historical Museum.) The Browning was jammed and no longer worked. But when a comparison was made between the bullets that had been removed from Lenin's body during his operation in 1922 and those that were removed from his corpse when it was embalmed in 1924, it was discovered that they were different. This was new evidence that a second person had taken part in the shooting. Who was that second shooter?

Immediately after the attack on Lenin, on the night of August 30, Alexander Protopopov, a former Left SR, was arrested and shot. In March 1918, he had been the head of the Cheka's counterintelligence unit; in April, he became the deputy commander of Dmitry Popov's Cheka military unit. On July 6, when Dzerzhinsky showed up at the headquarters of the Left SRs—who were being protected by Popov—and demanded that Blumkin be given up to the authorities, Protopopov personally arrested Dzerzhinsky, using force while doing so, and dealing Dzerzhinsky several blows. After the Left SRs were destroyed, Protopopov was arrested; but by August 30, he had been released.

This is the first direct piece of evidence that a highly placed Cheka operative—whom someone had released from jail well enough ahead of time— could have also had some connection to the attack on Lenin. Obviously, a person who had beaten up and arrested Dzerzhinsky on July 6 could have been released from jail only by Dzerzhinsky himself.

On September 2, 1919, the Cheka received a "top secret" report from Goryachev, a Chekist who claimed that he had "heard citizen Neyman say that a certain Zinaida Legonkaya had taken part in the assassination attempt, and that in fact this Legonkaya had allegedly done the shooting." This was the very same "Chekist-scout" who had accompanied Popova to the Lubyanka in the Red Cross truck. Consequently, on September 11 the Cheka issued an order—order No. 653—to arrest and search Maria Fedorovna Neyman and Zinaida Ivanovna Legonkaya.

On September 24, 1919, Legonkaya was interrogated (Neyman's interrogation is not in the Kaplan file) by the head of the Cheka's Special Department. She indicated that she had been a party member since 1917, that during the October Revolution she had served as an intelligence officer for the Zamoskvoretsky military commissariat, and that in October-November 1918 she had worked "behind enemy lines." In the concluding paragraph of her testimony, Legonkaya indicated that she had searched Kaplan and found "in her briefcase a Browning gun, a notebook with pages missing, cigarettes, a train ticket, needles, pins, and various trifles."

This testimony must be characterized as sensationalistic, since it contains the first mention of a Browning found on Kaplan's person. It is equally obvious that Legonkaya was not telling the truth. The results of the search, which was conducted at the Zamoskvoretsky commissariat by three women—Legonkaya, D. Bem, and Zinaida Udotova—are well known to us from the recorded testimony of Bem and Udotova, given on August 30, 1918. Zinaida Udotova testified:

> During the search, we undressed Kaplan completely and examined all of her things in minutest detail. We held up hems and seams to the light; every fold was smoothed out. Her shoes were meticulously examined; the insoles were removed; the lining was turned inside out. Each item was inspected two or three times. Her hair was combed and smoothed out. But despite the thoroughness of the search, nothing was discovered. She dressed partly by herself, partly with our assistance.

More or less the same thing was reported in her testimony on August 31, 1918, by Legonkaya herself:

> During the search, on Comrade Dyakonov's orders I stood by the door with a revolver at the ready. I did not touch her things at all and only watched Kaplan's hand movements. The search was thorough, even the hems and seams were examined; the footgear was examined on the inside and the lining was turned inside out. Her hair was combed; her naked body was also examined, between her legs, under her arms. But despite all of this thoroughness, nothing was discovered. She dressed partly by herself, partly with help from us.

The items discovered on Kaplan included: a train ticket to Tomlino, needles, eight hairpins, cigarettes, a brooch—all kinds of trifles. "Nothing else was discovered on Kaplan," Bem testified. In every other particular, Legonkaya's list was identical to Bem's: a notebook with pages missing, cigarettes, a train ticket, needles, pins...[56]

Where did the Browning in Kaplan's briefcase come from, then, and why was it never mentioned either before or after September 24, 1919? It may be supposed that in September 1919 Legonkaya's apartment was searched, that during this search a Browning was discovered, that a fingerprint analysis had revealed that Lenin had indeed been shot with the gun that was found in Legonkaya's possession. Legonkaya would have either had to confess that she had shot Lenin (and obviously be executed) or to explain how she had obtained "Kaplan's Browning." And she did provide such an explanation. Going against all of the established facts, she testified that she had found the Browning in Kaplan's briefcase during the search (while no one else had seen it). Whether this Browning was No. 150489 or some other model is not known. All of this, however, is merely a working hypothesis.

Legonkaya herself was not even arrested. She was made to sign a summons to appear before the Special Department of the Cheka upon request and released. About her subsequent fate, nothing is known, but it is curious that her file was reviewed by the NKVD in November 1934, and it is difficult to suppose that, having taken up her case once more, the NKVD left her at liberty.

Rumors that Kaplan was, in fact, never executed began to spread in the 1930s–1940s among convicts in prisons and concentration camps who had allegedly seen her working in the prison administrative office or the library in the Solovki Prison, in Vorkuta, in the Urals, and in Siberia. Persistent rumors circulated throughout the 1930s that she had been seen in the Verkhne-Uralsk and Solikamsk prisons, and that later the warden and the director of the prison had even pointed out her cell.

Fuel was added to the fire by the memoirs of Comintern activist Angelica Balabanova. Upon her return from Stockholm shortly after the assassination attempt, she visited Lenin and inquired about Kaplan's subsequent fate. He told her that the answer to this question would depend "on the Central Committee." He said this in such a tone of voice that she did not ask about Kaplan again. "It became clear to me," she wrote, "that the decision would be made by other people and that Lenin himself was not in favor of executing her.... Neither Lenin's words nor those of other people warrant the conclusion that an execution took place."

Balabanova wrote that her meeting with Lenin took place "at a secret location" where he had been taken "on the advice of physicians and out of precaution." "Physically, he had not yet recovered from the attack," and "he spoke about his health very reluctantly." The "secret location" was Gorki, where he and Krupskaya went on September 24–25. Therefore, Balabanova's meeting with him took place at the end of September or the beginning of

October 1918. It is inconceivable that by this time Lenin did not know about Kaplan's execution, if only because reports about it had appeared in *Izvestia* and in the Cheka's newsletter.[57] The way in which Balabanova describes taking leave of Krupskaya seems even more implausible. According to her account, Krupskaya embraced her and "with tears, said.... 'How frightening this is—to execute a revolutionary in a revolutionary country.'"[58] Today we know for certain that Lenin was not afraid of executing people, including revolutionaries. It is very difficult to believe that one month after the assassination attempt Krupskaya—who had spent all this time beside the recovering Lenin—should have shed tears on account of the executed and half-insane Kaplan. It is even more difficult to suppose that she did not know about the execution. Unless she was talking not about Kaplan, but about some other woman? But then everything described by Balabanova would have been tantamount to Lenin divulging a state secret by, and neither he nor Krupskaya would have ever agreed to that. However, rumors that Kaplan had not been executed had to be explained somehow. Perhaps people in the camps had seen another woman who had been convicted for shooting Lenin on August 30, 1918? Perhaps this was the woman who really had shot Lenin? Perhaps the NKVD had reviewed the case of Chekist Zinaida Legonkaya in 1934 and finally arrested her, and perhaps it was she who became known in the camps as the previously "pardoned" Kaplan?

Taken to the Kremlin after the shooting, surrounded by doctors, Lenin was convinced that he was about to die. Bonch-Bruevich, a man who was loyal to Lenin personally—his personal secretary and the executive secretary of the Sovnarkom—was the first to come to Lenin's side, along with his wife, Vera Velichkina, who had medical training. Only in her presence were doctors permitted to give Lenin morphine, an overdose of which could kill a sick person. The first injection was administered by Velichkina herself.[59] According to Bonch-Bruevich's memoirs, Lenin tried to understand whether he was badly hurt: "'What about the heart?... It is far from the heart... The heart cannot be hurt...' Lenin asked. And then he said something very strange, as if he thought that he was being killed by his own people: 'Why torture me? Why not just kill me at once...,' he said quietly and fell silent, as if falling asleep.'"[60]

Lenin's attitude toward the official account of Kaplan's shooting was skeptical. According to Sverdlov, by September 1, Lenin was "jokingly" cross-examining the doctors. Of course, not "jokingly" at all—he had no time for jokes. He was cross-examining the doctors quite seriously, trying to understand what had happened and what was happening.[61]

On September 14, Lenin talked to Malkov. One can imagine two alternative scenarios. Either Malkov told Lenin that he had shot Kaplan on Sverdlov's orders and destroyed the corpse without a trace. Or, on Sverdlov's orders, Malkov told Lenin nothing. In the former case, it would have become clear to Lenin that Sverdlov was covering his tracks and that the conspiracy had been organized by Sverdlov. In the latter case, we must suppose that Kaplan's execution was concealed from Lenin in order not to compromise Sverdlov. But it would have hardly been possible to keep this information secret for long.

It turned out, however, that even wounded, Lenin could make things difficult for Sverdlov as long as he remained in the Kremlin. Lenin was therefore sent away from Moscow—to Gorki. The analogy to Lenin, Stalin, and Gorki in 1922–1923 naturally comes to mind. Officially, in 1922–1923 Lenin was sent to Gorki to recover. The last chapter of this book will show how he was in fact squeezed out of his position by Stalin, exiled, and died in mysterious circumstances. But it was Sverdlov, not Stalin, who first thought of Gorki, in 1918. And reading about Sverdlov's "concern" for the health of the wounded "Ilyich," one is reminded of Stalin's "concern" for the ailing Lenin in 1922–1923. Let us refer to Malkov's memoirs:

> Ilyich started getting up from his bed. On September 16, for the first time after his illness, he took part in a meeting of the Central Committee of the Russian Communist Party, and on the same evening he chaired a meeting of the Sovnarkom. Ilyich had returned to work!

What good news! Could the overworked Sverdlov finally relax? Not quite. As Malkov goes on:

> In those days, I was summoned by Yakov Mikhailovich. I found the head of the Moscow provincial executive committee in his office; Yakov Mikhailovich instructed the two of us to find a decent house outside the city where Ilyich could be temporarily moved, so that he might rest and recover all his strength.
>
> "Keep in mind," Yakov Mikhailovich instructed us, "that no one must know about this assignment. Don't tell anyone anything. Do everything by yourselves and keep me informed."

This was how the famous Gorki came about. It was an estate that had once belonged to Reynbot, the former city governor of Moscow (who had married the widow of Savva Timofeyevich Morozov, the protagonist of this book's first chapter). Sverdlov "gave orders to prepare Gorki for Ilyich's move," Malkov recalls. "He again emphasized that everything must be kept strictly secret.... Dzerzhinsky assigned ten Chekists to provide security at

Gorki, subordinating them to me. I drove them to the location....and on the following day I drove Vladimir Ilyich and Nadezhda Konstantinovna to Gorki. This was around September 24–25, 1918."

Visitors to Gorki were few: Sverdlov, Stalin, Dzerzhinsky, and Bonch-Bruevich. As would happen repeatedly in 1922–1923, Lenin was impatient to return to the Kremlin, but he was not permitted to do so. In order to keep Lenin in Gorki, major repairs were started in his apartment in the Kremlin:

> By the middle of October, Vladimir Ilyich felt considerably better and began asking more and more often how the repairs were going and how soon he would be able to return to Moscow. I told Yakov Mikhailovich about this, and he replied:
> "Drag them out, drag out the repairs.... Let him stay a while longer where the air is fresh, let him rest."[62]

Sverdlov's main purpose was to demonstrate to party workers that the Soviet government could function perfectly well without Lenin. All of September and the first half of October, Sverdlov and Alexei Rykov took turns presiding over Sovnarkom meetings. All other top leadership posts—chairman of the VTsIK and secretary of the Central Committee, chairman of the Politburo and chairman of the Central Committee—already belonged to Sverdlov. "Look, Vladimir Dmitriyevich, we're surviving without Vladimir Ilyich,"[63] Sverdlov once said to Bonch-Bruevich. Can there be any doubt that Bonch-Bruevich reported this conversation to Lenin?

It should be noted that Sverdlov was not the only one who was surviving without Lenin: the same was true of Trotsky. Speaking on October 1, 1918 at a joint meeting of the Moscow Soviet and workers' organizations, he remarked:

> Over the relatively short period of time from the moment when the traitorous shot was fired at Comrade Lenin until today, the position of the Soviet army has stabilized. Every day, the Soviet army is taking gigantic steps forward.

Trotsky told his audience that he had visited Lenin "yesterday," and that he was "certain that the two bullets inside his body were not preventing him from keeping track of everything and from gently prodding everyone—which, of course, does not hurt."[64]

In other words, the wounded Lenin was not too much in the way, while the development of the army in his absence was "taking giant steps forward."

In October, the repairs to Lenin's apartment were finished. Apparently, Bonch-Bruevich, Lenin's personal friend and secretary, was the only person who did not want Lenin to rest and breathe fresh air: he immediately told Lenin that the repairs were completed and that he could return to the Kremlin.[65] Malkov recalls:

> About three weeks after moving to Gorki, Vladimir Ilyich met me during one of my visits with a kind of exaggerated courtesy.
> "So, Comrade Malkov, will the repairs in my apartment be over soon?"
> "Well, you know, Vladimir Ilyich, things are not so easy..."
> He suddenly became stern.
> "...The repairs in the Kremlin ended two days ago. I have found this out... Tomorrow, I'm going back to Moscow and returning to work. Yes, yes. Tomorrow. You can, by the way, let Yakov Mikhailovich know about this. Because I know who's giving you orders. So, remember—tomorrow!"
> And, sharply turning his back to me, Vladimir Ilyich went to his room. On the following day, he came back to Moscow.[66]

Thus, with the assistance of the evil Bonch-Bruevich, who wished to do him harm, Lenin returned from exile, where he had been sent by the good Sverdlov in order to relax under the gentle eyes of ten of Dzerzhinsky's Chekists.

By this time, Bonch-Bruevich—and Lenin, who was getting his information from him—had another reason to enter into conflict with Sverdlov. If Sverdlov, the conspirator, had had plans to dispose of the wounded Lenin, then he had been hampered in his designs inside the Kremlin by Bonch-Bruevich and his wife, Velichkina, who were always by Lenin's side. And it seems too suspicious a coincidence that, on September 30, i.e., five or six days after Lenin's departure for Gorki, Velichkina died in the Kremlin, officially of the Spanish flu.[67]

The coded language of the memoirs left by members of the Bolshevik old guard who had managed to survive Stalin's purges is not always easy to understand. Bonch-Bruevich's recollections contain the following lines:

> Fall of 1918.... In the Kremlin, over the course of two days, three women died of the Spanish flu. Vladimir Ilyich was in the country, recovering from his serious wounds. After receiving news of the deaths of the women, he expressed the most heartfelt condolences to their families and gave instructions for providing them with assistance. Not a month went by before Ya. M. Sverdlov came down with the same Spanish flu.... One had to see how concerned Vladimir Ilyich was.... By this time, he was already living in the Kremlin.... Despite doctors' warnings about the fact that the Spanish flu was highly contagious, Vladimir Ilyich came to the bedside of the dying [Sverdlov]... and looked right into Yakov Mikhailovich's eyes. Yakov Mikhailovich grew silent, became thoughtful, and whispered: "I am dying.... Farewell."[68]

On March 16, at 4:55 a.m. Sverdlov died.

This outwardly innocent passage from Bonch-Bruevich's memoirs tells us a great deal. First of all, Lenin would have never gone to see Sverdlov if he had been ill with the contagious Spanish flu.[69] No less important is the fact that one of the three women who died in the Kremlin over the course of two days in the fall of 1918 was Bonch-Bruevich's wife—a fact that Bonch-Bruevich "forgot" to mention. And it is clear why he forgot: three people over two days in the Kremlin—that sounds more like the elimination of undesirables than death from the Spanish flu, even during an epidemic.[70] Finally, Bonch-Bruevich deliberately shifted the dates: much more than one month had passed between the death of his wife and the death of Sverdlov. We are forced to read between the lines and conclude that the quote from Bonch-Bruevich is not all that innocent, that we are being given to know, first, that Sverdlov eliminated Velichkina and two other women, possibly medical workers;[71] and second, that Sverdlov himself was killed—"the same Spanish flu"—but now on orders from Lenin, who had recovered from the assassination attempt of August 1918.

Sverdlov returned to Moscow from another trip to the provinces on March 8, 1919. On March 9, i.e., immediately after his arrival, it was reported that he was "gravely ill." It was believed that he had caught a cold. However, already at that time persistent rumors were circulating that Sverdlov had been killed, that he had been attacked during a meeting. In November 1987, a documentary was broadcast on Soviet television with footage of Sverdlov's funeral. He was shown lying in his coffin with his head in bandages. Who had struck him is open to speculation.

Several years later, in 1922, at an open trial against the SR Party, the Soviet government formally acknowledged the fact that the assassination attempt against Lenin on August 1918 had been prepared by Cheka operatives G. I. Semenov and L. V. Konopleva (who had infiltrated the SR Party on assignment from the Cheka).

In order to sort out this part of the puzzle, let us state once more what we know about the attack on Lenin on August 30, 1918: he was shot and wounded; the shots were fired from two guns; one of the participants in the shooting may have been a woman; there is no evidence that the woman who fired the gun was Kaplan; there is no evidence that the woman who was shot by Malkov was Kaplan; there is no evidence that the woman who was shot was the same woman who had shot Lenin; the real participants in the assassination attempt were not arrested; the organizers of the assassination attempt remain unknown.

So who were Semenov and Konopleva? Obviously, they were not SRs.

From the beginning of 1918, both of them served in the Cheka. Before the Revolution, they would have been considered classic provocateurs. Today, they would be called intelligence agents operating inside the enemy's camp, classic "illegals." For this reason, it is absolutely pointless to go over the particular SR combat units that Cheka agents Semenov and Konopleva operated in, the particular Bolshevik leaders whom they planned to assassinate, and how and when they intended to proceed. All of Semenov's and Konopleva's work was Cheka secret service work inside the enemy camp (the SR Party). Some of this work was done by Semenov and Konopleva outside of Soviet Russia, which they left without any difficulty and to which they returned just as easily, and everything surrounding the work of these agents—their stories about being arrested by the Bolsheviks, about resisting the arrests, about planned escapes, and their repentance—must be characterized as Chekist fabrications, aimed at spreading disinformation. All of this was in preparation of Soviet Russia's first open political trial—the trial of 1922 against the SR Party.

We have seen the example of Blumkin, Cheka agent and participant in the assassination of Mirbach. Blumkin was soon pardoned, formally accepted into the ranks of the Bolshevik Party, and spent the remainder of his life working for Soviet counterintelligence, principally abroad. In 1929, he was arrested and shot for illegal contacts with Trotsky, who had been exiled from the USSR.

Semenov and Konopleva had similar careers. On orders from above—and obviously these orders could have come only from Dzerzhinsky—Semenov and Konopleva were preparing to assassinate Lenin. If the Left SR Blumkin, who killed Mirbach, had put the heads of the Left SRs on the executioner's block, then Semenov and Konopleva, who were "SRs," were putting the heads of the SR Party's leadership on the executioner's block.

The central committee of the SR Party always categorically denied any involvement in the attempt to assassinate Lenin. In the spring of 1918, the provocateur Konopleva proposed to Abram Gots, a member of the central committee of the SR Party, to assassinate Lenin, Gots replied: "Give up not only the work you are doing, but give up all work, go to your family, and take a rest."[72]

Even if we assume that the scenario presented by the Cheka at the SRs' trial was accurate—that Kaplan had shot Lenin, that she had made preparations to assassinate him because of a resolution passed by the central committee of the SR Party, and that she had worked under the supervision of Semenov and Konopleva—then we are still led to the conclusion that the attempt to assassinate Lenin was organized by the Cheka, under Dzerzhinsky's supervision, while Sverdlov's suspicious behavior, along with his sudden death in March 1919, brings us back full circle to where this account begins.

In January 1921, Semenov formally joined the Bolshevik Party with the recommendation of Avel Enukidze, Leonid Serebryakov, and Nikolai Krestinsky—prominent Bolsheviks, secretaries of the Central Committee, and members of the Central Committee. Konopleva joined in February 1921. After the decision was made at the end of 1921 to stage an open trial of the SR Party, Konopleva and Semenov were asked to prepare the necessary compromising documentation. On December 3, 1921, Semenov finished writing a pamphlet about the SRs' subversive activities. The manuscript of this pamphlet, which is stored in the archives of the SR trial, bears a handwritten note by Stalin: "I've read this. J. Stalin. (I think that the question of printing this document, the ways in which it might be used, and also the [future] fate of the diary's author should be discussed by the Politburo.) J. Stalin."[73]

On December 5, 1921—i.e., two days after completing the pamphlet that was reviewed by Stalin personally—Semenov submitted a "report" to the Central Committee of the Russian Communist Party about the anti-Soviet and subversive activities of the SRs.[74]

On January 21, 1922, the Politburo of the Central Committee of the Russian Communist Party issued instructions to intelligence agencies to ensure that Semenov's pamphlet would appear in print abroad within two weeks. On March 2, 1922, the Berlin newspaper *Rul'* for the first time mentioned Semenov's book, which had been published in Berlin.[75] Immediately after this, it was reissued in the RSFSR. Back then, the Chekists had a simple way of doing things, so the book that was published in Soviet Russia explicitly stated that 20,000 copies had been printed by the GPU printing office at the Lubyanka.[76]

Like Semenov, Konopleva wrote a number of documents that backed up her own false profile as an SR-turncoat, and traitor, who had gone over to the Soviet government. For the Chekists, it was important to have materials in the archives that showed that Konopleva (like Semenov) was a former SR and not just a Cheka operative. On January 15–16, she produced those documents. On January 15, 1922, she wrote a letter to the central committee of the SR Party where she let it be known that she was "informing the Central Committee of the Russian Communist Party about the military, combat, and terrorist activities of the SRs from the end of 1917 until the end of 1918 in St. Petersburg and Moscow."[77] On the same day, Konopleva gave elaborate testimony that the central committee of the SR Party had prepared terrorist attacks against Volodarsky, Uritsky, Trotsky, Zinoviev, and Lenin. In other words, she signed a death sentence for the members of the central committee of the SR Party. The letter's final words—"former member of the SR Party, member of the Russian Communist Party [Bolsheviks]"—manifestly spelled bad news for the central committee of the SR Party: Konopleva had been a Soviet agent provocateur within the SR Party.[78]

At the same time, on January 15–16, she wrote a personal letter to the secretary of the Central Committee of the Communist Party, Leonid Serebryakov. In this letter, she explained how and why she had gone over from the SRs to the Bolsheviks.[79] To accord with its contents, the letter would have to be backdated, to make it appear that it had been written before Konopleva joined the Communist Party. Apparently, this was the reason why it was decided not to use it, and the actual date of its writing remained. The letter to "dear Leonid Petrovich" was about whether Konopleva was ready—at this point—to join the party. In reality, it was written by a party member with over a year's standing:

> Dear Leonid Petrovich! I would like to have a talk with you, to share my thoughts. 1919 was the year when my old ideological worldview collapsed. And the outcome was that both in my views and in my work, I effectively became a communist, but considered it impossible to join the Russian Communist Party formally on account of my past. While still a member of the SR Party... I believed that it was our duty—mine and Semenov's—in the name of justice to open up to the International those pages of the history of the SR Party which are hidden from the masses.... The International must know all the dark, all the hidden aspects of the party's tactics during the Revolution. But how to do this, I don't know. This question, bound up with a difficult personal moral dilemma, stood in the way of my joining the Russian Communist Party. On the one hand, I felt that I had no moral right to join a party against which I had committed so many grave sins without telling it about them; on the other hand, I believed that that I could not reveal this information about my prior work in the SR Party without indicating the actual state of things, its connections to a number of specific individuals—everything was too tied up. I also considered this unacceptable from a moral point of view—plainly speaking, a betrayal of my old comrades. As much as I wanted to reveal my past to the International—an impartial judge—revealing it to the Central Committee or some other organ of the Russian Communist Party would have been unacceptable. One political party is no judge of another: both are interested parties, not impartial judges. Such was my belief. Before joining the Russian Communist Party, I told you more than once that my past prevented me from joining. But I decided to step over my past and I have joined the party, intending in my future work to compensate at least in part for my past, my mistakes and crimes against the Revolution.
>
> Going abroad, and reading the SR newspaper *Volya Rossii,* my old feelings returned with new force. This persecution of the Russian Revolution, of the Communist Party, that the SRs are fueling, by exaggerating and screaming about

the Russian Communist Party's mistakes, by trying to turn the Western European proletariat against us, by screaming about the horrors of the Central Committee and the Red Terror, has convinced me that the genuine face of the SR Party, its tactics, its crimes against the Revolution, must be revealed to the international and Russian proletariat in the name of the Revolution and the party.

I know that everything that is in the interest of the Revolution is permissible and just. The interest of the Revolution is our truth, our morality, and when Semenov and I discussed this question prior to his departure for Russia, we both decided that if the interest of the Revolution demands it, then we must, we are obligated to do this, even if it is unacceptable from the point of view of human morality... Just as a terrorist attack must be followed by the physical death of its perpetrator, so this action must be followed by a moral death. Or perhaps the death of the old morality? That is something I still do not know. Anything is possible. I know only one thing—everything must be done in the name of the Revolution!

I have asked myself, trying to test myself, whether maybe it is so difficult, so torturous for me to submit a request to the Central Committee of the Russian Communist Party because I still have something in common with the SRs, some kind of connection. In response to that, I told myself, and I am telling you: there is no connection left. As they are the enemies of the Revolution, the enemies of the Russian Communist Party, so they are also my enemies...

Dear Leonid Petrovich, I do not know whether you will be able to make sense of what I have written... I am completely alone here. I have tried to get to the bottom of this question, and frankly speaking, I have become completely confused about moral issues...

> All my very best to you.
> Lida
> January 15, 1922

Added to the letter:

> ...I am writing all of this to you as a comrade whom I value and respect, and as one human being to another. I repeat once more that I have not the least doubt or hesitation about what I must, what I personally must do for the Revolution; but to combine this with morality and ethics is something that I don't know how to do, can't do, and am afraid to do.
>
> Please forgive such a confused letter and write to me. January 16, 1922.
>
> > Lida
>
> P. S. In any event, let me know...that you have received the report and the letter. Please do this without fail.[80]

What is remarkable is both the fact that Konopleva, a former terrorist, who was supposed to have killed Bolsheviks, addresses the secretary of the

Central Committee "Dear Leonid Petrovich," and the fact that she is examining the question of her joining the party not in terms of whether or not the Bolsheviks will accept her, but in terms of whether she herself is morally prepared to join the party. Obviously, this letter is an unused rough draft, a part of the overall scenario of the SRs' trial. But it is addressed to an old close acquaintance, if not a friend. This is corroborated by the memoirs of Serebryakov's wife:

> It was quite typical that Lydia Konopleva, the Right SR who revealed her party's plans, who prepared terrorist attacks (the trial of Gots and others was heard around the world), came specifically to Serebryakov for a confessional conversation and made him the first to know everything that she knew about the bloody designs of her former party comrades. Subsequently, she constantly visited us: a quiet, blonde woman with an unremarkable appearance, who looked like a country teacher, and had a heavy look in her lightly tinted, womanly eyes. As it turned out, underneath this commonplace unattractiveness she concealed a tempestuous temperament and the slippery and detail-oriented mind of a cunning conspirator. She and her friend (I have forgotten his name) [Semenov] genuinely revered Serebryakov. After the SRs' trials, both of them went abroad on secret assignments.[81]

It is obvious that Serebryakov, the secretary of the Central Committee, could have been friends with Konopleva only if she was and remained a Communist. He could not have been friendly with a former militant SR. As for frequent visitors to Serebryakov's home with whom he was friendly:

> A great brotherly love over many years connected Sverdlov with Leonid. They had spent a long time together in exile, and had worked together from the first days of the October Revolution. Sverdlov's large family—his sisters, brothers, wife—continued to maintain close, friendly relations with Leonid after Yakov Mikhailovich's death.[82]

Thus, his best friend was Sverdlov. We read further: "Valery Mezhlauk once told me after quarrelling with Leonid over some trifle, both were serving as deputies for People's Commissar of Transport Dzerzhinsky that Leonid was wily and deceitful."[83]

What interests us here is not the personal characterization—which came from someone whose opinion may not have been entirely objective—but the fact that Serebryakov had been taken on as a deputy by Dzerzhinsky. The clear inference is that he was his right-hand man. Their work together was reinforced by friendly personal relations. Serebryakov's wife writes:

> Among Leonid's closest friends were very many Georgians, Abkhazians, and Armenians.... Gifts would constantly arrive from Tbilisi, Kutaisi, Yerevan—

wines, grapes, churchkhela, cheeses, and honey—which we, in turn, would give out to such intimate friends of Leonid's as Dzerzhinsky, Grigory Belenky, Bukharin, Voronsky, Sergei Zorin, Rudzutak, A. S. Enukidze, and Kalinin. It was a rare evening when one of these people did not visit us, and in the days of plenary meetings and congresses, a good dozen people would sleep over at our house.[84]

Thus, during the years 1918–1923, Serebryakov was friends with Sverdlov and Dzerzhinsky. And his home, which was visited daily by the likes of Dzerzhinsky, Bukharin, and Kalinin, was also visited by former SRs Konopleva and Semenov, who, on orders from the central committee of the Right SR Party, were preparing an attack on Lenin, which on August 30, 1918, almost ended his life. Can there be any doubt that Konopleva and Semenov were ordinary Soviet intelligence officers, operatives out of Dzerzhinsky's agency?

During the years 1922–1924, Konopleva served in the fourth directorate of Red Army headquarters; gave lectures on planting explosives to GPU operatives;[85] and then worked for the Moscow department of public education, in the publishing houses *Rabotnik prosvesscheniya* and *Transpechat'*. She was arrested in Moscow on April 30, 1937, "for possession of the Right SR Party archives" (i.e., materials from the 1922 trials, which she herself had helped to prepare), accused of having ties to Bukharin and Semenov, she was shot on July 13, 1913, and rehabilitated "for lack of a chargeable offense"[86] on August 20, 1960.

Semenov worked in the intelligence directorate of the Red Army. His major assignments in 1922 included organizing terrorist attacks against Kolchak and Denikin. In 1927, he was sent to China as a resident agent for Soviet intelligence. On February 11, 1937, he was arrested and charged with participating in an anti-Soviet right-wing organization since 1928, of having ties to Bukharin, being the leader of a "right-wing combat and terrorist organization," "organizing former militant SRs into a number of terrorist groups" on Bukharin's orders, "using these groups to prepare terrorist attacks against the All-Union Communist Party [Bolsheviks] and the Soviet government." On October 8, 1937, the Supreme Court's military tribunal sentenced him to death and executed him on the same day. On August 22, 1961, he was rehabilitated. The military tribunal ended his case because the charges against him could not be proved:

> An examination of the case has established that after 1918 Semenov did not create any terrorist groups and was not connected with the SRs. After his arrest on February 11, 1937, Semenov denied his guilt until June 15, 1937, and on June

4, 1937, during a confrontation with the convicted K. A. Usov, who was providing evidence against him, said: "You have worn Usov down with threats. Look at his appearance! That's why he's giving such evidence." For this comment, Semenov was put in solitary confinement, after which on June 15, 1937, he wrote a declaration, addressed to People's Commissar of Internal Affairs N. I. Yezhov, in which he admitted his guilt and promised to provide detailed testimony. The examination then established that in 1939, former NKVD agent M. L. Gatov, who had supervised the investigation and interrogated Semenov, was convicted for falsifying evidence and engaging in anti-Soviet activity in the organs of the NKVD.

Thus, the organizers of the attack on Lenin in August 1918 were rehabilitated in the USSR, not as part of the general wave of rehabilitations in 1956, when victims of Stalinist terror were being rehabilitated en masse, but through individual resolutions of the military tribunal in 1960 and 1961.

Claims that top Soviet leaders had some relation to the attack on Lenin in 1918 were first heard in 1938, during Bukharin's trial. In the spring of 1918, after the signing of the Treaty of Brest-Litovsk, the Left SRs started talking about forming a party together with the Left Communists in opposition to Lenin. To this end, they intended to "arrest the Sovnarkom," with Lenin at its head, declare war on Germany, and immediately release the arrested members of the Sovnarkom to form a new government with those who supported a revolutionary war. Pyatakov was to be appointed the head of the new Sovnarkom. The Left Communists themselves described those days as follows:

> On the issue of the Treaty of Brest-Litovsk, as is well known, at one time the situation in the Central Committee of the party was such that the opponents of the Treaty of Brest-Litovsk formed a majority in the Central Committee.... During a meeting of the VTsIK at the Tauride Palace, while Lenin was delivering a report on Brest-Litovsk, Pyatakov and Bukharin were approached by the Left SR Kamkov, [who]...half-jokingly said: "So what are you going to do if you get a majority in the party? Because in that case, Lenin will leave, and we and you will have to form a new Sovnarkom. In that case, I think that we will elect Comrade Pyatakov to be the head of the Sovnarkom."... After the signing of the Brest-Litovsk treaty...Comrade Radek came by...Proshyan's office in order to have some Left Communist resolution sent by radio. Laughing, Proshyan said to Comrade Radek: "All of you write resolutions. Wouldn't it be easier to arrest Lenin for a day, declare war on the Germans, and then again to unanimously elect Comrade Lenin as head of the Sovnarkom?" Proshyan was saying that, naturally, Lenin, as a revolutionary, if he were forced to put up a defense against the advancing Germans, while constantly berating both us and you ("you"—the Left Communists), would nonetheless be better than anyone else at conducting a defensive war.[87]

As early as January 1937 the GPU began collecting compromising information for Bukharin's trial. It was at this point that it remembered the old plan to "arrest" Lenin for a day and the names of Semenov and Konopleva. Both Soviet counterintelligence agents were arrested and, on instructions from the NKVD, provided compromising information against Bukharin, which was then presented to him in February 1937. His position was made worse because he had been among those who, by a resolution of the Central Committee, had given Konopleva a formal recommendation when she joined the party in 1921; and that in 1922, also by a resolution Central Committee, he had acted as defense counsel for Semenov during the SR trial, when the Soviet intelligence agent Semenov, on trial with the SRs, provided testimony that the Bolsheviks needed against them. On February 20, 1937, Bukharin tried to clear himself in a letter to the plenum of the Central Committee:

> I cannot pass by the monstrous charge against me that I allegedly gave Semenov terrorist directives.... No mention is made here of the fact that Semenov was a Communist, a party member.... I defended Semenov in accordance with a resolution by the Central Committee of the party. Our party believed that Semenov had done it a great service and accepted him into its ranks.... Semenov effectively gave away all of the SRs' combat groups to the Soviet government and the party. All of the SRs who remained SRs considered him a "Bolshevik provocateur." He appeared in the role of an informer at the trial against the SRs also. The SRs hated him and avoided him like the plague.[88]

During the preparations for the Bukharin trial Stalin was least of all interested in the truth, Bukharin's denial therefore changed nothing, and at the trial of the "anti-Soviet bloc of rightists and Trotskyites" in 1938, government prosecutor Andrei Vyshinsky continued to claim that Semenov had received terrorist directives from Bukharin personally. Later, the *Great Soviet Encyclopedia*, published under Stalin, added the finishing touches:

> By now it has been incontrovertibly proven that heinous Trotskyite-Bukharinite traitors were also involved in preparing the killing of the great Lenin. Moreover, the loathsome scoundrel Bukharin was an active organizer of the villainous assassination attempt against Lenin, which had been prepared by the Right SRs and took place on August 30, 1918. On that day, Lenin spoke at a workers' meeting in the Mikhelson Factory. While leaving the factory, he was gravely wounded by Kaplan, a White-SR terrorist. Two poisoned bullets had struck Lenin. His life was in danger.[89]

In 1938, many were surprised by the fact that Bukharin did not deny this most frightening of all accusations against him.[90] And here is why. The

NKVD prepared for the Bukharin trial with the utmost seriousness. And during the trial, the NKVD stood ready to introduce two important new witnesses: V. A. Novikov and...Fanny Kaplan.

On December 15, 1937, NKVD investigators had questioned former SR Vasily Novikov, who had been arrested long before. According to Semenov's allegations, Novikov had been one of the main participants in the attack on Lenin on August 30, 1918. Dressed as a sailor, he had made two appearances on the scene: he had caused congestion near the exit as Lenin was leaving the building; and after Lenin had been shot and was lying on the ground, he ran toward him with a revolver in order to finish him off but did not reach him and failed to do so. After the shooting, Novikov had allegedly escaped in a cab that was waiting for him, and after being arrested he had somehow managed not to get shot—although he should have shared "Kaplan's" fate for taking part in the terrorist attack—but was released instead. In short, Vasily Novikov was not involved in the attack on Lenin.

As a former SR, Novikov ultimately ended up in prison. In 1937, before the Bukharin trial, the NKVD remembered him:

Excerpt from the transcript of the interrogation of the convict Vasily Alexeyevich Novikov, born 1883, from December 15, 1937.

Question: Have you named all of the former members of the SR terrorist brigade with whom you met in subsequent years?

Answer: I omitted to mention the participant of the assassination attempt against V. I. Lenin, F. Kaplan, whom I met in the Sverdlovsk prison in 1932.

Question: Describe in detail the circumstances in which this meeting occurred.

Answer: In July 1932, in a transit prison in Sverdlovsk, during a walk in the prison yard, I met Fanny Kaplan accompanied by a guard. Despite the fact that she had greatly changed since our last meeting in Moscow in 1918, I nonetheless instantly recognized her. I did not have a chance to talk to her during this meeting. I don't know whether she recognized me—when we met, she gave no indication. Still doubting that this was Fanny Kaplan, I decided to check this and found proof that, indeed, it was really she.

Question: How?

Answer: One of the cells in the Sverdlovsk prison was occupied by Kozharinov, who was being transferred from solitary confinement in Chelyabinsk to internal exile. Kozharin had been recruited as a typist at the Sverdlovsk prison. I asked him to look through the lists of convicts to see whether Fanny Kaplan was among them. Kozharinov informed me that Fanny Kaplan—also known as Fanny Royd, transferred from political solitary confinement—was indeed listed among the inmates of the Sverdlovsk prison...

Question: From whom and what exactly did you hear about Kaplan in 1937?

Answer: On November 15, 1937, I was transferred from the Murmansk prison to the Leningrad prison, on Nizhegorodskaya Street. There I shared a cell with Matveyev. He and I started talking about my former work as an SR, and about Fanny Kaplan among other things. Matveyev, who was serving his sentence in Siberian concentration camps, told me that he knew that Fanny Kaplan—who participated in the assassination attempt against V. I. Lenin—was working in the directorate of the Siblag [Siberian labor camp] in Novosibirsk as a volunteer worker...

I have read this transcript and confirm its accuracy.
Novikov's signature.[91]

With such testimony from Novikov, it was safe to accuse Bukharin of organizing the attack on Lenin on August 30, 1918. Should the Bukharin trial have gone badly, the prosecution could have always introduced Kaplan and Novikov as witnesses—the former would have confirmed that she had received directives from Bukharin himself, and the latter would have confirmed that the witness on the stand was indeed Kaplan. For reasons that will never be known, Stalin decided not to use these "witnesses."

Tsar Nicholas II outside the imperial train on March 16, 1917.

Lenin in disguise in 1917.

Kamo returning from Germany
in shackles in 1909.

Left to right: Alexander Parvus, Trotsky and Lev Deutsch at
St Petersburg where they were arrested in 1905.

Lev Kamenev.

Grigory Zinoviev.

Alexander Parvus, whose real name was
Israel Lazaervitch Gelfand.

Trotsky.

Lenin at his desk reading *Pravda*.

The Bolsheviks in sketches; Trotsky, Zinoviev, Chicherin, Lunacharsky.

Kalinin, Sverdlov, Kollontai, Lenin.

Trotsky harangues the soldiers of the Red Army.

Kamenev, Lenin and Trotsky in November 1919.

Trotsky *(second from the left)* with Kamenev *(far right)* at the negotiations at Brest-Litovsk in January 1918.

Lenin and Stalin at Gorki. The photograph is probably a montage.

Lenin and Kamenev.

The Germans welcome the
Soviet delegation at Brest-Litovsk,
January 1918.

Yakov Yurovsky, the Bolshevik commissar
who carried out the murder of the Tsar
and the imperial family in 1918.

Lenin and Krupskaya in Gorki after his stroke in 1922.

Lenin recovering in Gorki.

The mansion in Gorki where
Lenin died in 1924.

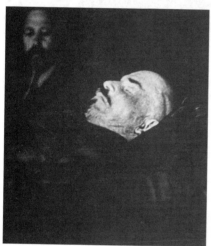

Two images of Lenin in death.

Lenin's funeral.

Dzerzhinsky carrying Lenin's casket.

Савва Тимофеевичъ
МОРОЗОВЪ.

21ᵍ Декабря 1904г.

Господамъ пайщикамъ Товарищества Московскаго Художественнаго театра. —

Милостивые Государыни
и милостивые Государи,
Глубоко тронутъ Вашимъ письмомъ. Всѣ мои старанія поддержать театру катиться подъ гору и спуститься до его теперишняго уровня были тщетны. —
Я считалъ и считаю сейчасъ, что дальнѣйшее участіе мое въ дѣлахъ театра, при наличномъ составѣ лицъ, управляющихъ имъ, совершенно безполезно, и я съ горечью ухожу изъ того дѣла, которое когда то любилъ. —
Отъ души желаю лучшей части пайщиковъ поднять вновь театръ до высоты, достойной тѣхъ хорошихъ побужденій, съ которыми работали лучшіе его участники и сберечь то огромное богатство, которымъ обладаетъ театръ въ лицѣ его талантливаго творца — Константина Сергѣевича Станиславскаго. —

Морозовъ's letter in his handwriting of 1904.

Suicide note found on Morozov's body but not in the victim's handwriting.

Въ моей смерти прошу
никого не винить.

ИМПЕРАТОРСКОЕ РОССІЙСКОЕ КОНСУЛЬСТВО
Симъ удостовѣряетъ подлинность …
… подпись …
… 2ᵍ … г. Казни
… Алексѣя …
Г. Ницца … VII дня, 1905 года
Генеральный Консулъ:

Two letters written by Krasin in 1917 and 1922 where the handwriting resembles the Morozov suicide note.

5.

Karl Radek and the Murders of
Karl Liebknecht and Rosa Luxemburg

The murders of the celebrated German revolutionaries Karl Liebknecht and Rosa Luxemburg on January 15, 1919, have been the subject of dozens of books and formal investigations by the German government. It would appear that in this case the facts are clear. But let us place this event in the context of German-Bolshevik relations during the first months of the Revolution and the picture changes completely.

The elimination of the leaders of the German Communist Party was useful to Lenin. Lenin's Treaty of Brest-Litovsk, however it may be assessed from the point of view of the interests of Soviet Russia, was undoubtedly a stab in the back for Liebknecht and the German revolution. A peace treaty with the Kaiser's government on the Eastern Front in March 1918 reduced the chances—such as they were—of a successful Communist uprising in Germany. Clearly, Liebknecht and Luxemburg stood for the defeat of their government in the world war, just as Lenin stood for the defeat of his government. At least since 1915, Luxemburg believed that the working class of other European countries lacked the strength to start a revolution and therefore that Germany's defeat increased the chances of a revolutionary explosion across Europe. A victory for German imperialism, with its enormous appetite and reactionary regime, Luxemburg argued, would set mankind back and lead to the demoralization of the international workers' movement. "Any military victory" by the German army, Luxemburg wrote, "means a new political and social triumph for reactionary forces within the government."

It was over the issue of the peace treaty that Rosa Luxemburg and the Lenin-led Soviet government had their first serious disagreements. "Her hopes that the Russian Revolution would bring the international proletariat to arms quickly faded," wrote Paul Frolich. "Rosa's greatest fear was that the Bolsheviks might play the German diplomatic game and accept a dangerous peace treaty, such as a 'democratic peace treaty' without annexations or reparations, in order to win over the German generals."[1]

However, neither Luxemburg nor Liebknecht could guess that Lenin's peace treaty would turn out to be far worse: he would sign an anti-democratic peace treaty with the German imperialists, which would include annexations, reparations, and additional agreements useful to the German government.

Naturally, Liebknecht and Luxemburg subjected Lenin's Brest-Litovsk policies to severe criticism, since they went against the interests of the German revolution. In the fall of 1918, this criticism became explicit and strident. "The old Bolshevism with its outdated objectives...no longer exists. Having abandoned the hope of an immediate revolution in Europe, it sets itself the goal of rebuilding the Russian economy on the basis of a combination of state capitalism and private capitalist and cooperative economic formations," Luxemburg wrote in September 1918 in the pamphlet, "The Russian Revolution."[2] Lenin's Treaty of Brest-Litovsk was described by Luxemburg as a "betrayal of the international proletariat."

However, Luxemburg did not confine her criticism of Lenin to the issue of Brest-Litovsk. She attacked the Sovnarkom's agrarian policy from the left: "What the Bolsheviks are doing must have exactly the opposite effect, since the division of land among the peasants seals off the path to socialist reforms." The terror unleashed by the Bolsheviks and the breakup of the Constitutive Assembly were characterized by Luxemburg as going against all democratic norms, freedom of speech, and freedom of the press: "Terrorism is only a proof of weakness, but it is aimed at domestic enemies.... When the European revolution comes, the Russian revolutionaries will lose not only their support, but, what is even more important, also their courage. Therefore, the terror in Russia merely expresses the weakness of the European proletariat."[3]

In other words, Rosa Luxemburg embraced a socialism that oppressed a minority of the population (as she imagined it, in "developed" Germany), while Lenin and Trotsky were building a socialism of the minority that oppressed the absolute majority and granted freedom—and even then, within limits—to only one party, the Bolsheviks.

It goes without saying that the Soviet government banned Luxemburg's pamphlet, while Luxemburg herself was subjected to harsh criticism by the Spartacist League—the pro-Bolshevik wing of the German Communist Party.⁴ Only in 1922, after breaking with Moscow, did Paul Levi, the head of the German Communist Party, publish the articles which Luxemburg had written in September 1918⁵—which, as he wrote, the party had ordered burned.⁶

A victory for the revolution in industrialized Germany was not in Lenin's interest, since agricultural Russia would then become secondary in importance, and Liebknecht and Luxemburg would become the leaders of the nascent Third International. What Lenin's role would have been in this scenario—since he had just signed a peace treaty with the German imperial government, and had previously accepted financial subsidies from the Germans, as was generally well known in Germany—one can only speculate. But it is obvious than neither the Left Communists in Russia nor the Communists in Germany could forgive Lenin for the Treaty of Brest-Litovsk.

Lenin's political career could be saved only by the defeat of the German revolution. It was for this reason that Lenin signed the Treaty of Brest-Litovsk in March 1918 and why he insisted on upholding it until the very last minute. Not by accident was the Brest-Litovsk agreement dissolved by a VTsIK resolution signed by Sverdlov and not by a Sovnarkom decree signed by Lenin: he was not prepared to dissolve the Treaty of Brest-Litovsk even in November 1918, when Germany had already lost the world war.

In order to hold on to power in Russia, Lenin sabotaged the German revolution. In his well-known letter to party and Soviet activists, published on October 4, 1918, in *Pravda* and *Izvestiya*, Lenin focused on two practical issues: the Soviet government had no intention of abolishing the Brest-Litovsk agreement, but it could raise a three million man army to provide support for the German revolution "by the spring" of 1919.⁷ In other words, Lenin was openly telling the Kaiser's government and the German Communists that at least until the spring of 1919, the Red Army had no intention of interfering in the German revolution already underway.

Paragraphs 15 and 19 of the peace terms read to the German delegation on November 8, 1918, in Compiègne, provided for the "repeal of the Bucharest and Brest-Litovsk agreements, as well as supplementary agreements... The return of Russian and Romanian money, confiscated and paid to the Germans." On November 13, Sverdlov announced the repeal of the Treaty of Brest-Litovsk. On December 14, the commander-in-chief of the Soviet army, Jukums Vacietis, sent a telegram to Lenin, Trotsky, and Krasin requesting support for units that were advancing westward into previously

German-occupied regions of the former Russian empire:

> The units that are advancing westward lack sufficient food provisions, especially bread. We advise you to assume personal responsibility and promptly arrange this matter so that the troops will not lack for anything. Report on what you undertake.

But Lenin was interested in exactly the opposite. His message to Trotsky's secretary, Sklyansky, read as follows: "Again and again: nothing to the west, a little to the east, everything (almost) to the south. Lenin."[8]

Only Lenin's lack of interest in seeing the German revolution succeed can explain his contradictory approach to foreign policy: extremely left-wing before coming to power, and then very right-wing immediately after capturing it. This did not mean that Lenin was against "world revolution." Only that was more important that the revolution should take place under his leadership. Not just the Russian Revolution, but the world revolution as well. Lenin had no use for independent revolutions, just as Stalin would have no use for them later on. Nothing illustrates this better than the history of the beginnings of the Comintern.

In theory, the Communist International was envisioned as a fraternal alliance among equal parties. In practice, Lenin intended to turn it into a foreign policy tool for the Soviet government. But it was difficult to hide these plans. And the main leaders of the world Communist movement came out against the hasty organization of the new Third International. "The memoirs of Paul Levi and other leaders of the Spartacist League show that Rosa Luxemburg was particularly insistent on this point: she did not want to allow the Comintern to become an appendage of Lenin's Central Committee," wrote to the well-known Social-Democrat and historian Boris Nicolaevsky.[9] Rosa Luxemburg hoped to revive the pre-war International, which had existed prior to 1914. Lenin was trying to split up the Second International in order to organize a new, Third International, under his own leadership. He therefore called for an international Communist congress. This was opposed by an influential wing of the German Communist Party headed by Rosa Luxemburg. She was a passionate defender of her views, wrote former Communist and historian Bertram Wolfe, but she did not resort to instigating splits. Lenin's method never varied: he fought for his view, splitting up those whom he could not control.[10] It was to this end that Karl Radek—Luxemburg's personal enemy from pre-Revolutionary times— was covertly sent to Berlin at the end of December 1918. How did this enmity begin?

Radek was personally an extremely unpleasant and totally unscrupulous man. The semi-conspiratorial conditions under which the Social Democrats operated in Europe led to constant wrangling, mutual suspicion, and endless intrigues. From 1911 on, Radek was plagued by constant problems. He was suspected of stealing things from his comrades, of engaging in financial improprieties, and even of acting as a provocateur and collaborating with the Austro-Hungarian government. As an Austrian subject, Radek belonged to the Social Democratic Party of the Kingdom of Poland and Lithuania. In 1912, Radek was expelled from the party on formal charges of theft. His case became famous because he claimed that he had been expelled from the party for political reasons. Radek was one of the most extreme leftists in the Polish-Lithuanian party, and his extremism created serious difficulties for the Social Democrats in Europe. Radek's case was discussed at the congresses of the Social Democratic Party of Germany (SPD) in 1912 and 1913. In 1913 the SPD passed a special resolution, as a result of his case, that persons who had been expelled from one Social Democratic party could not become members of other Social Democratic parties that belonged to the International Socialist Bureau. The German Social Democrats therefore tried to block Radek from entering the Russian or the German Social Democratic Party. However, the resolution was of little consequence for Radek's work and career. Radical newspapers continued to publish his writing. And Lenin had demonstratively taken Radek's side in this issue, writing an article in Radek's defense for the German Social Democratic newspaper *Vorwärts* (although the article was not published),[11] and admitting Radek into the Bolshevik Party. Radek remained a Bolshevik until 1936, when he was arrested by Stalin and killed in a labor camp in 1939. Joining the Leninist wing of the Social Democratic Party of Russia, he became Lenin's representative, particularly on issues relating to Germany, which Radek, according to his own admission, was an expert on.

It is not impossible, of course, that Rosa Luxemburg already suspected Radek of collaborating with Austrian or German intelligence, and therefore that the leaders of the Polish, the Russian, and later on the German Social Democratic parties fought for Radek's expulsion because of an insignificant theft. But having expelled Radek from the party, she had also become his personal enemy.

Luxemburg was not alone in her demands. The commission that clandestinely investigated Radek's activities was headed by Felix Dzerzhinsky, a Russian-Polish revolutionary and future head of the Cheka. Like Luxemburg, he insisted on holding Radek accountable for spending large sums of party and trade union money. But Dzerzhinsky did not speak out against Radek in public as Luxemburg had done.

At the end of 1914, in order to avoid being drafted into the army as an Austrian citizen, Radek moved to Switzerland. In Bern, he became friendly with Lenin and his group and embraced the Bolshevik party line on all fundamental issues. True, he did differ with Lenin on the topic of national self-determination and disagreed with his views on the transition from imperialist war to civil war. But at the socialist conferences in Zimmerwald (1915) and Kienthal (1916), Radek openly joined Lenin and Zinoviev as a leader of the radical group known as the Zimmerwald Left.

In 1916, in an article entitled "In the Grip of Contradictions," Radek polemicized against a certain Social Democrat who wrote under the pen-name "Junius," arguing that it was absurd to expect "spontaneous mass radical action" after two years of war. According to Radek, the Social Democrats could rely only on a rigid and ideologically monolithic party structure. Moving away from the conceptions of Rosa Luxemburg, which were based on the notion of a "revolutionary party of the masses," Radek had clearly shifted toward Lenin's idea of a "cadre party"—an organization of revolutionaries, with a mafia-like structure. It later emerged that "Junius" was the pen-name of Rosa Luxemburg. The enmity between Radek and Luxemburg thus came full circle, now also on a theoretical level: they were enemies both personally and ideologically.

When in April 1917, Lenin's group returned to Russia—passing through Germany and other European countries—Radek got off half way through. In Stockholm, he took charge of the Bolsheviks' international headquarters—the organization that was supposed to become the link between the up-coming proletarian revolution in Russia and its "most loyal and reliable ally," the German proletariat. In addition to Radek and his wife, the organization also included such well-known Bolsheviks of the Leninist wing as Ganetsky and Borovsky. Parvus (Alexander Gelfand), who rightly saw himself as a fourth member of the organization, paid frequent visits. Through Parvus, Professor Gustav Mayer, and the Swiss socialist Karl Moor—with whom Radek had been acquainted since 1904 (when he wrote for the newspaper *Berner Tagwacht*, which Moor edited)—the group remained in contact with the German government. It published two German newspapers in Stockholm: *Korrespondenz-Pravda* and *Bote der Russischen Revolution*. Most of the articles in both newspapers were written by Radek.

On Lenin's request, Radek sent articles on foreign policy to *Pravda*, trying to suppress anti-Leninist tendencies within the Zimmerwald movement and create an independent organization of leftists (he was assisted by the Italian Communist Angelica Balabanova and a number of Scandinavian leftists).

Thanks to their efforts, Stockholm became the site of a conference not of the whole socialist international, as the socialist parties of Europe had expected, but only of the Zimmerwald movement. But the Zimmerwald movement's attempts to publish a manifesto calling for a general international strike were not successful.

After returning to Russia, Radek occupied various posts in the Soviet government. His main work was promoting the idea of a world revolution. After coming into conflict with Lenin for the first time over the issue of the Brest-Litovsk agreement and refusing to support Lenin's Brest-Litovsk policy, Radek stated in a speech on October 7, 1918, following the start of the revolution in Germany, that only the German working class and the workers of Europe could help Soviet Russia finish what it had begun. "Without them, we will not win, and therefore it is our task to help them win. And therefore, comrades, we are entering the greatest but also the most dangerous period of the Russian Revolution."[12]

Radek soon received an invitation from the radically-oriented Berlin Workers' Council to come to the German capital to take part in the First All-German Congress of Workers' and Soldiers' Councils, scheduled for December 1918. Twice before this, in April and in August, Radek had tried unsuccessfully to cross the German border. Both times he had been sent back to the RSFSR. This time, the Soviet delegation that left for Berlin at the end of December consisted of five people: Bukharin, Rakovsky, Joffe (expelled from Germany on November 4 by Max von Baden's government for organizing revolutionary activities), Radek, and Ignatyev (the secretary of the delegation). However, German military personnel in Minsk refused to let the delegation cross the demarcation line. Bukharin, Rakovsky, Joffe, and Ignatyev returned home. Radek entered the country illegally, disguised as a returning prisoner of war, under his real name, Sobelsohn, which at that time was completely unknown. He was accompanied by two German Communists, Ernst Reuter and Felix Wolf. They traveled by sled, then by train, through Vilno, Eydtkuhnen, and Königsberg. At the beginning of January 1919, Radek arrived in Berlin and on January 15, Rosa Luxemburg and Karl Liebknecht were killed.[13]

Less than two months after the assassination, the participants of the first (constitutive) congress of the Comintern arrived in Moscow. Hugo Eberlein, the delegate from the German Communist Party, in accordance with the mandate from the party's central committee insisted that the official creation of the Comintern be postponed until the next congress. His demands were rejected. On March 2, the Comintern officially came into being, and the chairmanship of the executive committee went to Zinoviev, a prominent

Russian Bolshevik functionary who had not written a single serious theoretical work.[14]

The Germans found this difficult to accept. In protest, Eberlein even threatened that the German Communist Party would pull out of the Comintern. And yet, the Comintern was formed just as it had been envisioned by Lenin: it became an instrument to keep the German Communists in line, forcing them to submit to their Soviet comrades if only because the revolution had triumphed Russia but not yet in Germany. "Perhaps she would have spent her whole life arguing against the subjugation of German Communism to Russian Bolshevism," a German author wrote about Luxemburg.[15] But this assumption could no longer be verified.

Preparations for the assassination of Liebknecht and Luxemburg apparently began in November or early December 1918. During an investigation of Liebknecht's and Luxemburg's murders conducted in 1920 by the government of the Weimar Republic, Anton Fischer—who had been the deputy of Otto Wels, the military commandant of Berlin—gave written testimony that in November 1918 his agency began "searching and pursuing Liebknecht and Luxemburg to prevent them from engaging in agitation and organizational activities." On the night of December 9, 1918, soldiers from the second garrison broke into the editorial offices of the Spartacist newspaper *Die Rote Fahne*, intending to kill Liebknecht and Luxemburg. But they were not present. In the course of the investigation in 1922, several witnesses testified that already at that time Liebknecht and Luxemburg had a 100,000 marks reward on their heads. It had been promised by Philipp Scheidemann, one of the leaders of the right-wing Social Democrats, who from February to June 1919 was the head of the German government, and by his close friend Georg Sklarz, a businessman who had grown rich during the war as an army supplier in Germany.[16] Since the Kaiser's government only allowed its agents to grow rich on government orders, and since government orders were the simplest way of creating unregistered, secret funds to finance all illegal activities that the government might consider necessary, it was obvious that Georg Sklarz had been a German government agent since the time of the Kaiser.

Sklarz was also a collaborator of the famous political activist, revolutionary, and German government agent Alexander Parvus (*aka* Alexander Helfand or Gelfand). Thus, the plot to assassinate Liebknecht and Luxemburg was organized by three people: Scheidemann, the future head of the German government; Parvus, the German-Russian Social Democrat and agent of the German imperial government; and his collaborator Georg Sklarz, a revolutionary and a businessman. It was Sklarz who was supposed to pay a reward of 50,000 marks for each victim.[17]

It turned out that a "certain Russian baron" had provided funds to establish the Anti-Bolshevik League headed by von Tyzka. It was this league that had unsuccessfully attempted to assassinate Liebknecht and Luxemburg in early December 1918. With the permission of the city workers' council, in January 1919, the Guards Cavalry Division, which participated in the arrest and murder of Liebknecht and Luxemburg, occupied the Hotel Eden and established the Social Democrats' help service, the so-called Section 14.

In 1922, during an examination of the von Tyzka case, it was established that Section 14 had been headed by Scheidemann and Georg Sklarz, and that a reward of 100,000 marks had indeed been offered by them. According to the sworn testimony of Section 14 employee Hassel, its accountant Sonnenfeld, and officer Krasnik: "Fritz Henk—Scheidemann's nephew—confidently told us that there was a price on their heads and that the entire reward was in his possession." This was also confirmed by a group of Reichstag workers during the trial.

The order to kill Liebknecht and Luxemburg was given orally. It was stipulated that Liebknecht and Luxemburg were to be delivered to the hotel alive or dead and that those who would deliver them would receive 100,000 marks. Detectives searched for both revolutionaries, competing with one another. Prosecutor Weissman, who coordinated their actions sat in the commandant's office; he was appointed state secretary by Ebert in January.

These were the conclusions—rather unpleasant for the Germany's Social Democrats—reached during the investigation. It was obvious to everyone that the people involved in the assassination attempt of December 9-10, 1918, were most likely responsible for the murder that occurred on January 15, 1919. But there was, apparently, another person involved in organizing the murder of Liebknecht and Luxemburg on January 15: the Bolshevik Karl Radek. This conclusion was reached by the brother of Karl Liebknecht, Theodor, a well-known German lawyer and Social Democrat, who spent many years investigating the murder in an unofficial capacity.

The materials about his brother's murder that Theodor collected were destroyed during the bombing of Germany in November 1943.[18] Theodor evidently had no intention of returning to this subject. But in 1947, Boris Nicolaevsky, the well-known Russian historian and collector of archives, wrote Theodor Liebknecht a letter. Nicolaevsky was interested in a completely different issue, which was unpopular and dangerous at the time. He was unsuccessfully trying to prove that the revolutionary Social Democrat Karl Moor had been an agent of the German government, working under the code name "Baier":

The name of Karl Moor is well known to me. He was a German military intelligence agent and during his last years was associated with Colonel Nicolai. I have heard that he played some kind of role in the Swiss labor movement, but what interests me is the following: I have information from absolutely reliable people that this Karl Moor at one time (in 1917) had connected Lenin to the Germans and arranged the Bolsheviks' passage through Germany. On the other hand, he was also connected to Karl Radek and to Colonel Max Bauer when he [Radek] was arrested in Berlin in February 1919. I have every reason to suppose that your brother Karl met with Radek and Karl Moor in person shortly before his final arrest and had a very serious quarrel with Moor."[19]

In response to this, Theodor Liebknecht provided Nicolaevsky with information that must be characterized as sensational, which even Nicolaevsky refused to believe. The information concerned Radek's role in the murders of Karl Liebknecht and Rosa Luxemburg. It has not been possible to locate the letters from Liebknecht to Nicolaevsky that deal with this topic in the Nicolaevsky archive at the Hoover Institution; the correspondence between them is quite large, but it is mainly about Karl Marx. Nor are these letters in the Theodor Liebknecht archive at the International Institute of Social History in Amsterdam. Nicolaevsky tried to find Theodor Liebknecht's letters in his own archives, but without success. "I can't locate my old letters from Theodor Liebknecht, who wrote to me about the role of Moor (and Radek) in his brother's murder," Nicolaevsky wrote on March 24, 1962, to M. N. Pavolvsky, a contemporary and student of the dark pages of Bolshevik history, who at that time was working on German-Bolshevik ties during the First World War.[20] However, Nicolaevsky mentions this correspondence in letters to third parties. Since this is the only legal evidence against Radek— although it, too, must be considered indirect—we will provide a number of extended excerpts from Nicolaevsky's correspondence that deal with this far from trivial subject.

We should add that Nicolaevsky did not by any means immediately believe Theodor Liebknecht's stories. Radek's personal antipathy toward Rosa Luxemburg, who had insisted on expelling Radek from the Polish and German Social Democratic Parties, was known to Nicolaevsky. But this could have been precisely the reason for the rumors. The year 1947 was not the best time for sensational revelations of this kind. Radek, who had died in the purges, was considered a victim of Stalin's regime. Theodor Liebknecht had no proof—only the story that his brother had told him while fleeing from his pursuers. In the final analysis, Karl Liebknecht could have simply been mistaken: he might have imagined Radek's betrayal. Nicolaevsky said no more about the matter for ten years. Only after the death of Theodor Liebknecht himself, after the death of Stalin, after the revelations of the Twentieth Party Congress, and finally, after the publication in 1956, 1957, and 1958 of documents that revealed the connections that existed during World War I between the Bolsheviks (including Radek), on the one hand, and the Kaiser's government and its agents (above all, Parvus), on the other, did Nicolaevsky begin discussing to Theodor Liebknecht's conclusions in his letters.

The first such reference, apparently, dates from 1957. Here is what Nicolaevsky wrote to the former head of the French Communist Party, Boris Souvarine:

> I talked a lot about these topics with Theodor Liebknecht, who believed that both Radek and especially Karl Moor were agents of the German military. He assured me that Karl Liebknecht had come to the same conclusion about Radek. Theodor talked to him about it the last time they met. According to Theodor, Karl had been absolutely overwhelmed by information that he had received from someone at some point—Theodor did not know from whom. Theodor considered Moor to be the more dangerous of the two.[21]

Three years later, Nicolaevsky wrote about the same issue to Ryszard Wraga (Jerzy Niezbrzycki), who had spent the years 1934–1935 working for Polish intelligence:

> Radek must be dealt with separately. Theodor Liebknecht told me that Karl Liebknecht told him during their last meeting (a day before Karl's arrest) that he had learned "monstrous things" about Radek, who had just arrived illegally from Moscow, about which he promised to tell him the next time he saw him. They never saw each other again, and Theodor believed that Radek had betrayed Karl. In general, Theodor collected materials about the secrets of the German military. I should have his letters (if they were not destroyed...).... Do you know anything about the role of Karl Moor? Theodor Liebknecht thought that he was the German army's main agent among the socialists.[22]

On November 16, 1961, Nicolaevsky discussed Moor and Radek in a letter to Pavlovsky:

> Karl Moor was an old German agent (in military intelligence, I believe) about whom I heard a great deal from Theodor Liebknecht (brother of Karl). The transcripts of the Bolsheviks' Central Committee meetings contain an item to the effect that the Central Committee had refused to accept money from him, considering it to be of dubious origin. Moor introduced himself as a rich man and gave money (in small amounts) to emigrants who were in need, but he conducted himself poorly in every respect, and was treated with considerable dis-

trust. In 1921–1922, he really did come to Moscow, requested that the money which he had given earlier to various Bolsheviks personally be returned to him, and, I believe, got some of it back. But the reaction toward him was extremely negative (he was charged with seducing young girls from the Komsomol or something of the sort). In Berlin, he had a harsh run-in with the Left Communists, who practically accused him of being an agent of the Reichswehr. You must know that the Bolsheviks' old connections with the German military secret service were inherited by the Reichswehr. Theodor Liebknecht believed that Radek was responsible for the death of Karl Liebknecht. Theodor told me about his last conversation with Karl Liebknecht, who told him that he had become certain of the links between Radek and the Reichswehr, but could not give any details, since the conversation took place while they were walking outside. The connections between the Reichswehr and the Bolsheviks in general, and the connections of the period 1928–1933 in particular, are basically the old connection from the First World War. I consider 1909–1910 to be the beginning of all this, since it was at this time that the first links appeared between Polish Social Democrats from the opposition (Ganetsky, Unschlicht, and others) and the followers of Pilsudski, who were building the "Polish legions." The years 1910–1911 saw Lenin's break with the official leadership (Tysko [Jogiches], Rosa Luxemburg), which was opposed to deals with the military. Aas early as 1904, Luxemburg had warned the council of the RSDLP that the Japanese were giving money to the Finns. Tysko and Luxemburg were organizing the so-called Paris conference of revolutionary and oppositional parties (it was precisely for this reason that the RSDLP was not in Paris at that time), and the friendship between the opposition and Ganetsky and others. Ganetsky was the main *macher* behind Lenin's move to Cracow and all that followed.[23]

In a letter to the Italian socialist Angelica Balabanova from April 20, 1962, Nicolaevsky decoded what exactly it was that Karl Liebknecht knew concerning Radek:

> I now often recall my conversations with Theodor Liebknecht, who tried to prove to me that Radek had betrayed Karl. The day before Karl Liebknecht was arrested, he had met Theodor on the street and told him that he had information about Radek's ties with military circles and that he considered him a traitor. They agreed to meet on the following day, when Karl was supposed to tell him the details, but that night Karl Liebknecht was arrested and killed. For years, Theodor collected materials and told me that he was convinced of the accuracy of his brother's suspicions.... Moor also appeared in Theodor's stories as a person who, practically since the late 1880s, had been an agent of German military intelligence in Switzerland. Moor exerted influence on Radek, but the latter also had direct ties to Nicolai[24] and other leaders of German military intelligence.[25]

In 1962, Nicolaevsky began to write about Radek and Moor with considerable frequency:

> Regarding the fact that Karl Moor was a paid agent of German military intelligence over a period of many years, there can, I think, no longer be any doubt. I first learned about this forty years ago from Theodor Liebknecht. I think that Liebknecht also reported it in the press, in the weekly that he was publishing in Berlin at the time (under the title *Volkswille*, I believe), where he campaigned for an investigation into the murder of his brother, Karl. I should have Theodor's letters on this subject, but can't manage to find them at the moment. In any case, "Baier" is indeed Karl Moor. But here you come to the most critical question of the history of that period, namely, the question of how the Germans bribed the Bolsheviks.[26]

Nicolaevsky wrote several letters to M. N. Pavlovsky, who was then studying German-Bolshevik ties during the First World War:

> Theodor Liebknecht's stories are not about links with the foreign ministry, but about links with military intelligence, whose archives did not reach British and American secret services. And of course, Radek did not directly participate in the killing [of Karl Liebknecht]. The gist was that Radek had given them [German intelligence] Liebknecht's address and that, in return for this assistance, they saved Radek himself from arrest.... I must say that I'm not convinced that everything in Theodor Liebknecht's stories is wrong. He was undoubtedly an honest man, knew a great deal, was entirely correct with regard to Karl Moor, uncovered a lot about his brother's murder, with some good sources. That Radek had ties to highly placed people in German intelligence, I have no doubt whatsoever (Stalin did not shoot him in 1937 undoubtedly because he was planning on using those old connections), and therefore we may still discover much that is unexpected in this matter.[27]

With regard to the newly discovered documents in the German archives, many issues must be reconsidered. In particular, there is a lot to be said about Lenin himself, who had to know where the money that Ganetsky was sending him—hundreds of thousands and even millions—came from; and who knew even more about Radek. I often now recall my old conversations with Theodor Liebknecht, who tried to prove to me that Radek had betrayed Karl [Liebknecht]. For years afterward, Theodor collected materials and told me that he was convinced of the accuracy of his brother's suspicions. I admit, with regret, that at the time I did not take Theodor's stories seriously enough and did not write them down; but I must have some from his last letters from Switzerland. These stories also involved Moor, a person who since the end of the 1880s had been an agent of German military intelligence, that was seeking an alliance with the Bolsheviks for a campaign against France (there was another part which

sought an alliance with France for a fight against the Bolsheviks, it was headed
by General Hoffmann and later Ludendorff).[28]

For the contemporaries of those events therefore—the Social Democrats
Theodor Liebknecht, Bertram Wolfe, and Boris Nicolaevsky—the Soviet
government's interest in eliminating Luxemburg and Liebknecht was
obvious, and indeed was not exhausted by the agenda of the day (1918–
1919). Let us quote two long passages. Wolfe writes:

> On January 16, a little over two months after she had been released from
> prison, Rosa Luxemburg was seized, along with Karl Liebknecht and Wilhelm
> Pieck. Reactionary officers murdered Liebknecht and Luxemburg while "taking
> them to prison." Pieck was spared, to become, as the reader knows, one of the
> puppet rulers of Moscow-controlled East Germany today.
>   Leo Jogiches spent the next few days exposing the murder, until his arrest.
> He was taken to the Moabit Prison, along with Radek, Lenin's emissary to the
> Spartacists and to any German forces which the Russian ruler "might do
> business with." On March 10, Jogiches was dragged out and murdered, but
> Radek, having something of Lenin's governmental power, was permitted to sit in
> his cell, holding court for German officers and German heavy industrialists as
> well as German Communists, and begin the negotiations which led to the
> Reichswehr-Red Army secret military agreement, foreshadowing the future
> Stalin-Hitler Pact. In its way, the fate of the Russian emissary Radek and the
> "Russified" Pieck on the one hand, and that of Rosa Luxemburg on the other,
> are fitting symbols of the differences between Luxemburg's and Lenin's concep-
> tions of the relationship between socialist principles and power.[29]

In other words, Wolfe saw the elimination of Liebknecht, Luxemburg,
and Jogiches (and the fact that Wilhelm Pieck was allowed to live) not as an
accident, but as an entirely deliberate act, organized by the German and
Soviet governments through German military intelligence, on the one hand,
and Radek, on the other. This rather fantastic theory unexpectedly found
confirmation in Wilhelm Pieck's own recollections of the last days and hours
of Luxemburg's life. Pieck relates that Liebknecht and Luxemburg initially
used an apartment in Neukölln. But their work was too conspicuous, and in a
day or two they had to move. The move took place on the evening of January
14 and was extremely risky, since soldiers were stopping all vehicles to search
for weapons (this was the reason why Luxemburg and Liebknecht could not
leave Berlin). However, Pieck writes, "because of a betrayal that has still not
been solved, the White Guards had by the very next day already occupied
Rosa Luxemburg's and Karl Liebknecht's new hideout. When on the evening
of January 15, around 9 p.m., I wanted to stop by their apartment and bring

the necessary identification papers for both comrades in case the house was searched, their apartment had already been occupied by soldiers, and Karl Liebknecht had already been arrested and taken away. Rosa Luxemburg was still in the apartment, guarded by many soldiers. At the door of their apartment, I was arrested by the soldiers.... After some time, Rosa Luxemburg and I were taken to the Hotel Eden."[30]

When he was arrested, Pieck gave a false name. He was taken at first to the depot of the Guards Cavalry Division, and on the following day to a depot near the zoo, and finally to police headquarters, from where, on Friday, January 17, Pieck mysteriously managed to escape to neutral Switzerland.

But we will not accuse Pieck of cowardice, or of betrayal, without sufficient cause. It appears that he was allowed to escape. And if Wolfe is to be believed, this was by no means an accident. What is important for us is to establish that in Pieck's opinion, too, Liebknecht and Luxemburg were arrested and killed as the result of an "unsolved betrayal." An allusion to Radek's betrayal.

Moor was becoming a political traveling salesman who was trying to gain the trust of the Soviet government by diligently working on cementing an alliance, as Radek defined it, between German revanchist generals and Soviet militant Communists to collaborate against the West. This was an important period in Karl Moor's biography that begins when, on March 7, 1919, he showed up in Stockholm with instructions from Lenin. It was he who arranged the meetings between Radek and German military and intelligence officers, which Radek describes in his recollections about "November" in Germany.[31]

From his arrest in Berlin at the beginning of February 1919, Radek stopped concealing his ties to the German government. With the end of the German government's official legal proceedings against him on charges of engaging in subversive activities, Radek's isolation in a German prison cell ended as well. He still remained at Moabit prison, but he was allowed to receive a virtually unlimited number of visitors in the old apartment of the prison guard. Radek's "salon" was frequented by top-level German officers, on the one hand, and liaisons of the German Communist Party, on the other. Among the highly-placed guests of Radek's salon was Walther Rathenau, the future foreign minister of Germany, who signed the Treaty of Rapallo with the Soviet government in 1922 and was killed for doing so by right-wing extremists that same year.[32] Rathenau came to see Radek to discuss the terms for renewing diplomatic relations between Germany and Soviet Russia.[33]

Moor also brought Baron Eugen von Reibnitz to see Radek. The baron was a friend of Ludendorff's from the cadet corps. Having later lived for some time with Reibnitz, Radek called Reibnitz the first representative of "National Bolshevism." (The actual term "National Bolshevism" seems to have originated with Radek.) Reibnitz did indeed subsequently advocate an alliance with Soviet Russia aimed at liberating Germany from the Treaty of Versailles. However, National Bolshevist ideas resonated not only with officers and academics, but also with the German Communist Party, above all in Hamburg.

Radek's meetings were organized and false passports for his visitors were procured by his old acquaintance—Swiss Social Democrat and German government agent—Karl Moor, who had traveled to Russia shortly after the Bolshevik coup and with brief interruptions remained there for almost one-and-a-half years. In March 1919, he came to Berlin and tried to get the German government to agree to joint Soviet-German action against the Allied Powers and simultaneously became the main messenger between Radek and the outside world. Moor obtained the German authorities' permission to talk to Radek one-on-one and became his courier and go-between. A description of how meetings with Radek were arranged has been given by Ruth Fischer (Elfriede Friedländer, née Eisler), a prominent leader of the Austrian and subsequently the German Communist Party, who had moved from Vienna to Berlin in August 1919:

> Radek wanted to meet me and sent Moor to bring me to the Moabit prison. To my great surprise, Moor took me to the general headquarters of the army in Bendlerstrasse, where all doors automatically opened before us. An officer gave me a passport with an obviously false name and biographical information, and with this passport I had the right to visit Radek in his cell three times a week.[34]

In Ruth Fischer's opinion, Radek was beginning to lean toward National Bolshevism by October 1919. At that time, still in prison, he was preparing for the worst news from Russia—the collapse of the Soviet government—and hoping to reach an understanding with certain circles in the German army to secure protection for himself from Allied forces that might have demanded—and indeed did demand—his extradition as an enemy of the Allied Powers. It was at this time that he began receiving two prominent representatives of German (Hamburg) National Bolshevism, Heinrich Laufenberg and Fritz Wolffheim. Two months later, at the home of Baron von Reibnitz and in the apartment of Schönberg police commissioner Schmidt, waiting to leave for Russia, he discussed the idea of National Bolshevism with a German military intelligence officer Colonel Bauer and Rear Admiral Hintze, arguing, as he did in his "salon," that "Lenin wants an alliance with Germany against the victorious nations in the West."[35]

This was a continuation of Lenin's Brest-Litovsk policy. Its foundation lay in the clandestine German-Bolshevik ties formed before the Revolution. Its future became the Treaty of Rapallo, the secret Soviet-German military collaboration that successfully undermined the system of Versailles. Its apogee was the Soviet-German pact to divide Europe, signed in 1939 by Molotov and Ribbentrop. "The line of political relations between Germany and Russia, leading from Brest-Litovsk to August 23, 1939 and June 22, 1941... outwardly so capricious, is in reality perfectly straight—it is the line of a secret agreement, of a criminal pact!"[36] Thus ends the diary of Theodor Liebknecht, who had spent his life investigating his brother's murder.

6.

The Mystery of Lenin's Death

Lenin's illness and demise have long been shrouded in mystery. Yet it would be fitting to call it the starting point of departure for Soviet history. The view has been that Joseph Stalin may have had a hand in accelerating Lenin's death. At least, he has been seen as virtually the only Soviet leader who had no interest in seeing the chairman of the Sovnarkom regain his health. This chapter will show that Lenin had already been ousted from the Sovnarkom chairmanship by the middle of 1922, that the events that followed were tantamount to a government coup, that a wide conspiracy kept Lenin isolated until he died, and that the leaders of this conspiracy were, in all probability, Dzerzhinsky and Stalin.

In 1983, the issue of Lenin's death was addressed in an article by Abdurakhman Avtorkhanov, a historian who had emigrated from the Soviet Union during the Second World War. The article was entitled: "Did Stalin Kill Lenin?"[1] "Among the Georgian party elite," Avtorkhanov wrote, "... there were persistent rumors hat Lenin did not die of natural causes but had killed himself by swallowing poison given to him by Stalin. There are several versions of this story—Stalin was either supposed to have given this poison to Lenin at the latter's insistence, to save him from horrible torment, or else he was supposed to have poisoned Lenin through an agent-doctor... (who even had a name). According to another version, Stalin found a Georgian folk healer for Lenin... who did not heal Lenin, but medicated him to death with poisonous herbs. It is interesting that poison invariably figures in all versions of the story, as if Stalin really did bring Lenin a small vial of poison."[2]

Similar views were expressed by one of Lenin's American biographers, who wrote that after Lenin's death, communists who had known him would gather and whisper about the strange rumor that he had been poisoned by Stalin.[3]

Stalin's formal appointment to the post of general secretary of the party in April 1922 was not the beginning of his rise to power, but an acknowledgement of the fact that he had already concentrated unlimited power in his hands. Two factors had made Stalin's ascent possible at the very beginning of the 1920s: Lenin's ill health, which prevented this subtle psychologist of intraparty strife from noticing the rise of his political (and physical) destroyer; and Stalin's personal qualities.

Prior to the Eighth Party Congress, the position of general secretary was occupied by Yakov Sverdlov. The Secretariat of the Central Committee, it was said at the time, "was in his notebook." The Central Committee also had an executive secretary: this post was held first by Yelena Stasova, then by Nikolai Krestinsky, and then by Vyacheslav Molotov. Among the Politburo members who were elected after the Eleventh Party Congress (Lenin, Zinoviev, Lev Kamenev, Alexei Rykov, Stalin, Tomsky, Trotsky), Stalin was chosen as general secretary. Significantly, before Lenin fell ill, there were no political disagreements between him and Stalin. On March 28, 1922, Lenin publicly defended Stalin against Yevgeny Preobrazhensky, showing all of the delegates at the Eleventh Congress whose side he was on. Moreover, Lenin defended Stalin on the very issues over which he would start a war with him only a few weeks later: nationalities policy and the Workers' and Peasants' Inspection (Rabkrin).[4]

From December 1920 on, Lenin's illness is reported by many sources. On March 3, 1921, Lenin sent a note to Kamenev, which was published for the first time in 1989:

> I see that I probably won't be able to speak at the congress. The deterioration of the illness after three months of treatment is evident: they "comforted" me by saying that I was exaggerating... and while they acted so smart and comforted me and assured me, "you're exaggerating! hypochondria!"—they let three months go by. In a typically Russian, typically Soviet way. I will try to prepare.

But you should prepare, too. My speech is important for the congress and for the plenary meeting of the Central Committee. I'm very afraid that I won't be able to do it, neither here nor there.... I can't tolerate conversations and meetings more than once a decade, so to speak... Keep in mind that exchanging very short notes... is easier on my nerves (since I can think them over, put them aside for an hour, etc.). Therefore, I ask you please to get a stenographer and to send me (in front of the Politburo) notes of 5–10 lines more often. I will think for an hour or two and respond."[5]

To think for an hour or two over a note of several lines? This is no longer the Lenin of 1917!

Trotsky wrote about Lenin's illness: "Lenin's health deteriorated sharply at the end of 1921."[6] At the end of November 1921, Andreyeva visited Lenin before going abroad. She described this meeting—which turned out to have been their last—in a letter to Gorky on January 29, 1924, shortly after Lenin's death: "He was listening to something for a long time and then suddenly said: 'How young you still are, Maria Fyodorovna! You even have pink cheeks because you're nervous... You still know how to blush. Me—I've started to get tired. Very tired.'"[7]

Stalin—always observant—could not have been unaware that Lenin was falling ill. Note, too, that the year of 1921—when Lenin's note to Kamenev was written—was also the year that saw the beginning of the New Economic Policy (NEP), the second opportunistic step taken by Lenin after the Treaty of Brest-Litovsk. In terms of its unpopularity with the Communist Party nomenclatura, NEP could compare only to the treaty. More precisely, the compromise on the domestic front (NEP) was a consequence of the compromise on the international front (the Treaty of Brest). And since this is precisely what Lenin had been warned about by numerous opponents of the peace treaty, from Trotsky to the Left Communists, Lenin's proclamation of NEP was a form of deceit and a mockery of the party.

However, while during the signing of the Treaty of Brest both his supporters (namely, Lenin himself) and his opponents (namely, everyone else) were equally eager to point out that the treaty would not remain in effect for long, attitudes toward NEP were entirely different. In 1921, no one knew how long NEP might last and what its consequences might be. It is difficult to say how literally Lenin took his own pronouncement that NEP was being established "for real and for a long time." This slogan could certainly not have been received enthusiastically by everyone. A dispassionate analysis of the NEP system would make it obvious that there could be no peaceful co-existence between the all-powerful and well-armed, but poor and hungry communists, on the one hand, and the unarmed, well-fed, and wealthy "nepman," on the other. Either the communist would kill the "nepman," or the "nepman" would seize power away from the communist.

Lenin and his opponents took the lessons of Brest-Litovsk and used them in the intraparty strife of this period. Lenin was clearly impervious to open criticism, which he had been subjected to from all sides during the peace discussions in 1918. At the same time, he now tried to avoid an open discussion, which in 1918 had led to a split within the party and to his effective removal from power. With the apparent backing of the Politburo (whose support he did not and could never have regarding NEP), Lenin sharply changed the government's internal course, sincerely believing that in 1921 he had overcome his opposition more easily than in 1918.

But he was mistaken. Stalin's supporters in his fight against Lenin, which began in 1921 (but was not yet visible to large sectors of the party), came from faceless party functionaries, who found themselves ceding their power to the "nepman"—all because of Lenin. The New Economic Policy—the consequence of an earlier opportunistic policy (Brest-Litovsk)—was the last on the long list of Lenin's failures. At the top of this list were: the revolution in Europe, which failed to materialize because of the peace treaty; the defeat in the war with Poland (which was openly sabotaged by Stalin); the Kronstadt Rebellion of 1921; the peasant uprisings, the Tambov Rebellion is considered the largest only because of an accidental misunderstanding... Who should have been blamed for these disappointments if not the head of the government? And now this same person was deciding to place the party in another extreme situation—NEP.

Concluscions regarding the power struggle between Lenin and Stalin at that time can be based only on hints. On July 4, 1921 Lenin wrote a letter to G. L. Shklovsky in Berlin. Maria Ulyanova, one of Lenin's sisters, interprets this letter as Lenin's report to Shklovsky that he "was, so to speak, being undermined. By whom and how remains a mystery."[8] The mystery, however, may be easily solved by identifying the party member who was at that moment rising higher than the rest through the hierarchy. That person was Stalin. V. P. Naumov writes: "In mid-1921 the Politburo put him in charge of organizational work within the Central Committee. His job included preparing for Central Committee plenary meetings, TsIK sessions, and so forth, which meant that he was in essence carrying out the responsibilities of Central Committee secretary."[9]

On December 24, 1921, the party newspaper *Pravda* published a fable by the communist poet Demyan Bedny (Yefim Pridvorov).[10] This proletarian poet was an old party functionary. In 1910, he met Bonch-Bruevich, Lenin's future assistant and secretary. Bonch-Bruevich, in turn, introduced him to many Bolsheviks. From 1911 on, Bedny's work was published in the Bolshevik newspaper *Zvezda*, which was later renamed *Pravda*. In the middle of April 1912, Bedny met Stalin, Molotov and Sverdlov. During the same year, Bedny joined the party and, through an exchange of letters, became acquainted with Lenin, who valued his talent and did a lot to help him. In 1914, he met Gorky, then during the First World War, Lenin's sisters, Maria Ulyanova and Anna Yelizarova. In April 1917, he finally met Lenin and from April to June, he helped edit *Pravda*, without losing contact with Stalin. Stalin published an article in *Pravda* against Menshevik minister Tsereteli ("American Millions") and Bedny wrote a poem against Tsereteli ("Coalitional"). Stalin wrote an article in *Pravda* against Kornilov ("Conspiracy against the Revolution"). Bedny wrote a poem on the same subject ("Song"). After the unsuccessful July attempt to take over the government, Lenin went into hiding and Bedny, like Bonch-Bruevich, was with him.[11]

But the person to whom Bedny was closest was Stalin. "In the Kremlin, just as in the rest of Moscow, there was a constant battle over apartments, of which there was a shortage," wrote Trotsky, describing the year 1919.[12] As an intimate of Stalin's, Bedny managed to live in the Kremlin from March 1918 until the beginning of 1933, when he divorced his wife, Vera Rufovna Pridvorova, and moved to a private residence at 16 Rozhdestvensky Boulevard, leaving the Kremlin apartment to his wife. Bedny occupied half of this private residence. The other half was given over to the State Literature Museum, whose director was Bedny's old friend, Vladimir Bonch-Bruevich.

After the government moved to Moscow at the beginning of 1918, the entire Soviet leadership took up residence in the Kremlin. Lenin would drop in on Bedny from time and time, and so would Stalin. Bedny was also friendly with the Central Committee's secretary, Stasova, and he would visit the Secretariat, according to her, virtually on a daily basis. To rally troops on various fronts during the civil war, Bedny was given a private railway car (which had previously belonged to one of the grand dukes), and he seems to have been the only writer thus honored (the railway car remained his property practically until the 1930s). Bedny's awards were endless. In 1922, he was the first Soviet writer to become a member of the Moscow Soviet. A city in Penza Oblast—Bednodemyansk—was named in his honor, as well as a district in Odessa Province. The steamship *Demyan Bedny* was launched on the Volga. Bedny was given a dacha for his private use, in perpetuity, in Mamontovka Village. On top of this private dacha, he also obtained a government dacha and beyond his private car and chauffeur, he was given an official car with an official driver.

Perhaps the writer's biggest prize was his contract with the State Publishing House for the publication of his collected works. The contract was apparently signed at the end of 1922. The first volume came out in 1925. Up to 1934, when Bedny fell out of favor with Stalin, nineteen volumes were published, which included works written up to February 1932. In August 1934, speaking at a writers' congress, Bedny referred to the twenty volumes of his collected works, not yet aware that the twentieth volume would not be published.

Most of Bedny's writings were published in *Pravda*. Just how politicized his work was may be seen from his poem "In Defense of the Fable," written in 1936, after he returned to Stalin's good graces in the summer of 1935, when Stalin invited him to his dacha, stopping by his house in person to pick him up. Bedny spent New Year's Eve in 1935 at Stalin's dacha as well:

> And who can ever forget
> Whose genius it was
> That recognized its value?
> So that I should not aim
> At small game,
> But so that I should strike
> At hard-headed diehards
> Wandering in the woods
> And ferocious czarist dogs,
> The crosshairs of my fable
> Were often positioned by Lenin himself.
> By Lenin from far away, and by Stalin from nearby—
> While he was forging *Pravda* and *Zvezda,*
> When, looking out over the enemy's citadels, he
> Would point and say to me:
> "It wouldn't be a bad idea
> To lob a fable-missile here!

While giving Lenin his due, Bedny nonetheless indicated that Lenin was far away, while Stalin was nearby. It was clearly Stalin who supervised Bedny's work (if and when this work needed supervision). On October 17, 1921, Bedny gave Lenin his recently published novel in verse, *Tsar Andron,*[13] which he had completed on May 20, 1921. Critic N. V. Gamalii sums up this work as follows:

> The novel *Tsar Andron* describes how the peasants overthrow the Soviets and chase the Bolsheviks out of Moscow and Petrograd. Bourgeois parties immediately reappear in the country. The old czarist officials, industrialists,

bankers, and landowners return from abroad. The peasant czar does not trust them, but in order to fight them he needs to summon a workers' army, and Andron does not want to do this. Gradually, he becomes a puppet in the hands of domestic and foreign capitalists.... The people are once more in a state of bondage.... Revolutionary-minded workers, led by the Bolsheviks, overthrow Andron's government. The Soviet regime is restored, and Andron, dressed in sackcloth, flees from the palace in shame."[14]

Just as Kerensky once fled from the Winter Palace in Petrograd. In this way, Bedny was making a protest against the introduction of NEP, hinting to Lenin that he was turning into Tsar Andron. And since Bedny's protests were heard only under Lenin, and not under Stalin, we can conclude that he was not so much a sincere communist as an obedient scribe for the future general secretary. In the light of all these facts Bedny's fable "For No Other Reason," which was published in *Pravda* on December 24, 1921, needs to be considered:

> Vavila Anikeev, burly smith,
> Dropped by the lackeys' quarters one fine day
> And found them sobbing all, and so forthwith
> Said with great feeling: "Come what may,
> Your mistress is a vicious boor.
> Smacked you, did she?... Showed you all the door?..."
> "She'd never lift a hand to us, not she.
> Last night she almost died, sick as can be!"
> The lackeys told Vavila tearfully.
> "And here you're roaring fearfully!"
> "Indee-ee-eed we are!... The doctor, he was called.
> Paralysis is what he has foretold.
> She's soiling her own bed. Three days on end
> We've taken turns to watch our mistress dear:
> Bring things to drink, tuck in her sheets, stay near."
> "To drink!" the blacksmith sighed. "Oh, had I but an hour
> With yon crowbait, no drink but poison I'd commend.
> In Europe with the 'yellows' we'll have to reach a deal,
> Though not to last forever, I should add.
> And not, of course, so we could all together
> Help their mistress to regain her health."[15]

At first sight, this fable portrays a working man, a blacksmith who, entirely in keeping with the spirit of proletarian consciousness, offers to poison a dying mistress and member of the exploiting classes, while the politically unaware lackeys rally around her and grieve over her impending death. But the real subject was Stalin's plan to poison the ailing Lenin.

The "blacksmith" (who forges *steel* [*stal'*]) is, of course, Stalin. "Vavila," a Syrian name, hints at Stalin's non-Russian, Asiatic origins. The surname "Anikeev" relates to the legendary Anika the Victorious Warrior—another association with Stalin, who, while visiting Lenin (the "mistress"), sees the long faces of the Bolshevik leadership and thinks that they are miserable because Lenin has been reading them the riot act again. But it turns out that the doctors have determined that Lenin is becoming paralyzed. Told that the "lackeys," fearful of going on without Lenin, are taking turns keeping watch over the patient, Stalin, with his typical coarseness, remarks that if he could be at Lenin's sickbed, instead of bringing "you crowbait" or something to drink, he would give him "poison." One can only wonder whether Bedny was trying to warn Lenin of a plot being hatched against him or if he had perhaps written Lenin off and was simply making fun of the ousted chairman of the Sovnarkom. The moral of the fable is helpful in this regard.

"In Europe" means among the Europeans, the émigrés, which included those who, unlike the members of the "underground," had emigrated to wait for the 1917 Revolution—Lenin, Trotsky, Zinoviev, Karl Radek, and the rest. The underground included Stalin, Sverdlov, Kamenev, and others. "With the yellows" means with the hirelings (i.e., the lackeys who still followed Lenin), and primarily Bukharin. "We" meant Stalin and his supporters, predominantly Zinoviev and Kamenev. The "deal" to be made was the agreement between Stalin's faction and Lenin's men to allow Lenin to remain in power, but not "forever" and not for his own benefit ("help their mistress to regain her health"), but because the idea of being without him was still too daunting.

The fable did not pass unnoticed, and on March 27, 1922, Lenin, who until then had been fond of Bedny, criticized the poets of the Revolution on the pages of *Pravda*. Since Bedny was published in *Pravda* almost every day, it was easy to guess exactly who the intended subject of Lenin's criticism was. But Bedny—and Stalin, who stood behind him—were quick with a comeback. On March 31, *Pravda* published a reply to Lenin, in the form of a long-winded poem entitled "How Poets Should Be Read":

> He is, I know, as always, right;
> And yet I am no organ grinder
> Who'll play the tune for which I'm paid.

If one takes into account that during this time the editor of the newspaper of the party's Central Committee (or more precisely, the newspaper of the Secretariat of the Central Committee, i.e., Stalin's newspaper) was the former Left Communist and future Stalin ally Nikolai Bukharin, the innocent fables and poems of Demyan Bedny appear in an entirely different light.

On May 23, Lenin left for Gorki to get some rest, and it was here, while he was not working, that he had his first serious stroke on May 25–27, leaving his right arm and leg partially paralyzed and his speech impaired. On May 29, Doctor A. M. Kozhevnikov arrived with his nurse, M. M. Petrasheva, to give Lenin a bone marrow tap. "Vladimir Ilych's speech was impaired," Petrasheva recalled. "The doctors would ask him to name some object and he couldn't. They would ask him to write and he couldn't do that either. He would complain of paralysis, now in his arm, now in his leg. These were sudden bouts of paralysis, which passed quickly. When he began to walk, he fell down during one such incident.... The garden was full of lilac bushes, but he couldn't tolerate any strong smells. He was pleased when I brought him wild flowers.... He carried out the doctors' instructions very precisely. I remember that we decided to remove the books from his room. He was not allowed to read during this time."[16] In June, Lenin was allowed to get up from his bed. Gradually, he was able to take care of himself again, improved somewhat, and Petrasheva was dismissed.[17]

News of Lenin's illness and of his possible retirement was leaked out to the press. In Berlin, the White émigré newspaper *Rul'* assiduously collected all the rumors. As early as March 22, a front page article entitled "In the Dark" referred to Lenin as the "Kremlin prisoner." On March 26, the newspaper ran another front page story under the heading THE RIDDLE:

> The Sovnarkom is discussing what measures should be taken in the event of Lenin's unavoidable resignation from the government. Lenin's health is such that... his return to active participation in the government is absolutely out of the question.... The head of Moscow's city hall [Kamenev] has announced that it is not possible to expect Lenin to return to active participation in the government at the present time on account of his health.

On March 29, *Rul'* ran another front-page article entitled "Strange Illness": "The case of Lenin's illness is becoming more and more complicated, due mainly to the Bolsheviks themselves, who seem to be intent on deliberately arousing the public's distrust.... The issue of freeing Lenin from government duties has been put on the table; decrees are more and more frequently signed by Tsyurupa using Lenin's official title, the chairman of the

Sovnarkom.... The nature of Lenin's illness is being assiduously and persistently concealed. But it is also possible that the illness manifests itself in such strange and ambiguous ways that it is difficult to give it a definite diagnosis that could be understood by those who are not in the know. The fact is that Lenin has been taken into custody, as it were. Under the pretext that he needs rest, Lenin has been encouraged to step away from the affairs of state, while he, on the contrary, strives to participate directly in government (perhaps this is precisely what his illness consists in) and wants once again to assume control over the helm of the Soviet ship, which has fallen out of his hands. If this is the case, then it is clear why his illness is shrouded in such mystery and why it gives rise to so many contradictory reports. If Lenin and the Sovnarkom are engaged in a struggle, if he has in fact been taken into custody, then everyone who comments on the situation gives his reports one or another slant, depending on his own attitude toward this struggle and on the side that he is on.... Those who wish to see Lenin go express the hope that Lenin will submit to the medical diagnosis and resign. And as more and more rumors and contradictions pile up, it becomes more and more clear that Lenin's illness is in danger of turning into a catastrophe."

Printed in the same issue were excerpts from a letter by a private individual from St. Petersburg, which were published in the newspaper *Morning Post*: "Every day, Lenin's influence decreases and his supporters gradually become fewer and fewer in number, in tandem with the advancing decline of the country."

On March 30, the newspaper published a telegram from Reval, sent on March 28: "Lenin has progressive paralysis." "According to reports from a Soviet source, Lenin's attending physicians have established a diagnosis of progressive paralysis."

On May 4, *Rul'* published in a front-page article under the headline, THE SCREEN:

> This whole story of Lenin's illness is understandably perplexing. Soviet newspapers "refute" all "rumors" regarding Lenin's illness altogether, and only he himself has brought up it unexpectedly.... In any case, why is this whole story shrouded in such unfathomable mystery? Why are such great efforts being made to portray the situation as if nothing out of the ordinary has happened, that everything remains the same as it has been, while Lenin himself unexpectedly announces that he has been idle now for several months?... All of the evidence suggests that Lenin remains merely a screen. The Bolsheviks continue to act using his name, although he has effectively been deprived of all power.

On June 13, in an article entitled "The Soviet Triumvirate—Lenin's Deputy," the newspaper reported: "In view of the fact that Lenin's return to active participation in government seems unlikely, rumor has it that a 'troika' has been formed in Moscow to take charge of the affairs of the Soviet state. The group consists of Rykov, Bukharin, and Preobrazhensky."

In a press roundup, citing the German newspaper *Lokal Anzeiger*, *Rul'* reported:

"According to the newspaper's reports, which it received from sources close to Moscow, Lenin's illness is fatal and news of his death is imminent. This is cause for great worry in Moscow. Upon arriving in Berlin, Krasin immediately met with Rakovsky and Chicherin. This meeting resulted in a decision to establish a Directorate in Moscow before Lenin dies, consisting of Bukharin, Krasin, Litvinov, Rakovsky, and Chicherin."

An article entitled "Lenin's Illness" appeared in the same issue. The newspaper's reporter interviewed "a respected representative of the medical establishment": "The patient... was seen by the famous Bratslav psychiatrist, Dr. Foerster, considered an authority on parasyphilis, which sometimes takes the form of progressive paralysis."

On June 14, *Rul'* reported: "According to newspapers, member of parliament O'Grady, returning from Russia, has reported that Lenin is suffering from the consequences of an assassination attempt made against him one year ago, and that he will die in a matter of weeks. Two weeks ago the state of his health was very grave."

On June 15, citing the newspaper *Freiheit*, *Rul'* published a roster of names for another "troika": "In view of Lenin's departure from government, a 'troika' has been formed. The newspaper assures its readers that its members include Stalin, Kamenev, and Rykov, but that Trotsky is not a part of this group."

> On Tuesday [June 13], Chicherin received a letter from Litvinov in Moscow, which said that Lenin is fully conscious and that his illness is the result of overwork. In his current state, Lenin cannot occupy himself with government duties. However, his illness is of no immediate threat to his life. In Soviet circles, people claim that there has thus far been no talk at all about replacing Lenin with a triumvirate.

Within the upper echelons of the party, Lenin's illness unleashed an open struggle for power. On June 10, 1922, Serebryakov alludes to this fact in a letter to A. N. Vinokurov, people's commissar of social welfare. This letter mysteriously reached the editorial offices of *The Times* and was reprinted in *Rul'* on August 2:

"Return as soon as possible. Matters have become so muddled that the group will have to strain every nerve to restore the situation to what it once was. The leftists are insisting that a party congress be called immediately, but if that is done, we will be bankrupt and can count on only a pitiful minority. I have already written to Italy and to the Schwarzwald and have advised them to return home quickly, for otherwise their extended vacation will cost us and them dear.

The actions of our foreign guests (at the SR trial) have confused the situation greatly. Despite all the steps taken, Vandervelde's speech has gained wide currency not only in Moscow and Petrograd but also in the far-flung provinces. And we have raised the issue of expelling, if not all of the foreign supporters of the defense, then at least Vandervelde and Liebknecht, since, in addition to their speeches, there have also appeared various letters to workers. It is impossible to ascertain their authenticity, since their authors declare them to be base forgeries, although we know what a forgery is when a forgery is required. In the courtroom, Nikolai Ivanovich [Krylenko] has demonstrated his utter incompetence in matters of law in facing experienced jurists....The trial resembled a party conference more than a legal proceeding....

Things are so bad with Ilyich that we cannot even gain access to him. Dzerzhinsky and [Pyotr Gemogenovich] Smidovich protect him, like two bull-dogs, from all outsiders and permit no one in to see him or even to enter the house that he occupies. I believe this tactic to be senseless, since it leads only to the dissemination of fabrications and the most incredible rumors.

As yet the identities of the three are who are to constitute the Directory are not entirely clear. The TsIK has withdrawn Rykov's candidacy. It is true that Kamenev is fighting hard for him, but we well understand that he needs Rykov only as a screen, a loyal minion. As for Stalin, he has flatly refused to work with Kamenev, whose conduct in London he has yet to forget. At the same time, family squabbles are brewing among us, at the very moment when there is nothing we need less. I am most irritated by Radek, who has taken up a mysterious position simultaneously toward the TsIK and toward us, particularly with regard to Trotsky. He and Sklyansky are always together. He hangs about Lebedev and is conspiring in general or perhaps is cooking something up. There have been rumors that those people are creating a new trio headed by Trotsky, but I think that is all slander, since at the present time no one can stand forth openly except Dzerzhinsky, and Trotsky's much-vaunted popularity is simply a myth.

Something is brewing in the provinces. At least the Kremlin is daily beset by all kinds of delegations and people with petitions from the farthest reaches of the country, who represent not Soviet agencies but all kinds of circles and groups that have emerged outside the control of party organs. Many of them are genuine Russian peasants, whose attitude toward the government now is not nearly as favorable as it was earlier. One feels that a new mood has taken root in these distant places, and I am by no means convinced that it is in our favor. I am highly disturbed by the thought that we were so consumed with our actions abroad and with our recent first "ministerial crisis" that we have lost contact with the mood of the peasants and will not be capable of adapting it to our ends when this becomes necessary. I have already drawn attention to this, but all our colleagues are completely consumed by their own squabbles and rivalry, and they pay no attention to my words, with the sole exception of Stalin—who, it seems, is the only person to see things as they really are.

We are in the midst of an acute economic crisis. Moscow is surfeited with goods. No one is buying them, and they circulate in a narrow ring of speculators who finish by dropping out of sight. The speculator element is now beginning to decamp abroad. This is not a very auspicious symptom for the New Economic Policy. Indeed, Larin has been warning us about this for a long time already. The situation becomes more confused with every passing day. I do not know and cannot see an end to all this astonishing commotion. Heroic means will be needed to bend events in a favorable direction. And this is my reason for writing to you and asking you to come to Moscow as soon as you can. Here in the center we are all saying that "we'll get out of this somehow" but at the present moment I cannot see any chance of a turn for the good. Perhaps there is yet the faint hope that Pilsudski will extricate us from this situation; but, judging by Obolensky's reports, it is not he who decides what happens in Warsaw. Rather, the Sejm manipulates him.

Therefore, as early as June 10, there was talk that Dzerzhinsky had Lenin isolated and was the only party leader openly aspiring to Lenin's position—and that it was desirable to create a "directorate" as a counterweight to Lenin, on the one hand, and to Dzerzhinsky's pretensions, on the other (staffed, as we now know, by Stalin, Zinoviev, and Kamenev).

It could be claimed that what *The Times* had printed was a forgery. On June 18, however—a mere eight days later—*Rul'* printed another important document:

Official communique of Lenin's illness.

The Soviet government's communique of Lenin's illness states that: Vladimir Ilyich Lenin, former chairman of the Sovnarkom, is suffering from severe exhaustion whose effects have been complicated by poisoning. To regain his strength, Comrade Lenin must for an extended period of time, and at least until the fall, remove himself from all matters of government and refrain from any activity. He is considered likely to return to political work after a period of prolonged rest, since in the opinion of the medical authorities a restoration of his strength is possible.

In an editorial entitled "Lenin's Retirement," *Rul'* asked: "But when did this retirement come about? Why was there no announcement? Did he retire of his own volition, or was he forced out? Lenin's illness is classified as exhaustion complicated by poisoning.... But if this is so, if Lenin is already the former chairman, if a 'troika' has not been elected to take his place, then who is his replacement? Is there such a person? Why is this being hushed up at such a critical moment?"

Rul' has registered two points that are of interest: first, the removal of Lenin from the post of Sovnarkom chairman and, second, Lenin's worsening health, complicated by poisoning. Even though a White émigré newspaper, of course, was not and could not be the best informed source, it did print the communique, which was factually accurate. Since this official Soviet government communique appeared only in *Rul'*, it must be assumed that a leading party functionary had deliberately leaked this sensational document about Lenin's retirement, which was publicly disclosed in no other forum.

Three days later, on June 21, citing the Reval newspaper *Zhizn'*, *Rul'* reported:

> Recently, a joint meeting took place in Moscow between the Sovnarkom and the members of the Presidium of the VTsIK, at which People's Commissar of Health Semashko apprised top Soviet officials of the state of Lenin's health.
>
> According to Semashko's briefing, a panel of Russian and foreign doctors had seen fit to forbid Lenin to do any kind of serious work for an extended period of time, in order to avoid any tragic outcome of his illness. The Sovnarkom and the Presidium of the VTsIK, together with the members of the Central Committee of the Russian Communist Party, were therefore faced with the need to elect a worthy successor. After Semashko finished speaking, the candidacies of the most prominent figures in the Soviet government were discussed. The majority of those attending the meeting favored Trotsky as the most prominent communist leader.
>
> The candidacy of Kalinin, the current chairman of the VTsIK, was also put forth. Proposals were made to replace him at his current post with Yakovenko, Bukharin, Tsyurupa, or Rykov.
>
> The meeting lasted long into the night, but participants failed to settle on any one candidate.
>
> Some of the participants expressed the hope that "Ilyich's" health would soon improve, possibly some rest, and that the issue of a successor would become irrelevant: in any event, any decision can be postponed for one or two months, during which time Lenin can be replaced by his usual deputies in the Sovnarkom and the Soviet Council of Labor and Defense.
>
> Those attending the joint meeting felt it essential to maintain the matter of replacing Lenin in the strictest confidence, so as not to give the people occasion

to spread murky rumors, foremost among them was that Lenin has long been ill and mentally incompetent.

In its commentary on the report on the state of Lenin's health, which had appeared in *Die Rote Fahne*, *Rul'* emphasized that "Lenin feels well but is finding the inactivity prescribed by his doctors difficult to bear.... This last point forces one to conclude that Lenin's condition is such that comrades are having a hard time handling him; and herein lies the likely explanation for the fact that, despite Lenin's full recovery, he is no longer chairman of the Sovnarkom."

On June 30, in an article entitled "Lenin's Illness," *Rul'* quoted Prof. Klemperer, who had just returned from Moscow, where he had been invited to treat Lenin:

> First of all, Lenin's present condition has no relation to his wounds. Furthermore, rumors about Lenin's progressive paralysis have no basis in fact. We have performed a Wasserman test and have obtained negative results. Cerebral fluid was tested and showed no signs of syphilis and in general a diagnosis of progressive paralysis may be ruled out. Lenin is suffering from extreme exhaustion. One must take into account the fact that this man, who is already over fifty years old, has been working about 16 hours a day for the past three-four years.... Stomach poisoning has further exacerbated the state of his health. On Saturday evening [June 24], Lenin and I strolled together in the garden and he felt better. Therefore, I believe that the recent reports about the renewed deterioration of his health that have appeared in the press are not entirely accurate. Lenin cannot engage in intellectual work. Lenin cannot even read for long, since he becomes so exhausted that he starts suffering from headaches. And according to doctors' orders, he is not permitted to read the newspapers and to speak on the telephone. He receives only his close friends, as well as People's Commissar of Health Semashko and relatives. He requires absolute rest.... In the end, Lenin agreed to give up his work for three to four months and I think that during this time his health will revive, but of course it is difficult to guarantee this. It should be noted, however, that Lenin is aware of everything and keeps up with all political developments.

On July 19, *Rul'* reported on a letter from Riga written by Arthur Ransome, foreign correspondent for *The Manchester Guardian*, who had made several visits to Russia:

> "For the first time in his life, Lenin complained that he was incapable of doing his ordinary work. A person who saw him every day commented that he was ill, but not as much as he was making himself ill. Then new symptoms of

stomach disorders appeared, which were, however, also indications of mental fatigue rather than physical illness. At last, doctors made a final decision and prescribed absolute rest.

All this time, the Soviet government continued to function as it did before. Only on June 18, in a telegram sent from Moscow in connection with a discussion about the state monopoly on foreign trade, Rykov's name in the list of government officials present was followed by his new title of chairman of the Sovnarkom, from which it became clear that Rykov had replaced Lenin in the post of Sovnarkom chairman. It is as yet impossible to say whether or not this replacement is final. Besides Rykov, the most likely candidates are Bukharin, Stalin, Krestinsky, and Kamenev.

Kamenev has already temporarily replaced Lenin as head of the Moscow Soviet in 1918, while Lenin was recovering from the assassination attempt against him. Kamenev is married to Trotsky's sister, but he is Jewish and it is highly unlikely that that the communists have decided to hand their enemies such an effective weapon as the appointment of a Jew as Lenin's successor....

It is inappropriate to speak of Trotsky as a candidate for Lenin's post. He is Jewish and, although he has succeeded in garnering great popularity, even among the officers of the old army, his nationality still stands in his way. Besides, he has frequently been mistaken at many critical junctures during the first phase of the Revolution and is therefore to this day considered too excitable. One of his friends has said of him that he "should have been an aviator, since he is so apt to go up in the air." Furthermore, he is thought of as ambitious and therefore most communists would prefer someone else as head of state.

On August 1, *Rul'* reported:

According to reports from Moscow, foreign physicians have recently been called to see Lenin because he has had another, mild stroke. There is reason to fear that a third stroke would be fatal. The patient's condition is very grave. Reports that he has been transferred to one of the resorts on the Crimea or in the Caucasus have not been confirmed. At the present time, Lenin is in the country and takes no part in government activity."

For Lenin's successor, the Left Communists support Bukharin, while the right supports Semashko. Semashko is the head of the Commissariat of Health, a personal friend of Lenin's, and a supporter of NEP. At the present time, Lenin is being replaced by Rykov. The right and left Communists have agreed to let Rykov replace Lenin on a temporary basis as a compromise.

To round out the picture, let us cite one account alleging that Lenin was poisoned. The Associated Press reported on July 18, 1922, that Lenin "was poisoned on a train while on his way to a health resort in the Caucasus, and his corpse was thrown from the train as it crossed a bridge over the Don

River near Rostov. An informant reports that one of Lenin's visitors, a member of the executive committee of the Third International—who was, it is asserted, an accomplice to the murder—has now taken up the role of Soviet premier at that health resort."[18]

On August 15, the Soviet periodical *Soviet Russia*, which was published in English in the United States, ridiculed the Associated Press filing, calling it absurd. The story does indeed carry very little credibility. Since we have at our disposal only *Soviet Russia*'s retelling of the Associated Press report, it is impossible to determine whether or not the news agency thoroughly investigated the story before it was filed. There was, however, nothing absurd about the essence of this eccentric little piece. The Associated Press report claimed that Lenin had been ousted from power and that the government was now being headed by someone else. We would add that a few months later *The World*, a New York newspaper, ran a photograph of Krupskaya above a caption to the effect that this was "the wife of the former prime minister of the Soviet government." *The World* offered no gloss on what it meant by "former," apparently feeling that comment would be superfluous. *Soviet Russia*, though, called this "an exaggeration."[19]

The rumors about Lenin's illness (poisoning) and retirement can therefore be characterized as persistent. Since Lenin's retirement, which was announced only in *Rul'*, was kept so secret that even Lenin did not know about it, we are fully within our rights to call this a coup—that is, an act that was illegal from the viewpoint of the still-extant head of state (Lenin). But these are, all told, mere formalities. More important is the issue of the poison. The readers of *Rul'* naturally assumed that the poison had been administered via the bullets fired at Lenin by "Kaplan"—which, according to published Cheka sources, had been smeared with poison by a Socialist Revolutionary militant (actually Cheka agent) named G. I. Semenov.

The first person to announce that the bullets had been smeared with curare poison was People's Commissar of Health Nikolai Semashko. The same view was expressed by the Great Soviet Encyclopedia: "On leaving the factory, he [Lenin] was seriously wounded by Kaplan, a White SR terrorist. Two poisoned bullets hit him. His life was in danger."[20]

It is obvious, however, that the bullets were not poisoned. Thus, Cheka agent Konopleva, after reading the GPU-commissioned pamphlet by Semenov on the SRs' militant activities, reported to the Central Committee that the pamphlet contained "a series of factual errors and distortions, which deprive the report of a certain measure of its value as a historical document." The "smearing of the bullets with curare poison" was, in her view, one such inaccuracy.[21]

Prof. D. M. Scherbachev, a specialist who was consulted on the matter, gave a conclusive report on April 18, 1922, stating that "high temperatures of 100°C and higher do not destroy [curare] poison" (in other words, if the bullet had in fact been smeared with this poison, then Lenin would have died). This expert's opinion was not taken into account when the SRs were on trial. But in 1990, it was confirmed by the academician B. V. Petrovsky, who found that "there was no poisoning, supposedly carried by 'poisoned' bullets. It should be noted, incidentally, that bullets at that time were not filled with poison...poisoned bullets of any kind were absolutely out of the question."[22]

The *Brockhaus and Efron Encyclopedia* tells us that curare is invariably deadly: "If curare is applied to even a minor scratch on the body, the person or animal will unavoidably die.... Death comes as a consequence of suffocation [i.e., asphyxiation], while the subject retains full or almost unimpaired consciousness." Hence, if Lenin had really been shot with poisoned bullets, his life would have ended on the day of the assassination attempt.

Thus, the "poisoning" that was mentioned in official reports about Lenin's illness had no relation to the shots fired in 1918. What, then, did it refer to?

Let us turn to Trotsky. In 1939, when the show trials of party and government leaders were underway in Moscow and senior military officers were being executed, Trotsky's comrades-in-arms and friends, as well as members of his family, were eliminated one by one. Finally, after Stalin signed the non-aggression pact with Hitler, Trotsky wrote a sensational article in which he told about a possible poisoning of Lenin by Stalin. It is possible that this was Trotsky's first, cautious attempt to tell the truth. If his revelations, which bordered on the divulging of state secrets, had been received with interest in the West, perhaps Trotsky might have become more talkative. But the public and political spheres of the free world remained silent. No one was interested in Trotsky's exposé at the time. The Soviet Union's leftist sympathizers did not want to compromise Stalin and the socialist order, while the anti-Soviet right suspected Trotsky of being as much a liar as any other communist. No one understood the reach and scope of Stalin's criminality. Trotsky's article, written for *Life* and completed on October 13, 1939, never appeared in that magazine. On November 17, Trotsky wrote to his translator, Charles Malamuth: "I fear that the Stalinists are involving *Life* in machinations of some kind.... I have still not received any sort of reply from the editorial office. Do you happen to know what is going on?"[23]

On August 10, 1940, having wasted ten months, Trotsky gave up and published an abridged version of the article in the magazine *Liberty*. Ten days after that, he was murdered by an NKVD agent.[24]

What was it, then, that became the last straw for Stalin? Why was Mercader, who had already been part of Trotsky's circle for some time, given the order to kill Trotsky immediately after August 10? Might it have been because Trotsky had disclosed Stalin's most important secret? Trotsky had written:

> I am going to talk about an especially critical topic. Did [Lenin's] student [Stalin] take any measures to accelerate his teacher's death? I, more than anyone, understand the monstrosity of such an allegation. But what can one do if it is suggested by the situation, by the facts, and particularly by the personality of Stalin? Lenin warned us urgently in 1921: "This cook will prepare only spicy dishes." It turned out that the dishes were not just spicy, but poisoned, and not just figuratively, but literally.

> Two years ago, I first wrote down facts that were once (1923–1924) known to not more than seven or eight persons, and only in part. The only ones among them who are still alive, apart from myself, are Stalin and Molotov....

> The general secretary's behavior grew bolder and bolder as doctors' reports about Lenin's health became less and less favorable. In those days, Stalin walked around with a grim expression on his face, his pipe clenched firmly between his teeth and a sinister yellowness in his eyes; he did not reply to questions, but snapped back at people. His destiny was at stake. He decided to stop at nothing. This is what triggered the final rift between him and Lenin.... "You know Vladimir Ilyich, don't you?" Krupskaya triumphantly told Kamenev. "He would have never accepted a rift in personal relations if he did not consider it necessary to destroy Stalin politically".... Talking to me, Krupskaya told me about the deep distrust with which Lenin regarded Stalin during the last period of his life. "Volodya would say: 'He (Krupskaya did not say the name, but nodded in the direction of Stalin's apartment) has no basic honesty, no simple human honesty'"....

> Lenin tried to make his assessment of Stalin as inoffensive as he could. But his goal was nonetheless to remove Stalin from the only position that could give him power.

> After everything that had happened during the preceding months, Lenin's "Last Testament" could not have been a surprise for Stalin. Nonetheless, he took it as a cruel blow. When he first read the text that Krupskaya had given to him for the upcoming party congress—in the presence of his secretary Mekhlis, currently the political head of the Red Army, and the prominent Soviet politician Syrtsov, who has since then disappeared from the scene—he started spewing invective against Lenin, which expressed in genuine feelings toward his "teacher" at that time. Bazhanov, another one of Stalin's former secretaries, describes the Central Committee meeting at which Kamenev first read the "Last

Testament": "Everyone present was paralyzed with painful discomfiture. Stalin, sitting on the steps of the podium of the presidium, felt small and pitiful. I watched him carefully; notwithstanding his self-possession and seeming calm, one could clearly see that his destiny was at stake..."

Radek, who was sitting next to me at this memorable meeting, leaned over and said to me: "Now they won't dare to go against you..."

I replied to Radek: "On the contrary, now they'll have to go all the way, and as soon as possible."

Indeed, the "Last Testament" not only did not put an end to the infighting, which was what Lenin wanted, but on the contrary brought it to a feverish pace. Stalin could no longer have any doubts that Lenin's return to work would mean political death for the general secretary. And conversely, only Lenin's death could clear the way for Stalin....

During Lenin's second illness, probably in February 1923, at a meeting of the Politburo, after the secretary left, Stalin informed the members of he Politburo (Grigory Zinoviev, Lev Kamenev, and myself) that Ilyich had unexpectedly summoned him and demanded that poison be brought to him....

I remember how unusual, mysterious, and strange Stalin's face looked. The request that he had told us about was a tragic one; but his face was frozen in a half-smile, like a mask. I had observed a similar incongruity between his words and his facial expression on earlier occasions. This time, it was completely unbearable. The horror was further augmented by the fact that Stalin did not express any opinion about Lenin's request, apparently waiting to see what the others would say: did he want to get a sense of the others' reactions without committing himself? Or did he have some other idea in the back of his mind?... In front of me, I saw Kamenev, silent and pale... and Zinoviev, at a loss, as always during critical moments. Had they already known about Lenin's request before the meeting? Or had Stalin sprung unexpected news on his allies in the triumvirate as well?

"Obviously, fulfilling this request is out of the question!" I exclaimed. "Getye is not giving up hope. Lenin might get better."

"I told him all that," Stalin objected, not without disappointment, "but he just waves it off. The old man is in pain. He says he wants to have poison near him... he will resort to it if he becomes convinced that his situation is hopeless."

"All the same, it is out of the question," I insisted, this time, I believe, with Zinoviev supporting me. "He can fall prey to a temporary impression and take an irreversible step."

"The old man is in pain," Stalin kept repeating, looking absently past us and still not taking either one side or the other....

Stalin's behavior, his whole appearance, had a mysterious and frightening aspect. What does he want, this man? And why doesn't he remove that perfidious grin from his mask?... There was no vote, the discussion was not a formal one, but we parted with the self-evident conclusion that delivering poison was out of the question....

Several days before making his request of Stalin, Lenin added the merciless note to his "Last Testament." Several days after making the request, he broke off all relations with Stalin.... Lenin viewed Stalin as the only person who was capable of carrying out his tragic request since he was directly interested in its fulfillment.... At the same time, perhaps he also wanted to test Stalin: how exactly would the spicy-dish specialist rush to make use of this new possibility?... But I now ask myself another, more far-reaching question: Did Lenin really ask Stalin for poison? What if Stalin made up this whole story in order to prepare his own alibi? He didn't have the slightest reason to fear that we would check up on him: none of us would have asked the ailing Lenin if he had really asked Stalin for poison....

More than ten years before the famous Moscow trials, on a summer evening, on a veranda at a dacha, over a bottle of wine, Stalin confessed to his allies at the time, Kamenev and Dzerzhinsky, that the greatest pleasure in life was to clearly identify the enemy, to prepare everything thoroughly, to take one's revenge mercilessly, and then to go to bed....

I imagine events unfolding as follows. Lenin requested poison—if he requested it at all—at the end of February 1923. At the beginning of March, he once again became paralyzed. The medical prognosis at this time was cautiously pessimistic. Sensing a rise in uncertainty, Stalin acted as he would have if Lenin had already been dead. But the patient thwarted his expectations. His mighty constitution, supported by unbending willpower, let itself be known. By the winter, Lenin slowly began to recover. He started moving with greater ease, had people read to him, and started reading himself; he began to recover his speech. Doctors gave more and more optimistic prognoses. Of course, Lenin's recovery could not have prevented the supplanting of the revolution by a bureaucratic reaction. Not for nothing did Krupskaya comment in 1926: "If Volodya were alive now, he would be in prison"....

It was at this moment that Stalin must have decided for himself that he had to take immediate action. He was surrounded by collaborators whose fate was completely tied up with his own. The pharmacist Genrikh Yagoda was near at hand. Whether Stalin delivered poison to Lenin, with a hint that the doctors had given up all hope of recovery, or whether he resorted to more direct measures, I don't know. But I know for certain that Stalin could not just sit around and wait passively while his fate was hanging by a thread and he could resolve things simply by moving his hand....

[After Lenin's death] Stalin... might have feared that I would connect Lenin's death with the previous year's conversation about poison, that I would ask doctors to determine whether poisoning had taken place, that I would demand a special investigation. For all these reasons, therefore, it was safer to keep me far away until his body was embalmed, his inner organs cremated, and no professional investigation would any longer be possible.

When I questioned doctors in Moscow about the immediate cause of Lenin's death, which had come unexpectedly for them, they were at a loss for an answer. The autopsy, naturally, was performed with every formality: as general secretary, Stalin had seen to this before anything else. But the doctors did not look for poison, even if the more penetrating among them admitted the possibility of a suicide. They probably did not suspect anything else. In any case, they couldn't have had any inclination to go into the matter too deeply. They understood that politics was above medicine. Krupskaya wrote a very passionate letter to me in Sukhum; I did not bother her with questions about the matter. I renewed personal relations with Zinoviev and Kamenev only after two years, when they broke with Stalin. They clearly avoided talking about the circumstances of Lenin's death, giving one-word replies to my questions, and looking away. Did they know something or did they only suspect? In any case, they had been too closely connected with Stalin during the preceding three years and couldn't not be apprehensive that the shadow of suspicion would fall on them too. It was as if a leaden cloud was enveloping the story of Lenin's death. Everyone avoided talking about it, as if they were afraid of listening too closely to their own fear. Only the expansive and talkative Bukharin would privately sometimes make unexpected and strange insinuations. "Oh, you don't know Koba," he would say, with his frightened smile. "Koba is capable of anything."[25]

Thus, Trotsky revealed that Stalin had poisoned Lenin. All that remains is to determine how and when. If Bedny's December fable and *Rul"s* July report of a poisoning are not meaningless accidents, then we must conclude that the poisoning of Lenin began no later than May 1922. We may even suppose that Lenin's first serious stroke, on May 25–27, was caused by poison. We are somewhat helped here by a remark by the chekist Semenov about plans to murder Lenin, which he attributed to the SRs, but which were evidently occupying the minds of those who, by contrast with the SRs, were actually capable of poisoning Lenin, namely, Stalin and his ally Dzerzhinsky. "They more or less considered it possible to poison Lenin," Semenov wrote, "by putting something in his food or by sending him a doctor who would give him a shot causing a serious illness."[26]

In 1934, when he was already living abroad, Trotsky wrote in his diary: "Lenin created the party apparatus. The party apparatus created Stalin."[27] It was Stalin who became the man that replaced Lenin in the party; and it would be naive to think that during the years 1921–1923, Stalin was merely a middle-ranking party functionary.

"You don't understand those times. You don't understand the weight that Stalin had. The Great Stalin," Lydia Fotieva, Lenin's personal secretary, would later say about the years 1922–1923. "Maria Ilyinichna [Lenin's sister] told me during Vladimir Ilyich's lifetime, 'The smartest person in the party after Lenin is Stalin.... Stalin was an authority for us. We loved Stalin. He was a great man. And he said on more than one occasion, 'I am only Lenin's student.'"[28]

It is more difficult to determine when exactly the student outplayed his teacher and became "the Great Stalin." It appears that the latest date at which this could have happened was the month when Stalin was appointed general secretary: April 1922. Significantly, the date when Stalin was elected to this post is not mentioned in any document, which points to the absence of a formal written resolution concerning his appointment. Stalin became general secretary de facto, just as it happened for Sverdlov. It was this specific post that Stalin had settled upon for his ascent to absolute power. "He was never satisfied merely with the role of a political leader, who exerts power over his audience only through articles and speeches, and always aspired to have control over organizational connections as well: he knew perfectly well that this was the only way to control the top personnel among the party workers, who are necessary for the functioning of any organization." These words, which perfectly characterize Stalin, were written by Krupskaya about Lenin, the pre-Revolutionary Lenin of 1901.[29]

After doing away with the first aspirant to the post of general secretary, Sverdlov, Lenin had replaced him with a "suitable collective." But the perverse structure of the Bolshevik party had never been collegial in character. Lenin's hope that the party apparatus would be governed by several equal secretaries was utopian. Three years after Sverdlov's death, Stalin had concentrated "boundless power" in his hands, without any visible opposition from his colleagues in the Secretariat of the Central Committee. Thus, the Twelfth Party Conference, which ended on August 7, while Lenin was still ill, passed new bylaws for the party, which stipulated that "for secretaries of the regional committees, party membership prior to the October Revolution of 1917 is required, as well as confirmation from senior party officials (exceptions for newer party members are permitted only with the approval of senior party officials)." It would seem that the new provision was aimed at reinforcing the power of old party workers. In reality, this inconspicuous clause became Stalin's principal weapon: through it, he acquired the right to confirm the appointments of all regional secretaries personally (by checking the length of their party membership), and, by authorizing exceptions to the rule, the power to appoint those secretaries who, due to the short duration of their membership, would not have been able to become secretaries without Stalin's approval. The committee on the revision of the bylaws was headed by Molotov. The new bylaws were passed unanimously. Within a few months, the new general secretary had established his rule in the party.

It was during this time that enigmatic rumors about Lenin began to appear: the mysterious publication in *Rul'*, the idiotic reports in American newspapers about Lenin's corpse being thrown out of a train, the anecdotal accounts of bullets smeared with curare poison. And in all of these cases, poison was mentioned. Even in Demyan Bedny's fable. And when it seemed that the epidemic of rumors about Lenin's poisoning had passed, Stalin openly entered the game also—and with poison as well. He reported that Lenin, using the pretext of his deteriorating health, had asked that he provide him with cyanide. Stalin had a plan to poison Lenin.

We know about the fact that Lenin had asked Stalin for poison from the recollections of Lenin's secretary Lydia Fotieva, who by that time was already working for Stalin. When Fotieva was interviewed by the writer Alexander Bek, she told the following story about poison:

> I visited Stalin twice during this time. The first time had to do with the poison. But you can't write about this... Just don't write it down. And if you decide to publish it, then I will retract it... So then. First, about the poison. During the summer (of 1922), in Gorki, Lenin had already asked Stalin to send him some poison—cyanide. He told him: "If things get so bad that I can't speak, then I'll resort to poison. I want to have some on me." Stalin agreed. He said: "Fine." However, Maria Ilyinichna found out about this conversation and was categorically against it. She insisted that these kinds of illnesses had all kinds of reversals, that even if the ability to speak was lost, it could come back. In short, Vladimir Ilyich did not get his poison.[30]

In her memoirs. Maria Ulyanova indeed writes that Lenin asked Stalin to procure poison for him in May 1922, but this story is based on a later account by the same Fotieva, as will be shown below. In other words, Fotieva is quoting herself. Maria Ulyanova wrote:

> In the winter of '20–'21, '21–'22, V. I. was unwell. He had severe headaches and was unable to work. I don't know when exactly, but at some point during this time V. I. told Stalin that he will likely end up paralyzed, and he made Stalin give him his word that, should this happen, Stalin would help him to obtain cyanide and bring it to him. St[alin] promised. Why did V. I. turn to St[alin] with this request? Because he knew him to be a man who was firm, who was made of steel, who was not subject to any sentimentality. There was no one else for him to turn to with this kind of request. V. I. again made the same request of Stalin in May 1922, after his first stroke. V. I. Lenin decided then that everything was finished for him, and demanded that St[alin] be called to see him for a very brief visit. This demand was so insistent that people did not dare refuse. St[alin] spent only five minutes with V. I., no more. And when he came out of his room, he told me and Bukharin that V. I. had asked him to bring him poison, telling him

that the time had come to do what he had promised earlier. Stalin promised V. I. he would do so. They kissed and St[alin] left the room. But then, after discussing it all together, we decided that V. I. had to be encouraged, and St[alin] went back into his room. He told him that, after speaking to doctors, he became convinced that not everything was yet lost, and that the time to fulfill his request had not yet come.... They parted and did not see each other again until V. I. Lenin's condition started to improve.[31]

Even in this story, which comes from Lenin's sister, we hear only Stalin's retelling: Stalin left Lenin's room and told Ulyanova and Bukharin that Lenin was asking for poison. Apart from Stalin, no one actually heard this request. The source of all information about the poison, from December 1922 on, is also either Stalin or Stalin's underling—Lenin's secretary Fotieva—and moreover the time at which the request for poison is made coincides in a remarkable fashion with one more in a series of conflicts between Lenin and Stalin, on the one hand, and with the deterioration of Lenin's health, on the other. All that remains to be determined is whether the deterioration of Lenin's health was triggered by one more dose of poison, administered to Lenin by Stalin, or whether, indeed, every time that Lenin's condition grew worse, he inevitably asked Stalin for poison, like a patient asking his doctor for medicine. As Fotieva recalled,

> After another stroke in December, under strict secrecy, he again sent me to Stalin to ask for poison. I called him on the telephone and went to his home. After hearing me out, Stalin said:
>
> "Dr. Foerster has written me: 'I have no grounds to suppose that Vladimir Ilyich will be incapable of working in the future.' And he has stated that he can't give poison after reaching such a conclusion."
>
> I returned to Vladimir Ilyich empty-handed. I told him about my talk with Stalin.
>
> Vladimir Ilyich flew into a rage, started shouting. During his illness, he often became angry even over trifles—a broken elevator, for example (he had always been quick-tempered, but had fought against it).
>
> "Your Foerster is a quack," he shouted. "He is hiding behind evasive words."
>
> And I also remember Lenin saying:
>
> "What did he write? Did you see it yourself?"
>
> "No, Vladimir Ilyich. I did not see it."
>
> And finally, he lashed out at me:
>
> "Get out of here!"
>
> I left, but not without objecting:
>
> "Foerster is not a quack, but a world-famous scientist."
>
> Several hours later, Lenin called me.

He had calmed down, but was sad.

"Forgive me, I lost my temper. Of course, Foerster is not a quack. I got carried away."[32]

Lenin's humanity and kindness know no bounds. He did not order that Foerster be shot, arrested, or even exiled. In the fall of 1952, the academician Vinogradov gave Stalin a medical examination on someone's orders and found that the patient must be immediately relieved of all duties due to the state of his health. When Stalin learned of this diagnosis, he immediately had Vinogradov arrested. He recognized it for what it was: the first step in a government coup. A few months later, in March 1953, Stalin died. It seems that Lenin's type of death was applied to him as well.

In order to understand whether Lenin could have asked Stalin for poison, let us trace the chronology of Lenin's conflict with Stalin and Dzerzhinsky during the period of his illness. On August 10, the Politburo decided to form a committee in order to draft a resolution to improve federal relations between the RSFSR and the other Soviet republics. On August 11, the Central Committee's Organizational Bureau (Orgburo) approved the following members: Valerian Kuibyshev (chairman), Joseph Stalin, Grigory Ordzhonikidze, Grigory Sokolnikov, Christian Rakovsky, and the representatives of the republics—S. Agamaly-ogly (Azerbaijan), A. F. Myasnikov (Armenia), P. G. (Budu) Mdivani (Georgia), G. I. Petrovsky (Ukraine), A. G. Chervyakov (Belorussia), Ya. D. Yanson (Far Eastern Republic), and A. Khodzhayev (Khwarezm). By the beginning of September, the draft of the resolution was ready. Possibly, Lenin learned about this from Rakovsky, who visited him on August 25, and who generally had a negative attitude toward Stalin's draft.

On September 11, for the first time since the May stroke, a council of physicians that had convened in Gorki permitted Lenin to return to work at the beginning of October. On the following day, September 12, Lenin was visited by Stalin, who spoke with him for over two hours. It stands to reason that the conversation touched on the nationalities issue as well. On September 22, Lenin asked Stalin to acquaint him with the draft of the resolution and other documents pertaining to the nationalities issue, since a committee meeting had already been scheduled for September 23 in order to approve the final draft of the resolution. By this time, it was already known that Rakovsky's and Petrovsky's attempt (undertaken either on their own initiative or in concert with Lenin) to postpone the committee meeting until October 15 had failed: on Stalin's orders, the assistant to the general secretary, Amayak Nazaretyan, had replied that a postponement of the meeting was impossible. On September 19, the same reply was given by Kuibyshev (Stalin wanted to force the decision before the beginning of any active interference from Lenin).

The draft of the resolution prepared "by the committee under the chairmanship of Kuibyshev—but actually developed by Stalin—provided that Ukraine, Belorussia, Georgia, Armenia, and Azerbaijan would enter into the Russian Federation as autonomous republics. However, in the republics themselves, only the central committees of Armenia and Azerbaijan supported this proposal. The central committee of the Communist Party of Georgia came out against Stalin's plan, arguing that "unification by the grant of autonomous status to independent republics" was premature and insisting on the preservation of "all attributes of independence" in the republics. The Central Committee of the Communist Party of Belorussia favored a system of independent republics united through a series of treaties, while the Central Committee of the Communist Party of Ukraine had not discussed the proposal at all. But Rakovsky, as a member of the committee and one of Ukraine's party leaders, indicated in a letter on September 28 that Stalin's plans stood in need of revision.

Several days prior to this, at meetings on September 23 and 24 that were chaired by Molotov, who was not a member of the committee—but who was replacing Kuibyshev, who had gone on vacation—the committee voted to approve Stalin's plan in its basic form (with one member abstaining, Georgian representative Mdivani):

"1. It is considered advisable that treaties be concluded between the Soviet republics of Ukraine, Belorussia, Azerbaijan, Georgia, Armenia, and the RSFSR, providing for the formal entry of the first five republics into the RSFSR, with the question of Bukhara, Khwarezm, and the Far Eastern Republic being left open and limited to agreements with them on customs arrangements, foreign trade, foreign and military matters, and so on.

Note: The corresponding changes in the constitutions of the republics mentioned in par. 1 and of the RSFSR are to be made after enactment by Soviet procedure....

6. The present decision, if approved by the Central Committee of Russian Communist Party, shall not be published, but shall be passed on to the Central Committees of the republics as a circular directive to be enacted by Soviet procedure through the TsIK or the Congress of Soviets of the aforementioned republics pending the convocation of an All-Russian Congress of Soviets, at which it is to be declared as the desire of these republics' committees.[33]

Stalin was creating a new empire: "If we do not right now try to adapt the formal relations between the center and the periphery to the factual relations between them, which require that the periphery be absolutely subordinated to the center in all matters, that is, if we do not right now replace formal (factual) independence with formal (and at the same time real) autonomy, then in a year it will be incomparably more difficult to defend the unity of the republics," he wrote in a letter to Lenin of September 22, before the committee met.

On September 25, at Lenin's request, Nazaretyan sent to Lenin in Gorki the Orgburo committee's initial draft, materials from discussions in the central committees of the republics, and materials from two meetings of the Orgburo committee that had taken place on September 23 and 24. At the same time, without waiting for an answer or comments from Lenin and without coordinating his actions with the Politburo, Nazaretyan distributed the committee's resolution to the members and candidate members of the Central Committee of Russian Communist Party. On September 26, Stalin visited Lenin to discuss the situation. After a conversation that lasted two hours and forty minutes, Lenin wrote a letter to Kamenev (sending copies to all members of the Politburo), criticizing Stalin's resolution on the entry of the national republics into the RSFSR.

> "Comrade Kamenev! You have probably already received from Stalin his committee's resolution on the entry of the independent republics into the RSFSR.
>
> If you have not received it, get it from the secretary and read it, please, immediately. I talked about it yesterday with Sokolnikov, today with Stalin. Today I will see Mdivani (Georgian communist, suspected of "independentism").
>
> In my opinion, this issue is ultra-important. Stalin has a slight tendency to rush things. You must think it over carefully (you once planned to work on this matter and even worked on it a little bit); Zinoviev also.
>
> Stalin has already agreed to make one concession. In par. 1, instead of saying "entry" into the RSFSR, to say "the formal unification, along with the RSFSR, into a union of Soviet republics of Europe and Asia."
>
> The gist of this concession, I hope, is clear: we recognize ourselves to have the same rights as the Ukrainian SSR and others, and together with them and on the same footing enter into a new union, a new federation, the "Union of Soviet Republics of Europe and Asia"...
>
> It is important for us not to give fuel to the "independentists," not to destroy their independence, but to create another new layer of organization, a federation of republics with equal rights....
>
> Stalin has agreed to postpone submitting the resolution to the Politburo of

the Central Committee until my arrival. I am coming on Monday, 10/2.

This is my preliminary draft. I will add to it and change it on the basis of conversations with Mdivani and other comrades. I strongly urge you to do the same and to reply to me. Yours, Lenin."[34]

Stalin agreed to some of the amendments. In its new draft, the resolution proposed: "1. To recognize as necessary the formation of a treaty between Ukraine, Belorussia, the Federation of Transcaucasian Republics, and the RSFSR for the purpose of their unification into a Union of Soviet Socialist Republics, with each of them retaining the right freely to withdraw from the Union."[35] Yet this resolution—which was not reviewed by "Kuibyshev's committee," and whose force was therefore not entirely clear—skirted a whole series of questions, for example, whether the new Union represented a coalition of states with equal rights or a single state. Nothing was said about the independence of the equal republics. Instead of providing for direct entry into the Union for Azerbaijan, Armenia, and Georgia, the resolution provided for their entry into the Union through the Transcaucasian Federation.

But Stalin's main deception consisted in the fact that he had promised Lenin not to discuss this "ultra-important" question before Lenin's return on October 2 and... submitted this question for discussion at a Politburo meeting on September 27–28. It should be noted that Lenin's letter to Kamenev had been sent to all the members of the Politburo, that all of them knew about Lenin's agreement with Stalin, and that nonetheless they not only convened for a meeting of the Politburo, but went ahead and approved Stalin's new draft. A new alignment of forces within the Politburo thus came out into the open. The majority stood behind Stalin.

We know about Stalin's own reaction to Lenin's letter of September 26 from a response letter by Stalin, critical of Lenin, written for the members of the Politburo on September 27. In this letter, Stalin accuses Lenin of "national liberalism" and complains about his "haste." On the same day, he exchanges notes with Kamenev at the meeting of the Politburo. Kamenev: "Ilyich is getting ready to go to war to defend independence. He suggests that I talk to the Georgians. He even refuses to accept yesterday's amendments." Stalin: "In my opinion, firmness is needed against Ilyich. If a pair of Georgian Mensheviks influence the Georgian communists, and the latter influence Ilyich, then what does any of this have to do with independence?" Notes from September 28. Kamenev: "I think that, since Vl(adimir) Il(yich) insists, it will be worse to oppose him." Stalin: "I'm not sure. Let him do as he sees fit." Could Stalin really have acquiesced?

On October 2, 1922, Lenin returned to his Kremlin office and continued to work in the Kremlin for 74 days. The issue of the formation of the USSR was taken up at a Central Committee plenary meeting on October 6. But purely by chance (or perhaps due to a plan developed in advance), Lenin had a toothache and did not attend this meeting. The discussion lasted three hours. As Mdivani, the leader of the Georgian "deviationists," wrote to Tiflis from Moscow, "at first (without Lenin) they browbeat us and mocked us outright, but then, when Lenin interfered after we met with him [September 27] and gave him a detailed briefing, the tone changed in the direction of communist reason.... On the issue of interrelations, a voluntary union with equal rights for all members has been approved. As a result the stifling atmosphere against us has dissipated.... The plan, of course, is Lenin's, but its authors are listed as Stalin, Ordzhonikidze, and others, who immediately switched fronts.... The debates have revealed that a certain part of the Central Committee simply denies the existence of a nationalities problem and is infected with Great Russian traditions in general. But this part has received such a slap in the face that it will be long before it decides to stick its head again out of the hole into which Lenin has chased it (his intentions can be learned from his letter, which was read at the end of the meeting after the issue was decided)." The letter in question was a note that Lenin passed to Kamenev, to be read at the meeting: "Comrade Kamenev! I declare a war to the death against Great Russian chauvinism."[36] One can only imagine what Stalin must have thought of Lenin at this moment.

Meanwhile, Stalin sent Ordzhonikidze—who shared his views—to Georgia in order to establish order there. The Georgians were now refusing to enter into the Transcaucasian Federation (through which Georgia was supposed to have been pulled into an autonomous Union). The debates were heated. Ordzhonikidze did not mince words; he called one member of the Georgian Central Committee "a fool and a stooge," and another "a speculator, a tavern-keeper." But when Kabakhidze called Ordzhonikidze himself a "Stalinist ass," the latter hit Kabakhidze, in the presence of Rykov. On the night of October 20, several members of the Georgian Communist Party's Central Committee wired a message to the Russian Communist Party's Central Committee to the effect that joint work with Ordzhonikidze, who had been sent to Georgia to end the conflict, was impossible, since for Ordzhonikidze "intrigues and harassment are the main weapons against comrades who do not kowtow to him. It has become impossible to live and work under his bullying regime." On the same night, Stalin confirmed the receipt of this note "containing complaints and obscene language against Ordzhonikidze."

Initially, Lenin took Ordzhonikidze's side. On October 21, he sent an encrypted telegram to Tiflis, addressing it to the Georgian Central Committee, Tsintsadze, Kavtaradze, Ordzhonikidze, and the Secretary of the Transcauscasian Regional Committee Orakhelashvili: "I am surprised by the indecent tone of the wired note signed by Tsintsadze and others, which was passed to me by Bukharin for some reason and not by one of the secretaries of the Central Committee. I was certain that all disagreements had been resolved by the resolutions of the Central Committee's plenary meeting with my indirect participation and with the direct participation of Mdivani. Therefore, I strongly censure the invective against Ordzhonikidze and insist that you present your differences in a respectable and loyal fashion before the Secretariat of the Central Committee of the Russian Communist Party, to which I am wiring your letter."[37]

On October 22, 1922, the Central Committee of the Communist Party of Georgia submitted its resignation, which was approved by the Transcaucasian Regional Committee. Two days later, Stalin informed Ordzhonikidze that he was satisfying the "request for resignation submitted by the Central Committee of the Georgian Communist Party." And one month later, on November 24, the Secretariat of the Russian Communist Party's Central Committee established a committee "for restoring a firm peace within the Georgian Communist Party" and for an immediate review of the conflict, under the chairmanship of Dzerzhinsky and with the participation of Dmitry Manuilsky and Vincas Mickevičius-Kapsukas. "While welcoming the creation of this committee," writes E. Yakovlev, "Lenin nonetheless abstained from voting to select its members. It may be that he suspected what Zinoviev would in time say directly in conversation with Fotieva: the committee had already reached its conclusions before it left Moscow."[38] And it is clear why: all of its members were Stalin supporters.

December 12 began as usual. In the morning, Lenin came to Moscow from Gorki and at 11:15 a.m. he entered his office in the Kremlin; then he went to his apartment. At noon, he returned to his office and until 2 p.m. he talked with Rykov, Kamenev, and Alexander Tsyurupa, his deputies at the Sovnarkom and the Soviet Council of Labor and Defense (STO). At 5:30 p.m., Lenin came back to his office, spoke on the phone. From 6:00 until 6:45 p.m., he talked to Dzerzhinsky, who had returned from Tiflis, about the conflict between the Transcaucasian Regional Committee and the Georgian Central Committee. The rest of the day he devoted to the question of the foreign trade monopoly, and at 8:15 p.m. he went home.

"No one thought that December 12, 1922, would be Lenin's last day of work in his office in the Kremlin," writes V. P. Naumov.[39] So what happened?

Fotieva would go on to write down the following words, which she attributed to Lenin: "On the eve of my illness, Dzerzhinsky told me about the work of the committee and about the 'incident', and this had a very bad effect on me." So bad, that in the brief which he dictated to Fotieva on the very same evening in response to Trotsky's letter about "preserving and reinforcing the monopoly over foreign trade," Lenin notified Frumkin, Stomonyakov, and Trotsky that it was impossible for him to speak on this issue at the plenary meeting due to his illness, that he agreed with Trotsky in this matter, and that he wished them take upon themselves, in view of his condition, the defense of Lenin's position at the plenary meeting.

On December 13, citing his deteriorating health, Lenin officially announced that he was winding down his affairs. "All of the three subsequent days—December 13, 14, 15," writes V. P. Naumov, Lenin "was in a hurry."[40] Evidently, he understood that hurry was necessary. On December 13, Lenin had Fotieva take down a letter to Trotsky (with copies sent to Frumkin and Stomonyakov) in which he underscored his "uttermost agreement" with Trotsky on all questions and asked him "to take upon himself, at the upcoming plenary meeting, the defense of our common point of view about the categorical necessary to preserve and reinforce the monopoly over foreign trade."

Fotieva immediately informed Stalin about everything and Stalin realized that Lenin was trying to destroy him, through Trotsky, at the next plenary meeting. As early as December 14, Stalin and Kamenev attempted to remove the monopoly question from the day's agenda at the plenary meeting, on the grounds that this point should be discussed at the subsequent meeting with the participation of Lenin, who would certainly be better by then.

On December 15, Lenin wrote another letter to Trotsky: "I regard us as having reached a full agreement. I urge you to make an announcement about our solidarity at the next plenary meeting. I hope that our decision will pass."

Somewhat later, he received a letter from Frumkin, who informed Lenin about Stalin's and Kamenev's intrigues, and asked him to "talk this matter over with Stalin and Kamenev," since "further uncertainty about the situation will make all work impossible."

Then Lenin had Fotieva take down, over the telephone, another letter to Trotsky, the second on December 15:

> I am sending you the letter I received today from Frumkin. I also think that it is absolutely imperative to conclude this matter once and for all. If there are

apprehensions that this matter troubles me and may even affect the state of my health, then I think that this is completely wrong, since I am ten thousand times more troubled by the delay, which renders our policies on one of the cardinal issues completely unstable. Therefore I call your attention to the attached letter and strongly urge you to support immediate discussion of this matter. I am certain that if we are in danger of being defeated, then it is much more advantageous to be defeated before the party congress and then immediately to ally ourselves with a faction at the congress, rather than to be defeated after the congress. Perhaps the following compromise is acceptable: we can arrive at a decision about ratifying the monopoly now, and yet still raise this question again at the party congress—and we can agree upon this course of action right now. In view of our interests, we can accept no other compromise under any circumstances, in my opinion. Lenin.[41]

It may be said with certainty that this was Lenin's most courageous and principled act. It may also be claimed that Trotsky's agreement to defend Lenin's position on the monopoly issue was an expression of courage and loyalty toward Lenin. But something else is obvious, too: on December 15, 1922, Stalin signed not only Lenin's death sentence, but Trotsky's as well. Trotsky did not simply come out on the same side as Lenin (Lenin and Trotsky against Zinoviev, Stalin, Kamenev, and Bukharin): he also defeated Stalin. And this was something that Stalin could not forgive.

And so, on December 13–15, Lenin was not simply in good health, but working in the most active fashion: "He spoke on the telephone, received comrades at home, prepared for his speech at the Tenth Congress of the Soviets, wrote several letters and briefs on the foreign trade monopoly, on the division of responsibilities between the deputies of the Sovnarkom and the STO, expressed an interest in bread production from the harvest of 1922, social welfare, the census of the population, and other matters," writes Naumov.[42] In other words, Lenin was absolutely fit for work. So when did he become ill?

It seems that on December 12, Dzerzhinsky visited Lenin not to deliver a report on the Georgian affair, but in order to inform him that a decision had been reached (evidently by Stalin and Dzerzhinsky) to remove Lenin from power. On December 12, Dzerzhinsky succeeded in doing this, and Lenin agreed to wind down his affairs, leave the Kremlin, and effectively retire. In order to wind down his affairs, Lenin was given three days.

On the morning of December 16, Lenin had time to dictate another letter to Krupskaya. But at 11 a.m., Doctors V. V. Kramer and A. M. Kozhevnikov arrived and demanded that Lenin return to Gorki (which had probably been agreed upon with Dzerzhinsky on December 12). Lenin categorically refused. Offering to compromise, he asked that Stalin be informed that he was willing to not speak at the Congress of the Soviets, where, naturally, the first item on the agenda would be the nationalities policy. But Stalin no longer had any need of favors from Lenin, and the doctors, acting, naturally, on Stalin's orders, forbade Lenin to work.[43] "Being forced to give up his plans to speak at the congress greatly saddened Vladimir Ilyich," Naumov concludes. And from this sentence it follows that Lenin's illness grew worse whenever he was removed, demoted, isolated, deprived, and not the other way around. After all, what Lenin feared more than anything else was the loss of power.

On December 18, the previously postponed plenary meeting of the Central Committee took place, with Stalin presenting a draft for a treaty of union among the Soviet republics. Lenin did not take part in this meeting (obviously, Stalin would not have allowed him to take part in it), while Stalin himself, tired of Lenin's endless attempts to return to power, demanded formal authority for himself to decide Lenin's subsequent fate: through a special resolution, he took upon himself the "responsibility to ensure compliance with the treatment that doctors have established for Lenin."[44] This new treatment, which was established by Stalin, looked more than anything else like house arrest: "Comrade Stalin will assume personal responsibility for ensuring Vladimir Ilyich's isolation, in terms of both his personal contacts with colleagues and his correspondence."[45]

From a medical point of view, isolation is harmful for a patient. It was exactly this conclusion that was reached by Dr. Otfried Foerster—a famous German neuropathologist who was serving as a consultant to Lenin's attending physician—when he visited Lenin on December 20: "Had Lenin been kept in a state of inactivity from October 1922 on, he would have been deprived of the last great joy that he had his life. His continued complete isolation from any form of activity would not have been able to delay the progress of his illness. For Vladimir Ilyich, work was life, and inactivity signaled death."[46]

Everything suggests that the events of December 12–18 probably had no relation to Lenin's health. Lenin was banished from the Kremlin and Stalin was appointed (or more precisely, Stalin appointed himself) in charge of Lenin's penitentiary regime.

On December 21, Lenin had Krupskaya take down a letter to Trotsky. Note the purely formal way in which Krupskaya justifies her right to write down Lenin's letter to Trotsky by citing Foerster's permission:

Lev Davidovich,

Dr. Foerster has permitted Vladimir Ilyich to dictate a letter today, and he has dictated the following letter to you.

Comrade Trotsky,

It seems that the position has been taken without a single shot being fired, by a simple tactical maneuver. I urge you not to stop but to continue the offensive, and to this end put through a motion to raise at the Party Congress the question of strengthening the foreign trade monopoly and improving its implementation. This should be announced to the group of the Congress of Soviets. I hope you will not object and will not refuse to give a report to the group.

N. Lenin.

V. I. also asks that he be telephoned with a reply. N. K. Ulyanova.[47]

From this letter, Trotsky had to conclude that Lenin had lost his mind. He had just been expelled from his office and put under house arrest, forbidden to work, forbidden to meet with people, and forbidden to correspond with people, with Stalin officially appointed as his jailer (which Lenin, naturally, could not have known), and meanwhile he was writing about taking a position without firing a single shot. It was Stalin and Dzerzhinsky who were taking positions without firing a single shot in those days. It is not surprising that Trotsky did not reply to Lenin's letter: he had no intention of discussing this matter with the blinded Lenin.

Lenin was naive with respect to Stalin, but his naivete had its limits. It was not by accident that he had Krupskaya take down this letter, rather than his secretary. He was trying to reach an understanding with Trotsky confidentially. It appears, however, that this information did leak out. On the very next day, December 22, Stalin called Krupskaya, upbraided her, threatened her with punishment in accordance with the Party line and a Central Control Committee sanction, and told her that if this ever happened again, he would announce to the world that Alexandra Artyukhina, an early Bolshevik recruit, was Lenin's real widow. And on December 30, fearing that the service staff at Gorki had gone over or might go over to the side of Lenin and Krupskaya, Stalin gave orders to "replace the guard, replace the cooks! Everyone."

The accepted view is that Krupskaya did not tell Lenin about Stalin's call until March 5, 1923, the day Lenin wrote Stalin an emotional letter, threatening to break off relations. Krupskaya's secretary, Vera Drizdo, confirmed this in her memoirs:

> Why did a full two months elapse after Stalin had spoken so rudely to Nadezhda Konstantinovna before V.I. Lenin wrote him a letter demanding that Stalin apologize to her? I am possibly the only one who knows what really happened, since Nadezhda Konstantinovna often told me about it. It was in early March 1923. Nadezhda Konstantinovna and Vladimir Ilyich were talking about something. The telephone rang. Nadezhda Konstantinovna went to the phone (in Lenin's apartment, the phone was always in the hallway).
> When she returned, Vladimir Ilyich asked, "Who was it?"
> "It was Stalin. We've made peace."
> "What do you mean?"
> Nadezhda Konstantinovna had to recount all that had happened in December 1922, when Stalin had called her.... Nadezhda Konstantinovna asked Vladimir Ilyich to attach no importance to it, since everything had been smoothed over and she had forgotten about it. But Vladimir Ilyich was adamant.

It is obvious that Krupskaya did tell Lenin about everything on the very same day, which Stalin had to have expected. On the night of December 22, Lenin's health rapidly deteriorated (with Stalin's help or not?): according to Maria Ulyanova, on the night of December 23, Lenin's illness "spread, his right arm and his right leg became paralyzed. From then on, Vladimir Ilyich could no longer write on his own."

There are several indications that Lenin found out about Stalin's call to Krupskaya on December 22. First, this is confirmed by Trotsky, who cites Dmitrievsky: "Krupskaya, all in tears, immediately ran to complain to Lenin." Second, this is attested to by the fact that Lenin had another attack on the night of December 22. Indirectly, this is also confirmed by an interview with Fotieva: "Nadezhda Konstantinovna did not always comport herself as she should have. She could have told Vladimir Ilyich what she should not have told him. She was used to sharing everything with him. Even when it was wrong to do so.... For example, why did she tell Vladimir Ilyich that Stalin had upbraided her on the telephone?" Lenin's secretary Volodicheva also believed that Lenin found out about Stalin's rude behavior before March 5: "It is possible that he had known about this earlier. But he wrote the letter on March 5."[48]

At the same time, on December 22 Krupskaya wrote a letter to Kamenev, the de facto chairman of the Politburo, who was, along with Stalin, part of the anti-Lenin coalition. She would most likely not have written to him had she not told Lenin about the incident on the very same day, December 22:

> Lev Borisych, because of a short letter that Vlad. Ilyich dictated to me with the doctors' permission, Stalin yesterday allowed himself the rudest outburst toward me. I didn't join the party yesterday. In 30 years, I have never heard a single rude word from a single comrade. The interests of the party and Ilyich are no less dear to me than to Stalin. I now need as much self-possession as possible. I know better than any doctor what one can and what one cannot talk about with Ilyich, since I know what worries him and what doesn't, and in any case I know this better than Stalin. I turn to you and to Grigory (Zinoviev) as V. I.'s closest comrades and ask you to shield me from rude interference into my private life, unseemly abuse, and threats. I have no doubts about the unanimous decision of the supervisory committee, which Stalin permits himself to threaten me with, but I have no strength or time to waste on this stupid squabble. I'm also a living human being and my nerves are strained to the limit. N. Krupskaya.[49]

The cautious and cunning Stalin would not have accepted a break with Lenin if he did not consider him a political corpse. Stalin permitted himself to treat Krupskaya boorishly on 22 December because in so doing he risked nothing: in essence, he was calling her to tell her that he had decided to kill Lenin. That is the only way to explain Krupskaya's reaction to the call: "She was not herself at all: she sobbed, rolled on the floor, etc. She told V. I. about the reprimand a few days later," Maria Ulyanova attests.[50] Maybe the first attempt to get rid of Lenin for good was made on the night of December 22?

But the most important proof of the fact that Lenin found out about Stalin's phone call specifically on December 22 comes from Lenin himself: on December 23, one day after Stalin's phone call and his stroke, he began to write his "Last Testament."

By 1922, he knew very well what Stalin was. "Maria Akimovna," Alexander Bek would ask Lenin's secretary Volodicheva, "is there any chance of tracking down what Lenin actually said about Stalin?" "I never heard anything. Not even a hint," Volodicheva replied. "After all, Lenin was also a very careful man."[51] A very careful man, just like Stalin. Lenin did not reveal his intentions. He did not call or write to Stalin while still strongly affected by Krupskaya's account of her conversation. He understood that his days were numbered and that he had to dispense as many instructions as possible in the time he had left. At the same time, though, he had no intention of passively waiting for death at Stalin's hands, as can be judged from the number of articles, letters, and notes he produced after December 22. Lenin was pursuing two purposes as he began dictating those documents: on the one hand, to compile a testament; and, on the other, to assemble a file against Stalin that would undermine his authority in the party. History has shown that he would fail to reach both these objectives.

On December 23, Lenin asked the doctor on duty, A. M. Kozhevnikov, to let him dictate to a stenographer for five minutes, since he was "preoccupied with a certain question" and afraid that he would not fall asleep. Kozhevnikov, who suspected nothing, gave his permission. Shortly past 8 p.m., Lenin summoned Volodicheva:

> On December 23, 1922, I was told that Lenin wanted to see me. He was preoccupied with an important question and wanted to dictate something to a stenographer. I had already taken down Vladimir Ilyich's speeches and letters on earlier occasions. I wrote down his report at the April conference, received his telephone dispatches from Gorki, and now I had to take dictation from him on his sickbed. You can imagine how nervous I was! I remember seeing Maria Ilyinichna, Nadezhda Konstantinovna, and a group of doctors in Vladimir Ilyich's apartment. I was warned that Lenin was permitted to give dictation for no more than five minutes. Nadezhda Konstantinovna led me to a room where Ilyich was lying in bed. He looked unwell. He awkwardly gave me his left hand—his right hand was paralyzed. This shocked me. I did not expect him to be so sick. When we were left alone, I sat down at a desk beside the bed. Lenin said: "I want to dictate a letter to the congress. Take it down![52]

This was how Lenin dictated the first part of a letter to the upcoming Twelfth congress. During the dictation, no one besides Volodicheva was present:

> Nadezhda Konstantinovna did not take me into the room. They (Maria Ilyinichna, Nadezhda Konstantinovna, and the doctor) stood near the room where Lenin was lying. They only stepped aside to let me through. And I entered. Lenin dictated quickly. It seemed that he had thought through everything in advance. One could sense that he was ill. It was not easy for him to dictate. His voice was hollow; he didn't gesticulate as usual. He finished the dictation in the time allotted to him and became somewhat more cheerful. Meanwhile, I still didn't feel normal. It was as if I was in a fog.[53]

Lenin noticed Volodicheva's discomfiture and asked her, "why so pale?"[54] "Because Stalin will kill you for this," "because I must report everything to Stalin right now"—Volodicheva should have answered, but, as far as we know, she remained silent.

Lenin himself called these notes his "diary," believing that in this way he would fool the Politburo and not draw particular attention to his work. Let us look at what Lenin wrote and when, beginning with December 23:

23 December 1922—"Last Testament." part 1. Dictated to Volodicheva.

24 December—"Last Testament," part 2.

25 December—"Last Testament," part 3. Dictated to Volodicheva.

26 December—Note on increasing the size of the Central Committee to 50 or even 100 members. Dictated to Fotieva.

27 December—Part 4. "Granting Legislative Functions to the State Planning Committee." Dictated to Volodicheva.

28 December—Part 5. "Continuation of the Letter on the Legislative Nature of the State Planning Committee's Decisions." Dictated to Fotieva.

29 December—Part 6. "Continuation of Notes on the State Planning Committee." Dictated to Volodicheva.

29 December—Note on the State Planning Committee. Dictated to Volodicheva.

29 December—On increasing the size of the Central Committee. Dictated to Volodicheva.

30 December—"The Question of Nationalities or 'Autonomization,'" part 1. Dictated to Volodicheva.

31 December—"The Question of Nationalities or 'Autonomization,'" part 2. Dictated to Volodicheva.

31 December—"The Question of Nationalities or 'Autonomization,'" part 3. Dictated to Volodicheva.

2 January 1923—"Pages from a Diary." Published in *Pravda* on January 4, 1923.

4 January—addendum to the "Last Testament" with a proposal to remove Stalin. Dictated to Fotieva.

4 January—"On Cooperation," part 1. Published in *Pravda* on May 26, 1923.

6 January—"On Cooperation," part 2. Published in *Pravda* on May 27, 1923.

Not later than 9 January—an outline of the article: "What Should We Do with the Workers' and Peasants' Inspection?"

9 January—"What Should We Do with the Workers' and Peasants' Inspection?" part 1. Dictated to Volodicheva.

13 January—"What Should We Do with the Workers' and Peasants' Inspection?" part 2. Dictated to Fotieva.

13 January—"What Should We Do with the Workers' and Peasants' Inspection?" part 3. Dictated to Fotieva.

16 January—"Our Revolution (Apropos of N. Sukhanov's Notes," part 1. Published in *Pravda* on May 30, 1923.

17 January—"Our Revolution (Apropos of N. Sukhanov's Notes," part 2. Published in *Pravda* on May 30, 1923.

23 January—"How We Should Reorganize the Workers' and Peasants'

Inspection." Published in *Pravda* on January 25, 1923.

2 March—"Better Fewer, But Better." Published in *Pravda* on March 4, 1923.[55]

Let us run down the roster of Lenin's secretaries, as recorded in the "Journal of Lenin's Secretaries," from November 21, 1922 through March 6, 1923: Nadezhda Alliluyeva (until the morning of December 18), Shushanika Manucharyants (officially Lenin's librarian, until the evening of December 11), Sara Flakserman (only for December 3), Maria Glyasser (only for the evening of February 5), Maria Volodicheva (from the evening of November 27), and Lydia Fotieva (from December 13). Let us also note that, with the exception of Alliluyeva—Stalin's wife, whose life was tragically cut short—not one of these women was repressed during the purges. That is the best confirmation we can have that Stalin had no doubts as to their personal devotion, that none of them committed a single act of disloyalty to Stalin at that time, which was one of great danger for him. The same can be said of Vladimir Dmitrievich Bonch-Bruevich, Lenin's assistant and secretary, who lived on for many years, until he died in 1955. Bonch-Bruevich's brother, Mikhail—a general in the tsarist army and commander of the Northern Front prior to the Revolution—also remained unscathed. Mikhail Dmitrievich, who statistically speaking simply must have been executed sometime in the 1936–39 period, served out his career in the military, rising to the rank of lieutenant-general, and died in 1956.

How did Lenin's secretaries earn Stalin's lifelong indulgence? Through their loyal service and the impeccably kept "Journal of Lenin's Secretaries." This is an astonishing document. First published in 1963, it had been kept securely locked away until July 1956. What kind of "Journal" was it and why was it held in a safe for so long? On whose initiative was it begun? To whom did the people who made entries in it report? Who knew and who did not know of its existence? Who read it?

Not all of these questions can have clear answers. The "Journal" was begun on November 21, 1922. Evidently, on this day the Politburo, on Stalin's initiative, established surveillance over Lenin to the point of keeping a journal of his activities. Prior to the Revolution, Lenin had always placed Krupskaya as secretary at those political centers whose activities he wished to follow. In this instance, too, Stalin proved to be a worthy pupil. For the first few days after formal surveillance had been established, a particularly active secretary of Lenin's was Stalin's wife Nadezhda Alliluyeva. Naturally, she told Stalin whatever she would find out.

There is no indication that Lenin, Krupskaya, or Maria Ulyanova knew about the "Journal" and, if so, then one can fairly say that it was a secret document. Lenin's six secretaries could keep a secret journal only with permission from higher up in the chain of command—for example, from the Central Committee, the Secretariat of the Central Committee, or the Politburo. In other words, the order must have come from Stalin. From interviews with Fotieva and Volodicheva we know that the secretaries reported to Stalin and to Kamenev, the latter being chairman of the Politburo during the months in question. It is not known if Stalin read the "Journal" or was satisfied with oral briefings. But the fact that at least one secretary—Volodicheva—made her journal entries in shorthand, transcribing them later, would indicate that Stalin settled for oral reports.

The "Journal" breaks off on March 6, 1923, with the words "Nadezhda Konstantinovna asked..." The remainder of the text for that day is in shorthand, which Volodicheva deciphered on July 14, 1956. After March 6, 1923, the "Journal" was no longer kept. One gets the impression that while transcribing the entries for March 6, Volodicheva received a call from Stalin instructing her to stop keeping the "Journal" and to do no further work on it. Therefore it was dropped in mid-sentence.

The "Journal" is interesting not only for what it contains, but also for what has vanished from it. And a great deal indeed has disappeared. Entire days are omitted: 17 December 1922 and 19–22 December 1922. Recall that on December 18, Stalin was appointed Lenin's jailer, while December 22 was the date of the phone call from Stalin to Krupskaya, and if Krupskaya told Lenin about it, the secretaries' notes from December 22 must have contained accounts of Lenin's reaction. The period that began on December 25—while Lenin was dictating the third part of his "Last Testament," his memo on expanding the Central Committee, his notes on the State Planning Committee [Gosplan], his article on the nationalities issue, and, finally, the supplement to the "Last Testament," written on January 4, 1923, in which he recommends that Stalin be dismissed from the post of general secretary—is entirely omitted. Between December 25 and January 16 there are only two entries, for December 29 and January 5. Note how carefully those entries are arranged:

24 December.... Sukhanov's *Notes on the Revolution,* volumes 3 and 4 were taken out for Vladimir Ilyich.

29 December. Vladimir Ilyich asked through Nadezhda Konstantinovna for a list of new books. The doctors have permitted him to read. Vladimir Ilyich is

reading Sukhanov's *Notes on the Revolution* (volumes 3 and 4)....Vladimir Ilyich asked for the list of books to be divided into different categories.

5 January 1923. Vladimir Ilyich requested a list of new books from January 3 and Titlinov's book *The New Church.*

17 January [an entry by Volodicheva—Y.F.] Vladimir Ilyich... read and corrected the notes to Sukhanov's book on the Revolution.

The "Journal" has been censored in such a way as to create the impression that from December 25 until January 16 Lenin did nothing but read and work on the article on Sukhanov. Meanwhile, the final articles of his life were written during this time. After January 17, on the other hand, when entries in the "Journal" become relatively frequent, he wrote only two articles: "How We Should Reorganize the Workers' and Peasants' Inspection" and "Better Fewer, But Better."

The following dates are also missing from the "Journal": 27–29 January, 11 and 13 February, and 15 February–4 March 1923. Meanwhile, we know that Lenin was dictating on a daily, or almost daily, basis and, on the days when he did not dictate, the "Journal" always contains a note to this effect; for instance:

10 December, morning. Nothing from Vladimir Ilyich....
11 December, morning (entry made by Alliluyeva). There were no requests. Vladimir Ilyich did not telephone anyone. Check in the evening to make sure that the temperature in the office does not fall below 14 degrees.
11 December, evening (entry made by Manucharyants). There were no requests. Vladimir Ilyich did not telephone anyone....
18 December, morning (entry made by Alliluyeva). The plenum of the Central Committee is meeting. Vladimir Ilyich is not attending. He is ill—no requests or instructions.
18 December, evening. The plenum is meeting. Vladimir Ilyich is not attending. The plenary meeting has ended with an evening session....
18 January (entry made by Volodicheva). Vladimir Ilyich did not call for anyone....
21 January (entry made by Volodicheva). Vladimir Ilyich did not call for anyone.

Therefore, the days on which Lenin sent for no one and gave no dictation are noted. Does this mean that on all the days omitted from the "Journal" (or removed by its editors), Lenin did dictate something? Finally, it is unclear whether the "Journal" was continued after March 6, 1923. In any event, nothing after that date was published. It also appears that certain entries in the journal were made retroactively.

However, Lenin failed to anticipate that all of his secretaries reported about him to Stalin. By then the conspiracy against him had become so broad and so irreversible that Stalin could operate almost out in the open. The articles and letters that Lenin wrote against Stalin were immediately delivered by Lenin's secretaries to Stalin, who them made his own decisions about what to do with these documents. When Lenin's "Last Testament," dictated to Volodicheva, was brought to Stalin—in the presence of several party leaders—he ordered that it be burned. Volodicheva recalls:

> It was already late when I returned to the Secretariat. I sat there for a long time in a depressed state, trying to make sense of everything that I had heard at Lenin's. His letter seemed very alarming to me. I telephoned Lydia Alexandrovna Fotieva, told her that Lenin had dictated an extremely important letter to the next party congress, and asked her what I should do with it—whether I should show it to someone, perhaps Stalin. I don't want to put so much stress on how nervous I was—this was just the first time I had seen him in such a state. "Well then, show it to Stalin," said Lydia Alexandrovna. That was what I did....[56]
>
> In Stalin's apartment I saw Stalin himself, Nadezhda Sergeyevna Alliluyeva, Ordzhonikidze, Bukharin, and Nazaretyan (A. Nazaretyan, a party member since 1905, started working in the Central Committee of the Russian Communist Party in 1922). Stalin took the letter and asked Ordzhonikidze and Bukharin to accompany him to the next room. Everything took place in silence.... After approximately a quarter of an hour, Stalin came out. His steps were now heavy, his face expressed concern. He asked me into the next room, and Ordzhonikidze asked me how Ilyich was feeling.... I repeat: in Stalin's apartment, I saw Stalin himself, Alliluyeva, Ordzhonikidze, and Bukharin. It was important for me to let Stalin know that, although Vladimir Ilyich was confined to his bed, he was fully alert, that his speech was clear and lively. I formed the impression that Stalin was inclined to explain Lenin's letter to the congress by citing Ilyich's poor health. "Burn the letter," he told me. I carried out Stalin's instructions. I burned the copy of the letter that I had shown him, but I did not mention that there were four other copies of that document in the safe.
>
> On the following day, I told everything that had happened to Fotieva and Glyasser. "What have you done!" they cried. "Immediately replace the copy!" I immediately made a fifth copy."

By the morning of December 24, Lenin was not only practically forbidden to work (five minutes of dictation): he was literally prevented from opening his mouth. He is told to stop talking to the secretary and the stenographer. This demand came from doctors (in light of what was taking place, this word should be put in quotation marks, although the people in white coats around Lenin really were doctors). Then Lenin issued an ultimatum, like a prisoner in jail who is declaring a hunger strike, and it is clear that this ultimatum was meant not for the doctors, but for Stalin: if he is not allowed to dictate his "diaries" every day, at least for a short period of time, then he will "refuse to undergo treatment completely."[57]

The threat worked because Stalin knew that if Lenin refused to undergo treatment, his health might improve). The ultimatum, obviously, was discussed not by the doctors, but by Stalin's faction in the Politburo, which consisted of Stalin, Kamenev, and Bukharin, all the three, it is important to note, were acting in concert against Lenin. The Politburo reached the following decision:

> (1) Vladimir Ilyich Lenin is to be given the right to dictate for five to ten minutes a day, but he is not to write letters and not to expect a reply to his notes. Visits are forbidden. (2) Neither friends nor domestics are to convey to Vladimir Ilyich any information about politics, so as not to provide any occasion for reflection and agitation.[58]

In other words, Lenin the prisoner would have pen and paper issued to him in his cell for a few minutes a day, but, since his secretaries did all the writing, Stalin would promptly be brought up to date on what had been written. Lenin perceived his condition as nothing but incarceration: "If I were free (initially misspeaking himself, then repeating it with a laugh: if I were free), I could easily do all this myself," he said to Fotieva on February 1, 1923. But Lenin was no longer free. He lay in bed and expressed his disappointment: "You won't be able to stop me from thinking! I'm lying and thinking all the same!"[59] Krupskaya recalled: "That was the terrible thing during the time of the illness. When the doctors told him he couldn't read or work at all. I think that was wrong. Ilyich often said to me: 'They can't... stop me from thinking.'" Krupskaya herself also realized that Lenin was effectively incarcerated: "During the illness, there was a time when I told him, in the presence of a nurse, that, you know, you're recovering your speech, just slowly. Look at it as a temporary imprisonment. The nurse says: 'What are you saying, Nadezhda Konstantinovna? What kind of prison is this?' Ilyich understood: after this conversation, he started to exercise more self-control"[60]—in other words, he did not criticize his treatment in the presence of strangers.

On December 24, Lenin finished dictating the second half of the letter to Volodicheva. He was so concerned by the possibility of leaks that he repeatedly emphasized to her the need to maintain confidentiality: "What was dictated yesterday, December 23, and today, December 24, is highly classified." The diary was "highly classified. No one should know about it yet. Up to and including the members of the Central Committee." "He emphasized this on more than one occasion, and demanded that everything he dictated be kept in a special place, with strict accountability, and be considered absolutely classified." All of these demands of Lenin's were carefully recorded by Volodicheva in the journal she kept for Stalin.

"Afraid of upsetting Lenin, I did not tell him that Stalin was already familiar with the first part of his letter to the Congress," Volodicheva recalled, clearly downplaying the situation. What she should have said was "afraid of killing Lenin" or "afraid of striking Lenin down on the spot"... It is difficult even to imagine how Lenin would have reacted had he been told by Volodicheva that Stalin was getting word of what was happening and that, pursuant to a Politburo decision, his life was under minute surveillance, which had been formalized as the "Journal of Lenin's Secretaries."

Volodicheva's declaration that she had acquainted Stalin only with the first part of the "letter" is untrue. The discipline was strict: "We read nothing and told each other nothing," she recalls. "We did not ask each other anything.... We had a common journal... and each of us made the entry for her own day," but "we did not read it."

The secretaries lived in fear of Stalin. Here is some more from Bek's interview with Volodicheva:

> "Do you remember saying that when Lenin began to describe Stalin, you were struck by one word that he used in that description?"
> "Yes, *derzhimorda* [the bullying, blustering police chief in Gogol's *Inspector General*—Yu. F.]."
> "That was the letter about the nationalities issue?"
> "Where it was, in which transcript, I don't remember. At first I simply could not make it out; and when I did read it, I was too horrified to type any more."
> "And so that word never found its way anywhere?"
> "It did not."[61]

Volodicheva is obviously being less than accurate here, for *derzhimorda* did in fact find its way into Lenin's article "The Question of Nationalities or 'Autonomization'": "The Georgian who is dismissive about this aspect of the matter . . . is himself a crude, great-power *derzhimorda*."[62] Yet she accurately conveys the mindset of the time: while gutsy enough not to type up Lenin's dictation exactly, she was incapable of typing *derzhimorda* with reference to Stalin.

Even if Volodicheva really did not inform him on December 23 about the existence of four more copies of the "Last Testament," Stalin did not believe that only one copy of this document existed. Five copies were always made of Lenin's materials: one for Lenin, three for Krupskaya, and one—labeled "top secret"—to be sent to the Secretariat. Everything intended for publication in *Pravda* was retyped, reviewed once more by Lenin, and then given to Maria Ulyanova as the executive secretary of the editorial board. Three copies of the documents (Krupskaya's) were then sealed in an envelope.[63] Stalin, of course, knew about this.

After December 24, Stalin made some changes resulting in gaps in the "Journal" whenever Lenin dictated texts that were too inconvenient for Stalin. After December 24, everything that Lenin wrote is expansive, but completely innocuous in nature. This leads to the natural conclusion that a number of Lenin's materials were destroyed[64] or that the journal entries were fabricated retroactively. The "burning" of Lenin's texts could have been authorized only by Stalin as the party's general secretary. To suggest that Stalin was not interested in the contents of the notes dictated by Lenin after December 23 is absolutely impossible.

The behavior of Fotieva, the second secretary who worked with Lenin in December 1922-January 1923, was no different. Here is how she described what happened during those days in her interview with Bek:

"I handed over Lenin's nationalities letter myself."

"Immediately after he dictated it, you mean?"

"Yes. I can tell you, but don't write it down.... The second time I spoke to Stalin (after the conversation about poison) was about the nationalities letter that Vladimir Ilyich had dictated. That time I did not go to see him. I phoned instead: 'Comrade Stalin, Vladimir Ilyich has just finished a letter of a political nature in which he addresses himself to the congress. I believe it should be given to the Central Committee.' Stalin replied, 'Well, then, give it to Kamenev.' (They were together at that time.) So I did."

"But, Lydia Alexandrovna, you did not telephone Stalin because Vladimir Ilyich told you to?"

"No, Vladimir Ilyich knew nothing about it."

"Why did you not ask him?"

"In general, we asked him no questions. We were not to upset him."

"But someone told him later?"

"No. That would have upset him..."

"Then why did you not even consult with her?" [with Krupskaya—Y. F.]

"I did not report to Nadezhda Konstantinovna and did not ask her permission for anything."

"But Lenin's letter ["The Question of Nationalities or 'Autonomization'" —Y. F.] was directed against Stalin, wasn't it?"

"Not only against him. Also against Ordzhonikidze and Dzerzhinsky."

"Yes, yes, but mostly against Stalin, all the same. And you hand it over to him. That is, you arm him in advance. . . . But you could at least have consulted with Maria Ilyinichna."

"But Maria Ilyinichna had no power at all. She brought everything to Nadezhda Konstantinovna.... Had Vladimir Ilyich been well, he would definitely have invited Stalin over and would have spoken with him. But as it was, a letter stood in for a conversation."

"Why is there nothing about this in the 'Journal of Lenin's Secretaries'?"

"That was not at all the sort of thing we wrote about there...."

"But why, Lydia Alexandrovna, is there nothing in the journal about Vladimir Ilyich having dictated the last part of his 'Last Testament'—that is, the part in which he spoke about Stalin?"

"It was done secretly. That is why I did not note it down."

"But the preceding parts were secret too.... And Volodicheva tells us that he already knew about the 'Last Testament.' She herself, it seems, handed it over. And Stalin said, 'Burn it.'"

"Volodicheva is a sick person. Nothing of the sort happened." And then she was suddenly nervous—"Go away, go away with your questions!"[65]

Lenin dictated at a lively pace from December 23 through January 23, that is, for exactly a month, after which there was an unexpected but entirely plausible intermission. On January 24 he commissioned Fotieva "to ask Dzerzhinsky or Stalin for materials from the commission on the Georgian affair" and met head-on with strong opposition from both of them. Dzerzhinsky sent Fotieva to Stalin, who hid behind the Politburo resolution. Lenin began to suspect Fotieva of double-dealing: "First of all, about our 'conspiratorial' business: I know that you are being dishonest with me.' To her assurances to the contrary, he replied: "I have my own opinion about that." On January 25, which was a Thursday, Lenin asked if the materials had arrived. Fotieva replied that Dzerzhinsky would not be there until Saturday. On Saturday Dzerzhinsky said that Stalin had the materials. Fotieva wrote to Stalin but he was not in Moscow. On January 29 Stalin called and said that he could not hand over the materials without Politburo approval. He also questioned Fotieva suspiciously, wondering if she had told Lenin "more than she should have" and asking how he could be so "abreast of things." After all, the article on the Workers' and Peasants' Inspection (which Lenin had completed on January 23 and Stalin had already read) "indicates that certain circumstances are known to him." Fotieva vowed that she had told him nothing and had "no grounds for thinking that he was abreast of things." On December 30, having found out from Fotieva that Stalin was refusing to give him the materials from the Dzerzhinsky commission, Lenin declared that he would insist on obtaining the documents.

On February 1, the Politburo gave permission for the documents to be given to Fotieva for Lenin, but only on the condition that she would retain them for study (which is what Lenin apparently wanted) and would not brief Lenin on them without Politburo permission. In other words, the Politburo had handed over the materials but would not allow Lenin to have access to them, leaving them in the possession of Fotieva, Stalin's spy. Evidently on Stalin's orders, she dragged her feet and told Lenin that she would need four weeks to study them.[66]

Lenin was definitely heading into battle, but Stalin was not sitting idle either. On January 27, a few days before the tragicomedy involving the materials on the Georgian affair began, Stalin had a confidential letter on Lenin's most recent articles distributed to all the provincial committees of the Russian Communist Party. It was issued in the name of the Central Committee Politburo and its Organizational Bureau (Orgburo) and was signed by Politburo and Orgburo members Andreyev, Bukharin, Dzerzhinsky, Kalinin, Kamenev, Kuibyshev, Molotov, Rykov, Stalin, Tomsky, and Trotsky. The gist of the letter was that Lenin was ill and could no longer be held responsible for his own statements.[67]

It is not known if Lenin was aware of this letter or if his isolation, on the one hand, and the unwillingness of his nearest and dearest to disturb him, on the other, had reached the point where no one was telling him anything about Stalin's intrigues. However, on February 3, at the latest, Lenin received confirmation from Fotieva that a ban had been placed on conversations with him:

> Vladimir Ilyich called me in at seven o'clock for a few minutes. He asked if I had seen the materials. I replied that I had, but only from the outside, and that there did not seem to be as many as we thought. He asked if the issue had been raised in the Politburo. I replied that I was not authorized to talk about that. He asked, "You have been forbidden to talk about that specifically?" "No. I am not authorized to talk about current affairs in general." "So this is current?" I realized that I had committed a blunder. I repeated that I was not authorized to talk about it. He said, "I found out about it from Dzerzhinsky previously, before I fell ill. Has the committee made its report?" "Yes, it has. The Politburo gave overall approval to its decisions, as far as I remember." He said, "Well, I expect you will be making your report in about three weeks, and then I will follow up with a letter.[68]

On 12 February, a new round of sanctions designed to increase Lenin's isolation was instituted, and he had another attack. Fotieva made the following entry in the "Journal":

> Vladimir Ilyich is worse. A bad headache. He called me in for a few minutes. Maria Ilyinichna said that the doctors had upset him so much that his lips were trembling. The previous day, Foerster had said that he was categorically forbidden to have newspapers, to meet with anyone, or to receive any political information. . . . Vladimir Ilyich has gathered the impression that it is not the doctors who are giving instructions to the Central Committee, but the Central Committee that has given its instructions to the doctors.[69]

He was right, since Foerster believed that Lenin was harmed less by work than by the prohibitions laid on him. This was precisely why the suspicious Lenin was more and more often "categorically refusing to take his medications" and demanding that "he be relieved of the doctors' presence."[70] The patient realized that the people hired by Stalin were shortening his life. Lenin's hatred of Foerster had become so strong that the doctor had to hide in neighboring rooms.

On 14 February, two weeks after the materials came from the Politburo, Fotieva's entry reads:

> Vladimir Ilyich called me in at 1 p.m. He has no headache. He said that he is completely healthy. That his is a nervous illness and is such that he is sometimes completely healthy—that is, his head is completely clear—and sometimes he is worse. So we should make haste to carry out his instructions, since he most certainly wants to have something ready for the congress and hopes to be able to do that. But if we drag it out and thereby ruin it all, then he will be ever so cross.... He spoke again about his three points, and in particular about the one thing that bothers him most of all, i.e., the Georgian affair. He requested urgency. He gave some instructions.

The instructions also had to do with the Georgian affair:

> Hint to [Aron] Solts that he [Lenin] sides with the complaining party. Let any one of the complaining parties know that he sides with them. Three points: (1) there must be no fighting; (2) concessions are necessary; and (3) a large state must not be compared with a small one. Did Stalin know? Why did he not react? The designation "deviationist," given for deviating in a chauvinist and Menshevik direction, is proof that the backers of great-power policies are also deviating in the same direction. Collect printed materials for Vladimir Ilyich.[71]

It stands to reason that all this was passed on to Stalin before the day was out, and that he then took certain steps against Lenin that remain unknown to us. Lenin was evidently well enough to work between February 15 and March 5, since he finished the article "Better Fewer, But Better" on March 2. Although there are no entries in the "Journal" for the period from February 15 through March 4, we know something of the events of February 15 and following from Fotieva's memoirs:

> Solts, as a member of the presidium of the Central Control Committee, reviewed the announcement from the supporters of the Central Committee of the former Georgian Communist Party about the oppression to which they have been subjected. On February 16, as instructed by Vladimir Ilyich, I sent a note to Solts containing a request to hand over to me all the materials relating to the Georgian conflict. I still have the note I made:
> "Yesterday Comrade Solts told me that a comrade from the Central Committee of the Georgian Communist Party had brought him materials on all kinds of oppression of Georgians (supporters of the former Central Committee of the Georgian Communist Party)."
> As for the "incident" (meaning the insult leveled by Comrade Ordzhonikidze at Kabakhidze), the Central Control Commission had a statement from the victim, but it was lost. When I asked, "How was it lost?" Solts replied, "It just was."
> But it does not matter, since the Central Control Committee has an objective account of the incident from Rykov, who was present at the time.[72]

So Lenin's hints to Solts, Stalin's protégé, had done nothing to improve his situation. From a terse note written on February 25 we learn that Lenin was capable of working and was feeling well: that morning, he "wrote and talked about business.... In the evening, he read and dictated for over an hour."[73] What did he dictate? How many pages? Finally, we know that on March 3, Stalin authorized Fotieva to give Lenin her summary opinion of the Dzerzhinsky Committee's materials: "Lenin is to receive a memorandum and the summary opinions of L. A. Fotieva, M. I. Glyasser, and N. P. Gorbunov on the materials from the Politburo Committee dealing with the 'Georgian affair.'"[74]

This means that Lenin was well enough to work during the period from February 25 through March 3. But what exactly was happening during that time, and why is the "Journal" silent?

The Central Committee was meeting in plenary session in Moscow from February 21 to February 24. Apparently, this was one of the reasons for the lack of entries. Lenin had an interest in the plenum's business, "since it had reviewed the theses on the nationalities issue and the organizational issue; resolved not to publish them until Lenin had acquainted himself with them (with the permission of his doctors), and in the event that Vladimir Ilyich insisted on a reconsideration of these theses, to convene an extraordinary plenum. The plenum acknowledged the advisability of setting up a panel on the nationalities issue at the congress, which would be attended by all the deputies from the national republics and regions and was to invite up to twenty communists who were not delegates to the congress.

What had happened? Why this renewed respect for Lenin? What happened was that the theses of the plenum's general secretary had been deemed politically questionable and Lenin's expert appraisal was sought. How that happened, we can only guess. A powerful political force was exercising its pull here and proving more powerful than the influence of the Politburo majority with its general secretary in tow—a force that Stalin had not reckoned with, having already written it off. And such a force, as things stood at the time, could only have been—and was—Lenin's latest alliance with Trotsky.

The proposal to set up a panel on the nationalities issue at the congress, to be attended by all the deputies from the national republics and regions and invite up to twenty communists who were not delegates to the congress—a proposal that the plenum in fact adopted—seems too pivotal to have been just any old resolution. Had it come from Lenin? Did it not use the phrasing, or a paraphrase, of one of Lenin's letters or statements? For it is very likely that Lenin wrote at least one letter to the plenum. There may even have been several letters, since this plenary session was unusually long, lasting four days. What could the contents of that letter or those letters have been?

Trotsky provides some assistance at this point. His archive contains a document dated February 22, 1923, indicating that Trotsky clashed with the plenum majority (the Stalinists) and that on February 21 and 22 the plenum discussed a published article, a letter, and a draft (proposal) from Lenin. It would appear that the article was the one on the Workers' and Peasants' Inspection, since this was the only document that Lenin published around that time (it came out in *Pravda* on January 25, although the original idea had been to produce a single copy of that issue of *Pravda*, just for Lenin, making sure that no one else saw it). The letter was evidently the "Letter to the Congress" that had already been the subject of a Politburo discussion. Lenin's draft (or proposal) could have been a standalone document based on his the Workers' and Peasants' Inspection article.[75]

Lenin's view prevailed at the plenum. Stalin's theses were rejected and sent back to be reworked (by a commission chaired by Stalin). The document that the plenum passed on to Lenin for his examination and summary opinion was entitled "National Aspects of Party and State Building"; and it stated, in part, "Unifying the national republics into a Union of Soviet Socialist Republics constitutes the concluding stage in the development of a form of cooperation, which in this instance takes the shape of a military, economic, and political union of peoples in a single multinational Soviet state." Lenin had regained political control over Stalin: in demanding that the theses be reconsidered, he was effectively announcing the convocation of an extraordinary plenary session of the Central Committee.

March 5 can be considered a fateful day in Lenin's life. On that day at around twelve o'clock, he called Volodicheva in and asked her to take down two letters. Note that he was evidently well enough to work and there were no indications that he was feeling ill. More importantly, there were no indications of any kind of restriction: he was dictating what he wanted, to whom he wanted, and as much as he wanted. It would seem that during this entire time, beginning with his victory at the February plenary meeting, the prison sentence imposed on him by the Politburo had been lifted.

The first letter written on March 5 was to Trotsky: "I would greatly urge you to take up the defense of the Georgian case in the Central Committee. This case is currently being 'pursued' by Stalin and Dzerzhinsky, and I cannot count on their impartiality. Quite the contrary, actually. If you were to agree to take up the defense, then I could rest easy. If for some reason you do not agree, then return the entire case file to me. I will take that as a sign of your refusal."[76]

This letter to Trotsky was accompanied by a note from Volodicheva: "To Comrade Trotsky. In addition to the letter communicated to you by telephone, Vladimir Ilyich has asked [me] to inform you that Comrade Kamenev is going to Georgia on Wednesday and Vladimir Ilyich asks you to let him know if you want to send anything there from yourself personally."[77]

Lenin also passed all the relevant documents to Trotsky; and Trotsky did not return them, thereby signaling to Lenin that he would lend his support. This support would become known on April 16, in a letter written by Trotsky to "all the members of the Central Committee of the Russian Communist Party" and stamped "Top Secret":

Today I received the copy attached hereto of a letter from Comrade Fotieva, Comrade Lenin's personal secretary, to Comrade Kamenev on Comrade Lenin's article on the nationalities issue.

I received Comrade Lenin's article on March 5, along with three notes from Comrade Lenin, copies of which are also attached.

At that time I made a copy of the article for myself as being of exceptionally fundamental significance and based on it both my amendments to Comrade Stalin's theses (which Comrade Stalin has accepted) and my own article on the nationalities issue for *Pravda.*

The article, as previously stated, is of primary and fundamental significance, but it contains a sharp condemnation directed at three members of the Central Committee. As long as there remained even the faintest hope that Vladimir Ilyich had had time to give any instructions concerning this article with regard to the party congress—for which it was intended, as follows from the circumstances and in particular from Comrade Fotieva's note—I did not raise the article as an issue.

Under the present circumstances, which have been conclusively characterized by Comrade Fotieva's note, I see no alternative other than to convey this article to the members of the Central Committee, since it is in my view no less significant for party policy on the nationalities issue than the earlier article on the relationship between the proletariat and the peasantry.

If none of the Central Committee's members—due to intraparty considerations, of obvious significance—raises the issue of bringing the article, in one form or another, to the attention of the party or the party congress, then I will regard this as tacit consent, which will absolve me of personal responsibility for this article with respect to the party congress."[78]

The annotation in Lenin's *Complete Works* to the effect that Trotsky responded to Lenin's suggestion of March 5 with a refusal is therefore a deliberate fabrication.[79] Trotsky did assume the defense of Lenin's position and did not give it up even after March 6, when he could no longer count on any help from Lenin, who was completely out of action by that time. On March 28, 1923, Trotsky sent the following letter to the Secretariat of the Central Committee, with a copy to Glyasser (i.e., to Lenin):

Page 2 of Memo no. 57 on the Georgian affair contains only my suggestion on recalling Comrade Ordzhonikidze. I had made three suggestions; and since the first is mentioned, the other two, which were rejected, must also be presented: (1) to put on record the fact that the Transcaucasian Federation in its present form represents a distortion of the Soviet idea of a federation, in the sense that it is excessively centralized; and (2) to acknowledge that the comrades representing the minority in the Georgian Communist Party do not constitute a "deviation" from the party line on the nationalities issue—their policy on this issue is defensive in nature and is directed against the erroneous policy of Comrade Ordzhonikidze.[80]

This is yet more evidence that Trotsky did indeed respond positively to Lenin's note.

Lenin's struggle with Stalin peaked on March 5. Lenin, well-informed now, knew that, despite the plenary meeting's resolution in his favor, the Georgian affair had remained, in contravention of the Central Committee decree, in the hands of Stalin and Ordzhonikidze, which meant that Stalin's Secretariat with support from Dzerzhinsky's GPU had come out against Lenin and the party's Central Committee. He realized that the majority in the Politburo was also siding with Stalin, and that under such circumstances he had nothing to lose. Therefore, he decided to use his old trump card: Stalin's conflict with Krupskaya. Thus, Lenin wrote Stalin a letter that constituted an ultimatum: either you apologize, and thus acknowledge defeat, or start an open war. Lenin did not inform Trotsky about this letter, although it was precisely on Trotsky's help that he intended to rely in his fight with Stalin. From this it follows that Lenin was ready to accept Stalin's capitulation in private, without humiliating him in front of his party colleagues and keeping open the possibility of future cooperation:

Dear Comrade Stalin!

You were rude enough to call my wife on the telephone and berate her. Even though she let you know that she was amenable to forgetting what had been said, Zinoviev and Kamenev were still apprised of it through her. I have no intention of forgetting so easily what has been done to me, and it need hardly be said that what is done to my wife I consider to have been done to me. Therefore I ask you to consider whether you are amenable to taking back what was said and apologizing or whether you prefer to break off relations between us.

Respectfully, Lenin[81]

In the "Journal of Lenin's Secretaries," Volodicheva indicates that Lenin asked for this second letter "to be set aside for the time being, saying that today things were somehow coming out wrong."[82] What exactly was coming out "wrong," Volodicheva does not say. No corrections were made to the letter on the following day.

On March 6, Lenin asked Trotsky for a reply to his letter of March 5. "The telephoned reply was taken down in shorthand," Volodicheva noted in the "Journal," but she did not enter the content of Trotsky's reply there.

That must mean that the reply was not favorable to Stalin, since otherwise it would unquestionably have appeared in the "Journal" and, as we know, Trotsky was supporting Lenin. Lenin then went over the letter to Stalin again "and asked that it be delivered by hand [and] a reply obtained."

Thus, the letter that was dated March 5 was not sent until March 6. On the same day, Lenin dictated "a letter to the Mdivani group" (with copies to Trotsky and Kamenev), also directed against Stalin and constituting the last piece of officially acknowledged Leniniana: "I am following your case with all my heart. I am outraged by Ordzhonikidze's rudeness and the connivance of Stalin and Dzerzhinsky. I am preparing notes and a speech for you."[83]

This is one more indication that at this point Lenin definitely knew that he had Trotsky's support, why would he send Trotsky a copy of this letter had the latter refused to join forces with him against Stalin? It is also clear that Stalin was aware of this new alliance and quickly took whatever actions he needed to take. None of Lenin's notes and speeches on this issue were ever found, although we have reason to believe that he did at least begin to work on them.

While the "letter to the Mdivani group" was actually sent, the letter to Stalin was not, as of March 6, since, in Volodicheva's words, "Nadezhda Konstantinovna asked that the letter to Stalin not be sent."[84] Then Volodicheva "went to Krupskaya and reminded her that Vladimir Ilyich was waiting for a reply from Stalin and was worried. That argument, apparently, had the desired effect."[85] On March 7, after Krupskaya had consulted with Kamenev, the letter was delivered to Stalin, Kamenev, and, later, to Zinoviev, too.[86] Volodicheva recalled:

> I delivered the letter by hand. I asked Stalin to write back to Vladimir Ilyich, since he was waiting for a reply and was worried. Stalin read the letter right then, while I was still there. His face remained calm. He was silent for a while, thought a little, and said—slowly, articulating every word clearly, and making pauses between them, "This is not Lenin speaking. It is his illness speaking." And he continued, "I am not a doctor, I am a politician. I am Stalin. If my wife, a party member, had acted incorrectly and been punished, I would not have considered myself entitled to interfere. And Krupskaya is a party member. But, since Vladimir Ilyich insists, I am prepared to apologize to Krupskaya for being rude.[87]

According to Volodicheva, Krupskaya had insisted that the letter not be delivered. According to Fotieva, it was held back by Volodicheva, who was afraid to take such a sharply worded missive to Stalin.[88] Fotieva remembered that Lenin "was waiting for a reply. He was waiting from one minute to the next. But Volodicheva could not make up her mind to take the letter to Stalin, since it was so harsh. It was not until the next morning that I found out that the letter was still with us. I ordered Volodicheva to take it." Which of the two is telling the truth is hard to determine.

Having delivered Lenin's letter to Stalin, Volodicheva "recorded Stalin's brief reply to Vladimir Ilyich and was so worried" that there was something wrong with her handwriting, because it had changed almost beyond recognition.[89] And then Volodicheva did not carry Stalin's reply back to Lenin but went to Kamenev's apartment instead:

> My comrades advised me to do that, in particular Maria Ignatievna Glyasser.... She said that I absolutely had to stop by and show that letter to Kamenev, because Stalin might have written something that would disturb Vladimir Ilyich. Kamenev read it through and gave it back to me, saying that I could hand it over. After visiting Kamenev, I returned to my office. But the letter was not handed over, because it was already too late: Vladimir Ilyich was unwell.[90]

"Unwell" is not exactly an accurate description. On March 5–7 events took place, orchestrated by Stalin and his entourage, of which we are unaware. It appears that on March 6 or 7, Lenin was taken into custody: "It was officially intimated," Volodicheva recalled, "that as of March 6 or even the day before, Vladimir Ilyich was in no condition to read or work or have any visitors or do anything. There could be no contact with him." "It was officially intimated....there could be no contact with him": the clear implication is that Lenin was under arrest. This means that Volodicheva had told Stalin about the letter that had been written by Lenin but not yet sent, and about the letter to Trotsky, on March 5 or 6.

"What was happening to Nadezhda Konstantinovna is not known either," Volodicheva continued, from which it follows that Krupskaya was also arrested at the same time, on March 5–7. Maria Ulyanova, evidently also under arrest, was permitted to make a telephone call to Stalin. What was said in that conversation is not known, but from the scraps of yelling heard on the other end of the line it was possible to gather that she was demanding to be released immediately and threatening that otherwise she would appeal to the workers in Moscow for help, on Lenin's behalf.[91]

On March 6 Volodicheva wrote in the "Journal": "The letter has still not been given to Vladimir Ilyich, since he has fallen ill." This is the last complete sentence in the "Journal." "There is no way to say with absolute certainty whether Lenin knew about Stalin's reply. Yes, later—when we were at the dacha, when he was feeling better—it is possible. Possible, though, not certain!"[92] is how Volodicheva ended her account of Lenin's last fight. But whether or not the powerless Lenin knew after March 6 about the return note from Stalin that had been dictated or read to Volodicheva and approved by Kamenev is not all that important. On the night of March 9, 1923, his health took another turn for the worse and he lost the power of speech. A week later, Stalin, citing Krupskaya as his authority, reported to the Politburo that the time had come to poison Lenin:

> On Saturday, March 17, Comrade Ulyanova (Nadezhda Konstantinovna) informed me, under the utmost secrecy, of "Vl. Ilyich's request to Stalin—that I, Stalin, should assume the responsibility of obtaining and delivering to Vladimir Ilyich a dose of cyanide. N. K. has told me, among other things, that "Vladimir Ilyich is suffering unbelievably," that "it is unthinkable to go on living like this"; she was most inflexibly insistent that I "not refuse Ilyich's request." In view of N. K.'s particular insistence and in view of the fact that V. Ilyich was demanding that I agree... I did not consider it possible to reply with a refusal, so I declared, "I ask Vladimir Ilyich to calm himself and to rest assured that when the need arises I will unwaveringly fulfill his request." Vladimir Ilyich did indeed calm down. I must, however, declare that I lack the strength to fulfill V. Ilyich's request and must refuse this mission, no matter how humane and necessary it may be, whereof I hereby inform the Politburo of the Central Committee.[93]

This is the first and last indication that the general chorus of well-wishers suggesting that Lenin be poisoned turns out to include the voice of his own wife! Yet for some reason we are again hearing about this from Stalin rather than through a letter from Krupskaya, which would have been more natural.

It was this note that appears to have been the subject of the conversation described by Trotsky in his article of 1939 (he erroneously places it in February or early March 1923).

And several days later, on March 22, an expanded session of the Politburo took place. Stalin's theses, which had been rejected at the February plenary meeting, were discussed and approved and on March 24, they were published in *Pravda*. Since due to their importance these theses could be approved only by a plenary meeting of the Central Committee, on March 23 Trotsky wrote a letter of protest. It was at this point that the collective leadership that made up the Stalinist majority declared open war on Trotsky, the very same war about which Trotsky had warned Radek. On March 29, a letter from Politburo members and candidate members Zinoviev, Stalin, Kamenev, Tomsky, Rykov, Bukharin, Kalinin, and Molotov was sent to the participants of the expanded session of the Politburo: the extraordinary plenary meeting. The letter officially informed party members that differences of opinion with Trotsky had become irreconcilable.[94] Lenin was not mentioned in that document at all. Trotsky was explicitly declared as the main obstacle to party unity (that is, the only voice of the opposition that supported Lenin). Formally, of course, the Soviet leadership's complaint was written due to disagreements with Trotsky regarding the "theses on industry,"[95] although in the letter they were mentioned only once, at the very beginning. On March 30–31, a plenary meeting of the Central Committee approved the Politburo's amendments to Trotsky's theses and instructed him to produce a new draft of the document. Stalin was retaliating against Trotsky for his criticism on the nationalities issue. The new draft was not accepted. Instead, Trotsky once again came under criticism:

> But even after this, Trotsky so distorted the amendment on the peasant question that had been approved at a plenary meeting of the Central Committee that it acquired a completely different meaning and a new resolution by the Politburo was required so that the amendment on the peasant question could be added to the theses in its entirety. As may be seen from the contents of his report at the congress, Trotsky departed from the theses that had been approved by the Central Committee, failed to provide an analysis of the fundamental issues involved in the industry problem, and reduced the issue of the governing role of the party to the misguided, anti-Leninist thesis of the dictatorship of the party.[96]

In short, the Politburo unexpectedly discovered an underachiever in its midst, who was incapable of handling his everyday work and moreover was heading in a misguided, anti-Leninist direction.

On April 17, the Twelfth Party Congress convened without Lenin. "Vladimir Ilyich could not and does not know the items on the agenda of our congress or the resolutions prepared by the Central Committee," Kamenev informed the delegates. A day before the congress began, Fotieva officially submitted to the Politburo (the presidium of the congress) the text of Lenin's article, "The Question of Nationalities or 'Autonomization.'" Since this work of Lenin's had already been making the rounds among party activists and had been copied and distributed primarily by the Georgian delegation, it was decided to read it in committees without the right to publicize it. Zinoviev and Kamenev supported Stalin. The Georgian "deviationists"—Makharadze, Mdivani, and others—were censured, with Ordzhonikidze coming out as their accuser. Bukharin urged delegates to vote for the "outstanding theses of the Central Committee and Comrade Stalin." And Yenukidze made a speech that can only be characterized as an outright lie:

> Now about Comrade Lenin's letter. Comrade Mdivani in his speech has constantly invoked the name of Comrade Ilyich and he wanted to create the impression that Comrade Lenin supposedly wrote this letter on purpose in order to

support the deviationist comrades and to provide a wholesale justification of their policies. [Bukharin: "Of course, that was the purpose."] That was not the purpose, Comrade Bukharin I will permit myself to say that we also know Comrade Lenin a little and that we have also had occasion to meet with him in connection with various issues, and in particular in connection with the Georgian question. And I claim, comrades, and I hope that when Comrade Lenin's health improves, he will agree with the fact that often the positions that have been advanced here by the deviationist comrades were known to him, but that when they were correctly explained and interpreted, he agreed with the policies that were carried out there by Comrade Ordzhonikidze.... Comrade Lenin has become the victim of one-sided, erroneous information....

Stalin, as the victor, was lazy and magnanimous. "Might I be permitted to say a few words about this topic which everyone is tired of..."

On April 22, 1923, Lenin's birthday, Stalin presented him with an entirely Stalinesque gift by awarding Demyan Bedny the military Order of the Red Banner for his role in the civil war. Since the award—made to a poet and political agitator, which was in itself unprecedented at that time—was being given not on Red Army Day (February 23) and not even in the year when the civil war ended but much later, one must assume that the quick-witted Stalin was thinking of an entirely different civil war, the one being waged within the Bolshevik Party against Lenin.

In Stalin's mind, Bedny's role in that war had been great indeed. So Bedny received his medal and the right to have his biography included in 1924 in a volume published by the *Great Encyclopedia* and entitled *Activists of the USSR and the October Revolution*, thus becoming one of the 248 names in the top party hierarchy. On April 13, 1933, his fiftieth birthday, Bedny was the first Soviet writer to receive the Order of Lenin.

This excursus into the events of December–March has been necessary in order to understand if Lenin could possibly—as Stalin and Fotieva have claimed he did—have secretly asked Stalin for poison in December 1922, when the battle was at its height. The answer is obvious: he could not. The allegation that he did was fabricated by Stalin himself at various times and in a strikingly dogged way, as if someone were accusing him of being Lenin's poisoner.

The story of how Stalin created his alibi is a separate criminal narrative that is worthy of study in its own right. It could be isolated in a separate subchapter: "Stalin's Alibi."

"At the beginning of the 1930s"—as will be shown below, sometime after October 1932—Maria Ulyanova decided out of the blue to write her memoirs; and these were not ordinary memoirs, but her recollections of how

Lenin fell ill and died. Since Ulyanova—who had never been known for her civic courage and was an obedient party worker—was able to use unpublished archival documents in her memoir project (i.e., was allowed access to secret party papers but did not insist that they be published), one can only infer that she was acting on someone else's orders. That someone else had to be Stalin. And he, being predominantly interested in the question of the poison, made yet another document fabricated after the event available to her, one that had been signed by yet another impartial eyewitness to the events—Fotieva. He also forced Ulyanova to quote that document. Fotieva had written:

> On 22 December Vladimir Ilyich called me in at 6 p.m. and dictated the following: "Do not forget to take all measures to acquire and... deliver cyanide in the event that the paralysis affects my speech, as a humane measure and in emulation of Lafargue " [Paul Lafargue, Karl Marx's son-in-law, who committed suicide with his wife in 1911, at the age of seventy]."

The absence of this note from the "Journal of Lenin's Secretaries" had to be explained. Fotieva reported that Lenin himself had asked for this in confidence while Fotieva, who remained obedient to Stalin before and after this incident, for some reason decided this time to betray Stalin and obey Lenin:

> He added, "This note does not go into the journal. You understand, don't you? You understand? And I hope that you will do as I say."

Why, then, did Fotieva not tell anyone about the note later, in a separate memo—on December 23, for instance? And what has become of that note? There never was any such note. And the reason given for not making an entry in the "Journal" was most unoriginal: "There was a phrase omitted at the beginning that I could not remember." And at the end? "At the end—I could not make it out, because he was speaking very quietly. When I asked him about it, he did not answer. He ordered me to keep it in strictest secrecy."[97]

Every word in this document is a fabrication. Ulyanova does not say where Fotieva's note of December 22 came from and when it was made. Despite its importance, Fotieva "forgot" to put it into the "Journal of Lenin's Secretaries." She did not write down the second sentence of the document not because she forgot it, but because she was unable to make it on December 22 (but she was able to make it out "at the beginning of the 1930s"?).

Stylistically as well, the note smacks of forgery. Lenin could not have "dictated" the phrase: "Do not forget to take all measures to acquire and... deliver." Only Stalin could have dictated that. Nor could Lenin have said that he was intending to do away with himself "as a humane measure and in emulation of Lafargue." That phrase also, in its entirety, could have come from Stalin. On December 22, a day before he started to work on his "Last Testament," Lenin would hardly have been thinking about how best to emulate Lafargue. The instruction that "this note does not go into the journal" is another falsification, since Lenin did not know and could not have known that the "Journal" even existed. Nor could he have intended "journal" to mean his own personal notations, since they could not have been called that until December 23, when Lenin began to write his testament.

From March 7, 1923, until January 21, 1924, Lenin was unable to function as a political figure.[98]

In this situation, Krupskaya's and Ulyanova's sole task was to prevent Lenin from being murdered by Stalin. Only this can explain Krupskaya's public support of Stalin in his conflict with Trotsky. Even so, on at least two occasions Krupskaya revealed her real opinions. On October 31, 1923, she wrote a letter to Zinoviev, Stalin's ally, which was first published in the USSR in 1989:

> Dear Grigory.... Trotsky is by no means the only one who is to blame for this whole disgrace. Our group is also to blame for all that has happened: you, Stalin, and Kamenev. You could have averted this disgrace, of course, but decided not to do so. If you could not it would prove the complete powerlessness of our group, its complete helplessness.... Our side took on a false, unacceptable tone. It is wrong to create an atmosphere of squabbling and personal issues. The workers... would have firmly censured not only Trotsky, but you as well. The workers' healthy class instinct would have forced them to speak out firmly against both sides, but even more firmly against our group, which is responsible for the general tone.... We are forced to conceal the whole incident from the workers.[99]

Discussing her husband's sufferings, Krupskaya pointedly writes "our group," "our side," "we"—to an audience consisting of Stalin, Zinoviev, and Kamenev. But still she cannot keep her views to herself:

> Also completely unacceptable is the misuse of Ilyich's name that occurred at the plenary meeting. I can imagine how outraged he would be if he knew how his name was being misused. It is a good thing that I was not present when [Grigory Ivanovich] Petrovsky said that Trotsky is to blame for Ilyich's illness. I

would have cried out, "It is a lie!" It was not Trotsky who concerned Vladimir Ilyich most of all but the nationalities question and the mores that have taken hold in our upper echelons. You know that Vladimir Ilyich saw the danger of a schism not only in the personal qualities of Trotsky but also in the personal qualities of Stalin and others. Therefore, because you know this, the references to Ilyich were unacceptable, disingenuous. They should not have been permitted; they were hypocritical. Those references were excruciatingly painful to me personally. I thought: is it now worth it to him to improve, when his closest comrades in the cause treat him so, have so little consideration for his opinion, misrepresent him so?...

The time is too serious to create a schism and to make it psychologically impossible for Trotsky to work. We should try to come to terms with him in a comradely fashion. Formally, all of the blame for the schism has now been assigned to Trotsky. But only formally, but then wasn't Trotsky forced to do what he did? I don't know the details, and they're not the point anyway... the point is that we have to take Trotsky into account as a force within the party, and we have to be able to create a situation in which this force would be used to the greatest benefit of the party.[100]

This letter, in addition to reflecting Krupskaya's views, demonstrates that Lenin was no longer being informed about what was taking place at the Joint Plenary Meeting, that Lenin was on Trotsky's side, not Stalin's, who was the guilty party in the "nationalities question," and that it was "inadvisable" for Lenin's health to improve, since he meant nothing to his "comrades and colleagues," something that Krupskaya must have already realized no later than March 5, 1922.

The second letter in which Krupskaya speaks of being on Trotsky's side in the conflict with Stalin was written on January 29, 1924, shortly after Lenin's death: "Dear Lev Davydovich.... The attitude that Vladimir Ilyich developed toward you when you came from Siberia to visit us in London did not change in him up to his very death. I wish you strength and health, Lev Davydovich, and I send you a firm embrace."[101]

So emotionally loaded is this note that it could well be called a farewell. Did Krupskaya know that Trotsky really was at the time a hair's breadth away from death? That in January 1924 Stalin had tried to dispose of Trotsky, too? Trotsky described the attempt on his life in more than modest terms, confining himself to a single phrase: "In the latter half of January 1924 I traveled to the Caucasus, to Sukhumi, in an attempt to rid myself of a mysterious infection that had been hounding me, whose nature the doctors have not divined to this day. The news of Lenin's death came while I was en route."[102]

That is all that Trotsky has to say about the January 1924 coup d'état organized by Stalin. Just before his departure from Moscow, on January 18, Trotsky was twice visited by Getye. On January 21, a few days after Trotsky left the capital, Lenin died; and once Trotsky recovered, he was never able to regain the political clout he had once had. Since the mysterious nature of the illness that doctors could not diagnose was eminently clear to Trotsky, however, he never again went to the Kremlin pharmacy to have his prescriptions filled.[103] These safety measures saved him only to a point: within three years, Trotsky would be exiled; in another year, he was expelled from Russia; and then he was killed. Ultimately, he could not escape the same fate as Lenin.

Sinister rumors about Lenin's poisoning did not subside after 1924. Lydia Shatunovskaya was sentenced to 20 years in prison "for the intention to emigrate to Israel" and spent seven years in solitary confinement in the Vladimir prison. She was released shortly after Stalin's death (March 5, 1953), and soon afterward, at the Porechye Sanatorium near Moscow, she ran into her old acquaintance, Ivan Gronsky (1894–1985), a critic, reporter, editor, and party functionary. In 1932–1933, he was the head of the Soviet Writers' Union steering committee; in 1928–1934, he served as managing editor of the newspaper *Izvestiya*, and during the years 1932–1937, he was the editor-in-chief of the magazine *Novy Mir*. In addition, Gronsky was something like a commissar of literature under Stalin. "Through him, Stalin obtained information about everything that went on in literature, and stayed in contact with writers' circles.... Gronsky was one of the very few people who was allowed to enter Stalin's office without being announced. Among his other duties, he was entrusted with the very delicate task of carrying out surveillance over Gorky."[104]

In 1937, Gronsky was arrested, convicted, and spent 16 years in prisons and labor camps. In 1953, he was released. And it was then, at the Porechye Sanatorium, that he met his fellow ex-prisoner, Lydia Shatunovskaya. As she recalled:

> After we renewed our acquaintance, Ivan Gronsky and I often took walks together and told one another about many things.... During one of our walks Gronsky, a very smart and careful man, shared with me, a woman and not a party member, his suspicions about Lenin's death and about the mysterious role played by Stalin in speeding it up.... He candidly told me of his conviction that Stalin had actively and deliberately accelerated Lenin's death, since no matter how sick Lenin was, as long as he lived the path to absolute dictatorship remained closed to Stalin.[105]

What did Gronsky tell her? On October 19, 1932, during one during a meeting with writers at which, along with everyone else, he had had a fair amount to drink, Stalin "to Gronsky's horror began to talk to those present about Lenin and about the circumstances of his death." Shatunovskaya writes:

> He mumbled something to the effect that he alone knew how and why Lenin died.... Gronsky... carried the drunken Stalin to another room and laid him on the sofa, where he promptly fell asleep.... When he woke up he spent a long and agonizing time remembering what had happened the night before; and when he did remember, he leapt up in horror and fury and pounced on Gronsky. He shook him by the shoulder and yelled frantically, "Ivan! Tell me the truth. What did I say about Lenin's death yesterday? Tell me the truth, Ivan!" Gronsky tried to calm him, saying, "Iosif Vissarionovich! You didn't say anything yesterday. I simply saw that you were not feeling well, so I brought you into the study and put you to bed. Besides, all the writers were so drunk that no one could either hear or understand a thing."
>
> Stalin was gradually beginning to calm down when another thought entered his head: "Ivan!" he yelled. "You weren't drunk, though. What did you hear?"... Gronsky, of course, tried in every possible way to assure Stalin that nothing had been said about Lenin's death and that he, Gronsky, had heard nothing and had taken Stalin away only because everyone present had been drinking far too much.... From that day on, Stalin's attitude to Gronsky changed completely, and in 1937 he was arrested."[106]

There is also the testimony of Boris Nicolaevsky, a well-known and respected historian, who collected a vast archive on the Russian Revolution, which is now stored at the Hoover Institution:

> Trotsky... told about one extremely important episode which will possibly force historians to admit that Stalin was Lenin's killer... in the literal meaning of this word, a poisoner.... The fact that Lenin made such a request of Stalin is open to serious doubt: by this time, Lenin no longer trusted Stalin, and it is not clear how he could have turned to him, of all people, with such an intimate request. This fact acquires particular significance in light of another story. The author of this article was acquainted with an émigré of the war years.... In the Chelyabinsk pretrial detention facility, she had met an old convict who in 1922–1924 had worked as a cook in Gorki, where the ailing Lenin was living at the time. This old man confessed to my acquaintance that he had added drugs to Lenin's food that made his condition worse. He did this on the instructions of people whom he considered to be Stalin's representatives.... If we consider this story to be true, then Stalin's announcement to the Politburo—as related by Trotsky—has a definite meaning: Stalin was creating an alibi for himself in case people should find out about the work of the poisoner-cook.[107]

This episode, as retold by Nicolaevsky, echoes the recollections of Elizabeth Lermolo, who was arrested on the night of December 1, 1934, in connection with the murder of Kirov. Once out of the Stalinist camp system, she found her way to the West after World War II and published her memoirs after Stalin's death. These memoirs contain an identical episode— Lenin, Gorki, a cook, poisoning—except that in her narrative the cook is just a bystander, not the poisoner. Here is her account:

> One day a man was added to my exercise shift. He was an old-time prisoner, Gavriil Volkov, a Communist. Until then he had been allowed to take his walks only in solitude. Through the window of my cell I had often seem him, all hunched over, wandering by himself around the deserted yard. Although his cell was two doors away from mine, I had never had an opportunity to exchange a single word with him. He looked frightened and at the same time frightening. There was something about him that made you avoid having a conversation with him. There were rumors that he was being held in "strictest isolation" on direct orders from the Kremlin. And no one knew what he was charged with and why he was in prison....
>
> Until 1923 he was employed in the Kremlin as the manager of a dining room that was maintained there for the highest placed party functionaries. Later he became chef at the Kremlin sanatorium in Gorki.... Volkov had been arrested and brought to the prison from the "Silver Pines" in 1932. The third anniversary of his stay in solitary confinement had just passed.
>
> To my usual questions regarding his term of imprisonment and reason for imprisonment, he gave some surprising answers. He didn't know the term of his sentence; as for the reason for his imprisonment, he could only guess. He had never stood trial. No one had ever interrogated him.
>
> "Not only was I never interrogated but no official was even permitted to discuss my case with me." In response to my surprise, he explained that people who had any connection with the Kremlin would rarely be subjected to interrogation or made to stand trial if they fell into disfavor. Usually, the sentence was issued in absentia....
>
> "For a period of eleven years I have kept a frightful secret buried deep within my soul, which I had not shared with anyone.... What's more, I know that I shall never get out of here alive. I must tell you my story.... When Lenin became ill in 1923," Volkov went on to say, "the decision was made to hospitalize him in the Kremlin sanatorium at Gorki." Volkov was sent there to serve as Lenin's personal chef. Lenin's wife, Nadezhda Krupskaya, approved of Volkov's selection for she had known him in the Kremlin as a trusted and thoroughly dependable person.
>
> He had to work hard and was alone to cook and serve Lenin, his wife, and the doctors. He worked for almost a year without a single day off, since he knew that it was his duty to do everything possible to hasten the recovery of his party's

leader. Lenin and his wife clearly valued Volkov's loyalty.

Although Lenin did not feel well, the doctors were promising to get him back on his feet quickly. Occasionally, he would begin to feel better, and would come out on the terrace to sit in the sun. From time to time, he had visitors. Stalin came to see him several times. But for the most part Lenin remained alone, apart from Nadezhda Krupskaya.

Initially, things went smoothly. Lenin's condition, it seemed, gave no cause for alarm. Then, toward the end of the year , shortly before New Year's—"the winter was bitter cold," Volkov recalled. "Nadezhda Krupskaya was unexpectedly summoned to Moscow on urgent business. She was kept there for two days, and during her absence Lenin's health took a drastic turn for the worse.

"When Krupskaya returned and saw Lenin, she gasped. That's how bad he looked. Naturally, special treatments were prescribed and soon he improved. Everyone felt relieved, and life returned to normal."

About ten days later Nadezhda Krupskaya was called back to the Kremlin on some party matter. This time she stayed longer, and Lenin again took a turn for the worse. As Volkov was bringing him his tea one morning, Lenin seemed very upset. He couldn't speak. He made signs to Volkov, who couldn't figure out what he wanted. There was no one in the room except the two of them. Volkov asked him, "Shall I call the doctor?" Lenin shook his head categorically and continued to gesticulate. Only after long questioning did Volkov finally understand what Lenin wanted. He was asking him to get through to the Kremlin somehow, to tell Krupskaya that he was feeling worse and to ask her to drop everything and return to Gorki. Lenin warned Volkov not to telephone Krupskaya, but to see her in person.

"Needless to say," Volkov continued, "I made every effort to do as he asked, but I couldn't get out of Gorki. For one thing, a severe snowstorm made all the roads impassable, by foot or car. And, more importantly, Stalin phoned from the Kremlin and ordered all physicians as well as the entire staff at Gorki to remain at their posts until the health of 'our dearly beloved Comrade Lenin' had improved. In short, Nadezhda Krupskaya did not return from the Kremlin, and Lenin's condition grew worse and worse until he was no longer able to get out of bed."

And then on January 21, 1924....at eleven in the morning, as usual, Volkov took Lenin his second breakfast. There was no one else in the room. As soon as Volkov appeared, Lenin made an effort to rise, and extended both his hands, uttering unintelligible sounds. Volkov rushed over to him and Lenin slipped a note into his hand.

As Volkov turned, having hidden the note, Dr. Yelistratov, Lenin's personal physician, ran into the room, apparently having been attracted by the commotion. The two of them got Lenin back to bed and gave him an injection to calm him. Lenin quieted down, his eyes half-closed. He never opened them again.

The note, scratched in a nervous scrawl, read: "Gavrilushka, I've been poisoned... Go fetch Nadya at once... Tell Trotsky... Tell anyone you can."

"Two questions," Volkov said, "have troubled me all these years. Did Yelistratov see Lenin give me that note? And if he did, did he inform Stalin? These questions have ruined my peace, poisoned my existence. I have felt every minute that my life is hanging by a thread.

"What a horror!" I cried.

"Later on, I ran into Dr. Yelistratov a few times, but we never exchanged a word. We merely looked at each other, that was all. I thought I detected in his eyes the same torment of a deeply hidden secret. I may be wrong, but it seemed to me that he was also the slave of a secret. What became of him, I don't know—he soon disappeared from Gorki.

Volkov fell silent, but a minute later he added:

"Alas, I was never able to carry out Lenin's request. I told no one about the note. You are the first. You can ask me why I have kept silent for so long," he said. "Believe me, it was not only out of fear that Stalin would have me shot. I understood that in order to conceal the truth about Lenin's death, he would not stop at destroying my relatives, friends, and acquaintances—anyone he could suspect of knowing my secret. That's why I kept my lips sealed. I even stopped seeing my fiancée, for fear of endangering her life.

When our walk ended that morning, Volkov took me to the door of my cell. And I never saw him again.[108]

Lenin had many cooks. From time to time, they were replaced. Naturally, it is easier to assume that there was a poisoner-cook, rather than a rescuer-cook, whom the dying Lenin addressed not formally as "Comrade Volkov," but as "Gavrilushka." It also does not seem to be the case that during this period Lenin was capable of writing, talking, or even whispering.[109] Finally, both stories could have been true. The cook Gavriil Volkov could have added poison to Lenin's food, following the orders of Stalin's agents. Meanwhile, the poisoned Lenin, unaware that he was being poisoned by his cook, could have written his note...

The responsibility for the operation to poison Lenin apparently belonged to Genrikh Yagoda. In his book *The Real Stalin*, Yves Delbars—citing a story told by Stalin's secretary Grigory Kanner, which Kanner had heard from another one of Stalin's secretaries, who remains unnamed and who escaped abroad (apparently Boris Bazhanov)—describes the following episode, which occurred on January 20, 1924:

Kanner saw Yagoda enter Stalin's office accompanied by two doctors, who had treated Lenin.

"Fyodor Alexandrovich [Getye]," Stalin said to one of these doctors. "You must immediately go to Gorki and urgently examine Vladimir Ilyich. Genrich Georgievich [Yagoda] will accompany you."

That same evening—it was January 20, 1924—Kanner, who was in and out of the room, overheard parts of a conversation between Stalin and Yagoda: "There will soon be another attack. The symptoms are there. He has written a few lines [Kanner saw a few lines in Lenin's distorted handwriting] to thank you for sending him a means of deliverance. He is terribly distressed by the thought of another attack...."

On January 21, 1924, the fatal attack occurred. It was terrible, but it did not last long. Krupskaya left the room for a moment in order to telephone. When she returned Lenin was dead. On his bed-table were several small empty bottles. At a quarter-past seven the telephone rang in Stalin's office. Yagoda announced that Lenin was dead.[110]

Once again the myth that Lenin asked Stalin for poison and that this poison was delivered to Lenin on January 21, 1924, by Yagoda, who had gone with Getye to examine Lenin is revived.

Before his death, Lenin asked Krupskaya to read him Jack London's story "The Love of Life." Two travelers are crossing an ice-cold river. One twists his leg and can go no further. The other does not turn around and goes on. The man who is hurt goes as far as he can, then falls down from weakness and exhaustion. In order not to die of hunger, he eats raw fish. He fights a wolf that attacks him and tears apart its throat with his teeth. Finally, fishermen notice the dying man on the shore, rescue him, and bring him back to life.[111]

Up to the very end, Lenin was hoping that he would survive, that he would be able to overcome the enemy that had attacked him, that he would be rescued by his comrades. Could such a man have committed suicide? Could he have asked Stalin for poison?

On January 22, at 11 a.m.—in other words, 16 hours after Lenin's death—an autopsy was performed. Nine doctors were present during the autopsy, which ended at 4 p.m. The medical report stated that Lenin had died of "disseminated sclerosis." A week later, Dr. Vaysbrod, who was present during the autopsy, wrote in *Pravda* that doctors were not yet able to assemble all the details of Lenin's illness into a single clinical picture. Evidently, Vaysbrod was implying that he was not satisfied by the medical report that had come out after the autopsy. Indeed, the report did not include a toxicological analysis and did not describe the contents of Lenin's stomach; it indicated only that his stomach was empty and that the walls of the stomach had contracted, although it was known that Lenin had eaten two meals on the day of his death. The report referred to irregularities in the spleen and liver, but did not go into details. On the whole, the doctors avoided discussing those organs in where traces of poisoning might have been detected. Nor had they done a blood analysis.

It was around this time that another tradition was offered: the committee that organized the funeral of a dead leader would always be headed by the main pretender to the power of the deceased. And the person appointed to head the committee to organize Lenin's funeral by the USSR's TsIK was Dzerzhinsky—who was also the first among Lenin's pallbearers, as photographs show.[112] Lenin's funeral was the subject of the March and April issues of the Soviet government's English-language photo-journal *Soviet Russia Pictorial*. Beneath one of the photographs were listed the men who carried Lenin's coffin: Stalin, Zinoviev, Kamenev, Bukharin, Molotov, Rudzutak, Dzerzhinsky—Lenin's successors. But where was Trotsky? The answer to this question was given in the June issue, which contained a photograph of Trotsky and his attending physcian, Dr. Getye, in Sukhumi, on the Black Sea: Trotsky was vacationing on the sea (while Lenin's other devoted comrades-in-arms stood freezing at the funeral).

However, it appears that Dzerzhinsky was also to share Lenin's fate. The rumors that he did not die of natural causes have had remarkable staying power. Here is what Nicolaevsky wrote on September 1, 1954, to Nikolai Valentinov-Volsky (1878–1964), the revolutionary, historian, and journalist who emigrated in 1930, first to France and then to the United States:

> Stalin's favorite technique for a long time was to use doctors to poison people.... Personally I first refused to believe that Dzerzhinsky had been poisoned...but later I heard the same story... from a man who was the head of one of the groups that worked for Georgy Malenkov, the secretary of the party's Central Committee. "Now, reading Reiss's notes"—Reiss was a Soviet intelligence agent who had fled to the West and was killed on Stalin's orders in Switzerland in September 1937—"I came across [NKVD head Nikolai Yezhov's words to the effect that] Dzerzhinsky was unreliable. Under such circumstances, I am no longer as categorical in my rejection of any possibility of poisoning." "I know that Dzerzhinsky opposed placing the GPU under Stalin's control... I know, furthermore, that Stalin's apparatus began to carry out major operations in the fall of 1926," i.e., after Dzerzhinsky's death; "that Stalin brought the apparatus in other countries under his control in 1927–1928. And that Stalin undoubtedly made use of Dzerzhinsky's death, since it was useful to him...[113]

Let us cite the testimony of one more informed contemporary observer of these events, Ryszard Wraga, former agent of Polish intelligence. On June 20, 1960, in a letter to N. Valentinov-Volsky, Wraga wrote:

"Dzerzhinsky's death represents a sharp break in the tactics and methods of the GPU—it unleashed such a police state and led to such a rejection of revolutionary methods in favor of a state-sponsored security regime, that I don't think that it will ever be possible to get to the bottom of it or evaluate it.... This was a man who was completely lacking in cynicism and had no profit-seeking motives. I think that he represented quite a constraining beginning for Stalin and that, had he lived, all of Stalinism would have looked different. But these are considerations of a more literary nature and not very serious."[114]

Nicolaevsky's and Wraga's epistolary evidence may be supplemented by documentary evidence. On June 2, 1937, Stalin gave a long speech about the discovery of a military-political conspiracy at an extended session of the Military Council of the People's Commissariat of Defense. Concerning Dzerzhinsky, Stalin said the following:

"It is often said that in 1922... Dzerzhinsky voted for Trotsky, and not just voted for him, but openly supported Trotsky, under Lenin and against Lenin. Did you know this? He was not a man who could remain passive in anything. He was a very active Trotskyite and he wanted to bring the entire GPU to Trotsky's defense. He was unable to do this."[115]

Can there be any doubt that "he was unable to do this," in Stalin's language, meant that Dzerzhinsky had had to be eliminated? It is no surprise that when Viacheslav Menzhinsky, chairman of the OGPU (successor of the GPU), came to the Politburo on November 14, 1932, with a draft resolution on establishing an Order of Felix Dzerzhinsky, Stalin entered a motion against it.[116]

Epilogue

Perhaps it is indeed necessary that our old comrades should so easily and simply go down to their graves.

Joseph Stalin
Speech at the Funeral of Mikhail Frunze
November 3, 1925

There can be no doubt that the assumption that Lenin was murdered, supported by a growing mass of materials and research, will force us to look at many matters that appeared to be very clear. The subject of Lenin himself—not as a great man, or a necessary man, but as someone who interfered and was oppressive—will be one of the first to be reconsidered. The chronology of Stalinist crimes will evidently have to be shifted over to a starting point at least twenty years earlier—from December 1, 1934, when on Stalin's orders his rival for the post of general secretary, Sergey Kirov was killed by a "terrorist," to April 1922: the beginning of the operation to poison Lenin. The top leadership of the Communist Party of the USSR—which found it expedient to enter into a conspiracy with Stalin to eliminate the leader of their party—now appears in an entirely new light.

Such spectacular beginnings were bound to lead to things no less spectacular. Starting in 1924, many party members died in circumstances that have never been fully explained. A partial list begins even before Lenin's death, on the evening of June 14, 1922, Simon Ashkovich Kamo (real name: Ter-Petrosian), the well-known Russian revolutionary, fighter, and Stalin's collaborator in pre-Revolutionary dealings and expropriations, died after being hit by a truck in Tiflis. The bicycle that Kamo was riding when he was run over had been given to him as a present by Yakov Sverdlov. Stalin continued exacting revenge on Kamo even after his death—his monument in Tbilisi was torn down and his sister was arrested.[1]

On March 25, 1924, shortly after Lenin died and an open conflict with Trotsky began, Ephraim Sklyansky—Trotsky's deputy in military affairs, the factual head and coordinator of the Red Army's campaign during the civil war, the deputy head of the Revolutionary Military Council—was removed from his post. It was obvious that Sklyansky's transfer to a new position—the chairmanship of the Mossukno state textile trust—was a prelude to Trotsky's own removal. In April 1925, by a Central Committee resolution, Trotsky was forced to resign as head of the armed forces. He was replaced by Mikhail Frunze. On August 27, 1925, during a trip to the United States, Sklyansky drowned in a lake.

In November 1925, Frunze also died while undergoing surgery. The post of people's commissar was filled by Stalin's protégé, Kliment Voroshilov. Immediately after Frunze's death, rumors that Frunze had been killed on Stalin's orders began to circulate. Here is what Trotsky wrote about the matter in his draft of an unfinished biography of Stalin:

> He was not destined to remain long at his post as head of the armed forces: in November 1925, he died under the surgeon's knife. But during those few months, Frunze showed too much independence in protecting the army from the GPU.... Frunze aimed to free the command staff from the GPU and in a relatively short time he abolished the commissariat corps. Zinoviev and Kamenev subsequently assured me that Frunze was on their side and against Stalin. In any even, the fact is that Frunze did not want to go into surgery. Already at that time, his death gave rise to a series of theories.... Subsequently, they hardened into a direct accusation against Stalin. Frunze had been too independent at his military post, had identified himself too closely with the command staff of the party and the army, and had undoubtedly hindered Stalin's attempts to gain control of the army through his personal agents.
>
> Based on the facts of the case, the following course of events may be deduced. Frunze had a stomach ulcer, but believed—following the opinion of doctors who were close to him—that his heart would not be able to handle chloroform and was firmly set against having an operation. Stalin ordered the Central Committee's doctor—in other words, his own trusted agent—to convene a specially selected consultation board. This board recommended a surgical intervention. The Politburo ratified the recommendation. Frunze had to submit, in other words, to face death through an anesthetic.... The circumstances surrounding Frunze's death were reflected in a short story by the famous Soviet writer Pilnyak. Stalin immediately confiscated the short story and subjected its author to official disfavor. Pilnyak later had to offer public repentance for his "mistake." At the end of 1925, Stalin's power was already so great that his

administrative plans could easily include an obedient medical consultation board, chloroform, and the surgeon's knife.

Writing about Boris Pilnyak, Trotsky has in mind his "The Tale of the Unextinguished Moon." The story, which was completed in January 1926 and published in the journal *Novy Mir*, No. 5, 1926, that never reached its readers, since the whole run of the journal was confiscated.[2]

It appeared that Frunze had been killed in order to bring the army under the control of the OGPU, which was headed by Dzerzhinsky. This meant that the next clash would be between Stalin's Secretariat and Dzerzhinsky's OGPU. We know who won that battle: on July 20, 1926, Dzerzhinsky suddenly died of a heart attack.

Stalin's wife and Lenin's secretary Nadezhda Alliluyeva died tragically either at Stalin's own hands or by suicide. On April 10, 1956, the Paris newspaper *Russkaya Mysl* published a short article on this topic under the undiplomatic heading, STALIN—ALLILUYEVA'S MURDERER. As the newspaper reported:

> The Foreign Office has confirmed incoming reports that Stalin in Moscow is being openly accused of killing his second wife, Nadezhda Alliluyeva. This information first appeared in London newspapers on April 3. They referred to the Moscow periodical *Sovietsky Kommunist*, which reported that Stalin had "personally shot his second wife".... This charge is being read at all Communist Party meetings across the Soviet Union, as the head of the Foreign Office's press department has confirmed. Alliluyeva died under mysterious circumstances in 1932. As is well-known, the Soviet government announced that she died "after a prolonged and difficult illness." However, people did not lend credence to this report and said that she had committed suicide.

Vyacheslav Menzhinsky, who replaced Dzerzhinsky as head of the OGPU, died in 1934. At his public trial in Moscow in 1938, Genrikh Yagoda—the former people's commissar of internal affairs—admitted that he had organized Menzhinsky's murder with the assistance of medical doctors. In his unfinished draft for a biography of Stalin, Trotsky wrote:

> Doctor I. N. Kazakov has given his testimony:

> "As a result of my conversation with Yagoda, L. G. Levin and I developed a method to cure Menzhinsky that actually destroyed his last strength and accelerated his death. In this way, Levin and I practically killed Menzhinsky. I gave Levin a mixture of lysates, which, in combination with alkoloids, produced the desired result, i.e., Menzhinsky's death."

Kazakov's colleague Levin—the attending physician of the Soviet Union's top government officials—also testified that he had accelerated Menzhinsky's death on Yagoda's orders.

But can the transcripts of the public trials be believed? This question is an extremely complicated one and has no simple answer. The truth and lies of the Moscow trials are a separate and intricate subject.

From 1932 to 1939, Trotsky's secretary and bodyguard in Turkey, France, Norway, and Mexico was Jean van Heijenoort, of French origin. In 1939, he left Trotsky and moved to New York. His final rift with Trotskyism came in 1948. In the 1950s, he taught mathematics at New York University, and from 1965 until 1977 he taught the history and philosophy of logic at Brandeis University. For 30 years, Heijenoort served as consultant for the Trotsky archive at the Houghton Library at Harvard; he wrote a book, *With Trotsky in Exile: From Prinkipo to Coyoacan.*[3] In 1986, he was killed by his own wife—ironically, in Mexico. It is difficult to find a person who knew Trotsky better during those years. And yet one very significant pronouncement by Heijenoort has remained unremarked by historians. Referring to the Moscow trials, he said that nothing had been falsified and nothing had been concealed.[4]

Menzhinsky died on May 10, 1934. On the following day, Gorky's son, Maxim Alexeyevich Peshkov, died as well. Four years later, during the aforementioned trial, Yagoda, Kazakov, and Levin confessed to the murders of Valerian Kuibyshev (1888–1935) and Gorky (1868–1936). Trotsky writes:

> Yagoda had a special cabinet with poisons. When he needed to, he took out precious vials from this cabinet and gave them to his agents along with corresponding instructions. The head of the GPU—a former pharmacist, by the way—always displayed an exceptional interest in poisons. He had several toxicologists at his command, for whom he had created a special laboratory, funding for which was supplied in unlimited amounts and without monitoring. It cannot be supposed for a moment, naturally, that Yagoda constructed such an enterprise for his own personal needs.... "Next to Yagoda on the defendants' bench sat four Kremlin doctors who were accused of killing Maxim Gorky and two Soviet ministers: "I plead guilty," testified the venerable Doctor Levin, who was once my own doctor, "to applying medical treatments that were counterindicated for the illness." In this way, "I caused the premature deaths of Maxim Gorky and Kuibyshev."

Trotsky goes on:

> Kazakov was particularly useful in this respect, since, according to Doctor Levin, he had operated on his patients using medications that he prepared him-

self without any monitoring in his own laboratory, so that he alone knew the secret of his injections.... "I never doubted that this was Kazakov's doing," Levin says.... Yagoda did not like Gorky's son's way of life. He felt that he was a harmful influence on his father and surrounded his father with "undesirable people." This led Yagoda decide to eliminate him and he invited Doctor Levin to assist in liquidating Gorky's son.... Yagoda told [P. P.] Kryuchkov, Gorky's secretary and his own agent: "Gorky's activity needs to be reduced, Gorky's activity is constraining certain individuals".... The testimony of Doctor Levin, an old man who is 68, made the most shocking impression. According to him, he had deliberately helped accelerate the deaths of Menzhinsky, Kuibyshev, and Maxim Gorky as well. He was acting on Yagoda's instructions, since he feared that "his family would be destroyed." Doctor Levin told Doctor [D. D.] Pletnev that, if his orders were disobeyed, "Yagoda will definitely destroy us, and you will not save yourself from Yagoda. He stops at nothing, he forgets nothing." These words pertain not to Yagoda, but to his boss [Stalin], who stops at nothing, and forgets nothing. The security of the Kremlin, and Stalin's personal security in particular, were concentrated in Yagoda's hands. Had he been a conspirator, and not an agent of Stalin's, on any given day he could have found favorable circumstances to get rid of the dictator....

During the trial, that consisted mainly of lies, the charges and the confessions of poisoning an old and sick writer seemed to me a phantasmagorical episode. Subsequent information and a more attentive analysis of the circumstances have compelled me to revise this assessment. Not everything in the trials was a lie. There were people who had been poisoned and there were people who had done the poisoning. The main mover among them [Stalin] controlled the trials by telephone....

Why, however, didn't the authoritative and respected Kremlin doctors complain to members of the government, whom they knew well since they were their own patients? Doctor Levin's list of patients alone includes 24 top officials, many members of the Politburo and the Council of People's Commissars!

The answer is that Levin, like everyone in the Kremlin and around the Kremlin, knew perfectly well whose agent Yagoda was. Levin took his orders from Yagoda because he was powerless against Stalin.

People in Moscow knew and whispered about Gorky's dissatisfaction, about his attempt to escape from Russia, about the fact that Stalin had refused to give him an international passport. After the writer's death, suspicions arose at once that Stalin had helped the destructive power of nature. Another purpose of the Yagoda trial was to clear Stalin of this suspicion.[5]

Reading the biographies of Soviet and party leaders of the Stalin era, one discovers that almost none of them died of natural causes. By now, much has been written about the mysterious death of Stalin himself,[6] who was killed by four conspirators: Lavrenty Beria, Georgy Malenkov, Nikita Khrushchev, and

Nikolai Bulganin. The conspirators were led by Beria. It was he who aspired to the Stalin's position as head of the party and the state. However, Beria, who had headed the NKVD since December 1938, was too hateful to the entire party elite. In June 1953, Beria was arrested by his own co-conspirators and, after a brief stay in prison, he was shot on or about December 22, 1953, by Soviet Army Marshal Pavel Batitsky.

On November 22, 1954, the principal prosecutor of Stalin's trials, the general prosecutor of the USSR and subsequently the USSR's representative to the UN, Andrei Vyshinsky, was poisoned in New York. The poisoning was carried out by an agent of the Soviet security services, who had come to New York from Moscow specifically for this purpose.

News of Stalin's death found Vyshinsky in New York. He left for the funeral and soon returned, in order to head the Soviet delegation to the UN. After receiving news that Beria had been killed, Vyshinsky understood that his career and his life were hanging by a thread. People who observed him at the UN at that time noted that he seemed pale, aged, and had somewhat toned down the previous brazenness of his speeches. This was particularly apparent during the autumn months of 1954. At the end of October or the beginning of November, he was summoned back to Moscow "to deliver a report and to receive new instructions." As the general prosecutor, Vyshinsky himself had more than once sent such "summonses" to Moscow to Soviet diplomats who would be arrested upon arrival and he understood perfectly well why he was now being summoned back. Under various pretexts, he delayed his return. Consequently, on November 19, a "diplomatic courier" with a special mission arrived in New York. On November 22, at 9:15 a.m., the Soviet delegation announced that Vyshinsky had suddenly died of a heart attack during breakfast at the USSR's UN mission at 680 Park Avenue. No outsiders—diplomats, reporters, policemen wishing to examine Vyshinsky's corpse—were allowed into the building. Vyshinsky's death certificate was signed by "Dr. Alexei Kassov," the official doctor of the Soviet embassy in Washington D.C. and the Soviet delegation to the UN. On the following day, the morning of November 23, a special flight chartered by the Soviet delegation carried Vyshinsky's body to Moscow, along with Dr. Alexei Kassov and the "diplomatic courier."[7]

Thus ended the era of Stalinism in the Soviet Union. The party leaders who replaced Stalin, Beria, and Vyshinsky reformed the system in a radical fashion. They gave themselves the right to die of natural causes even in those cases when they had fallen out of favor. This was a new development, previously unknown in Soviet history. The leaders put an end to the mass killings of the members of their organization. Abolishing the system of mass terror both with respect to themselves and to the rest of the population, they became accustomed to a peaceful existence, only occasionally amusing themselves with small military conflicts of a local nature. However, those who replaced Brezhnev were not willing to enter history as bloody executioners even on the scale of the war in Afghanistan. The communist leadership of the USSR lost its nerve. Having endured for three quarters of a century, it threw its power away as hastily as it had captured it.

Abbreviations

Cheka	All-Russian Extraordinary Commission
CPSU	Communist Party of the Soviet Union
FSB	Federal Security Service of the Russian Federation
GPU	State Political Directorate (state security), former Cheka
IISH	International Institute of Social History
KGB	Committee for State Security
NEP	New Economic Policy
NKVD	State Political Directorate (state security, former OGPU)
OGPU	Joint State Political Directorate (state security, former GPU)
PPS	Polish Socialist Party
RSDLP	Russian Social Democratic Labor Party
RSFSR	Russian Soviet Federative Socialist Republic
SR	Socialist-Revolutionary Party (the SRs)
SPD	Social Democratic Party of Germany
SSR	Soviet Socialist Republic
TsIK	Central Executive Committee
TsK	Central Committee
USSR	Union of Soviet Socialist Republics
VTsiK	All-Russian Central Executive Committee

Bibliography

Books

Anikeev, V. *Deyatelnost' TsK RSDRP(b) v 1917–1918 godah*. M., 1974

Ardov, M., Ardov, B., Batalov, A. *Legendarnaya Ordynka*. Collection of Memoirs. *Inapress*. SPb, 1995

Baumgart, V. D. *Brest-Litovsk and the "Reasonable" Peace Treaty with the West*. — In: Versailess — St. Germaim — Trianon. Umbrich in Europa vor funfzig Jahren. R. Oldenbourg, Munchen und Wien, 1971

Bedny, Demyan. *Collected Works* in 8 vol., vol. 4. Poems 1920-1922. M., 1965

Bedny, Demyan. *Collected Works* in one vol., 1909–1922. Moscow—St. Petersburg, published by the satirical press *Krokodil* under the aegis of *Rabochaya Gazeta*, 1923

Bol'shaya Sovetskaya Entsiklopediya, 1st ed., vol. 62

Bothmer, *Mit Graf Mirbach in Moskau*. Tubingen, 1922

Bonch-Bruevich, V. *Collected Works*, vol. 2. M., 1961

Bonch-Bruevich, V. *Pokushenie na V. I. Lenina v Moskve 30 avgusta 1918 goda*. (Personal recollections.) M., 1924

Bonch-Bruevich, V. *Vospominaniya o Lenine*. 2nd ed. M., 1969

Carmichael, J. Trotsky. An appreciation of His Life. New York, 1975

Chubaryan, A. *Brestskii mir*. M., *Nauka*, 1964

Dalinsky, S. — *Pamyat'*, No 2

Dekrety sovetskoi vlasti, vol. 2. M., 1959

Delbars, Yves. *The Real Stalin*. George Allen & Unwin Ltd, London, 1951

Dokumenty vneshnei politiki SSSR, vol. I. M., 1959

Dumova N. *Moskovskie metsenaty*. M., *Molodaya gvardiya*, 1992

Dvenadtsatyi s'ezd RKP(b). Transcript. M., *Politisdat*, 1968

Dzerzhinsky, F. *Izbrannye stat'i i rechi*. M., 1947

Fanni Kaplan. Ili Kto strelyal v Lenina? Collected documents. Kazan, 1995

Fanni Kaplan: "Ya strelyala v Lenina". (An attempt at a documentary investigation of the assassination attempt against V. I. Lenin). Edited, compiled, and annotated by B. Sudarushkin, 1990

Felshtinsky, Yu. *Bolsheviki i levye esery. Oktyabr 1917, iul 1918. Na puti k odnopartiinoi diktature*. Paris, 1985

Felshtinsky, Yu. *Krushenie mirivoi revolutsii. Brestskii mir. Oktyabr 1917 — noyabr 1918*. M., *Terra*, 1992

Fischer, Ruth. *Stalin und der Deutsche Kommumsmus*. Frankfurt am Main, 1950

Frelih, P. *K istorii germanskoi revolutsii*, vol. 1, 1927

Frolich, Paul. *Rosa Luxemburg*. Gedanke und Tat. Europaische Verlagsanstalt, Frankfurt am Main, 1967

Halveg, V. *Vozvrachshenie Lenina v Rossiu v 1917 godu*. M., *Mezhdunarodnye otnoshenoya*, 1990

Gamalii, N. Pishu i dumau ob Il'iche. M., *Sovetskaya Rossiya*, 1983

Geller, M, Nekrich, A. *Utopiya u vlasti*. Overseas Publications Interchange, 1986

Germany and the Revolution in Russia, 1915–1918: Documents from the Archives of the German Foreign Ministry by Z. A. B. Zeman. Oxford University Press, London, 1958

Goldbach, Marie-Louise. *Karl Radek und die deutsch-sowjetischen Beziehungen 1918-1923*. Verlag Neue Gesellschaft GmbH. Bonn-Bad Godesberg, 1973

Gorokhov, I, Zamyatin, L., Zemskov, I. G. V. *Chcherin — diplomat leninskoi shkoly*. 2th ed. Editor A. Gromyko. M., 1974

Gusev, K. *Krah partii eserov*. M, 1963

Haffner, S. *Revolutsiya v Germanii 1918/19. Kak eto bylo v deistvitelnosti?* Trans. for the German. M., *Progress*, 1983

Halveg, V. *Vozvrachshenie Lenina v Rossiu v 1917 godu*. M., *Mezhdunarodnye otnoshenoya*, 1990

Heijenoort, Jean van. *With Trotsky in Exile: From Prinkipo to Coyoakan*. Harvard University Press, 1978.

Hilger, G, Meyer, A. *The Incompatible Alli*es. *A Memoir-History of Soviet German Relations 1918–1941*. New York, 1953

Hoffmann, General. *Voina upuchshennyh vozmozhnostei*, GIZ, 1925

Ioffe, S. *Memuary Stalina o Lenine v zapisi Demyana Bednogo*, unpublished 115-page study (Palo Alto, CA)

Iroshnikov, M. *Sozdanie sovetskogo tsentralnogo gosudarstvennogo apparata. Sovet narodnyh komissarov I narodnye komissariaty, oktyabr 1917 — yanvar 1918 g.* 2nd ed. L., 1967

Iz istorii Vserossiiskoq Chrezvychainoi komissii(Cheka) (1917–1921). Collection of documents, M., 1958

Izmailovich, A. *Posleoktyabrskie oshibki. Revolutsionnyi sotsializm* Publishing. M., 1918

Kamenev, U. *Dve partii*. L., 1924

Kamenev, U. *Dve partii*. With V. Lenin's preface. Published *Rabochaya Gazeta,* Paris, 1911

Kamkov, B. *Dve taktiki. Revolutsionnyi sotsializm* Publishing, M., 1918

Katkov, G. *The Trial of Bukharin*. New York, 1969

Kostin, N. *Sud nad terrorom*. M., *Moskovsky rabochii*, 1990

Krasnaya kniga Cheka, vol. 1., 2nd ed., annotated. M., *Politizdat*, 1989

Kreml za reshetkoi (Podpolnaya Rossiya). Berlin, *Skify* Publishing, 1922

Krupskaya, N. *O Lenine*. Collection of articles and speeches. 5th ed. M., *Politizdat*, 1983

Krupskaya, N. *Pereezd Il'icha v Moskvu i pervye mesyatsy ego raboty v Moskve.* — In: *Vospominaniya o Vladimire Il'iche Lenine*, vol. 2. M., 1957

Krupskaya, N. *Vospominaniya o Lenine*. M., *Partisdat*, 1932

Kuusinen, O. *Before and After Stalin. A Personal Account of Soviet Russia from the 1920s to the 1960s.* London, 1974

Kuznetskaya, L., Mashtakova K. *Vstrecha s Leninym Sovetskaya Rossiya*, M., 1987

L'Allemagne et les problèmes de la paix pendant la premiere guerre mondiale. Documents extraits des archives de l'Office allemand des Affairs étrangères, pub. Et ann. Par A. Scherer et J. Grunewald. Liv. III. De la revolution Sovietiquea la paix de Brest-Litovsk (9 Novembre 1917 — Mars 1918). Paris, 1976

Lenin, V. *Collected Works*, 4th ed., vol. 27, 34

Lenin, V. *The Complete Collected Works*, 5th ed., vol. 5, 36, 37, 45, 50

Lermolo, Elizabeth. *Face of a Victim.* Harper & Brothers Publishers, New York, 1955

Levi, Paul. *Russkaya revolutsiya. Kriticheskaya otsenka slabosti Rozy Luksemburg* [The Russian Revolution. A Critical Assessment of Rosa Luxemburg's Weakness]. Berlin, 1922

Lopukhin, V. *Bolezn', smert' i bal'zamirovanie V. I Lenina. Pravda i mify.* M., *Respublika*, 1997

Lunacharsky, A. V. *Siyauchshii dorogoi genii.* Speech delivered on January 21, 1929, at a formal assembly commemorating the fifth anniversary of Lenin's death. Transcript in *Dialog. M.,* 1995, No 3

Malkov, P. *Zapiski komendanta Kremlya.* M., 1967

Malkov, P. *Zapiski komendanta Kremlya.* 3rd ed. M., 1987

Mandelstam, N. *Vospominaniya.* New York, 1970

Martov, L. *Spasiteli ili uprazdniteli?* Paris, 1911

Maiorov, M. *Borba Sovetskoi Rossii za vyhod iz imperialisticheskoi voiny.* M., 1959

Mints, I. *God 1918-i.* M., 1982

Morozova, T. P. *Zagadochnaya smert' Savvy Morozova.* — *Otechestvo.* Regional Almanac. M., *Profizdat*, 1997, p. 243

Nicolaevsky, B. *Tainye stranitsy istorii.* M., 1995

Payne, Robert. *The Rise and Fall of Stalin.* Simon and Schuster, New York

Perepiska sekretariata TsK RSDRP(b) s mestnymi partiinymi organizatsiyami. March-July, 1918. Collected documents, vol. 3. M., 1967

Peters, Ya. *Vospominaniya o rabote Cheka v pervyi god revolutsii* — *Byloe,* No 2, 1933 (Paris)

Petrenko, N. (Ravdin). *Lenin v Gorkah* — *bolezn i smert.* — *Minuvshee.* Historical Almanac, No. 2, Paris, 1986

Pomper, P., Felshtinsky, Yu. *Trotsky's Notebooks, 1933–1935.* Columbia University Press, New York, 1986

Protokoly Pyatogo s'esda RSDRP. Published by Marx-Engels-Lenin Institute, Moscow, 1935

Protokoly s'esdov i konfrentsii Vserossiiskoi kommunisticheskoi partii (b). Sed'moi s'ezd. March 1918. Editors D. Kin and V. Sorokin. M.-L., 1928

Protokoly Tsentral'nogo komiteta RSDRP(b). August 1917 — February 1918. M., GIZ, 1958

Protokoly zasedanii VTsIK IV cozyva. (Transcript.) M., 1920

Radek, K. *Der Zusammenbruch des Imperialismus*. 1919.

Rauch, G. *A History of Soviet Russia, 6th edition*, New York, 1976

Rosa Luxemburg Ein Leben fur die Freiheit. Reden — Schriften — Briefe. Ein Lesebuch. Herausgegeben von Frederik Hetmann. Fischer Taschenbuch Verlag, Frankfurt am Main, 1980

RSFSR. VtsIK. Transcript. M., 1919

Russkie pisateli 1800–1917. Biographical Dictionary, vol. 1. M., 1992

Sed'moi ekstrennyi s'ezd RKP(b). March, 1918. Transcript, M., 1962

Semenov, G. *Voennaya i boevaya rabota partii sotsial-revolutsionerov za 1917–1918 gg.* Berlin, 1922

Shatunovskaya, L. *Zhizn' v Kremle*. New York, Chalidze Publishing, 1982

Shestak, Yu. *Taktika bolshevikov po otnosheniu k partii levyh eserov i otkolovshimsya ot nee partiyam "revolutsionnyh kommunistov" i "narodnikov-kommunistov"*. M., 1971

Shesternin, S. *Realizatsiya nasledstva posle N. P. Shimidta i moi vstrechi s Leninym.* — in *Staryi bol'shevik*, vol. 5 (8). M., 1933

Solomon, G. *Sredi krasnyh vozhdei*, vol.1. Paris, 1930; reissued in Moscow in 1995

Steinberg, I. *Pochemu my protiv Brestskogo mira*. [Why We Are Against the Treaty of Brest-Litovsk]. M., *Revolutsionnyi sotsializm*, 1918

Spiridonova, M. *Prosh Prosh'yan. K biografii Prosh'yana.* — *Katorga i ssylka*, book 9. M., 1924

Spirin, L. *Klassy i partii v grazhdanskoi voine v Rossii. 1917–1920*. M., 1968

Spirin, L. *Krah odnoi avantury (Myatezh levyh eserov v Moskve 6-7 iulya 1918 g.)*, M., 1971

Stalin, I. The Collected Works, 1946–1952. M., 1997

Stasova, E. *Stranitsy zhizni I borby*. M., *Politizdat*, 1957

Steinberg, I. N. *In Workshop of the Revolution*, New York – Toronto 1953

Stupochenko, L. *Proletarskaya revolutsiya*, 1923, book. 4

Sverdlov, Ya. *Izbrannye proizvedeniya*, vol. 2–3. M., 1959-60

Sverdlova, K. *Yakov Mikhailovich Sverdlov*. M., 1976

Tikhomolov, S. *Vosem let s Dzerzhinskim*. In: *O Felikse Edmundoviche Dzerzhinskom. Vospominaniya, stat'i, ocherki sovremennikov*. M., 1977

Trotsky's archive, vol. 1. M., 1990

Trotsky, L. *O Lenine. Materialy dlya biografa*. M., 1924

Trotsky, L. *Portrety revolutsionerov*. M., 1991

Trotsky, L. *Sovetskaya respublika i kapitalisticheskii mir,* vol. 17, part 1. Speech at the Seventh Congress of the Russian Communist Party

Trotsky, L. *Stalinskaya shkola falsifikatsii. Granit* Publishing, Berlin, 1932

Trudy I Bserossiiskogo s'esda Covetov narodnogo hozyaistba. May 26 — June 4, 1918. (Transcript), M., 1918

Toman, B. *Za svobodnuu Rossiu, za svobodnuu Latviu...* M., 1976

The Trotsky Papers, 1917–1922, vol. 1. Hague, 1964

Ulyanova, M. *O Lenine*. M., 1969

Uprochenie sovetskoi vlasti v Moskve i Moskovskoi gubernii. M., 1958

Vacietis, J. *Iulskoe vosstanie v Moskve 6 i 7 iulya 1918 g.* — *Pamyat'*, vol. 2. M., 1977; Paris, 1979

Valentinov-Volsky, N. *Nasledniki Lenina.* M,. Publishing House *Terra*, 1991
Valentinov-Volsky, N. *Maloznakomyi Lenin.* Paris, 1972
Varsky, A. *Roza Luksemburg. Takticheskie problemy*, Hamburg, 1922
V borbe za pobedu Oktyabrya. Collected articles. M., 1957
Velikaya Oktyabrskaya cotsialisticheskaya revolutsiya. Encyclopedia. M., 1987
Voitinsky, V. *Gody pobed i porazhenii*, vol. 2. Berlin, 1924
Volkov, F. D. *Stalin's Rise and Fall*, M, 1922
Vystrel v serdtse revolutsii. Edited by N. D. Kostin, *Politizdat*, 1983
Yaroslavsky, Em. *Ocherki po istorii VKP(b)*, vol. 1. M., 1937
Zapiski Instituta Lenina, vol. 3. M., 1928
Zinoviev, G. Collected works, vol. 7. L., 1925

Periodical Press

Andriasova, T. *Byla li killerom Fanni Kaplan?* — *Novoe russkoe slovo.* April 8, 1996
Avtorkhanov, A. *Ubil li Stalin Lenina?* — *Novyi zhurnal*, vol. 152
Bezelyansky, Yu. *Nichego ne pomnu, krome horoshego go…* — *Novoe Russkoe Slovo*, No. 44, March 15, 1996
Boinov, V., Kudryashov, S. *Otravlennse puli. Dve versii pokusheniya na V. I. Lenina.* — *Komsomolskaya pravda*, August 1990
Bukharin, N. *Pamyati Il'icha.* — *Pravda*, January 21, 1925
Chernin, O. *Brest-Litovsk.* — *Grani*, No 153, 1989
Delo Radeka. — *Voprosy istorii*, No 9, 1997
Delo Georga Sklartsa — *Voprosy istorii*, No 10–11, 1997
Deyatelnost' Tsentral'nogo komiteta partii v dokumentah (sobytiya i fakty). — *Izvestiya TsK KPSS*, 1989, No 4
Dokumenty germanskogo posla v Moskve Mirbaha. Publication by S. Drabkina. — *Voprosy istorii.* 1971, No 9
Doroshenko, V. *Lenin protiv Stalina. 1922–1923.* — *Zvezda*, 1990, No. 4
Heifits, M. *Dve puli dlya Lenina I obe raznye.* — *Novoe russkoe slovo*, December 19, 1997
July 6—In the Bolshoi Theater. — *Prozhektor, No 27 (145), 1928*
Kostin, N. *Sud nad terrorom.* — *Istochnik*, 1993, No 2
Kuda hotel bezhat' Sverdlov? Ed. V. Lebedev. — *Istochnik*, 1994, No 1
La Lutte Ouvrière, June 12, 1936, No 1
Lenin, V. *Pamyati Prosh'yana.* — *Pravda*, December 10, 1918
Levchenko, Stanislav; Kalugin, Oleg. *Ya rad, chto pomog razvalit' vsemoguchshii KGB.* — *Novoe Russkoe Slovo*, April 26, 1996
Litvin, A. *V Lenina "strelyal" Dzerzhinsky?* — *Rodina*, 1995, No 7
Maksimova, E. *Sledstvie po delu Fanni Kaplan prodolzhaetsya.* — *Izvestiya*, March 4, 1994; *Istochnik*, 1993, No 2
Orlov, B. *Mif o Fanni Kaplan.* — *Vremya i my* (Israel), December 1975, No. 2
Orlov, B. *Mif o Fanni Kaplan.* — *Istochnik*, 1993, No 2

Orlov, G. *Brest-Litovskii mir I den' osnovaniya Krasnoi armii.* — *Russkaya mysl,* March 25, 1958

Pavlov, D. Petrov, C. *Polkovnik Akasi i osvoboditel'noe dvizhenie v Rossii (1904—1905.)* — *Istoriya SSSR,* 1990, No 6

Rech I. V. Stalina v Narkomate oborony. U. Murin's publication. — *Istochnik,* 1994, No. 3

Record of G. A. Aleksinsky's conversation in Geneva, 1915 — International Review of Social History (Amsterdam), 1981, vol. 26, No 3. Published by Samuel Baron

Rubnev, D., Tsypkov, C. *Sledovatel respubliki* — *Volga,* 1967, No 5

Rykov, A. I. *Vospominaniya* — *Izvestiya,* October 2, 1918

Serebryakova, G. *Moei docheri Zore o ee ottse.* Published by Z. Serebryakova. — *Rodina,* 1989, No 6

Soobchsheniya s severa. — *Golos Kieva,* No 54, June 21, 1918

Sotsial-demokrat, February 20, 1918, No 28

Spiridonova, M. *Otkrytoe pis'mo Tsentralnomu komitetu partii bolshevikov.* — *Grani,* 1986, No 139

Strubel, G. *Ich habe sie richten lassen* (article devoted to the seventieth anniversary of the assassination of Luxemburg and Liebknecht) — *Die Zeit,* January 13, 1989, No. 3

Topolyansky, V. *Kto strelyal v Lenina? Iznanka pokusheniya.* — *Literaturnaya gazeta,* November 10, 1993, No 45 (5473)

M. Ulyanova ob otnoshenii V. I. Lenina k I. V. Stalinu. — *Izvestiya TsK KPSS,* No. 12, 1989

Vasilyev, O. *Pokushenie na Lenina bylo instsenirovkoi.* — *Nezavisimaya gazeta,* August 29, 1992

Vospominaniya o Lenine. April, 1938. A. I. Marshak's publication. — *Sputnik,* April 1990, No. 4

Wolfe, Bertram. "Rosa Luxemburg and V. I. Lenin: The Opposite Poles of Revolutionary Socialism." *The Antioch Review,* Summer, 1961. The Antioch Press, Yellow Springs, Ohio

Yakovlev, E. *Poslednii intsident. Konspect dramy Vladimira Il'icha.* — *Moskovskie Novosti,* January 22, 1989, No. 4

Zapiski Teodora Libknehta. — *Voprosy istorii,* No 2, 1998

Archival documents

Balabanova A. collection, folder 219 — International Institute of Social History (IISH, Amsterdam)

Balabanova A. collection, letter from Nicolaevsky to Balabanova from April 20, 1962 — International Institute of Social History (IISH, Amsterdam)

Krasnaya kniga Cheka — Harvard University and Hoover Institution copy.

Nicolaevsky's collection at Hoover Institution (Stanford University), N. Valentinov-Volsky collection, box 4. L. Dan correspondence. Letter from L. Dan to N. Valentinov-Volsky, May 1, 1961, p. 2.

Nicolaevsky's collection at Hoover Institution, box 18, folder 1. Transcript of foreign policy report from the conference [of the Kadets in Yekaterinodar?], May 14, 1918, pp. 8–10. The author is not named.

Nicolaevsky's collection at Hoover Institution, box 18, folder 27. From the press office of the RSFSR's authorized representation in Estonia. August 9, 1921

Nicolaevsky's collection at Hoover Institution, box 198, folder 23, sheet 12

Nicolaevsky's collection at Hoover Institution, box 392, folder 4. V. Zenzinov. *Stranichka iz istorii rannego bol'shevizma.*

Nicolaevsky's collection at Hoover Institution, box 475, folder 8. Burtsev to Nicolaevsky, June 10, 1931

Nicolaevsky's collection at Hoover Institution, box 478, folder 21. Letter from Nicolaevsky to H. Eckert from April 14, 1954

Nicolaevsky's collection at Hoover Institution, box 478, folder 21. Letter from Nicolaevsky to H. Eckert from December 26, 1962

Nicolaevsky's collection at Hoover Institution, box 496, folder 3. Letter from Nicolaevsky to Pavlovsky from August 11, 1962

Nicolaevsky's collection at Hoover Institution, box 496, folder 3. Letter from Nicolaevsky to Pavlovsky from September 2, 1962

Nicolaevsky's collection at Hoover Institution, box 496, folder 3. Letter from Nicolaevsky to Pavlovsky from November 16, 1961

Nicolaevsky's collection at Hoover Institution, box 500, folder 19. Letter from Nicolaevsky to Otto Schüddekopf from August 25, 1962

Nicolaevsky's collection at Hoover Institution, box 508, folder 48. Letter from Nicolaevsky to R. (Jerzy Niezbrzycki) Wraga from July 15, 1960

Nicolaevsky's collection at Hoover Institution, box 591, folder 13. Letter from Abramovich to Valentinov-Volsky from December 24, 1957, pp. 1–2

Nicolaevsky's collection at Hoover Institution, box 591, folder 13. Letter from Valentinov-Volsky to Abramovich from December 30, 1957, p. 2

Nicolaevsky's collection at Hoover Institution, box 786, folder 6; box 475, folder 8; B. I. Nicolaevsky to V. L. Burtsev, June 6, 1931, p. 1

Suvarin's collection, letter from Nicolaevsky to Suvarin from April 11, 1957 — International Institute of Social History (IISH, Amsterdam)

Trotsky's archive, bMs Russ 13. T-3742 — Houghton Library, Harvard University

Ves Petrograd na 1916 god (Address Directory)

Valentinov-Volsky N. collection at Hoover Institution, box 8

Notes

Chapter 1 – The Money for the Revolution

1. A. V. Lunacharsky. *Siyauchshii dorogoi genii*. Speech delivered on January 21, 1929, at a formal assembly commemorating the fifth anniversary of Lenin's death. Transcript in *Dialog (M.)* 1995, No 3, p. 66.
2. *Ya rad, chto pomog razvalit' vsemoguchshii KGB*. Interview by Stanislav Levchenko with Oleg Kalugin in *Novoe Russkoe Slovo*, April 26, 1996, p. 12.
3. Hoover Institution at Stanford University, B. I. Nicolaevsky's collection (hereafter Nicolaevsky's collection), box 392, folder 4. V. Zenzinov. *Stranichka iz istorii rannego bol'shevizma*.
4. Letter from Lenin to A. I. Rykov from February 25, 1911, in V. Lenin, *Collected Works*, 4th ed., vol. 34, p. 389.
5. Nicolaevsky's collection, N. Valentinov-Volsky collection, box 4. L. Dan correspondence. Letter from L. Dan to N. Valentinov-Volsky, May 1, 1961, p. 2.
6. N. Valentinov-Volsky. *Maloznakomyi Lenin*. Paris, 1972, pp. 82–84, 88.
7. Interview conducted by Yuri Felshtinsky with O. A. Kavelina, granddaughter of Anna Timofeyevna Karpova, née Morozova, sister of Savva Timofeyevich Morozov.
8. T. P. Morozova. *Zagadochnaya smert' Savvy Morozova*. — *Otechestvo*. Regional Almanac. M., *Profizdat*, 1997, p. 243.
9. Ibid, p. 238.
10. M. Ardov, B. Ardov, A. Batalov. *Legendarnaya Ordynka*. Collection of Memoirs. *Inapress*. SPb, 1995, p. 211.
11. N. Dumova. *Moskovskie metsenaty*. M., *Molodaya gvardiya*, 1992, pp. 139–141, 143, 144, 146, 148, 150–152.
12. *Russkie pisateli 1800—1917*. Biographical Dictionary, vol. 1. M., 1992, p. 649.
13. Lenin, V. *The Complete Collected Works*, 5th ed., vol. 5, pp. 369–370.
14. Nicolaevsky's collection, box 392, folder 4. V. Zenzinov. *Stranichka iz istorii rannego bol'shevizma*.
15. N. Valentinov-Volsky. *Maloznakomyi Lenin*, p. 107; N. Dumova. *Moskovskie metsenaty*, p. 161; B. Nicolaevsky. *Tainye stranitsy istorii*. M., 1995, p. 12; *Protokoly pyatogo s'esda RSDRP*. Published by Marx-Engels-Lenin Institute, M., 1935, p. 631.
16. T. P. Morozova. *Zagadochnaya smert' Savvy Morozova*, p. 245.
17. N. Dumova. *Moskovskie metsenaty*, p. 162.
18. *Bol'shaya sovetskaya entsiklopediya*, 1st ed., vol. 62, p. 556.
19. *Vospominaniya A. I. Rykova* — *Izvestiya*, October 2, 1918, p. 2.
20. N. Valentinov-Volsky. *Maloznakomyi Lenin*, pp. 109–110.
21. Nicolaevsky's collection, box 392, folder 4. V. Zenzinov. *Stranichka iz istorii rannego bol'shevizma*.
22. V. Voitinsky. *Gody pobed i porazhenii*, vol. 2. Berlin, 1924, p. 103.
23. L. Martov. *Spasiteli ili uprazdniteli?* Paris, 1911, pp. 20–21.
24. See S. Shesternin. *Realizatsiya nasledstva posle N. P. Shimidta i moi vstrechi s Leninym*. — in *Staryi bol'shevik*, vol. 5 (8). M., 1933, p. 153.
25. Ibid, p. 155.
26. U. Kamenev. *Dve partii*. L., 1924, p. 184; N. Valentinov-Volsky. *Maloznakomyi Lenin*, p. 116.
27. U. Kamenev. *Dve partii*. With V. Lenin's preface. Published *Rabochaya Gazeta*, Paris, 1911.
28. N. Valentinov-Volsky. *Maloznakomyi Lenin*, p. 117. In Kamenev's pamphlet, for reasons of secrecy Andrikanis is referred to as "Z." Valentinov-Volsky changed "Z" to "Andrikanis " to make the text easier to read.
29. See L. Martov. *Spasiteli ili uprazdniteli?*
30. Ibid, pp. 20–21.
31. N. Valentinov-Volsky. *Maloznakomyi Lenin*, p. 102.
32. See S. Shesternin. *Realizatsiya nasledstva posle N. P. Shimidta i moi vstrechi s Leninym*, p. 155.
33. Nicolaevsky's collection, box 392, folder 4. V. Zenzinov. *Stranichka iz istorii rannego bol'shevizma*.
34. *Collected Works*, 4th ed., vol. 34, p. 345.
35. See Em. Yaroslavsky. *Ocherki po istorii VKP(b)*, vol. 1. M., 1937, p. 204.
36. See N. Valentinov-Volsky. *Maloznakomyi Lenin*, pp. 118–120.

37. Nicolaevsky's collection, box 786, folder 6; box 475, folder 8; B. I. Nicolaevsky to V. L. Burtsev, June 6, 1931, p. 1.
38. Ibid.
39. Ibid.
40. Nicolaevsky's collection, box 475, folder 8. Burtsev to Nicolaevsky, June 10, 1931, p. 2.
41. V. Halveg. *Vozvrachshenie Lenina v Rossiu v 1917 godu.* M., *Mezhdunarodnye otnoshenoya*, 1990; *Germaniya i russkie revolutsionery v gody pervoi mirivoi voiny.*—in: B. Nicolaevsky. *Tainye stranitsy istorii*, pp. 238-390.
42. D. Pavlov, C. Petrov. *Polkovnik Akasi i osvoboditel'noe dvizhenie v Rossii (1904–1905.)*—*Istoriya SSSR*, 1990, No 6, p. 53.
43. Ibid, p. 58.
44. V. Bonch-Bruevich. *Collected Works*, vol. 2. M., 1961, p. 329.
45. Record of G. A. Aleksinsky's conversation in Geneva, 1915—International Review of Social History (Amsterdam), 1981, vol. 26, No 3, p. 347. Published by Samuel Baron.
46. D. Pavlov, C. Petrov. *Polkovnik Akasi...*, pp. 54, 62–63, 65–66, 71.

Chapter 2 - The Treaty of Brest-Litovsk

1. Quote from: *Izvestiya TsK KPSS*, January 1989, No 1, p. 233.
2. *Velikaya Oktyabrskaya cotsialisticheskaya revolutsiya.* Encyclopedia. M., 1987, pp. 464–465.
3. V. Baumgart, *Brest-Litovsk and the "Reasonable" Peace Treaty with the West.* — In: Versailess — St. Germaim—Trianon. Umbrich in Europa vor funfzig Jahren. R. Oldenbourg, Munchen und Wien, 1971, s. 60.
4. Trotsky's archive, Houghton Library, Harvard University, bMs Russ 13. T-3742.
5. L. Trotsky. *O Lenine. Materialy dlya biografa.* M., 1924, pp. 78-79.
6. Ibid, p. 79.
7. Nicolaevsky's collection, box 198, folder 23, sheet 12.
8. L. Trotsky. *Stalinskaya shkola falsifikatsii.* Berlin, *Granit*, 1932, p. 39.
9. *Sed'moi ekstrennyi s'ezd RKP(b).* March, 1918. Transcript, M., 1962, p. 111.
10. L. Trotsky. *O Lenine*, pp. 82–83.
11. Trotsky's archive. *Kommunisticheskaya oppozitsiya v SSSR, 1923–1927*, vol. 1. M., 1990, pp. 138–139.
12. M. Maiorov. *Borba Sovetskoi Rossi za vyhod iz imperialisticheskoi voiny.* M., 1959, p. 210; A. Chubaryan. *Brestskii mir.* M., *Nauka*, 1964, pp. 140–141.
13. M. Maiorov. *Borba Sovetskoi Rossii*, p. 211; A. Chubaryan. *Brestskii mir*, p. 141.
14. M. Maiorov. *Bor'ba Sovetskoi Rossii*, p. 211.
15. V. Lenin. *The Complete Collected Works*, 5th ed., vol. 35, p. 332.
16. Trotsky's archive, T-3742; O. Chernin. *Brest-Litovsk —Grani*, No 153, 1989, p. 173.
17. General Hoffmann. *Voina upuchshennyh vozmozhnostei.* GIZ, Moscow-Leningrad., 1925, p. 186; Trotsky's archive, T-3742. P. Frelih. *K istorii germanskoi revolutsii*, vol 1, p. 225.
18. O. Chernin. *Brest-Litovsk*, p. 173.
19. Trotsky's archive, T-3742. L. Stupochenko — *Proletarskaya revolutsiya*, 1923, book. 4, pp. 97–98.
20. G. Zinoviev. *Collected Works*, vol. 7. L., 1925, part. 1, pp. 499–500.
21. A. Chubaryan. *Brestskii mir*, pp. 220–221.
22. Trotsky's archive, T-3742.
23. *Dokumenty vneshnei politiki SSSR*, vol. I. M., 1959, p. 106; L'Allemagne et les problèmes de la paix pendant la premiere guerre mondiale. Documents extraits des archives de l'Office allemand des Affairs étrangères, pub. Et ann. Par A. Scherer et J. Grunewald. Liv. III. De la revolution Sovietiquea la paix de Brest-Litovsk (9 Novembre 1917 — Mars 1918). Paris, 1976, doc. No 263, February 19, 1918. Bussche's telegram to the German emabassy in Vienna.
24. G. Orlov. *Brest-Litovskii mir I den' osnovaniya Krasnoi armii.* — *Russkaya mysl*, March 25, 1958.
25. February 21, 1918. Schüler's telegram to the German foreign ministry. — Germany and the Revolution in Russia, 1915–1918: Documents from the Archives of the German Foreign Ministry by Z. A. B. Zeman. Oxford University Press, London, 1958, doc. No 278.
26. *Sotsial-demokrat*, February 20, 1918, No 28.
27. *27 Protokoly Tsentral'nogo komiteta RSDRP(b).* August 1917–February 1918. M., GIZ, 1958, pp. 211–212.
28. Ibid, pp. 212–213.
29. Ibid, p. 215.
30. K. Sverdlova. *Yakov Mikhailovich Sverdlov.* M., 1976, pp. 312–313.

31. Ibid, p. 314.
32. *Protokoly Tsentral'nogo komiteta RSDRP(b)*, pp. 219–228.
33. *Dokumenty vneshnei politiki SSSR*, vol. 1, p. 119.
34. V. Lenin. *Collected Works*, 4th ed., vol. 27, p. 57.
35. *Sed'moi ekstrennyi s'ezd RKP(b)*. March 1918. Transcript. M., 1962, p. 235.
36. Ibid, p. 191.
37. Ibid, p. 192.
38. *Protokoly s'esdov i konfrentsii Vserossiiskoi kommunisticheskoi partii (b). Sed'moi s'ezd.* March 1918. Editors D. Kin and V. Sorokin. M.–L., 1928, p. 4.
39. G. Rauch. *A History of Soviet Russia, 6th edition*, New York, 1976, p. 76; A. Chubaryan. *Brestskii mir*, pp. 189–190; *Trudy I Bserossiiskogo s'esda Covetov narodnogo hozyaistba.* May 26–June 4, 1918. (Transcript), M., 1918, p. 15. K. Radek's speech.
40. Sed'moi ekstrennyi s'ezd RKP(b), pp. 33–50.
41. Ibid, pp. 41–44.
42. Ibid, pp. 49–51.
43. Ibid, pp. 57–61.
44. Ibid, p. 76.
45. Ibid, pp. 88–89.
46. Ibid, pp. 77–78.
47. Trotsky's archive, T-3742; L. Trotsky. *Sovetskaya respublika i kapitalisticheskii mir*, vol. 17, part 1, p. 138. Speech at the Seventh Congress of the Russian Communist Party.
48. *Sed'moi ekstrennyi s'ezd RKP(b)*, pp. 65–69, 71–72.
49. Ibid, pp. 101–103.
50. Ibid, p. 109.
51. Ibid, pp. 110–114.
52. Ibid, pp. 123–124.
53. Ibid, pp. 125–126.
54. Ibid, p. 127.
55. *Perepiska sekretariata TsK RSDRP(b) s mestnymi partiinymi organizatsiyami.* March-July, 1918. Collected documents, vol. 3. M., 1967, p. 32.
56. Ibid, p. 136.
57. G. Zinoviev. *Collected Works*, vol. 7, part. 1, p. 511.
58. Eleven issues of *Kommunist* did come out. The newspaper was shut down on March 19 (*Protokoly s'esdov i konfrentsii*, p. 258).
59. On April 20, Bukharin, Radek, Smirnov, and Obolensky (Osinsky) began publishing *Kommunist* as a weekly journal in Moscow, but only four issues came out, and in June the journal was shut down.
60. G. Zinoviev. *Collected Works*, vol. 7, part. 1, p. 535.
61. *Sed'moi ekstrennyi s'ezd RKP(b)*, pp. 65–69, 71–72.
62. Nicolaevsky's collection, box 157, folder 2. V. [G.] Kolokoltsev [Ukrainian minister of agriculture from May 15 to October 19, 1918], A Brief Account of Agrarian Issues in Ukraine during the Hetman Government from May 1, 1918, until December 15, 1918, p. 1.
63. Nicolaevsky's collection, box 157, folder 3. *Kievskaya mysl*, No 64, April 29, 1918. Lesser Rada session of April 27, prime minister's speech.
64. *Dokumenty germanskogo posla v Moskve Mirbaha.* Publication by S. Drabkina. — *Voprosy istorii.* 1971, No 9, pp. 123-124; I. Gorokhov, L. Zamyatin, I. Zemskov. *G. V. Chcherin — diplomat leninskoi shkoly.* 2th ed. Editor A. Gromyko. M., 1974, p. 87.
65. *Deyatelnost' Tsentral'nogo komiteta partii v dokumentah (sobytiya i fakty).* — *Izvestiya TsK KPSS*, 1989, No 4, pp. 148–149.
66. *Pravda*, May 24, 1918, No 101. The letter was written on May 22; V. Lenin, 5th ed., vol. 36, p. 375–376.
67. *Deyatelnost' Tsentral'nogo komiteta partii v dokumentah*, p. 150.
68. J. Vacietis. *Iulskoe vosstanie v Moskve 6 i 7 iulya 1918 g.* — *Pamyat'*, vol. 2. M., 1977—Paris, 1979, p. 43.
69. G. Solomon. *Sredi krasnyh vozhdei*, vol.1. Paris, 1930, p. 85.
70. *Protokoly zasedanii VTsIK IV cozyva.* (Transcript.) M., 1920, pp. 376, 388.
71. Karl von Botmer. *S grafom Mirbahom v Moskve.* M., 1996, p. 64. Note from June 13, 1918.
72. *Soobchsheniya s severa.* — *Golos Kieva*, No 54, June 21, 1918.
73. Nicolaevsky's collection, box 18, folder 1. Transcript of foreign policy report from the conference [of the Kadets in Yekaterinodar?], May 14, 1918, pp. 8–10. The author is not named.
74. A. Izmailovich. *Posleoktyabrskie oshibki.* M., *Revolutsionnyi sotsializm* 1918, p. 13.

75. I. Steinberg. *Pochemu my protiv Brestskogo mira. [Why We Are Against the Treaty of Brest-Litovsk].* M., *Revolutsionnyi sotsializm,* 1918, pp. 26–27.
76. B. Kamkov. *Dve taktiki.* M., *Revolutsionnyi sotsializm,* 1918, pp. 27–28.
77. I. Steinberg. Pochemu my protiv Brestskogo mira, p. 15.
78. Ibid, pp. 24–25.
79. Ibid, p. 27.
80. B. Kamkov. *Dve taktiki,* pp. 28–29.
81. I. Steinberg. Pochemu my protiv Brestskogo mira, p. 12.
82. A. Izmailovich. *Posleoktyabrskie oshibki,* p. 13.
83. General Hoffmann. *Voina upuchshennyh vozmozhnostei,* p. 194.
84. *Trudy I Bserossiiskogo s'esda Covetov narodnogo hozyaistba,* pp. 15–16.
85. L. Trotsky. *O Lenine,* pp. 88–89.
86. *Deyatelnost' Tsentral'nogo komiteta partii v dokumentah,* p. 142.
87. The transcripts of Central Committee meetings from May 6 and 10 have not been found (Ibid, p. 141; V. Anikeev. *Deyatelnost' TsK RSDRP(b) v 1917–1918 godah.* M., 1974, p. 268).
88. V. Lenin, vol. 36, pp. 322–326, 608; *Deyatelnost' Tsentral'nogo komiteta partii v dokumentah,* p. 142.
89. V. Anikeev. *Deyatelnost' TsK RSDRP(b)* p. 271; *Deyatelnost' Tsentral'nogo komiteta partii v dokumentah,* p. 155, note 8.
90. *Deyatelnost' Tsentral'nogo komiteta partii v dokumentah,* pp. 146–148.
91. Ibid.
92. Ibid, p. 140.
93. V. Anikeev. *Deyatelnost' TsK RSDRP(b)* p. 263.
94. Ibid.
95. General Hoffmann. *Voina upuchshennyh vozmozhnostei,* pp. 199–200.
96. Quote from: B. Nicolaevsky. *Tainye stranitsy istorii.* M., 1995, p. 385. Riezler's report from June 4, 1918.
97. *Dokumenty germanskogo posla v Moskve Mirbaha,* p. 125.
98. Nicolaevsky archive, box 18, folder 1. Transcript of foreign policy report at conference from May 14, 1918.
99. B. Nicolaevsky. *Tainye stranitsy istorii,* pp. 384–386.
100. Lenin, V. *The Complete Collected Works,* 5th ed., vol. 36, pp. 483–486.
101. Ibid, pp. 493, 495, 497.
102. *Sed'moi ekstrennyi s'ezd RKP(b),* p. 63.
103. *Protokoly zasedanii VTsIK IV cozyva.* Transcript, M., 1920, p. 171.
104. J. Vacietis. *Iulskoe vosstanie v Moskve 6 i 7 iulya,* pp. 24, 25.

Chapter 3 - The Assassination of Count Mirbach and the Destruction of the Left SR Party

1.   *Krasnaya kniga Cheka,* vol. 1., 2nd ed., annotated. M., *Politizdat,* 1989. The first edition of the book came out in 1920 and was immediately confiscated. Until its reissue in 1989, historians could use only the typewritten manuscript of the book, preserved on microfilm in major American archives.
2.   K. Gusev. *Krah partii eserov.* M, 1963, pp. 193–194; I. Mints. *God 1918-i.* M., 1982, pp. 408–409.
3.   *Krasnaya kniga Cheka,* pp. 185–186.
4.   Ibid, pp. 295–298, 308.
5.   M. Spiridonova. *Prosh Prosh'yan. K biografii Prosh'yana. — Katorga i ssylka,* book 9. M., 1924.
6.   V. Lenin. *Pamyati Prosh'yana. — Pravda,* December 10, 1918.
7.   *Krasnaya kniga Cheka,* pp. 295–309.
8.   *Krasnaya kniga Cheka,* p. 264.
9.   M. Iroshnikov. *Sozdanie sovetskogo tsentralnogo gosudarstvennogo apparata. Sovet narodnyh komissarov I narodnye komissariaty, oktyabr 1917 — yanvar 1918 g.* 2nd ed. L., 1967, p. 73.
10. According to the address directory *Ves Petrograd na 1916 god,* in 1916 Baron Roman Romanovich Mirbach resided at Furshtadskaya St., 9, and served as a special assignments clerk at the Main Directory of His Imperial Majesty's Chancellery founded by the Empress Maria (*Ves Petrograd na 1916 god.* St. Petersburg directory of names and addresses, published in 1923, edited by A. Shashkovsky, p. 448). Roman Mirbach's subsequent history cannot be traced; he is not mentioned in post-Revolutionary directories. Katkov does indicate in his article that "according to rumors, the nephew of the German ambassador" lived in France; but these were only unverified rumors.

11. *Krasnaya kniga Cheka*, p. 197.

12. Ibid, p. 198.

13. Ibid, p. 200.

14. Ibid.

15. G. Solomon. *Sredi krasnyh vozhdei*, vol.1. Paris, 1930, p. 81. Reissued in Moscow in 1995 (in 2nd ed., p. 55).

16. Quote from: L. Spirin. *Krah odnoi avantury (Myatezh levyh eserov v Moskve 6-7 iulya 1918 g.)*, M., 1971, p. 75.

17. *Krasnaya kniga Cheka*, p. 297.

18. N. Mandelstam. *Vospominaniya*. New York, 1970, pp. 112–113.

19. *Iz istorii Vserossiiskoq Chrezvychainoi komissii (Cheka) (1917–1921)*. Collection of documents, M., 1958, p. 154.

20. *Krasnaya kniga Cheka*, pp. 264, 183, 261.

21. N. Mandelstam. *Vospominaniya*, p. 113.

22. *Iz istorii Cheka*, pp. 151–154. By agreement with the German government, the ChK had no right to arrest German embassy workers (even if they were Soviet citizens) without the embassy's approval. Dzerzhinsky did not have time to receive an answer to his request.

23. *Krasnaya kniga Cheka*, p. 261.

24. M. Geller, A. Nekrich. *Utopiya u vlasti*. 2nd ed., 1986, p. 69. Chapter written by M. Geller.

25. For a more detailed account, see Yu. Felshtinsky. *Bolsheviki i levye esery. Oktyabr 1917, iul 1918. Na puti k odnopartiinoi diktature*. Paris, 1985, pp. 164–257; Yu. Felshtinsky. *Krushenie mirivoi revolutsii. Brestskii mir. Oktyabr 1917 — noyabr 1918*. M., Terra, 1992, pp. 432–512.

26. G. Solomon. *Sredi krasnyh vozhdei*, p. 83 (2nd ed.: pp. 56–57).

27. D. Karmaikl. *Trotskii*. Jerusalem, 1980, p. 143.

28. O. Kuusinen. *Before and After Stalin*. M., 1974, p. 36–37.

29. L. Spirin. *Klassy i partii v grazhdanskoi voine v Rossii. 1917–1920*. M., 1968, p. 29, 174.

30. Karl von Botmer. *S grafom Mirbahom v Moskve*. M., 1996, p. 80.

31. V. Bonch-Bruevich. *Vospominaniya o Lenine*. 2nd ed. M., 1969, p. 299.

32. See F. Dzerzhinsky. *Izbrannye stat'i i rechi*. M., 1947, p. 112, editor's note.

33. L. Trotsky. *O Lenine. Materialy dlya biografa*. M., 1924, p. 117.

34. Ibid., p. 118.

35. Ibid.

36. "Mitleid" and "Beileid" mean "compassion" and "condolence," respectively.

37. L. Trotsky. *O Lenine*, pp. 118–119.

38. F. Dzerzhinsky. *Izbrannye stat'i i rechi*, p. 112, note; K. Sverdlova. *Yakov Mikhailovich Sverdlov*. M., 1976, p. 362.

39. P. Malkov. *Zapiski komendanta Kremlya*. M., 1967, pp. 208, 209; L. Spirin. *Krah odnoi avantury*, p. 40; B. Toman. *Za svobodnuu Rossiu, za svobodnuu Latviu...* M., 1976, p. 180.

40. *Zapiski Instituta Lenina*, vol. 3. M., 1928, p. 42; V. Lenin. *The Complete Collected Works*, 5th ed., vol. 50, p. 112–113.

41. Subsequently a note was added to the extensive instructions sent to the district Soviets of Moscow pertaining to the destruction of the Left SR Party: "The present announcement is not subject to publication as yet, but is intended only for internal use." (*Krasnaya kniga Cheka*, p. 243).

42. L. Spirin. *Krah odnoi avantury* p. 14.

43. This deleted line has not received due attention from historians. It appears only in one edition of Lenin's writings: *Zapiski Instituta Lenina*, vol. 3, p. 42.

44. *Krasnaya kniga Cheka*, p. 195.

45. *Iz istorii Vserossiiskoq Chrezvychainoi komissii (Cheka) (1917–1921)*, p. 155.

46. *Krasnaya kniga Cheka*, pp. 195–196.

47. V. Bonch-Bruevich. *Vospominaniya o Lenine*, p. 303–304.

48. G. Hilger, A. Meyer. *The Incompatible Allies. A Memoir-History of Soviet German Relations 1918–1941*. New York, 1953, p. 7.

49. *Krasnaya kniga Cheka*, p. 271.

50. S. Tikhomolov. *Vosem let s Dzerzhinskim*. In: *O Felikse Edmundoviche Dzerzhinskom. Vospominaniya, stat'i, ocherki sovremennikov*. M., 1977, p. 139.

51. V. Bonch-Bruevich. *Vospominaniya o Lenine*, p. 309.

52. *Krasnaya kniga Cheka*, p. 271.

53. L. Spirin. *Krah odnoi avantury*, p. 15.

54. *Izvestiya VtsIK*, July, 1918.

55. Ibid, July 14, 1918.
56. Ya. Peters. *Vospominaniya o rabote Cheka v pervyi god revolutsii* — *Byloe*, No 2, 1933 (Paris), pp. 107–108; *Krasnaya kniga Cheka*, pp. 261–262.
57. Ibid.
58. *Prozhektor, No 27 (145), 1928, p. 12.* July 6—In the Bolshoi Theater (under the byline "E.").
59. K. Sverdlova. *Yakov Mikhailovich Sverdlov*. M., p. 361; Ya. Peters. *Vospominaniya o rabote Cheka v pervyi god revolutsii*, pp. 107–108.
60. *Prozhektor, No 27 (145)*, 1928, p. 12. July 6—In the Bolshoi Theater (under the byline "E.").
61. K. Gusev. *Krah partii eserov*, p. 207; *Prozhektor, No 27 (145)*, 1928, p. 12.
62. F. Dzerzhinsky. *Izbrannye stat'i i rechi*, p. 113.
63. F. Dzerzhinsky. *Izbrannye proizvedeniya v dvuh tomah, vol. 1. M., 1957*, pp. 268–269; Ibid, vol. 1. 2nd ed., 1967, pp. 264–265.
64. *Krasnaya kniga Cheka*, p. 286.
65. Ibid, p. 301.
66. M. Spiridonova. *Otkrytoe pis'mo Tsentralnomu komitetu partii bolshevikov.* — *Grani*, 1986, No 139, p. 194.
67. F. Dzerzhinsky. *Izbrannye stat'i i rechi*, p. 116.
68. *Krasnaya kniga Cheka*, pp. 271–172.
69. Ibid, pp. 209–210.
70. Ibid, p. 263.
71. *Izvestiya VtsIK,* July 8, 1918.
72. *Krasnaya kniga Cheka*, pp. 265, 272, 266.
73. J. Vacietis. *Iulskoe vosstanie v Moskve 6 i 7 iulya 1918 g.* — *Pamyat'*, vol. 2. M., 1977—Paris, 1979, pp. 27–28.
74. S. Dalinsky. — *Pamyat'*, No 2, p. 79.
75. J. Vacietis. *Iulskoe vosstanie v Moskve*, p. 32.
76. *Krasnaya kniga Cheka*, p. 237.
77. L. Spirin. *Krah odnoi avantury*, p. 66.
78. B. Toman. *Za svobodnuu Rossiu, za svobodnuu Latviu…*, pp. 183–184.
79. J. Vacietis. *Iulskoe vosstanie v Moskve*, p. 38. Perhaps it was because of this that on August 30, 1918, he proposed to Trotsky to shoot Vacietis (*The Trotsky Papers 1917–1922*, vol. 1. Hague, 1964, p. 116). But Vacietis was saved by the assassination attempt against Lenin, which took place on the same day; and the idea of shooting him was forgotten. Only in 1937 did Stalin execute Lenin's sentence—by executing Vacietis.
80. According to the report of the Moscow regional military commissariat from July 11, 1918.
81. P. Malkov. *Zapiski komendanta Kremlya*, p. 211.
82. *Uprochenie sovetskoi vlasti v Moskve i Moskovskoi gubernii*. M., 1958, p. 142.
83. *Dekrety sovetskoi vlasti*, vol. 2. M., 1959, pp. 536–537.
84. *Uprochenie sovetskoi vlasti v Moskve i Moskovskoi gubernii*, p. 142.
85. L. Spirin. *Krah odnoi avantury*, p. 53.
86. *Izvestiya TsK KPSS*, No 5, 1989, pp. 145, 146. The document is in Sverdlov's handwriting.
87. L. Spirin. *Krah odnoi avantury*, p. 54.
88. Quote from: D. Karmaikl. *Trotskii*, p. 43.
89. *Stenograficheskii otchet Pyatogo Vserossiiskogo s'ezda Sovetov*. M., 1918, p. 209.
90. Ya. Sverdlov. *Izbrannye proizvedeniya*, vol. 2. M., 1959, p. 246.
91. *RSFSR. VtsIK. Sozyv V*. Transcript. M., 1919, pp. 57, 58, 61, 62.
92. Quote from: Yu. Shestak. *Taktika bolshevikov po otnosheniu k partii levyh eserov i otkolovshimsya ot nee partiyam "revolutsionnyh kommunistov" i "narodnikov-kommunistov".* M., 1971, p. 101.
93. *Pravda*, July 8, 1918, No 139.
94. V. Bonch-Bruevich. *Vospominaniya o Lenine*, p. 316.
95. *Izvestiya VtsIK,* July 8, 1918, No. 141.
96. Ya. Peters. *Vospominaniya o rabote Cheka v pervyi god revolutsii*, p.110. On August 22, 1918, Dzerzhinsky was reinstated as head of the Cheka. (See: *V borbe za pobedu Oktyabrya*. Collected articles. M., 1957, pp. 297–298.)
97. V. Bonch-Bruevich. *Vospominaniya o Lenine*, p. 316.
98. Ya. Peters. *Vospominaniya o rabote Cheka v pervyi god revolutsii*, p.109.
99. L. Spirin. *Krah odnoi avantury*, p. 79.
100. Steinberg I. *In Workshop of the Revolution*, London, Gollancz, 1955, p. 222.

101. G. Solomon. *Sredi krasnyh vozhdei*, pp. 82–83. Alexandrovich's testimony was not published by the Soviet Chekists. However, there is every reason to believe that his testimony, as well as Spiridonova's testimony, published in *Krasnaya kniga Cheka,* was forwarded to the Germans in Berlin. This is indicated by the fact that Spiridonova's testimony, as it appears in *Krasnaya kniga Cheka,* is preceded by the word "Berlin." In the new, 1989 edition, on p. 268, this word was removed by the editors, but it appears in the manuscript of *Krasnaya kniga Cheka* preserved in the Hoover Institution's archives, and on the microfilm copy of this manuscript preserved in the Harvard University library. (p. 319 of the copy). The fact that some kind of testimony by Alexandrovich and Spiridonova was forwarded to Berlin at the time follows from a document stored in the Trotsky archive (Trotsky's archive, T-564). Also, Spiridonova's testimony begins with paragraph "b." Paragraph "a" was not pubished by the Chekists (see p. 319 of the copy).

102. M. Spiridonova. *Otkrytoe pis'mo Tsentralnomu komitetu partii bolshevikov,* p. 194.

103. Dostoevsky has a wonderful description of the state that Lenin must have been in at that time in the episode in which Raskolnikov returns to the scene of his crime: "He walked, looking at the ground. Suddenly, someone seemed to whisper something in his ear. He lifted his head and saw that he was standing at that house, at the very gate.... An overwhelming and unexplainable desire drew him. He entered the house, passed through the whole gateway, then into the first entrance on the right, and began climbing the familiar stairs.... For some reason, he had imagined that he would find everything exactly as it had been before... perhaps even the corpses on the same spots on the floor. But now: bare walls, no furniture; strange! He walked up to the window and sat down on the windowsill."

104. N. Krupskaya. *Pereezd Il'icha v Moskvu i pervye mesyatsy ego raboty v Moskve.* — In: *Vospominaniya o Vladimire Il'iche Lenine,* vol. 2. M., 1957, pp. 192–193. Soviet historians have offered very convincing explanations of Lenin's behavior. For example, the editors of the book *Lenin v Moskve* [Lenin in Moscow] write: "After the defeat of the Left SR rebellion in Moscow, Vladimir Ilyich went to inspect the Morozov mansion, which had been the Left SRs headquarters. According to the memoirs of N. K. Krupskaya, Vladimir Ilyich became interested in finding out why the SRs had chosen this house for their headquarters and how they had organized its defense" (*Lenin v Moskve,* M., 1957, pp. 61–62.) But the Left SRs did not "choose" the Morozov mansion—it was here that Popov's unit was quartered. And no defense had been "organized." Lenin was drawn to the mansion because he wanted to see the results of his actions. Lenin's visit to the mansion took place in such secrecy that not even the soliders who were guarding the approaches to the mansion knew about it. And they were so suprised by the appearance of a car heading toward the mansion in the evening hours that they opened fire on Lenin's vehicle (M. Ulyanova. *O Lenine.* M., 1969, p. 128).

105. *RSFSR. VtsIK. Sozyv V.* Transcript, pp. 89–90. From Chicherin's speech. The fact that Blumkin would not be arrested was very hard to believe. Even many years later, a French newspaper confidently claimed in an article on Blumkin that after the assassination of Mirbach, Blumkin had been "arrested and put in prison" (article by *Ya. Blumkin* in: *La Lutte Ouvrière,* June 12, 1936, No 1, p. 1). It was difficult even to suppose that this had not been the case.

106. *Kreml za reshetkoi (Podpolnaya Rossiya).* Berlin, *Skify,* 1922, p. 10.

107. *RSFSR. VtsIK. Sozyv V.* Transcript, p. 61.

108. Sablin declared the Left SRs' actions—starting with Dzerzhinsky's arrest—an act of self-defense. Spiridonova likewise rejected the charge that there had been an "uprising": "Everything that has happened is the result of the Russian government's precipitate defense of the murdered agents of German imperialism and the self-defense of the central committee of the party of the man who carried out this murder" (*Krasnaya kniga Cheka,* p. 269).

109. Quote from: D. Rubnev, C. Tsypkov. *Sledovatel respubliki — Volga,* 1967, No 5, p. 122.

110. *RSFSR. VtsIK. Sozyv V.* Transcript, p. 58.

111. *Krasnaya kniga Cheka,* pp. 304–307.

112. *Kreml za reshetkoi,* pp. 12–13.

113. *Izvestiya TsK KPSS,* 1989, No 5, c. 155.

Chapter 4 - Vladimir Lenin and Yakov Sverdlov

1. A. Lunacharsky. *Siyauchshii dorogoi genii.* Speech delivered on January 21, 1929, at a ceremonial assembly commemorating the fifth anniversary of Lenin's death. Transcript—*Dialog (M.)* 1995, No 3, p. 66.

2. *Kuda hotel bezhat' Sverdlov?* V. Lebedev.—*Istochnik,* 1994, No 1, pp. 3–4; *Argumenty i fakty,* August, 1966, No 33 (826), p. 16.

3. *Fanni Kaplan. Ili Kto strelyal v Lenina?* Collected documents. Kazan, 1995, p. 27.

4.. E. Stasova. *Stranitsy zhizni I borby*. M., *Politizdat*, 1957, p. 103.
5. Nicolaevsky's collection, box 591, folder 13. Letter from Abramovich to Valentinov-Volsky from December 24, 1957, pp. 1–2. Nicolaevsky's collection, box 591, folder 13. Letter from Valentinov-Volsky to Abramovich from December 30, 1957, p. 2.
6. N. Bukharin. *Pamyati Il'icha*. — *Pravda*, January 21, 1925.
7. A. Lunacharsky. *Siyauchshii dorogoi genii*, pp. 65, 67.
8. *See* B. Orlov. *Mif o Fanni Kaplan*. — *Vremya i my* (Israel), December 1975, No. 2, pp. 153-163; January 1976, No 3, pp. 126–159; V. Boinov, S. Kudryashov. *Otravlennse puli. Dve versii pokusheniya na V. I. Lenina*. — *Komsomolskaya pravda*, August 1990, p. 2; *Fanni Kaplan: "Ya strelyala v Lenina"*. (An attempt at a documentary investigation of the assassination attempt against V. I. Lenin). Edited, compiled, and annotated by B. Sudarushkin, 1990.
9. E. Maksimova. *Sledstvie po delu Fanni Kaplan prodolzhaetsya*. — *Izvestiya*, March 4, 1994; *Istochnik*, 1993, No. 2, p. 88.
10. *Fanni Kaplan. Ili Kto strelyal v Lenina?* p. 25.
11. E. Maksimova. *Sledstvie po delu Fanni Kaplan prodolzhaetsya*.
12. T. Andriasova. *Byla li killerom Fanni Kaplan?* — *Novoe russkoe slovo*. April 8, 1996, p. 4.
13. V. Bonch-Bruevich. *Pokushenie na V. I. Lenina v Moskve 30 avgusta 1918 goda*. (Personal recollections.) M., 1924, pp. 20, 89. First published on November 7, 1923, *Molodaya Gvardiya*.
14. Ya. Sverdlov. *Izbrannye proizvedeniya*, vol. 3, M., 1960, p. 5.
15. Ibid.
16. The notice was also published in *Ezhenedelnik chrezvychainyh komissii po borbe s k-r i spekulyatsiei* (October 27, 1918, No 6). The section on the Red Terror in *Po Sovetskoi Rossii* includes a list of people executed by the Cheka (p. 27). The thirty-third entry on this list is "Kaplan, Right SR, for attempting to assassinate Comrade Lenin."
17. Central Archive of the Ministry of Security of the Russian Federation, N-200, v. 10. Testimony of the assistant military commissar of the Fifth Moscow Soviet Infantry Division from August 30, 1918 — Quote from: *Istochnik*, 1993, No. 2, p. 80; *Proletarskaya revolutsiya*, 1923, No 6-7, pp. 279–280 (with minor differences); *Fanni Kaplan. Ili Kto strelyal v Lenina?*, pp. 106–108.
18. *Proletarskaya revolutsiya*, pp. 277–278; N. Kostin. *Sud nad terrorom*. — *Istochnik*, 1993, No 2, p. 80.
19. B. Orlov. *Mif o Fanni Kaplan*, p. 159; A. Litvin. *V Lenina "strelyal" Dzerzhinsky?* — *Rodina*, 1995, No 7; V. Boinov. *Otravlennse puli*.
20. V. Topolyansky. *Kto strelyal v Lenina? Iznanka pokusheniya*. — *Literaturnaya gazeta*, November 10, 1993, No 45 (5473).
21. *Fanni Kaplan. Ili Kto strelyal v Lenina?*, p. 122.
22. *Proletarskaya revolutsiya*, 1923, No 6–7, p. 282; *Fanni Kaplan. Ili Kto strelyal v Lenina?*, p. 123.
23. *Istochnik*, 1993, No 2, p. 84.
24. *Fanni Kaplan. Ili Kto strelyal v Lenina?*, p. 162. Transcript of A. Sukhotin's testimony from August 30, 1918.
25. Quote from: *Istochnik*, 1993, No. 2, p. 81.
26. *Fanni Kaplan. Ili Kto strelyal v Lenina?*, p. 131.
27. Ibid, p. 138.
28. V. Topolyansky. *Kto strelyal v Lenina?*
29. B. Orlov. *Mif o Fanni Kaplan*. — *Istochnik*, 1993, No. 2, p. 71, Transcript of Kaplan's testimony.
30. B. Orlov. *Mif o Fanni Kaplan*. Ibid.
31. During questioning on August 31, it emerged that the assassin was dressed in a way that was not entirely adequate for her designs. The insides of her shoes had exposed nails and no insoles; and even the escort guards who searched Kaplan took pity on her and gave her two envelopes to cover the nails. Kaplan testified: "The papers that were found inside my shoes were probably those that were given to me in the commissariat, when I asked them to give me something to put inside, because I had nails inside my shoes. Those papers were given to me either by the people who were searching me or by soldiers, I don't remember." The Red Army soldiers guarding the "arrested criminal F. Kaplan "at the Zamoskvoretsky district military commissariat were "strongly reprimanded through the military commissariat of the Zamoskvoretsky district for allowing this criminal, who had attemped to assassinate Comrade Lenin, to use blank envelopes from the Zamoskvoretsky district military commissariat as insoles inside her shoes in order to relieve her of a minor inconvenience" (Central Archive of the Ministry of Security of the Russian Federation, N-200, v. 10. Transcript of testimony given by D. Bem, who searched F. Kaplan, on August 30, 1918. Quote from: *Istochnik*, 1993, No. 2, p. 81; *Fanni Kaplan. Ili Kto strelyal v Lenina?*, pp. 122, 149).

32. *Fanni Kaplan. Ili Kto strelyal v Lenina?*, p. 136; V. Topolyansky. *Kto strelyal v Lenina?* After she went blind, Kaplan learned Braille. After being released in February 1917, she was able to recover her sight in part at the Kharkov ophthalmology clinic.

33. O. Vasilyev. *Pokushenie na Lenina bylo instsenirovkoi.—Nezavisimaya gazeta*, August 29, 1992.

34. *Istochnik*, 1993, No. 2, p. 76.

35. V. Topolyansky. *Kto strelyal v Lenina?* Topolyansky's assumption is confirmed by one of the witnesses: "But when Comrade Lenin started to put his hand on the handle of the car door, a woman whom I had been watching crouched down and started shooting. The crowd scattered in all directions.... at this time, some gentleman ran up to her, knocked the revolver out of her hand, and started to lift up Comrade Lenin. She moved a few paces away and we immediately caught her and led her to the Zamoskvoretsky military commissariat" (*Fanni Kaplan. Ili Kto strelyal v Lenina?*, p. 146, testimony of S. I. Titov from August 31, 1:50 a.m.).

36. The case itself is preserved in the central archive of the FSB. It has been published, but several pages have been removed from it and are now stored in the president's archive. No one is allowed to see them. They contain the testimony of those witnesses from the Mikhelson Factory who a man shooting at Lenin.

37. His first words after he came to were: "Did they catch him or not?" (*Istochnik*, 1993, No. 2, p. 80).

38. P. Malkov. *Zapiski komendanta Kremlya*. 3rd ed. M., *Voenizdat*, 1987, p. 146.

39. Quote from: *Vystrel v serdtse revolutsii*. Edited by N. D. Kostin, *Politizdat*, 1983, p. 65.

40. Soviet Russia Pictorial, 1924, May, p. 119.

41. Quote from: *Vystrel v serdtse revolutsii*. Publication by N. Kostin. Second, expanded edition. M., *Politizdat*, 1989, pp. 78–79.

42. *Proletarskaya revolutsiya*, 1923, Nos. 6–7, pp. 277–278; N. Kostin. *Istochnik*, 1993, No. 2, p. 80. Kostin refers to Central Archive of the Ministry of Security of the Russian Federation, N-200, v. 10. Testimony of S. K. Gil from August 30, 1918. "N" is the archive of unrehabilitated persons; *Fanni Kaplan. Ili Kto strelyal v Lenina?*, p. 118.

43. Ibid, p. 162, from the testimony of A. Sukhotin, August 31, 1 a.m.

44. B. Orlov. *Mif o Fanni Kaplan.—Vremya i my*, pp. 156–157.

45. V. Bonch-Bruevich. *Pokushenie na V. I. Lenina*, pp. 6–13.

46. Quote from: Yu. Felshtinsky. *Bolsheviki i levye esery*. Paris, 1985, p. 203.

47. P. Malkov. *Zapiski komendanta Kremlya*, p. 148. In accordance with the resolutions published by the Central Committee in *Pravda* on April 4, 1925, and February 12, 1927, memoirs about Lenin had to be approved by various offices prior to being published, including the Institute of Marxism-Leninism and its branches (N. Petrenko (Ravdin). *Lenin v Gorkah — bolezn i smert. — Minuvshee. Historical Almanac*, No. 2, Paris, 1986). In addition to these censors, the memoirs of Kaplan's executioner Malkov passed through an even more stringent form of censorship: Malkov wrote them together with the son of Yakov Sverdlov, Andrei Sverdlov, who had a degree in history and was a former high-ranking NKVD official. (P. Malkov. *Zapiski komendanta Kremlya*, p. 5.)

48. Ibid, p. 149.

49. B. Sudarushkin. In: *Fanni Kaplan: "Ya strelyala v Lenina"*, p. 62.

50. "We will not bury Kaplan. Destroy her remains completely..." said Sverdlov, according to Malkov's recollections. (P. Malkov. *Zapiski komendanta Kremlya*, p. 160).

51. *Istochnik*, 1993, No. 2, p. 73.

52. B. Sudarushkin. In: *Fanni Kaplan: "Ya strelyala v Lenina"*, p. 61. The car squadron was located exactly across from the children's half of the Bolshoi Palace, where Kaplan was being held.

53. *Istochnik*, 1993, No. 2, p. 73.

54. M. Heifits. *Dve puli dlya Lenina I obe raznye. — Novoe russkoe slovo*, December 19, 1997, p. 10.

55. *Fanni Kaplan. Ili Kto strelyal v Lenina?*, p. 178.

56. Ibid, pp. 171, 172, 174, 177; Central Archive of the Ministry of Security of the Russian Federation, N-200, v. 10. Transcript of the interrogation of Z. I. Legonkaya from September 24, 1919 — Quote from: *Istochnik*, 1993, No. 2, p. 80; *Fanni Kaplan. Ili Kto strelyal v Lenina?*, pp. 155–156. Testimony of Z. F. Udotova, August 31, ibid., pp. 153–154. Testimony of Z. I. Legonkaya, August 31; *Istochnik*, 1993, No. 2, pp. 80–81; *Fanni Kaplan. Ili Kto strelyal v Lenina?*, p. 121; Central Archive of the Ministry of Security of the Russian Federation, N-200, v. 10. Transcript of the interrogation of Z. I. Legonkaya from September 24, 1919 — Quote from: *Istochnik*, 1993, No. 2, p. 80.

57. Kaplan's name also appeared on a list of executed individuals compiled by Chekist A. Ya. Belenky: "The alphabetical list of people shot in 1918-1919, which was kept by Comrade Belenky, includes Kaplan's last name (without initials). Head of the 6th section of the 8th department of the GUTV NKVD, Senior State Security Lieutenant Ivanov." (See: *Fanni Kaplan. Ili Kto strelyal v Lenina?*, p. 179.)

Kaplan's registration card for case No. 2153, filled out at the end of September, indicates the same thing: "Kaplan.... accused of attempting to assassinate Comrade Lenin (executed)" (*Fanni Kaplan. Ili Kto strelyal v Lenina?*, pp. 138–139).

58. IISH (Amsterdam), A. Balabanova collection, folder 219.
59. "A few minutes later, Vera Mikhailovna was already injecting morphine into Vladimir Ilyich's leg and measuring his pulse" (V. Bonch-Bruevich. *Pokushenie na V. I. Lenina*, p. 11).
60. V. Bonch-Bruevich. *Tri pokusheniya na V. I. Lenina*. M., *Federatsiya*, 1930, p. 81.
61. "The patient jokes, tells the doctors that he is sick of them, does not want to submit to discipline, jokingly cross-examines the doctors, and is generally unruly." (Quote from: *Vystrel v serdtse revolutsii* [A Shot at the Heart of the Revolution], 1989, p. 148.)
62. P. Malkov. *Zapiski komendanta Kremlya*, pp. 150–152.
63. V. Bonch-Bruevich. *Tri pokusheniya na V. I. Lenina*, p. 102.
64. *Pravda*, October 2, 1918, p. 4.
65. P. Malkov. *Zapiski komendanta Kremlya*, p. 154.
66. Ibid, pp. 152, 154.
67. On October 1, 1918, *Pravda* published a death notice: "On the night of September 30, at 2:15 a.m., Vera Mikhailovna Bonch-Bruevich died quietly of pneumonia." "Vera Mikhailovna departed somehow completely unexpectedly," wrote M. Savelyeva in an obituary in the same newspaper. A death notice and an obituary were published in *Izvestiya* (October 1, 1918, p. 1), which also indicated the suddenness of the death: "and suddenly she died—one could say that she was consumed in a few days." Velichkina was less than 50 years old.
68. V. Bonch-Bruevich. *Lenin v Petrograde i Moskve*. M., *Polinizdat*, 1982, pp. 55–56.
69. "Needless risk-taking—for the sake for risk-taking—no": this was how Krupskaya characterized Lenin in a questionnaire. (N. Krupskaya. *O Lenine*. Collected articles and speeches. 5th ed. M., *Politizdat*, 1983, p. 88).
70. Lenin's letter of condolence to Bonch-Bruevich on account of his wife's death, written on October 1, 1918, was first published only in 1958.
71. Unfortunately, it is not clear who the other women were. On October 1, 1918, *Izvestiya* reported that Vera Velichkina "died at 2:15 a.m. on the night of September 30" in the presence of two medical workers who were on duty by her bedside: Doctor Anna Georgievna Pozern and Nurse Poletayeva. Maybe they were the two women who died in the Kremlin around the same time?
72. Main Archive of the Russian Federation, file 1005. Transcript of day 31 of the trial 31. — Quote from: *Istochnik*, 1993, No. 2, p. 72.
73. B. Orlov. *Mif o Fanni Kaplan*. — *Istochnik*, 1993, No. 2, p. 72.
74. *Fanni Kaplan. Ili Kto strelyal v Lenina?*, p. 19.
75. G. Semenov. *Voennaya i boevaya rabota partii sotsial-revolutsionerov za 1917-1918 gg.* Berlin, 1922. Price 12 marks. 44 pages.
76. G. Semenov. *Voennaya I boevaya rabota partii sotsial-revolutsionerov za 1917–1918 gg.* M., *Gosudarstvennoe izdatelstvo*, 1922.
77. This document received the name: "Report of L. V. Konopleva to the Central Committee of the Russian Communist Party (Bolsheviks)." Clearly, an arrested militant SR could not have made a "report" to the Central Committee. An arrested party could give testimony to the Cheka. Only a Bolshevik could make a report to the Central Committee. Konopleva did also testify before the Cheka: but this was for the trial against the SRs.
78. See: N. Kostin. *Sud nad terrorom*. M., *Moskovsky rabochii*, 1990, p. 10.
79. Ibid, pp. 11–12.
80. Ibid.
81. G. Serebryakova. *Moei docheri Zore o ee ottse*. Published by Z. Serebryakova.—*Rodina*, 1989, No, 6, p. 31.
82. Ibid, p. 31.
83. Ibid.
84. Ibid, p. 32.
85. V. Topolyansky. *Kto strelyal v Lenina?*
86. M. Heifits. *Dve puli dlya Lenina I obe raznye*.
87. *Pravda*, December 15, 1923, No 285; December 16, 1923, No. 286; *Pravda*, January 3, 1924, No. 2; *Bulleten oppozitsii*, April 1938, No. 65, pp. 13–14.
88. *Materialy fevralsko-martovskogo plenuma TsK VKP(b) 1937 g.* — *Voprosy istorii*, 1992. No. 2–3, pp. 27–28.

89. *Bolshaya sovetskaya entsiklopediya*, editor-in-chief O. Shmidt, vol. 36, OGIZ, 1938, article *Lenin i leninizm*, p. 374.
90. *Pravda*, March 3, 9, 12, 1938; G. Katkov. *The Trial of Bukharin*. New York, 1969, p. 172–180.
91. *Istochnik*, 1993, No. 2, pp. 86–87.

Chapter 5 - Karl Radek and the Murders of Karl Liebknecht and Rosa Luxemburg

1. Paul Frolich. Rosa Luxemburg. Gedanke und Tat. Europaische Verlagsanstalt, Frankfurt am Main, 1967, S. 284.
2. Nicolaevsky's collection, box 6, folder 12. Rosa Luxemburg on the Bolsheviks. Russian Social Democratic Labor Party leaflet. Reprinted from *Sotsialisticheskii vestnik*, No 1, 1922. Published by the Petrograd RSDLP committee, February 1922, p. 2.
3. A. Varsky. *Roza Luksemburg. Takticheskie problemy*, Hamburg, 1922, p. 7.
4. Bertram Wolfe (1896–1977) was the head of a faction in the American Communist Party and in 1929 was expelled from the party for factionalism. Until the end of 1937, he supported the charges made at the Moscow trials against the "opposition." At the end of 1937, he publicly renounced his former views and came out against the trials. Later, he renounced Communist activity altogether and became a respectable professor. He is the author of a number of books, the most of famous of which is *Three Who Made a Revolution*.
5. Paul Levi published a book with the title *Russkaya revolutsiya. Kriticheskaya otsenka slabosti Rozy Luksemburg* [The Russian Revolution. A Critical Assessment of Rosa Luxemburg's Weakness]. Berlin, 1922.
6. Wolfe. 'Rosa Luxemburg and V. I. Lenin: The Opposite Poles of Revolutionary Socialism." *The Antioch Review*, Summer, 1961. The Antioch Press, Yellow Springs, Ohio, p. 222.
7. V. Lenin. *The Complete Collected Works*, 5th ed., vol. 37, p. 99.
8. *The Trotsky Papers, 1917–1922*, vol. 1. Hague, 1964, p. 200.
9. Nicolaevsky's collection, box 510, folder 1.
10. Wolfe. *Rosa Luxemburg and V. I. Lenin*, p. 216.
11. For greater detail, see *Delo Radeka. — Voprosy istorii*, No. 9, 1997, pp. 15–34; Marie-Louise Goldbach. *Karl Radek und die deutsch-sowjetischen Beziehungen 1918–1923*. Verlag Neue Gesellschaft GmbH. Bonn-Bad Godesberg, 1973.
12. K. Radek. *Der Zusammenbruch des Imperialismus*. 1919, s. 44.
13. Wolfe. *Rosa Luxemburg and V. I. Lenin*, p. 216.
14. Eberlein, who fled from Hitler to the Soviet Union, was shot in 1937.
15. Gustav Strubel. *Ich habe sie richten lassen* (article devoted to the seventieth anniversary of the assassination of Luxemburg and Liebknecht) — *Die Zeit*, January 13, 1989, p. 41.
16. See: S. Haffner. *Revolutsiya v Germanii 1918/19. Kak eto bylo v deistvitelnosti?* Trans. for the German. M., Progress, 1983, pp. 158, 163.
17. See: *Delo Georga Sklartsa* — *Voprosy istorii*, No 10, 1997, pp. 33–33; No 11, 1997, pp. 3–24.
18. See: *Zapiski Teodora Libknehta*. — *Voprosy istorii*, No. 2, 1998, pp. 3–29.
19. Nicolaevsky's collection, box 489, folder 2. Letter from Nicolaevsky to Th. Liebknecht from December 16, 1947. One page in German.
20. Nicolaevsky's collection, box 489, folder 3. Letter from Nicolaevsky to M. N. Pavlovsky from March 24, 1962. One page.
21. IISH (Amsterdam), Suvarin's collection, letter from Nicolaevsky to Suvarin from April 11, 1957.
22. Nicolaevsky's collection, box 508, folder 48. Letter from Nicolaevsky to R. (Jerzy Niezbrzycki) Wraga from July 15, 1960. One page.
23. Nicolaevsky's collection, box 496, folder 3. Letter from Nicolaevsky to Pavlovsky from November 16, 1961. One page.
24. Colonel Walter Nicolai was the head of the third bureau—Germany's military intelligence. After WWI, formally retired, he remained in the intelligence service. Records indicate that in July 1932 he traveled from Berlin to Munich in order to meet with Nazi leaders, including Himmler and Hess, at the apartment of Ernst Röhm, the commander of the German SA.
25. IISH (Amsterdam), Balabanova collection, letter from Nicolaevsky to Balabanova from April 20, 1962. One page.
26. Nicolaevsky's collection, box 500, folder 19. Letter from Nicolaevsky to Otto Schüddekopf from August 25, 1962; one page. Box 478, folder 21. Letter from Nicolaevsky to H. Eckert from April 14, 1954, one page, in which he quotes his own letter to Schüddekopf.

27. Nicolaevsky's collection, box 496, folder 3. Letter from Nicolaevsky to Pavlovsky from September 2, 1962. One page.
28. Nicolaevsky's collection, box 496, folder 3. Letter from Nicolaevsky to Pavlovsky from August 11, 1962. Two pages.
29. Wolfe. *Rosa Luxemburg and V. I. Lenin*, p. 222.
30. *Rosa Luxemburg Ein Leben fur die Freiheit. Reden — Schriften — Briefe. Ein Lesebuch*. Herausgegeben von Frederik Hetmann. Fischer Taschenbuch Verlag, Frankfurt am Main, 1980, pp. 308–309.
31. Nicolaevsky's collection, box 478, folder 21. Letter from Nicolaevsky to H. Eckert from December 26, 1962, p. 2.
32. Rathenau did not have much regard for his partner at the negotiating table. In February 1922, Rathenau said the following about Radek in conversation with Lord D'Abernon, the British ambassador in Berlin: "This is a slovenly character, a sleazy little Jew." Lenin once said that after talking to Radek, he always had an urge to wash himself from head to foot.
33. Nicolaevsky's collection, box 18, folder 27. From the press office of the RSFSR's authorized representation in Estonia. August 9, 1921, p. 2.
34. Ruth Fischer. *Stalin und der Deutsche Kommumsmus*. Frankfurt am Main, 1950, S. 251.
35. Gustav Strubel. *Ich habe sie richten lassen* (article devoted to the seventieth anniversary of the assassination of Luxemburg and Liebknecht) — *Die Zeit*, January 13, 1989, No. 3.
36. Zapiski Teodora Libknehta, p. 29.

Chapter 6 - The Mystery of Lenin's Death

1. A. Avtorkhanov. *Ubil li Stalin Lenina?* — *Novyi zhurnal*, vol. 152, pp. 240–259.
2. Ibid, p. 251.
3. Robert Payne. *The Rise and Fall of Stalin*. Simon and Schuster, New York, pp. 332–333.
4. Lenin, V. *The Complete Collected Works*, 5th ed., vol. 45, p. 122.
5. *Izvestiya TsK KPSS*, 1989, No. 1, p. 215.
6. L. Trotsky. *Portrety revolutsionerov*. M., 1991, p. 67.
7. Quote from: Yu. Bezelyansky. *Nichego ne pomnu, krome horoshego go...* — *Novoe Russkoe Slovo*, No. 44, March 15, 1996.
8. *Izvestiya TsK KPSS*, 1989, No. 12, pp. 197, 201.
9. *Pravda*, February 26, 1988, No. 57.
10. Here and below, writing about Demyan Bedny, we are relying on the unpublished 115-page study by philologist Solomon Ioffe (Palo Alto, CA): *Memuary Stalina o Lenine v zapisi Demyana Bednogo*, which has been graciously made available to us.
11. V. Bonch-Bruevich. *Pokushenie na V. I. Lenina v Moskve 30 avgusta 1918 goda*. (Based on Personal Recollections.) M., 1924, p. 14. First published on November 7, 1923, *Molodaya Gvardiya*.
12. L. Trotsky. *Portrety revolutsionerov*, p. 54.
13. Demyan Bedny. *Collected Works* in one vol., 1909–1922. M.—St. Petersburg, published by the satirical press *Krokodil* under the aegis of *Rabochaya Gazeta*, 1923, pp. 295–334.
14. N. Gamalii. Pishu i dumau ob Il'iche.. M., *Sovetskaya Rossiya*, 1983, p. 172.
15. Demyan Bedny. *Collected Works* in 8 vol., vol. 4. Poems 1920–1922. M., 1965, p. 258.
16. *Vospominaniya o Lenine*. April, 1938. A. I. Marshak's publication. — *Sputnik*, April 1990, No. 4. *Vospominaniya Marii Makarovny Petrashevoi, medsestry*. From S. Marshak's archive, p. 50.
17. Ibid.
18. *Soviet Russia*, vol. VII, August 15, 1922, p. 121.
19. Ibid, December 1922, p. 290.
20. *Lenin i leninizm*. — Bol'shaya sovetskaya entsiklopediya, vol. 36, p. 374.
21. *Fanni Kaplan. Ili kto strelyal v Lenina?* — Collection of Documents. Kazan, 1995, pp. 31–32.
22. *Pravda*, November 25, 1990.
23. L. Trotsky. *Portrety revolutsionerov*, p. 80.
24. On June 6, 1941, People's Commissar of Internal Affairs Lavrenty Beria submitted report No. 1984/6 to Stalin, requesting that Trotsky's murderers be awarded top state honors.
25. L. Trotsky. *Portrety revolutsionerov*. Article *Sverh-Bordzbia v Kremle*.
26. *Istochnik*, 1993, No. 2, p. 70.
27. P. Pomper, Y. Felshtinsky. *Trotsky's Notebooks, 1933–1935*. Columbia University Press, New York, 1986, p. 129.

28. *Toward a History of Lenin's Last Documents*. From the archives of the writer A. Bek, who in 1967 interviewed Lenin's private secretaries. — *Moskovkie Novosti*, No. 17, April, 1989, pp. 8–9 [Hereafter: Bek's archive].
29. N. Krupskaya. *Vospominaniya o Lenine*. M., *Partisdat*, 1932, p. 45.
30. Bek's archive.
31. M. Ulyanova ob otnoshenii V. I. Lenina k I. V. Stalinu. — *Izvestiya TsK KPSS*, No. 12, 1989, pp. 198–199.
32. Bek's archive.
33. Lenin, V. *The Complete Collected Works*, 5th ed., vol. 45, pp. 551–558.
34. Ibid, pp. 211–213.
35. Ibid, pp. 558–559.
36. Ibid, p. 214.
37. Ibid, vol. 54, pp. 299–300.
38. E. Yakovlev. *Poslednii intsident. Konspect dramy Vladimira Il'icha*. — *Moskovskie Novosti*, January 22, 1989, No. 4, pp. 8–9.
39. *Pravda*, February 26, 1988, No. 57.
40. Ibid.
41. Published in: *The Trotsky Papers*, vol. 2, Hague, 1964, pp. 786, 788
42. *Pravda*, February 26, 1988, No. 57.
43. L. Kuznetskaya, K. Mashtakova. *Vstrecha s Leninym* (based on materials from the museum "V. I. Lenin's Office and Apartment in the Kremlin"). — *Sovetskaya Rossiya*, M., 1987, pp. 259–260.
44. Lenin, V. *The Complete Collected Works*, 5th ed., vol. 45, p. 710.
45. E. Yakovlev. Poslednii intsident.
46. *Pravda*, February 26, 1988, No. 57
47. Published in: *The Trotsky Papers*, vol. 2, c. 788.
48. Bek's archive.
49. *Izvestiya TsK KPSS*, 1989, No. 3, pp. 130–131.
50. Ibid, 1989, No. 12, p. 198.
51. Bek's archive.
52. Ibid.
53. Ibid.
54. *Pravda*, March 25, 1988, No. 85.
55. Lenin, V. *The Complete Collected Works*, 5th ed., vol. 45, pp. 343–406.
56. Bek's archive.
57. Lenin, V. *The Complete Collected Works*, 5th ed., vol. 45, pp. 591–592.
58. Ibid, p. 710.
59. *Vospominaniya o Lenine*. April, 1938. A. I. Marshak's publication, p. 50.
60. N. Krupskaya. *O Lenine*. Collection of articles and speeches. Fifth edition. M., *Izdatel'stvo Politicheskoi Literatury*, 1983, pp. 84–85.
61. Bek's archive; Lenin, V. *The Complete Collected Works*, 5th ed., vol. 45, p. 474.
62. Trotsky's archive. *Kommunisticheskaya oppozitsiya v SSSR, 1923–1927*, vol. 1. M., 1990, pp. 76–77.
63. L. Kuznetskaya, K. Mashtakova. *Vstrecha s Leninym*, p. 262.
64. See: V. Doroshenko. *Lenin protiv Stalina. 1922–1923*. — *Zvezda*, 1990, No. 4.
65. Bek's archive.
66. Lenin, V. *The Complete Collected Works*, 5th ed., vol. 45, p. 478.
67. See Preface by V. Loginov in his publication *"Is arhiva Beka."*
68. Lenin, V. *The Complete Collected Works*, 5th ed., vol. 45, p. 479.
69. Ibid, p. 485.
70. E. Yakovlev. *Poslednii intsident*
71. Lenin, V. *The Complete Collected Works*, 5th ed., vol. 45, pp. 485–486, 607.
72. L. Fotieva. *Iz zhizni Lenina*. M., *Politizdat*, 1967, pp. 313–314.
73. Lenin, V. *The Complete Collected Works*, 5th ed., vol. 45, p. 714.
74. Biograficheskaya hronika V. I. Lenina, vol. 12, M., 1982, p. 585.
75. Trotsky's archive, vol. 1, pp. 29–32.
76. Lenin, V. *The Complete Collected Works*, 5th ed., vol. 54, p. 329.
77. Trotsky's archive, vol. 1, p. 35.
78. Ibid, p. 53.
79. "Citing his illness, Trotsky replied that he could not take on such an obligation" (V. Lenin. *Collected Works*, 5th ed., vol. 54, p. 674).
80. Trotsky's archive, vol. 1, p. 51.

81. Lenin, V. *The Complete Collected Works*, 5th ed., vol. 54, pp. 329–330.
82. Ibid, vol. 45, p. 486.
83. Ibid, vol. 54, p. 330.
84. Ibid, vol. 45, p. 486.
85. Bek's archive.
86. Lenin, V. *The Complete Collected Works*, 5th ed., vol. 45, p. 486.
87. Bek's archive.
88. Ibid.
89. Ibid.
90. Ibid.
91. Ibid.
92. Lenin, V. *The Complete Collected Works*, 5th ed., vol. 45, p. 486; Bek's archive.
93. I. Stalin. *The Collected Works, 1946–1952*. M., 1997, p. 252.
94. *Dvenadtsatyi s'ezd RKP(b)*. Transcript. M., *Politisdat*, 1968, pp. 816–820.
95. Trotsky's archive, vol. 1, pp. 35–51.
96. *Dvenadtsatyi s'ezd*, p. 873.
97. *Izvestiya TsK KPSS*, 1991, No. 6.
98. N. Petrenko (Ravdin). *Lenin v Gorkah — bolezn' i smert'. — Minuvshee* (Historical Almanac), No. 2, Paris, 1986; *Grani*, 1987, No 146, pp. 145–174. Frankfurt am Main, *Posev*; U. Lopukhin. *Bolezn', smert' i bal'zamirovanie V. I Lenina. Pravda i mify*. M., *Respublika*, 1997.
99. N. K. Krupskaya — G. E. Zinoviev. October 31, 1923. — *Izvestiya TsK KPSS*, 1989, No. 2, pp. 201–202. Krupskaya is referring to the conflict between Trotsky and his opponents at the joint plenary meeting of the Central Committee and the Central Control Committee of the Russian Communist Party on October 25–27, 1923. The transcript of this meeting has not been found.
100. Ibid, p. 202.
101. Trotsky's archive, vol. 1, p. 89.
102. L. Trotsky. *Portrety revolutsionerov*. Article *Sverh-Bordzhia v Kremle*, p. 77.
103. See: N. Valentinov-Volsky. *Nasledniki Lenina*. M., *Terra*, 1991, appendix 8, p. 214.
104. L. Shatunovskaya. *Zhizn' v Kremle*. New York, Chalidze Publishing, 1982, pp. 227, 229, 230.
105. Ibid, pp. 232–233.
106. Ibid, pp. 234, 235.
107. B. Nicolaevsky. *Tainye stranitsy istorii*. M., 1995, pp. 228–229.
108. Elizabeth Lermolo. *Face of a Victim*. Harper & Brothers Publishers, New York, 1955, pp. 132–137.
109. See: N. Petrenko (Ravdin). *Lenin v Gorkah — bolezn' i smert'*.
110. Yves Delbars. *The Real Stalin*. George Allen & Unwin Ltd, London, 1951, pp. 124–130. The chapter "Lenin's Testament" (translated from English). The book first came out in French, in two volumes, under the title *Le Vrai Staline* (Paris, 1950–1951).
111. See: Jack London. *Collected Works*, M., 1954, vol. 2, pp. 39–49.
112. *The Unknown Lenin. From the Secret Archive*. Ed. by R. Pipes, Yale University Press, 1996, p. 77.
113. See: N. Valentinov-Volsky. *Nasledniki Lenina*, pp. 214, 216–217.
114. Hoover Institution archives, Valentinov-Volsky collection [Valentinov-Volsky. Box 8].
115. See: *Rech I. V. Stalina v Narkomate oborony*. U. Murin's publication.—*Istochnik*, 1994, No. 3, pp. 72–88.
116. *Istochnik*, 1996, No. 4, p. 103.

Epilogue

1. F. D. Volkov, *Stalin's Rise and Fall*, M., 1922, pp. 36–37.
2. In 1987, the novella was reprinted by the Moscow journal *Znamya*, No. 12.
3. Jean van Heijenoort. *With Trotsky in Exile: From Prinkipo to Coyoakan*, Harvard University Press, 1978.
4. See also A. B. Feferman. *Politics, Logic, and Love. The Life of Jean van Heijenoort* (Wellesley, Mass., 1993), p. 140.
5. Partly published in L. Trotsky: *Portrety revolutsionerov*. M., 1991, pp. 75–76.
6. See, for example, "*The Demise*. From the memoirs of A. L. Myasnikov, a participant in the council of physicians by Stalin's bed" in *Literaturnaya Gazeta*, March 1, 1989, No. 9 (5231). Published by L. Myasnikov.
7. *Russkaya Mysl*, April 24, 1956.

Index